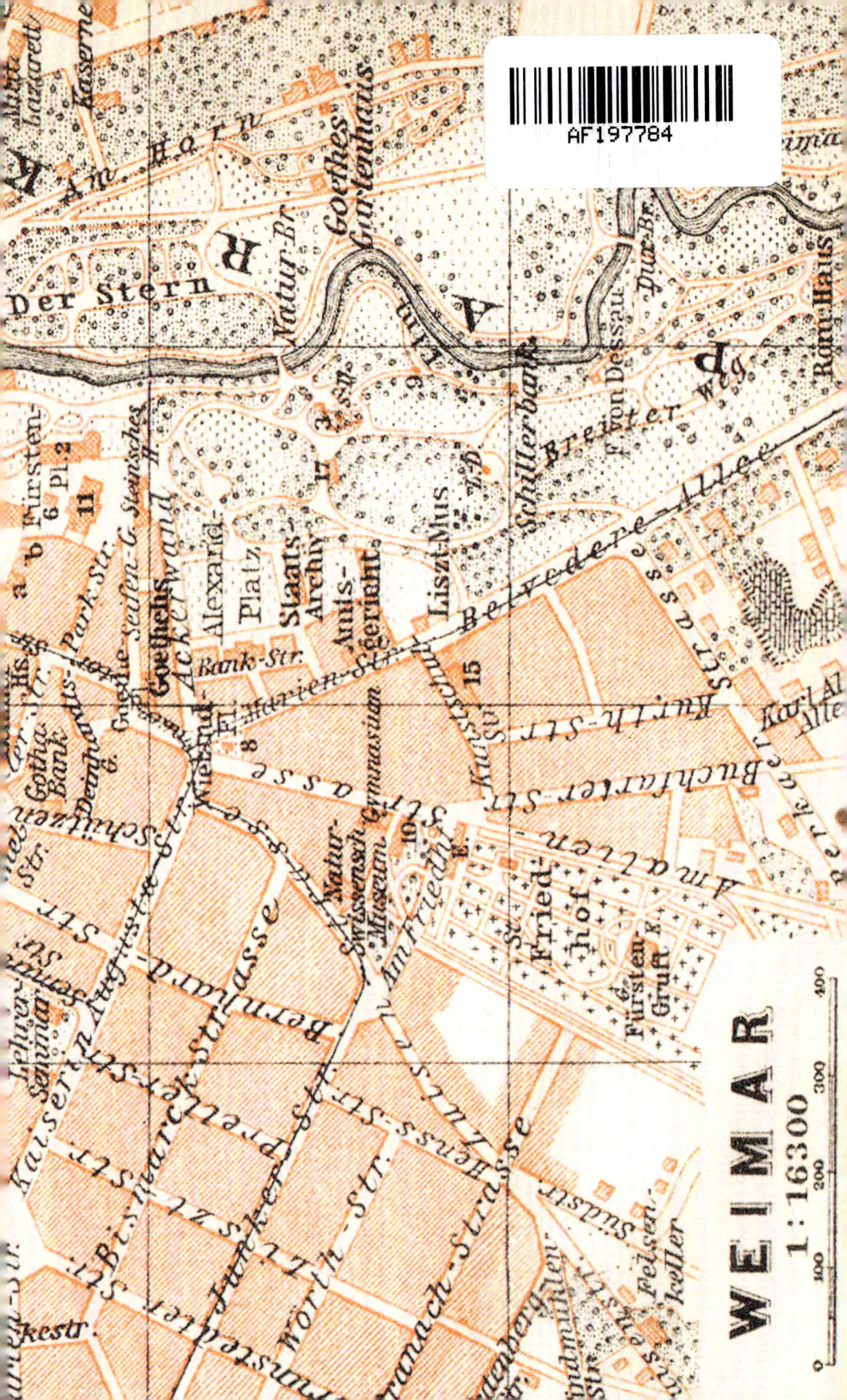

Weimar

Weimar

Life on the Edge of Catastrophe

KATJA HOYER

ALLEN LANE
an imprint of
PENGUIN BOOKS

ALLEN LANE

UK | USA | Canada | Ireland | Australia
India | New Zealand | South Africa

Allen Lane is part of the Penguin Random House group of companies
whose addresses can be found at global.penguinrandomhouse.com

Penguin Random House UK
One Embassy Gardens, 8 Viaduct Gardens, London SW11 7BW

penguin.co.uk

Penguin
Random House
UK

First published in Great Britain by Allen Lane 2026

001

Copyright © Katja Hoyer, 2026

Penguin Random House values and supports copyright.
Copyright fuels creativity, encourages diverse voices, promotes freedom
of expression and supports a vibrant culture. Thank you for purchasing
an authorized edition of this book and for respecting intellectual property
laws by not reproducing, scanning or distributing any part of it by any
means without permission. You are supporting authors and enabling
Penguin Random House to continue to publish books for everyone.
No part of this book may be used or reproduced in any manner for the
purpose of training artificial intelligence technologies or systems. In accordance
with Article 4(3) of the DSM Directive 2019/790, Penguin Random House
expressly reserves this work from the text and data mining exception.

The moral right of the author has been asserted

Set in 12/15pt Dante MT Std
Typeset by Six Red Marbles UK, Thetford, Norfolk
Printed and bound in Great Britain by Clays Ltd, Elcograf S.p.A.

The authorized representative in the EEA is Penguin Random House
Ireland, Morrison Chambers, 32 Nassau Street, Dublin D02 YH68

A CIP catalogue record for this book is available from the British Library

ISBN: 978–0–241–68124–4

Penguin Random House is committed to a sustainable future
for our business, our readers and our planet. This book is made from
Forest Stewardship Council® certified paper.

MIX
Paper | Supporting
responsible forestry
FSC® C018179

In memory of my papa

Contents

CONTENTS

List of Illustrations

Every effort has been made to contact copyright holders. The author and publisher would be glad to amend in future editions errors or omissions brought to their attention.

Endpapers

Front: Map of Weimar in 1913, produced by Karl Baedeker. Courtesy of Alamy.

Back: A tourist map of Weimar produced by the Elephant Hotel, 1938. Courtesy of Landesarchiv Thüringen – Hauptstaatsarchiv Weimar, Nachlass Hermann Giesler Nr.1.

Illustrations in the text

Karlsplatz in central Weimar, 1907 (today: Goetheplatz). Postcard, via Wikimedia Commons.

Arthur Schmidt, in Alexandria, 1908 © Marie-Luise Seyfarth, Weimar. Taken from ". . . und unweigerlich fuehrt der Weg nach Buchenwald": Der Geist von Weimar hinter Gittern by Udo Wohlfeld.

Rosa and Ernst Schmidt, 1915 © Marie-Luise Seyfarth, Weimar. Taken from Jüdische Familien in Weimar by Erika Müller and Harry Stein.

Elisabeth Förster-Nietzsche, 1910. Photo by Louis Held, via Wikimedia Commons.

Theatre Square in Weimar, before the opening of the National Assembly on 6 February 1919. Published in the Leipziger Illustrirte Zeitung, 20 February 1919. Illustration by Felix Schwormstädt.

Harry Graf Kessler, 1909. Courtesy of DLA Marbach.

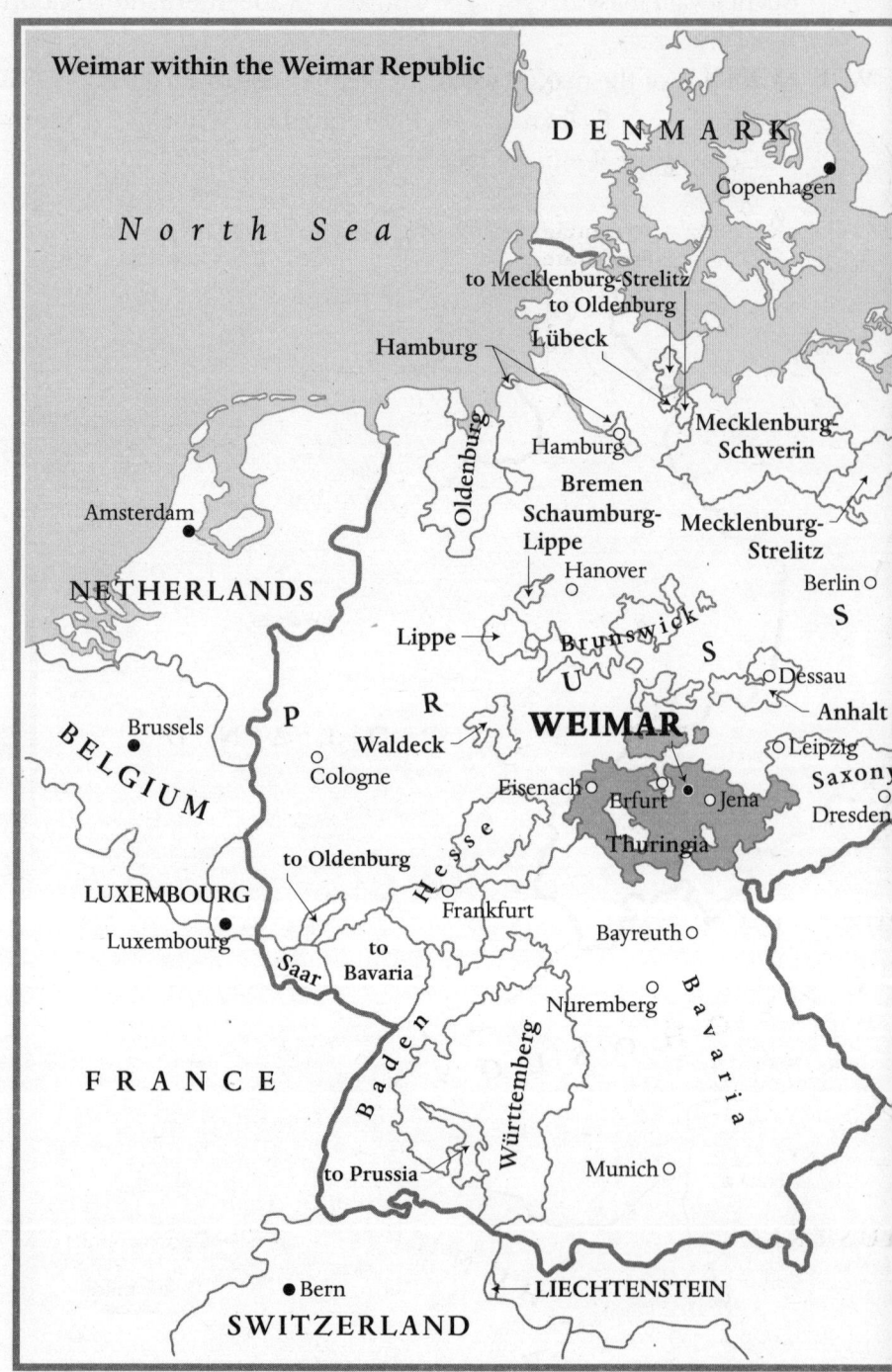

Weimar within the Weimar Republic

DENMARK

Copenhagen

North Sea

to Mecklenburg-Strelitz
to Oldenburg
Lübeck

Hamburg

Mecklenburg-
Schwerin

Amsterdam

Oldenburg

Hamburg

Bremen
Schaumburg-
Lippe

Mecklenburg-
Strelitz

NETHERLANDS

Hanover

Berlin

S

Lippe

Brunswick

S

U

S

Dessau

Anhalt

Brussels

P

R

WEIMAR

Leipzig

BELGIUM

Waldeck

Eisenach

Erfurt

Jena

Saxony

Cologne

Dresden

LUXEMBOURG

to Oldenburg

Hesse

Thuringia

Luxembourg

Saar

to
Bavaria

Frankfurt

Bayreuth

FRANCE

Baden

to Prussia

Württemberg

Nuremberg

Bavaria

Munich

Bern

LIECHTENSTEIN

SWITZERLAND

Introduction

Germany in a nutshell

Carl Weirich stared at the crematorium ovens. Six gaping holes framed by iron and brick. Their heavy doors stood open, revealing cavities filled with lumpy piles of ash. Something white protruded from the dark mess. Fingers perhaps, or ribs. Carl was nearly sixty years old and had never seen anything so horrifying in his life. He was surrounded by friends and neighbours, but there was no comfort in that. Everyone in the room was alone with their thoughts.

Someone coughed. A couple of women sobbed quietly. They looked incongruous in their brightly coloured spring dresses, shaky hands pressing handkerchiefs to their faces against the stench of death and misery. Some of the men and women kept their eyes fixed on the American soldier. Standing in between the two rows of ovens, he explained in a firm voice that they had been used to burn the bodies of tens of thousands of human beings and that there were more death mills like this one all over Europe. As he spoke, he looked at the ashen faces of the townspeople in front of him to ensure everyone was listening. For years, he said, ordinary Germans like them had lived under the thick black plumes of Nazi crematoria. Each and every one of them had been a bystander to mass murder.

Carl felt sick and lightheaded. He hadn't eaten anything since the morning, when he and more than 1,000 fellow German civilians had been forced to undertake a two-hour march to come to this place. It was 16 April 1945. Four days earlier, US Army units had occupied the town of Weimar in central Germany, where Carl lived. Eight kilometres north-west, they had made a terrible discovery. Amid the beech forests of the Ettersberg hill lay Buchenwald concentration camp. What the Americans had found there was so horrific that they feared people would find it hard to believe. They decided that, on behalf of German civilians everywhere, Weimarers were to be confronted with the horrors that had unfolded in their midst.

Carl Weirich was among the throngs that set off from Weimar train station at 10 o'clock in the morning. A bookbinder by trade, he ran a stationery shop in the heart of the old town. He had been too old to be drafted to fight for Nazi Germany on the front lines, but he was fit enough to undertake the hike up the steep banks. He had done it many times. The Ettersberg hill was a popular destination for Weimarers seeking relaxation. In the summer months, its forests offered shady walks and splendid views over the town. In the winter, it was excellent for sledging and skiing.

It felt odd walking the familiar paths out of Weimar and up the hill, surrounded by many friends and neighbours. Even Acting Mayor Erich Kloss was there. It was an unseasonably warm and sunny day. Many Weimarers seemed almost glad to get out of the rubble of their bomb-ravaged town for a while. People talked among themselves as the long column made its way up the Ettersberg. Kloss noted that 'because the sun was shining, the whole thing felt like a spring day out . . . women and girls engaged in lively chatter, curious and expectant, among the men, too, there were no glum faces'.[1]

That changed when the Weimarers walked through the gates of Buchenwald. The sheer moral depravity of what had taken place here hit them with blunt force. There was evidence of torture. Prisoners explained the ways in which they had been tormented by their captors. Carl and the others saw the gallows where prisoners had been executed, a wooden block over which they had been bent to be flogged, a long pole around which their arms had been bent backwards until joints dislocated and tendons tore.

They saw corpses piled up on carts, their gaunt faces evidence of the suffering endured in the last moments of life. The stench of bodies decomposing in the spring sun was so strong that some of the women fainted. Teenager Edelgard Schlegelmilch hesitated when she was told to step over a corpse. She just couldn't bear it any longer. She froze and shut her eyes. An American soldier ordered her to open them. After all, that's what they had been brought here to do: open their eyes to Nazi crimes. Edelgard did as she was told, walking through the dystopian scenes as if in a trance. 'This can't be true,' she thought. 'You must be dreaming.'[2]

The nightmare wasn't over yet. The Weimarers were shown evidence of medical experimentation on the prisoners, and the over-crowded barracks. Inmates presented festering wounds and injuries. Many were so thin that they looked like living skeletons. Mass graves had been dug up, revealing countless bodies that had been carelessly discarded. Perhaps most incredible of all was a table displaying samples of human skin that had been collected by the former camp commandant and his wife. There were shrunken heads and a lamp-shade made from human skin. Weimarers insisted again and again that they hadn't known, that they had no idea such things had taken place, let alone a mere walk away from the beds in which they slept.

The US Army filmed the townspeople the day they were con-fronted with Buchenwald. The resulting documentary, called *Death Mills* or *Die Todesmühlen*, put the blame for Nazi atrocities squarely on the shoulders of ordinary Germans like Carl. 'These Germans, the ones who said they didn't know, were responsible too,' the nar-ration insists. 'They had put themselves gladly into the hands of criminals and lunatics. They tell you now they meant no evil, that they knew nothing of what was going on or could do nothing even if they knew . . . Today, these Germans who cheered the destruction of humanity in their own land, who cheered the attack on helpless neighbours, who cheered the enslavement of Europe, plead for your sympathy.'[3]

To Carl, visiting Buchenwald felt like 'running the gauntlet'. He wrote that 'it took strong nerves to see the terrible things in the crematorium and also in the barracks, where a number of sick pris-oners still lived'. He may not have admitted this to the Americans, but he confided in his diary that what he witnessed up on the Etters-berg had been 'atrocious crimes committed by us'. His heart had filled with disgust and shame about 'our German downfall'.[4] There was no getting away from it. Not far from his home, tens of thousands of people had been murdered by a regime cheered on by millions of Germans. Carl had been no exception.

Like many Germans of his generation, Carl did not spend much time pondering his own responsibility for what had happened. He focused his mind on the immediate threats to himself and his family, on grief, trauma, hunger and destruction. It would fall to later generations to draw conclusions from one of the darkest chapters in human history and to decide what to learn from it.

The question of how and why a nation that prided itself on its culture and civility enabled the catastrophe of Nazism haunts us to this day because we fear a repeat. It is no mere historical question. 'It happened, therefore it can happen again,' warned Holocaust survivor Primo Levi. Despite the many pages written on the rise and rule of the Third Reich, the matter is worth re-examining at the granular level. How did Germany, within a few years, turn from one of the most liberal democracies in the world to a genocidal dictatorship? What choices did individual Germans make that enabled this? A crucial piece of this twentieth-century puzzle is the town of Weimar.

Weimar lies in the heart of Germany. On a map of the country, it sits slightly off-centre, about halfway between Hamburg and Munich. It is a quaint town, conscious of history and tradition, both of which it has in abundance. Its cobbled streets are home to timber-framed houses, elegant villas, churches, palaces and deep green treetops. Situated in the valley of the River Ilm, its leafy parks are so expansive that one nineteenth-century writer joked that 'Weimar is really a park that has a town.'5 Weimar has attracted many famous residents. Johann Wolfgang von Goethe, widely regarded as Germany's national poet, lived and worked here with his friend and fellow writer Friedrich Schiller. Johann Sebastian Bach resided in Weimar for years, as did fellow composer Franz Liszt and the philosopher Friedrich Nietzsche. Weimar's place in German cultural history far exceeds its physical size.

'Weimar is Germany in a nutshell,' the former German

President Roman Herzog once said, 'a town in which not only culture and thought were at home but also philistinism and barbarism.'[6] Weimar has long been Germany's beacon of culture, but for a time it was also its heart of darkness. It represents all the country gained, lost, suffered and inflicted. At no time was this more true than during the tumultuous period between the two world wars, from 1919 to 1939.

The town that had once been home to some of Europe's greatest minds seemed the ideal place for Germany to reinvent itself after the horror and humiliation of the First World War. It was here that, in 1919, a new constitution inaugurated a new Germany, eventually stamping the town's name on to the country's first attempt at a fully fledged democracy: the Weimar Republic. Few people outside of Germany could point to the town of Weimar on a map. Yet its name conjures powerful notions of noble experiments and fallen ideals.

Over the course of the next twenty years, Weimar also captured the imagination of those who sought to destroy democracy. It was precisely the town's allure as the locus of German culture and tradition that caused Adolf Hitler to visit over forty times and that led the Nazi Party to choose it as the place to regroup after its early defeats. The first formal Nazi Party rally was held in Weimar in 1926, before they were staged in Nuremberg. Weimar was where the Hitler Youth received its name and where central Nazi rituals like the Hitler salute were first presented to the public. The state of Thuringia, of which Weimar was the capital, lifted sanctions on Hitler and the Nazi Party earlier than other German states after his botched coup attempt in Munich in 1923. Weimar became a safe haven for the movement, a testing ground for Nazi ideas. Early support for Nazism also meant that many of Hitler's most trusted lieutenants came from Weimar, men such as Hitler Youth leader Baldur von Schirach and Hitler's private secretary Martin Bormann. It is not without bitter irony that Hitler was also one of the first to coin the term 'Weimar Republic'. Officially, the state was still called the German Reich. But in 1929, the future dictator and other enemies of the fragile democracy used its tenth anniversary to deride it as a supposedly un-German system, using the term 'Weimar Republic' in a derogatory fashion shortly before its demise.

Between 1919 and 1939, the people of Weimar were carried away by the historical tides that engulfed their country. Many of its residents contributed to the storms of the interwar era. Weimar became the birthplace of the influential Bauhaus school of art and design, but also the place from which it was evicted as conservative reaction against its experimental art grew. The National Theatre in the town thrived in the tension between traditionalism and avant-garde culture that marked the period. Its new, liberal-minded director Ernst Hardt wanted it to become a standard-bearer for both traditional and modern drama, and the town itself to become a beacon of a new German culture.

In the early 1920s, creative minds were drawn to Weimar, which was rapidly becoming a focal point for the existential crisis that gripped Germany after the Great War. When Walter Gropius agreed to settle in Weimar and build up the Bauhaus, the town had managed to attract one of the most influential names in architecture. Many other illustrious figures followed, among them the Russian painter Wassily Kandinsky and Swiss-born artist Paul Klee, who lectured at Gropius's school. By 1924, nationalist pressure on the town's liberals had intensified to levels that many found unbearable. Theatre director Hardt buckled under biting personal attacks on him and resigned. Increasingly, nationalists and Nazis began to use the theatre for their conventions.

As a place of German culture, Weimar was visibly Nazified once fascism took hold. Hitler's favourite hotel, the Elephant in the town centre, was demolished and rebuilt to his specifications, including a private apartment for his exclusive use. While more such projects were planned, Weimar was the only regional capital in Nazi Germany that received a 'Gau Forum', a local Nazi Party complex, complete with marching square, 'People's Hall' and administrative buildings for organizations like the Gestapo, the feared secret police. For this, the street layout was remodelled, which continues to shape the townscape to this day.

Most Weimarers turned a blind eye to the establishment of the infamous Buchenwald concentration camp on their doorstep and would continue to do so even as tens of thousands of prisoners arrived at their railway station. Set up in 1937, it would become the largest such camp in the German Reich, incarcerating nearly 280,000 people in total on the main site and its sub-camps. It was located very close to Ettersburg Castle, where Goethe, Schiller and other figures of the German literary canon once talked and wrote. Its proximity to the idealized heart of German culture was such that even pro-Nazi organizations found it uncomfortable. Weimar's chapter of the National Socialist Culture Community, keen to put distance between the barbarism that was to take place there and the country's literary heroes, impressed on the planning committee that under no circumstances was the place to be named after the famous hill, or the castle or anything else associated with the 'classic era' of the town. The neutral name 'Buchenwald' ('Beech Forest') was chosen, allowing Weimarers to disavow any connection to the monstrous crimes that took place there. In the first year alone, forty-eight people died at Buchenwald. By April 1945, when it was liberated, the death toll reached 56,000.

The connection between Buchenwald and Weimar cannot be severed. It was at the town's train station where the prisoners first arrived. It was in the town crematorium where the bodies of those who died there between 1937 and 1940 were brought to be burned and buried before the camp built its own crematorium. Weimar's citizens shared facilities such as the camp's zoo, which was set up for the entertainment of SS personnel. The inscription on the camp gate, which read 'Jedem das Seine' ('To Each His Own'), was designed by former Bauhaus student Franz Ehrlich, who had been arrested by the Nazis in 1935 and became one of Buchenwald's first prisoners in September 1937. He used a Bauhaus typeface for the inscription. The concentration camp Weimar was so keen to disassociate itself from was now branded with a product of the culture that the town had first fostered, then expelled.

Many Weimar residents not only looked the other way but

actively promoted Hitler's ideology. Nazi election results in Weimar were higher than the German average. It was the seat of the first state government to appoint a Nazi minister, in 1930, three years before Hitler became Chancellor of Germany. Yet the town also continued to be home to the Cranach Press publishing house, run by the liberal Anglo-German diplomat and writer Harry Graf Kessler, who promoted the League of Nations. In its juxtaposition of the heights of modernity with the abyss of Nazism, Weimar was interwar Germany in a nutshell.

Many of those whose formative years were spent in Weimar in the 1920s made remarkably contrasting choices in the 1930s. Take the eighteen-year-old Marlene Dietrich, who was sent to Weimar to learn from the best musicians and artists of the day. Or Walter Gropius, the founder of the Bauhaus school. Neither found life in Nazi Germany bearable. Both chose to live in the US rather than remain in a country run by Hitler. Dietrich renounced her German citizenship in 1939 and became an American. Other inhabitants of Weimar made different choices that linked them intricately to the nation's fate. Emmy Sonnemann worked as an actress at the German National Theatre in Weimar from 1922. Ten years later, her life would change forever. One day in 1932, she happened to be sitting in the Kaiser Café when an important-looking man in uniform stepped in. It was Hermann Göring. The two became a couple and married in 1935. Hitler was their best man.

Weimar, the town that was meant to give its name to Germany's democratic renewal, became synonymous with the catastrophic failure of this political experiment, and this is reflected in the contrasting lives of its residents. What roles did they play in this process? Were the American occupiers right to suggest that they 'were responsible too', because 'they had put themselves gladly into the hands of criminals and lunatics'? No one is entirely free to act outside of the circumstances in which they find themselves. But this doesn't mean people don't have agency. Interwar Germany has long fascinated scholars and the public because it embodies the tension between the individual and the collective, between inevitability and responsibility.

To many Germans, it seemed their lives permanently teetered on the edge of catastrophe after the First World War. They felt trapped by forces greater than any one individual and would later tell the world and themselves that there was nothing they could have done to prevent their nation's fall. Others were wracked by what-if questions concerning personal tragedies. Could they have saved a loved one, their families or themselves from misery, grief or annihilation? The way we tell and teach the story of interwar Germany today suggests not only that they could but that they should have acted differently, that there was a way of pulling history back from the brink. It's a moment in time we return to for lessons because the stakes could hardly have been higher. The fate of democracy, of Germany, of tens of millions of ordinary lives and of Europe itself hung in the balance.

This book tells the stories of Weimar's people – the illustrious and the ordinary – to examine the impact and often also the futility of personal decisions made in the face of seismic historic forces. At the centre of the story is Carl Weirich, a middle-class shop owner who came to Weimar in 1914 with great hopes for the future, only to find that two world wars and a multitude of crises would hit his business and his family. The bookbinder was fascinated by paper, ink, typewriters and the written word. He kept a meticulous diary, which details his life story. I have cross-checked events and people referenced in it for historical accuracy and have found his records to be correct wherever specifics are mentioned. Carl's writing is often surprisingly frank, giving a unique and granular insight into his life between the wars. His and all other direct speech quoted in this book stems from historical records.

Weimar's women were also caught up in events and tried to shape their own destiny within the means available to them. There was Rosa Schmidt, a Jewish hotelier who operated the Hotel Hohenzollern right by the train station. She was married to Arthur Schmidt, who came from an old Weimar family and fought in the First World War. The couple struggled to keep their business afloat during the challenging post-war years and hyperinflation. Their

Hotel Hohenzollern is where Hitler stayed during his early Weimar visits.

At the other end of town, Elisabeth Förster-Nietzsche ran an archive that contained the literary remains of her late brother Friedrich Nietzsche. After the famous philosopher suffered a mental breakdown, his sister became his carer and the self-appointed steward of his legacy. Permanently cash-strapped, she and the Nietzsche Archive relied on funding from generous donors and the various governments of the interwar era. While not impressed by Hitler to start with, Elisabeth soon embraced Nazism, and Nazism embraced Nietzsche. Despite her politics, Elisabeth's oldest friend remained the liberal Harry Graf Kessler. The pair wrote frequent, lively letters to one another in which they often referenced personal conversations that took place during Harry's visits to Elisabeth's villa in Weimar. Together with Harry's detailed diary entries, they form a rich pool of historical sources.

A few Weimarers actively resisted Nazism. One of them was Kurt Nehrling, a young social democrat who returned from his brief war service with a debilitating case of tuberculosis. Neither this nor personal blows of fate deterred him from fighting for his convictions. This put both himself and his family in grave danger, though his actions were never enough to harm the Nazis in their course. Kurt's life story is reconstructed through letters, official documents and descriptions from his friends and comrades.

These and many other Weimarers form the human tableau of this book. Though they represent different age groups, genders, social classes and responses to the tumultuous era they lived through, they should not be seen as types. Each individual was a real human being with their own complex circumstances, motives and room to manoeuvre. While their stories combine into what many may regard as a cautionary tale, it is difficult and often unhelpful to judge people's behaviour from our vantage point a century later. I have kept my commentary and analysis as a historian to a minimum, allowing you, the reader, to observe events, decisions and developments as they unfolded.

If we are to avoid the mistakes made by people in the past, the first step is to understand why they were made. Democracy and civilization are maintained or destroyed by the choices we make as individuals and as societies. No amount of history, tradition and culture is sufficient to safeguard against the takeover of a ruthless totalitarian ideology. There is no better case study of this than Weimar between the wars.

Prelude: War

Blood and thunder

Carl Weirich stepped out of the sunshine and into the little shop in the middle of Weimar. The air inside smelled of books and leather. Cramped shelves and glass cabinets displayed pens, postcards, typewriters and ink pots. Notebooks, rulers, pencils and paintbrushes waited for children to pick up supplies for the next school year. Carl's heart filled with a mixture of awe and anxiety. This was it, his new life in Weimar.

It was 28 April 1914 and Carl had travelled the 75 kilometres from his home town of Eisenach by train in the morning. He had arrived at Weimar's elegant train station and walked down Sophienstraße, the long, broad avenue that led down to the old town. He tried to take it all in: the hotels that surrounded the large square in front of the station, the Grand Ducal Museum that came up after a short walk, the viaduct and park in front of it. The main road was shared by horse-drawn carriages, the odd car and a one-cart tram taking visitors and Weimarers back and forth between the town centre and the train station. It all seemed wonderful. Weimar. This famous town in the heart of Germany had once been home to many of the country's greatest poets, thinkers, musicians and philosophers. It would soon be Carl's home.

Excited at the prospect, he passed the post office, crossed Karls-platz underneath its large trees and turned left into Geleitstraße. The sound of water tinkled in the air as he walked the cobbled street past a fountain and the Hotel Chemnitius. When he reached Number 10, he stopped and looked up. The sign above the large window read 'Richard Straubel'. This well-established stationery shop was up for

Weimar's Karlsplatz in 1907.

lease. It was Carl's chance to grow roots and build something for himself. His life and profession revolved around books, writing and printing. What better place for new beginnings than Weimar?

Carl felt it was about time he settled. He had taken more time than most to learn a trade, travel and see the world. He was now twenty-eight years old, a slender man with bright blond hair, a pointy nose and a friendly, open face. The youngest of five siblings, he was the only one in his immediate family still living this kind of life. Born in 1885 to the bookbinder Andreas Weirich, who ran a successful stationery business in Eisenach, he grew up in the shadow of the famous Wartburg Castle, where Martin Luther had translated the New Testament of the Bible into German and unleashed a religious revolution that would change the world. Eisenach attracted a steady and lucrative stream of tourism from all over Europe. The Weirichs ran a thriving shop that offered both bookbinding services and Wartburg souvenirs. Financially comfortable, if not outright wealthy, Carl had an idyllic childhood, hiking in the mountains and singing folk songs with his family. In their Protestant household the 'iron strictness' of his father was offset by his mother's kindness.[1] Both his parents worked hard in the shop so that, one day, they would be able to help all their children make the best of their own lives. And now it was Carl's turn.

He was offered a chance to start his own business when the ageing stationery shop owner Richard Straubel decided it was time to retire after running his business in the heart of Weimar's old town for twenty-eight years. It was ideally placed next to the Hotel Chemnitius and not far from many restaurants and tourist attractions, able to supply locals with school equipment, paper and bookbinding services while visitors bought postcards and souvenirs. It would change hands for 1,000 marks in rent and 11,500 marks to purchase the stock wholesale, a sum of which Carl's parents would pay 7,000 now and 4,500 with interest in 1917. His brother Arno, a master bookbinder and twelve years his senior to the day (they were both born on 9 November), accompanied Carl to take stock and reassure. Both men loved what they saw. The matter was settled. Carl would move to Weimar. 'And so my path was well paved through parental love and support,' he reflected in his diary.[2]

Carl's parents also bought a spartan set of furniture for their son. On 1 May, he moved into the small room above the shop until he got married and started his own family. An iron spiral staircase led up to Carl's simple abode, which contained little more than a bed, a table and a chair. He ate his lunches at Frau Gerlach's butcher shop next door and was grateful when Frau Straubel, the wife of the previous owner, made him a cup of tea from time to time. The elderly Straubels continued to live in the building, which was enormously helpful for Carl, who didn't have any contacts in Weimar. Frau Straubel regularly popped into the shop, appearing side by side with the young man to ease the transition for regular customers with a cheerful 'May I introduce our successor Weirich to you?'[3] But Frau Straubel made it clear that her services were time-limited, urging Carl to get married so that someone else might make tea for him and help in the shop. She soon guessed that he didn't need to be told twice. On the day he moved in, eight 'fiery red roses' arrived at Geleitstraße 10 in celebration of the new job and the new life in Weimar.[4] They were from Carl's girlfriend Friedel.

★

Rosa Schmidt screamed and writhed as the pangs of labour gripped her again and again. She was fighting a lonely battle to give birth to her third child in Alexandria, Egypt. She was thirty-one years old and thousands of kilometres away from home. Her family hailed from Żółkiew, now Zhovkva in western Ukraine. The medieval town had been a Polish settlement but was in the Austro-Hungarian Empire when Rosa was born there in 1882. Headed by her mother Sarah Grill-Freimann, the family lived alongside Jews, Ukrainians, Armenians and Poles.

All that lay in the past. Rosa Grill-Freimann was now Rosa Schmidt, a petite woman with wavy hair and warm, brown eyes. Her new name had opened a new chapter in her life. Together with her husband Arthur, who was three years older, she had settled in Alexandria in British-controlled Egypt. There the newly-weds began running a busy hotel together. Arthur, a slim, elegant man whose sharp-featured face was framed by a side parting and a neatly trimmed goatee beard, worked as head waiter. Rosa helped out where she was needed while raising their first two children, nine-year-old Alexandra and seven-year-old Arthur.

The pair had first met years earlier on a cruise liner where Arthur had worked as a steward and chef and Rosa as a childminder. Travelling the seas together, they fell in love and soon got married. Their work and love for adventure had brought them together even though they had very different backgrounds. Rosa came from one of the Jewish families that constituted half of Żółkiew's population. Arthur was born into a Protestant household in Weimar. His father Hermann Schmidt had been a brush-maker but his son did not follow in his footsteps. Something drew the young man out of his sleepy home town. Working on a cruise ship would allow him to see the world despite his modest upbringing. Like her future husband, Rosa also wanted to travel and work and signed up to look after the children of wealthy passengers on the same vessel. The adventurous spirit that brought the couple together would shape their lives. As Herr and Frau Schmidt, they settled in Alexandria, founded a family and built a life for themselves thousands of kilometres away from their home towns.

As much as he loved his wife, Arthur wasn't there to support Rosa

Arthur Schmidt in Alexandria, 1908.

while she was giving birth to their third child. He was 3,000 kilometres away in Weimar, visiting family. He had taken Alexandra and Arthur with him while their heavily pregnant mother had stayed behind to look after the business and also because a long journey over land and sea would have been perilous in her state. Rosa managed. On 28 January 1914, she gave birth to a healthy boy who would be christened Ernst. She couldn't wait to introduce the baby to his father and siblings, who were due to return in a few months. She had no idea that history would soon scupper these plans and change her life forever.

As Carl Weirich moved to Weimar in the spring of 1914, Johannes Wagner, called Hanns, was leaving. The teenager left his home town and rented a small room in the university city of Jena, a few kilometres to the south-east of Weimar. There, he wanted to learn the art of book printing. A blond, bright-eyed seventeen-year-old, Hanns came from a family of book printers. His grandfather Robert had founded the 'Printing House R. Wagner' in Weimar in 1879, and upon his death in 1893 had passed it on to his son Alfred. Hanns was born four years later, and, being Alfred's only son, he knew he would one day take over the business.

Growing up surrounded by books and seeing them made, he fell in love with reading from an early age – so much so that his parents tried to rein him in. He was particularly beguiled by the German thinker Arthur Schopenhauer, whose philosophy has always attracted those in search of meaning and purpose. The boy read by candlelight until the small hours of the morning. His attic room in the impressive four-storey building his father had built at Rollplatz 7 became a much-cherished sanctuary.

Hanns also loved animals and nature. He kept an aquarium with salamanders, water snails and frogs. One day, when he introduced a small turtle to this microcosm, he learned a hard life lesson. Hanns was doing his homework when he heard a terrible noise of anguish. He realized it came from the aquarium and rushed over to find the head and arms of a frog dangling out of the turtle's mouth. It had already swallowed one of the creature's legs and a bit of its rump. The frog squealed pitifully and seemed to look accusingly at Hanns through eyes shining with mortal pain. The boy didn't know what to do. Stunned, he watched the poor creature slowly being devoured alive. 'It was gruesome,' he later remembered, 'and for the first time I gained a lasting impression of the cruelty of nature.'[5]

On 1 August 1914, Germany and Russia sent each other declarations of war, setting in motion a chain of events that would leave no life in Europe untouched. Nine million people would die in military combat during the First World War, which raged through Europe from August 1914 to November 1918. Two million Germans would be among the dead.

Throughout August 1914, Weimar experienced the same electric mix of jubilation and fear as the rest of the country. It was a strange transformation. A place that took pride in its civility and high culture suddenly became a garrison town. Its professional soldiers, part of the 5th Thuringian Infantry Regiment No. 94, found out that their country was at war while engaged in a regular exercise at Ohrdruf in central Thuringia. When the men had set off from their local train stations on 28 July, there had already been unease. A local reporter noted: 'Now, in this fateful hour, the sight of departing military trains impresses the observer in a particular manner.' Some of the soldiers even wondered whether they would ever see their home town again. 'Well, surely it won't be as bad as that,' the journalist commented.[6]

Upon the outbreak of war, the men were immediately recalled. They returned to their barracks, nicknamed the 'Weimar Acropolis' as the imposing building towered high above the town centre on a hill to the east. In addition to the regular troops, many volunteers, reservists and militia forces of the so-called Landwehr flooded into town. Their frenetic energy was infectious and shook sleepy Weimar into a hub of activity.

Within days, things escalated. On 3 August, Germany and France declared war on one another. The next day Germany invaded neutral Belgium, causing Britain to declare war on Germany. Both excitement and alarm spread like wildfire. Local farmers worried what would become of the harvest should they be drafted. Panic buying ensued. The Weimar branch of the Social Democratic Party (SPD) warned that 'Our German fatherland stands on the brink of an abyss . . . our fatherland will be exposed to a national catastrophe of a scale the world has never seen.'[7]

Foreigners were regarded with wild-eyed suspicion. No exceptions were made for Weimar's celebrity residents like Henry van de Velde. The much-venerated Belgian designer and architect had become one of the most prominent figures of the Jugendstil movement, Germany's answer to Art Nouveau. Now he was placed under police surveillance. Actual criminals convicted of petty crimes such as theft or fraud received an amnesty from Wilhelm Ernst, Grand Duke of Saxe-Weimar-Eisenach, so that they could be drafted for military service.

All the political parties represented in the Reichstag, the German parliament, agreed to support the war effort wholly, and their local chapters followed suit. The Weimar SPD cancelled a 'Down with the War!' event, scheduled for 3 August.[8] The few dissenting voices were either silenced or silenced themselves in the name of national unity.

On 7 August, the Weimar infantry battalion was deemed ready for departure to Belgium. At noon, the men gathered for a celebratory goodbye in the courtyard of the Schloss, Weimar's palace and the ancestral residence of the Grand Dukes of Saxe-Weimar-Eisenach.

The mood was sombre as the soldiers stood in formation, listening to a service delivered by the court cleric Karl Trainer, who declared that Germany's enemies had 'pressed the sword into our hands'.[9] The next day, Regiment 94 left Thuringia for St Vith, a picturesque town by the Belgian border. The trains were decorated with flowers and crowds gathered at the station to see them off with cheers and good wishes. The *Jenaer Volksblatt* reported that 'The brave defenders of the fatherland, who now pass through the Weimar-Gera station in long trains, display not only a confident battle optimism but also a refreshing sense of humour.'[10] Someone had painted an image of Deutscher Michel, a well-known personification of Germany, on the side of the locomotive. Wearing his customary nightcap, Michel leaned back in his chair, smoking a pipe. His right foot casually rested on a 'bunch of Russians and Frenchmen who bent pitifully under the weight'.[11] But the left-leaning *Weimarische Volkszeitung* detected an undercurrent of unease. Once one of the trains was out of sight, it claimed, the station quietened and 'the seriousness of the hour became a certainty'.[12]

Grand Duke Wilhelm Ernst was desperate to be seen to do his part. He pleaded with the High Command and even with the Kaiser himself to allow him to command troops, but in vain. He simply didn't have enough experience. He accompanied his men to the Western Front without really knowing what exactly he would do there. When he eventually received the Iron Cross, first class, he confided in a letter to his wife Feodora that he thought 'for us, who have after all done nothing, it is too much'.[13] Wilhelm Ernst was doomed to look on as his Weimarers shed blood.

In August 1914, life changed drastically for all Weimarers, from the grand ducal court to ordinary families. Arthur Schmidt, who had intended to return to Rosa in Alexandria to reunite his young family, now found that he couldn't do so. Britain was establishing a naval blockade to restrict the supply of goods to Germany. From the autumn the North Sea, Germany's only sea access to the oceans, became a war zone. The resulting lack of food would claim the lives of over half a million German civilians through the next four years. In August 1914, it also meant Rosa Schmidt was stuck in Alexandria with her baby son Ernst. Her two older children would soon have to face life in Weimar without both their parents. Arthur volunteered to fight and was sent to the Western Front. Rosa was determined to find a way through to her children, even if it meant embarking on a dangerous journey with her seven-month-old baby.

Hanns Wagner was also convinced that he should help defend his country. The book-printing apprenticeship in Jena would have to wait. His parents disagreed. They were not happy to see their only son interrupt his education. At seventeen, he was not yet legally of age but his parents couldn't stop him attending an evening course for treating illness and war injuries in Jena, and so that's what he did while continuing to implore his parents to sign the permission slip. It didn't take long before they relented. On 26 August, Hanns began his military training in Oberweimar, just south-east of his home town. 'Exhausting and stupid', as that seemed at times, he resolved to get through it to defend Germany.[14]

No amount of practice could have prepared Hanns for the savagery of mechanized warfare. In October, just a few weeks after completing his basic training, the teenager was cowering in a half-finished trench somewhere between Ypres and Menin in Belgium. Around him fountains of mud erupted. Shells tore through the air, exploding with ear-splitting noise upon impact – each barrage louder than the previous one. Hanns knew that the deadly wall of fire behind him was encroaching on his pathetic shelter. British artillery got closer and closer to its target. But what to do? Ahead of him enemy soldiers sat in their trenches, their rifles trained on the German lines. Anyone who dared crawl out from the chest-high mud wall that blocked the line of fire risked getting shot. Trapped, nobody moved as the relentless bombardment crept towards them. Hanns was certain the next barrage would hit the trench. He wanted to live. So he threw his bag over his shoulder, grabbed his rifle and climbed over the top.

Ignoring the deafening chaos around him, he concentrated on moving forward. After a few hundred metres, he finally found shelter. The bloated body of a horse lay still in the otherwise feature-less landscape, and Hanns crawled as close as he could to the carcass. He waited. Hours passed. When dusk settled over the inferno of war, the bombardment subsided, and Hanns finally dared to move. Under the shelter of darkness, he crept back to his unit. Where the trench had been just a few hours earlier, he now found only broken earth. He was reluctant to use his torch, for fear of making himself a target, but he couldn't help it. He had to know. In the brief flashes of light he glimpsed scenes of sheer horror. Severed limbs. Shreds of human flesh. The lifeless, pale faces of boys who had, just a few months earlier, been his school friends in Weimar.

Bookbinder Carl Weirich felt no urge at all to become a soldier. He was busy building a life for himself and he wouldn't let war get in the way. While Hanns Wagner was losing friends and his youthful naivety in the bloody trenches of the Western Front, Carl also began a new chapter of his life. At 3 p.m. on 21 October 1914, he married his long-term girlfriend Friedel in her home town of Oranienburg, just north of Berlin. It was a bittersweet experience for him. His father Andreas had been gravely ill when he met Friedel for the first time in the summer and approved of the match. He had died shortly after and 'didn't live to receive the news that Germany was at war', Carl noted in his diary.[15] In tribute to the stern but supportive father, the couple had chosen his parents' wedding day, 21 October, to get married.

The party in Oranienburg was a welcome distraction from war for the many guests in attendance. It was hard to get away from it. While Carl had run his new stationery business in Weimar success-fully enough to meet the monthly credit repayments, the military conflict had found its way into the shop. Decorative boxes in which letters from the front lines could be collected by anxious relatives were selling well, as were postcards of the victorious military leaders who had made advances on the Eastern Front. But in Oranienburg all that was forgotten for a few precious hours. The wedding party went on until midnight.

In Belgium, Hanns Wagner couldn't find a single living soul as he searched what was left of the trench he had fled a few hours earlier. His entire company seemed to have been wiped out and there was no point in lingering among their lifeless bodies. So he wandered around until he found a nearby group of infantry soldiers.

He joined them just as they attempted to make their way through a forest under constant fire from British troops. Hanns fired blindly into the distance. Shot after shot until his rifle was glowing hot. Suddenly he broke down in pain. He had been hit in the foot, but in the chaos of battle nobody noticed. It seemed to take a long time before he was finally found by medics in the evening and carried on a stretcher along a dark road. Every time the group came under fire, the medics set down the stretcher and sought shelter while Hanns lay on the road, immobile and helpless, hearing bullets hiss back and forth above his head.

Eventually, they reached a field hospital where Hanns was patched up by a medic working by candlelight. The boy sank into feverish dreams that brought some relief from pain and fear. Soon after, he was transported by train to a makeshift military hospital near Düsseldorf where Hanns was treated by an ear, nose and throat specialist with no experience or interest in treating open wounds. The doctor never bothered changing his bandages and the gaping hole in his foot soon began to fester. Resting the wounded limb on a stool next to the bed so the pus that oozed out from the bandages could drop on to the floor, he was driven to near insanity by the clockwork regularity of the sound. Soon, the indifferent doctor asked him to decide whether he wanted his leg amputated above or below the knee. Hanns spent night after night listening to the drip-drip-drip of his wound, considering these terrible options. He still hadn't come to terms with spending the rest of his life with just one leg, when a senior physician came to inspect the hospital. Hanns told him about his woes and the doctor took a look at the festering hole in the teenager's foot. There was no need to amputate, he decided, and ordered that the bandages be changed and the wound cleaned regularly, staff shortages or not. Hanns's foot soon began to heal, causing his physician to sneer: 'If you carry on making such progress and the war lasts a bit longer, you might yet be able to die a hero's death for your Grand Duke after all.'[16]

Carl and Friedel Weirich knew little of the tragedy unfolding on the front lines. They had their own concerns in Weimar. On 29 November, they enjoyed their first evening at the Court Theatre together. They watched the French opera *Mignon*. Based on Goethe's novel *Wilhelm Meister's Apprenticeship*, it tells the story of a young man on a journey to educate himself and find a meaningful life. Carl found it 'wonderfully staged' and was relieved to see that his 'darling wife' loved the songs.[17] It was a welcome respite for both of them. Friedel was extremely unhappy in Weimar and permanently homesick. Her husband, though working hard to keep the shop afloat, tried and failed to cheer her up. On occasion it worked, like when he bought her a cake for her twenty-fourth birthday on 13 November, and her mother had visited from Oranienburg. Then, he wrote in his diary, 'the streams of Friedel's tears stopped flowing and we showed her dear mother jubilantly how much we loved each other'.[18] They also went hiking in the surrounding mountains, spending what Carl fondly described as 'the happiest moments of our life together'. But Friedel's mind was never at ease. Sobbing bitterly, she would speak of her beloved Oranienburg. She missed her parents and her siblings. Carl felt this was unfair. He too had left his home town to build a new life in Weimar, and he was trying hard to make it work. So why couldn't she? 'You're a man,' Friedel cried, 'you don't know what longing is.'[19]

Weimar's children also saw their lives upended. Jutta Hecker, a ten-year-old girl with wavy, blonde hair and large round eyes, listened intently as a letter was read out to her class in December 1914. It was from Dr Glaser, her affable headteacher at the Sophienstift school for girls. At forty-two, he had been a dynamic school leader. Now he was gone. He had been called up for military service immediately when war broke out, and the pupils had packed parcels with warm clothing and small Christmas presents for him and the other soldiers. Dr Glaser's long letter was full of praise and gratitude. He wouldn't live to see the end of the terrible war that had engulfed him and his town. He would die on 14 November 1917.

The war cut short what would have been a sheltered childhood for Jutta in a middle-class household. The youngest of three, she was doted upon by her good-natured mother Lili and her loving father Max, who had worked at the Goethe and Schiller Archive since 1900. Max Hecker found a willing disciple in his youngest child. The girl was fascinated when he recited poetry or told her about Weimar's famous writers of years gone by. Jutta remembered later that she realized then 'that there was a realm made of rhyme and rhythm, which stands above daily life'.[20]

Max and Lili were both from Cologne and had no social network in Weimar. They decided they might as well move to the outskirts of town where the rent would be cheaper and they were closer to the countryside. They lived in one of twelve houses on the Lindenberg, a hill to the east of the town centre. Max now had a short commute to the archive on foot, walking past the Altenburg house where the famous Hungarian composer Franz Liszt once lived. Jutta had to walk half an hour down the steep street to the Sophienstift school for girls, which had been founded in 1854 by the Grand Duchess Sophie of Saxe-Weimar-Eisenach for the 'Daughters of the Upper Classes'. Her daily walk to school with friends led her past some of Weimar's most famous sights: the Ilm Park, the Schloss, the library and the old town. Jutta was no stranger to uniforms, as many officers lived on the Lindenberg, and she was friends with their sons and daughters.

When war broke out, Jutta's life changed immediately. The officers left for battle, cheered on by their fellow Weimarers. By Christmas the first of her Lindenberg neighbours was dead, leaving a son and a daughter behind. At school, life also changed. Male teachers were drafted, foreign teachers sacked. Jutta's French teacher, fifty-three-year-old Mathilde Borst, had to leave because she was from Strasbourg, which was then part of Germany but continued to be a hotbed of separatists who wanted it to become French again. Annie Royston, a Cambridge graduate who had taught English at Jutta's school for twenty-four years, was also dismissed.[21] Pupils were frequently set homework in lieu of lessons that had to be cancelled.

After school, Jutta and the other children visited wounded soldiers at Weimar's military hospital, performing plays or songs for them. They collected scrap metal and other materials that could be repurposed or sold to raise funds for the increasing number of invalids returning from the front lines. They organized donations of books and clothes for soldiers and of money for their widows and orphans. Horses needed hay and farms help with the harvest. By Christmas 1914, it was abundantly clear to everyone in Weimar that there was no end in sight. There would be more hardship, more sacrifice, more death.

As his wound still hadn't closed and Hanns Wagner was in no fit shape to return to the front, he was allowed to come home for Christmas on a four-week leave. That was great news in principle, but what would his parents think? He was reduced to 'skin and bones, a skeleton limping along on crutches'.[22] His uniform, while cleaned and brushed, was tattered. But he was looking forward to returning to his childhood home at Rollplatz 7 for a while. His parents gave him a warm welcome and bought a large shoe made of felt for their son so he could get his bandaged foot into it, which he still had to have cleaned at Weimar's military hospital every three days. He hobbled around the cobbled streets in good cheer, and was pleased to bump into Margarete Deinhardt, a girl his age with whom he had chatted through the last dance of the ball in his final school year. That all seemed a lifetime ago. Margarete was now a volunteer at the military hospital, where she saw first hand what the fighting did to the young men in her home town. The pair no longer indulged in inconsequential small talk. When they met for coffee at the busy Café Grenzdörffer, there was only one topic: the war.

The Wagners, on the other hand, were optimistic. The war was surely as good as won, they told their wounded son. It was a surprise it hadn't already ended before Christmas. There was really no point for Hanns to go back. Why didn't he resume his apprenticeship? And anyway, there was no glory in soldiering. Hanns wasn't even a glamorous officer but a mere infantry soldier. His parents were ashamed at the state of his uniform and made him limp over to the tailor to have a new one made. In the end, Hanns was almost glad to go back to the front. He had changed and there was now a gulf between son and parents that was hard to bear. He wouldn't return to Weimar for Christmas again until the war was over.

In their increasing desperation to win the war, the German authorities were drawing on all available human resources whether they volunteered their services or not. On 1 May 1915, a group of new recruits was being inspected. It was an unseasonably summery day and the men had been ordered up to the Webicht area, a forest as popular with hikers and dog walkers as it was with landscape painters and blue-blooded hunting parties. In 1911, the Weimar Association for Air Traffic, a hobby club for flying enthusiasts, established a small airfield there, called Weimar-Lindenberg, or more informally Ninety Acres. It was there that Carl Weirich was now running around with his fellow would-be soldiers.

Carl was feeling hot and nauseous. The bookbinder wasn't cut out for military life. He had hated every minute of it since he had been recruited to the Landsturm unit on 21 February 1915. For one thing, his shop depended on him. Friedel was trying to step in but she had no experience in bookbinding or dealing with customers. So Carl's mother had to come from Eisenach to help out with the household, while Frau Straubel, the elderly wife of the previous owner, kindly agreed to help and train Friedel. But it wasn't easy. Friedel had developed a permanent cough that often left her wheezing and feeling dizzy. She was also pregnant.

Apart from the strain it put on everyone, soldiering just wasn't for Carl. Grown men were 'trained like schoolboys', he grumbled, 'perhaps 10 years earlier this may have been fun for me'.[23] The inspection at Ninety Acres certainly turned out to be no fun at all. Panting, Carl ran around in full kit, the blazing sun beating down on his head. The heavy rucksack, nicknamed 'monkey' by the men because of its outer fur lining, clung to his sweat-soaked back. He could barely hold up his rifle when the world around him swam out of view and he collapsed right in front of a senior officer. Semi-conscious, Carl was dragged into the mercifully shady Webicht forest to cool down. It was clear that he was useless as a soldier. He was released from military duty, for now.

Rosa Schmidt had known that it wouldn't be easy to journey across the Mediterranean Sea and then hundreds of kilometres across a war-torn continent with her infant son Ernst. Leaving her home and work in Alexandria behind, she had battled her way through Italy and Switzerland, finally making it to the German border in Gottmadingen on 5 October 1915. As the official stamped her passport, allowing mother and child to cross into Arthur's home country, she knew it would be a matter of days until she was finally reunited with her two eldest children. It would take longer still for her husband to finally meet their youngest boy. Arthur was fighting amid the deadly

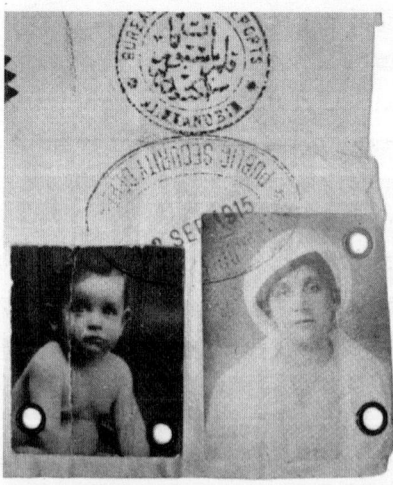

Rosa Schmidt and her baby son Ernst in 1915. The photographs were riveted to the official document that allowed them to sail out of Egypt in wartime.

stalemate on the Western Front and there was no telling when or if he would return to Weimar.

The 21st of October 1915 marked Carl and Friedel Weirich's first wedding anniversary. It should have been a happy occasion. Their daughter Wilfriede was born on 27 August, and many family members had come all throughout September to meet the baby. Carl had used the opportunity to go on a long-distance autumn hike, all the way from Weimar to Eisenach, and felt revived by it. On 26 September, the family had celebrated Wilfriede's christening at the church of St Peter and Paul in Weimar, commonly known as Herderkirche.

The fleeting moments of joy didn't last. On their wedding anniversary, Friedel collapsed in a coughing fit, bringing up vast amounts of blood. A doctor was rushed in and diagnosed severe bleeding from the lungs. Friedel would need a lot of care and bed rest. Carl couldn't look after his desperately sick wife, his newborn daughter and his shop all alone. He needed help. Friedel's mother came from Oranienburg the next day. She and the Weimar doctor Herr Mannes nursed Friedel through three weeks of high fever and coughing fits. When she had stabilized, her mother travelled back to Oranienburg and took little Wilfriede with her. Friedel was in no state to look after her tiny daughter. Christmas 1915 was lonely and miserable for the Weirichs. Carl put the tree next to Friedel's bed and the two prayed for a better 1916.

The year of 1916 brought more pain to many Weimarers. As his customers bought postcards to send to their sons, husbands, brothers and fathers in the trenches, Carl Weirich was fighting to keep the business afloat. Much to his relief, his mother arrived from Eisenach on 29 May. She had agreed to stay with her youngest son at Geleitstraße 10 because he was hopelessly overworked. Carl was still working hard to make enough money to settle the repayments of the loan for his stock every month. Friedel had recovered somewhat since receiving an injection against her illness and was able to get out of bed again. But her doctor still judged it best that she recover fully in a specialized lung sanatorium in Römhild in southern Thuringia. Such facilities had been popular in Germany since the second half of the nineteenth century to deal with the huge number of people suffering from tuberculosis. The disease, also known as the white death or consumption, usually affects the lungs of its victims, causing them to cough up mucus and blood. Gradually, the condition gets worse with fever, weakness, weight loss and eventually death. Urbanization and rapid population growth in Europe in the 1800s had made the disease an epidemic. It is estimated that a quarter of all deaths at the time were caused by it.

Friedel departed for Römhild, leaving her husband trying to run his shop amid an ever-worsening supply situation in which bartering and being in the right place at the right time were vital. Carl's mother not only proved incredibly helpful with these practicalities but also joined him on his long hikes that always had a soothing effect on him. Together they met friends and family, visited Friedel and made the best of a difficult time. When Friedel returned from the clinic in the summer of 1916, she was 'fit as a fiddle', her husband rejoiced, and 'a new delirium of love and happiness ensued'.[24]

On the Western Front, happiness had become a rare commodity. The men were growing increasingly cynical, trapped between the futility and barbarity of their endeavour to break through enemy lines. Weimar soldiers tried to find ways of coping mentally and physically with the incomprehensible scale of bloodshed. Many tried to use the precious moments of calm to think of home. On 30 June 1916, the thunder of artillery fire rumbled across the Somme valley in the distance as a young soldier from Weimar stepped out into the summer air. There had been heavy rain for days, soaking the surrounding fields and waterlogging the trenches in which his comrades were holding out while British shells continued to pound their defensive positions. But now the clouds had finally cleared and made way for a spectacular sunset. As the wide French skies turned a hazy golden colour, soon to give way to a moonless night, the soldier sat down and began to write a letter.

It was Ludwig Sckell's twenty-sixth birthday, and he longed to be with his family. Germany had been at war for nearly two years and it had torn the Sckells apart. Ludwig had lost his youngest brother August in 1914. His wife Gertrud, his newborn son Otto Max, his parents Maria and Otto and his younger siblings Paul and Charlotte were at home in Weimar, 700 kilometres away. Ludwig had no idea when or if he would see them again. Having finished his shooting practice for the day, he wrote to his parents and siblings. But even as he thought of home and family, there was no escaping the situation. Ludwig could hear the ferocious roar of industrialized warfare boom across the fields. In an effort to end the deadly stalemate, British and French forces had been planning to break through by sheer force in the region of the River Somme, not far from where Ludwig was about to put pen to paper. Their preparatory barrage had dropped 1.5 million shells over the last week.

'The food here is great,' wrote Ludwig, 'even better than in W[eimar]. Several times a week, we get butter, cheese, jam etc., good lunches, every day a third of a loaf of bread, plenty – so there are no shortages here.'[25] This was more than a bit of trivia to distract from the bloodletting of the battles raging in the distance. Ludwig was better fed than his family in Weimar. The British naval blockade was in full force, preventing Germany from importing food.

At home in Weimar, ration cards were given out for essentials like flour, barley, potatoes and skimmed milk.[26] A few months into the war, the *Jenaer Volksblatt* had already warned of bread and potato shortages: 'Potatoes at the price of 5 or 6 marks[27] for 50kg are becoming a luxury item for poorer parts of the population who can't afford them. What now?'[28] Ludwig wrote his birthday letter 'in the hope that all of you loved ones at home are in good health'.[29]

If his life on the Western Front was comparatively comfortable, it was because it was atypical. The Sckells had been court gardeners in Weimar for generations, and as chief gardener Ludwig's father Otto was responsible for all the green spaces owned and maintained by the Duchy of Saxe-Weimar-Eisenach. In 1914, Ludwig had been appointed as chief gardener at Dornburg Castle, the summer residence of the Grand Duke high above the banks of the River Saale. When his superiors at the Western Front realized who he was, Ludwig had been relieved of regular duty and tasked with cultivating several gardens behind the front lines. This had suited him down to the ground. 'There is much to do,' he wrote excitedly, 'planting vegetables, even though it [is] very late for that already, picking strawberries, weeding, maintaining paths, transforming wasteland into a good, usable state etc. etc.'[30]

Ludwig's comrades found it difficult to be as enthusiastic about his cushy posting while they risked life and limb in the muddy trenches at Verdun and the Somme. 'Now, there are many people who begrudge one such a task,' the letter complained, 'but at the end of the day this doesn't matter. – Maybe father could send me some seeds as there is very little in terms of flowers and generally nothing or little of this type of thing here; we mostly grow vegetables. – M[aybe] some things that can be sown here and now, and if there are perennial species, which will bloom next year. Maybe I could do with some grass seeds too, but I'll have to discuss that with the sergeant first.'[31]

A few hours after Ludwig had put his pen down and folded up pieces of paper that spoke of grass seeds and perennial flowers, whistles rang out across Allied lines a few dozen kilometres northeast of him. At 7.30 a.m. on 1 July 1916, they broke the silence of a serene French summer morning, shrieking the signal for eleven British and five French divisions to climb out of their trenches and attack the German positions along the Somme valley. The Battle of the Somme had begun. It would last 140 days and involve over 3 million men, of whom a million would be killed or wounded, making it one of the bloodiest battles in human history.

As the summer of 1916 turned into early autumn and there was no end in sight to the carnage on the Western Front, Hanns Wagner was concerned that an army physician would soon deem him 'k.v.' – *kriegsfähig* or 'fighting fit'. The wound in his foot had healed enough for him to be judged *garnisondienstfähig*, capable of doing garrison duties, and he had been posted to Strasbourg. But on marches and drills, his war wound had repeatedly caused him grief. At one point, bone splinters had come loose and bored themselves through his tissue, causing infection. Professor Ledderhose, a well-known surgeon, had operated on the foot. When Hanns had woken up, the bearded physician had dangled his patient's amputated middle toe in front of him. He'd had to remove it to get to the splintered bone and joked, 'Now you can attach it to your watch chain.'[32]

Injured enough not to be sent to the front lines but not so much as not to be useful for the war he was still sure Germany would win, Hanns stayed in his reserve unit in Strasbourg. His time was filled with guard duties, drills and playing the piano for his comrades. After a year, he took part in officer training. As a freshly minted *Unteroffizier*, his task was now training new recruits in drill. He would always think of Strasbourg as the 'beautiful city'.[33] But the spectre of the Western Front loomed large. Hanns had to take the new arrivals for training near the front lines so they had time to get used to the deafening noise and the soul-hardening sight of utter devastation. He took the young men to a battle-ravaged and deserted village not far from Verdun where he continued their training to a soundtrack of explosions and the bone-shaking boom of what he suspected was Germany's Big Bertha in action, one of the largest artillery weapons ever used in combat. The fear was ever present that one day he himself might be sent into the arms of the 'bloodsucking vampire of Verdun who drinks relentlessly and in large gulps', as he put it.[34] Almost everyone from his unit was called up to the 'cursed Western Front' eventually.[35] But when Romania entered the war on the side of the Allied powers on 27 August 1916, Hanns managed to be sent there instead. With a group of new recruits – all middle-aged married tradesmen, Hanns noticed – he headed east.

In early 1917, Weimar's new train station was inaugurated even though the neoclassical building that was to be its crowning glory was as yet unfinished. Works had begun in 1914 but stopped in 1916.

Finished or not, the train line was needed to transport further men and goods to the front lines. Max Hecker, who was keen to continue his work at the Goethe and Schiller Archive, was commandeered to guard the station at night. Civilians at the home front were now exposed to extreme material hardship. In their despair, people were tempted to procure essentials whichever way they could, including theft from parked trains.

Max's twelve-year-old daughter Jutta looked on in sorrow as long columns of horses were sent off to battle. She reflected later that this made her realize what war really means: 'Humans, animals die, but culture and outlook are damaged too.'[36] Bread had been rationed since 1915 and this year meat rationing was adding to the pressures. There was no longer enough fuel and Weimarers had been freezing throughout the cold winter of 1916/17. Jutta's school had to close for four weeks.

Despite his pitiful showing during training two years earlier, Carl Weirich hadn't been forgotten by the rapacious military machine. He had been declared unfit for combat but not for work. So on 27 May 1917, he was drafted into a unit of recovering soldiers. They were based at the Hotel Hohenzollern at Brennerstraße 42, right next to the train station. There, they were put to use completing administrative duties. It could have been a lot worse. His older brother Arno was recruited for soldiering at the age of forty-four, despite suffering from chronic kidney disease. The intense training proved too much for him. Arno collapsed and died. Carl meanwhile was allowed to stay in a desk role, a twenty-minute walk from his home. Friedel ran the shop in his absence and the couple continued to sleep in the same bed, as Carl was allowed to return home most evenings.

The Hohenzollern was not a bad place to work. Manager Willy Wischeropp ran a modern hotel. The handsome white building had twenty-three rooms with gas heating and electric lights. There were flushing toilets. In 1912, a cinema had been installed. It was by no means Weimar's finest address. It didn't have the old-fashioned grandeur and legendary reputation of the Hotel Elephant in the town centre where such illustrious figures as Goethe, Schiller and Wagner had stayed and dined. But it was a neat and long-established place and, most importantly for Carl, it wasn't the front lines.

There was other good news too. The Weirichs' 'dear little daughter Wilfriede' finally came home.[37] The girl was now nearly two years old and had stayed with her grandmother in Oranienburg for most of her young life while Frieda was recovering from tuberculosis. Carl was glad to see that this family reunion 'was a glimmer of light for my dear wife in an otherwise dark existence in serious times of war'.[38]

Ludwig Sckell would never see his young family again. While the Weirichs had at least their Sundays to go on long walks together with little Wilfriede in her pram, he had been given a farm to run on the Western Front. His civilian workers were 'all old people over the age of forty who have been commandeered for the task', Ludwig complained in a letter to his father Otto. 'The animals are of course all gone, and so there are only empty stables.'[39] Germany's military situation had become desperate, making it increasingly obvious to Ludwig and many other Germans that their suffering had lost all purpose. In addition to the lack of imports and ongoing logistical problems caused by the lack of manpower, the potato harvest had also largely failed that year, leaving German civilians exposed to starvation and disease as they subsisted on a diet of root vegetables normally intended as animal feed. Whatever was left was sent to the front lines, leaving little for women and children in the so-called turnip winter. The rate of female mortality had gone up by 11.5 per cent in 1916 compared to pre-war levels. By 1917, it was up by 30 per cent. Ludwig's wife Gertrud, whom he had only married a year before he had left for France, perished in 1916. His baby son Max Otto died in 1917 not yet a year old. 'And what have I lost!' Ludwig wrote to his parents. 'Two dear brothers, my wife and the little boy, whom I was not to see again.'[40]

No matter how hard such personal tragedies hit German families, there was no end in sight to their misery. The High Command resumed its policy of unrestricted submarine warfare from February 1917, which included attacks on merchant ships. This drew the United States into the conflict with its vast resources and overwhelming manpower, dashing German hopes of victory once and for all. Yet war raged on as the military dictatorship that had taken over the running of the country insisted on getting something out of the war. Blind to the suffering of its fellow Germans, the regime pursued a policy of 'Siegfriede' – 'Victory Peace'. There would be no peace until Germany had either gained something from the war or was destroyed by it.

Hanns Wagner continued to fight in the foothills of the Carpathian Mountains in Romania. Life alternated between long periods of intense boredom and short bursts of extreme danger. Even something as mundane as going to the toilet could turn dangerous, as Hanns found out one morning when he got up to relieve himself. He heard a whistling sound and seconds later a shell exploded nine metres away. A jagged piece of shrapnel hissed through the air and landed right in front of him. Strangely fascinated by the fact that the Russians (who were supporting Romanian infantry) had chosen to use artillery fire on a single man, he reached out and picked up the piece of metal. It was still red hot and he dropped it instantly.

Getting a field kitchen to the moving front lines was difficult as the Romanians had begun to attack supply efforts. So the men marched on hard tack and tea. When they discovered a nearby vineyard, they supplemented their meagre rations with small purple grapes. After a while Hanns noticed that his stool had turned red. Assuming this was from the grapes, he didn't say anything. A doctor visited the front lines soon to check for diseases such as malaria, cholera, typhoid and dysentery that the men contracted all too easily in the unhygienic conditions of the trenches. The physician measured Hanns's temperature and told him to go straight to the field hospital without getting into contact with anyone. There were enough dysentery cases as it was.

In Weimar, Christmas of 1917 was another lonely one for Carl and Friedel Weirich. Friedel was still not fully cured from her lung problems but had to help in the shop while Carl worked long shifts in the military administration at the Hohenzollern. Neither had time to look after their child. On their third wedding anniversary in October, they had sent Wilfriede back to Oranienburg to live with her grandmother. The absence of the little girl was painfully obvious in the small flat at Christmas. Like most Weimarers the Weirichs were tired and dejected. The lack of proper nutrition, heating and things as basic as soap was affecting their health. Death was everywhere. People anxiously checked the lists of war casualties to see if their loved ones were among the latest batch of Weimarers killed or injured. Those who stayed behind got sicker and thinner by the week.

Carl and Friedel Weirich were looking forward to seeing their daughter again in the summer of 1918. Wilfriede was nearly three years old now and would have learned new words and skills in the care of her doting grandmother. Her parents had done their best to take their minds off the heartbreaking separation from their only child. They had seen nine plays at the theatre through the dark months of January and February. As winter gave way to spring, they had visited family and gone hiking with friends or Carl's mother, who came to visit from Eisenach. The time until they would see Wilfriede again went by in a flurry of work and distraction. But there was no getting away from the fact that she was growing up without them, had playmates they didn't know and was learning to walk and talk with her grandmother rather than her parents. That would have to change as soon as the war was over. Then Friedel would have time to recover properly, Carl could concentrate on the shop, and both would be reunited as a family when their child came home.

Such daydreams got Carl through the difficult weeks and months, but they came to an abrupt end in late June. Carl received a message from Friedel's sister Hedwig in Oranienburg that hit him 'like lightning'.[41] Little Wilfriede was gravely ill. 'Outwardly seemingly unperturbed but with a heart deep in pain,' Carl told his wife nothing of the news, but urged her to travel to Oranienburg immediately. He pleaded with his commanding officer and was granted leave to follow shortly after his wife had departed.

When Carl arrived at the house of his parents-in-law on 3 July 1918, he walked into a living nightmare. Friedel and her mother were in a 'heart-wrenching' state of anguish. Wilfriede, his 'dear girl', lay still and lifeless in a small white coffin. The child had suffered an inflammation of the brain and passed away in the arms of her mother and grandmother. Carl and Friedel were inconsolable. Numb with pain, they followed the procession carrying the small wooden box that contained the lifeless body of their only child to Oranienburg's cemetery. Pastor Thiele, the priest who had married them four years earlier, spoke at her tiny grave. The next day the bereaved parents travelled back to Weimar alone and bereft.

The rest of the summer of 1918 went by in a dismal blur for the Weirichs. Wracked by self-recrimination, they asked themselves again and again: why did we miss so much of our daughter's short life? Whenever they saw other families and their 'lively children', pangs of guilt and pain jolted the couple. But there was no time to grieve. The food situation had become so drastic that their own health would soon deteriorate if they didn't spend what little spare time they had procuring food from somewhere.

They embarked on 'hamster raids' into the countryside, as did many of their fellow Germans. Outside the town boundaries 'no law applied', Carl noted in his diary. The strict rationing system enforced by military law no longer provided enough nutrition. But in villages deals could be struck. Carl combined these outings with the hiking excursions that had so often preserved his sanity. One day, he walked to the Cospeda Mill in nearby Jena where he got some flour. Another time he walked to the town of Magdala with Friedel where friends gave them some precious meat. Cooking fat was also a permanent problem. The Weirichs regularly foraged in the forests for beechnuts from which oil could be pressed. No matter how desperate their own situation was becoming, nothing could fill the hole the loss of their daughter had ripped into the fabric of their lives.

The Weimarers on the Western Front faced absolute carnage in the last months of the war. By September 1918, each of the three battalions in Regiment 94 had on average forty soldiers left. The 94ers were constantly depleted and refilled as men died, were wounded or got ill in their futile struggle. It became increasingly difficult to draft new recruits from the civilian population. At the beginning of October, Grand Duke Wilhelm Ernst wrote to his wife in bitter understatement, 'the overall situation unfortunately doesn't look so rosy'.[42]

That applied to those at home in Weimar too. In October, Jutta Hecker's school was closed again. It had appointed a new headmaster, the forty-four-year-old Professor Dr Julius Voigt, who had served in the war for over three years before being recalled in the spring of 1918 to take over the Sophienstift from his late predecessor Dr Glaser. Voigt was a well-educated man who had spent time in France, England and Constantinople between 1900 and 1903.[43] But no matter how capable he may have been, it was impossible to keep the school running in the autumn of 1918 when one of the deadliest pandemics in history struck. Globally, the Spanish Flu killed tens of millions of people while infecting nearly a third of the world's population.

In Weimar, the disease tore through factories, hospitals and schools. People were asked not to attend if they were ill. The closure of the Sophienstift was one of a number of desperate measures to hold the pandemic at bay. The fourteen-year-old Jutta now had time to watch columns of war-ravaged soldiers march home along the Lindenberg road. It was a sorry sight: ragged grey uniforms, some with their shoulder pieces torn off. On that road, Jutta reflected later, she watched history happen.

Late in the evening of 7 November, August Baudert returned from Berlin to Weimar by train. He was a little anxious but determined to be home in these troubled times. Now fifty-eight years old, he had deep-set eyes framed by thinning hair and a moustache. Baudert had grown up in a working-class family around 20 kilometres south of Weimar. He had been a master textile worker before becoming politically active. In 1906, he had moved to Weimar to take up a position in the local chapter of the Social Democratic Party, of which he had been a member for the best part of four decades.

In order to help Weimar's workers link up and coordinate strikes and political campaigns, he had pressed for the construction of a brand-new headquarters for their movement. The Volkshaus or People's House was opened in 1908 and Baudert hoped it would 'now and for all times honour its name'.[44] The handsome, yellow, two-storey building immediately drew famous German socialists and communists such as Clara Zetkin, Rosa Luxemburg and Karl Liebknecht to Weimar who all spoke in its great hall before the war. It was home to clubs and offered a library and educational courses. There were even plans for a bowling alley.

Having made his mark on Weimar with the Volkshaus, Baudert went on to become the town's constituency representative in the German parliament in the 1912 election. In that capacity he had seen and heard things in the German capital in the first week of November 1918 that had smacked of revolution. US President Woodrow Wilson had made it abundantly clear that there would be no peace for Germans unless the monarchy was abolished and the political system democratized from the ground up. For many German workers, who had suffered the brunt of the brutal war the Kaiser and his government had waged to the bitter end, this wasn't good enough. For the radicals among them, the chance to overthrow the entire social order had arrived and it might never come again. Hadn't the October Revolution in Russia sprung from misery and defeat in war almost exactly a year earlier? Perhaps there would be a November Revolution in Germany. The thought thrilled some and frightened others.

What would the end of the war mean for Germany? Anyone tied to the Kaiser feared the worst. His cousin, Russia's Tsar Nicholas II, had been captured by the revolutionaries and murdered in a basement together with his entire family on 17 July 1918. Now, it seemed, a similar sequence of events had been set in motion in Germany. The war was lost and sailors in the port of Kiel mutinied on 3 November. The SMS *Thüringen*, a dreadnought class battleship named in the presence of Grand Duke Wilhelm Ernst in 1909 and mainly staffed by Thuringian sailors, was among the first to rebel. The Kiel mutiny unleashed a revolutionary wave that rolled across Germany, breaking bulwarks of authority in its path. It was only a question of time before it reached Berlin. The capital hummed with frightful gossip and hopeful jubilation. 'There was a hubbub that is impossible to describe,' Baudert wrote in his memoirs. 'The wildest rumours were spread.'[45]

In Weimar, Baudert had watched military discipline break down months ago. In the early summer of 1918, he had observed soldiers drinking in 'merry rounds' after they had 'allegedly "got separated" from their units on their way and had thought it best to come home'.[46] Baudert's reminders that there might be punishment were met with sarcastic remarks. The atmosphere in the barracks became charged as the ratio of politicized workers in them increased. Some, particularly from the town's only large industrial compound, Weimar Werke, had previously been spared the draft because their labour on the home front was essential. But as the regime became desperate, more were called up. The workers left neither their political views nor their contempt for the regime at the barrack gates. Unrest and desertion became commonplace in the last year of the war.

One of the trains that left Weimar at the beginning of 1918, with 200 men on board, arrived with only fifty at the front lines.[47] The rest absconded, taking their time to reappear in Weimar. Rumours made the rounds that one soldier had fired on the grand ducal palace. Those drafted for the regime's last desperate throw of the dice were concerned not only for their own lives but also for those of loved ones left behind. 'Misery has reached its peak,' Baudert had noted in his diary in August 1918, 'we are starving and now weeks without meat are upon us, and all that on 3 pounds of bread in 7 days without any spread. Sad times!'[48]

Ignited by the mutiny in Kiel, the German Revolution spread south, sparking rebellion in barracks and air bases across the country. It reached Weimar when, despite the impending end of the war, one of its reserve companies received marching orders on 7 November. Resentful soldiers shuffled into the courtyard in the evening, but one of them had had enough. He stepped out of formation and threw his rifle on to the ground. For a moment everyone went deadly quiet. Then a few of the officers snapped out of their stunned disbelief at this open display of contempt and dragged the young man off. His comrades were marched to the train station to be deployed, but more soldiers ran away, leaving their rifles behind. In the night, while their MP Baudert returned from Berlin, the remaining soldiers at the Weimar barracks discussed what they should do. Scraps of paper were passed around. They had made up their minds. They would resist any future orders. Weimar would not sit out the revolution.

Baudert awoke the next morning to find it was a grey and misty November day. He was glad to be home. Germany was a powder keg and so was Weimar. He wanted to be here with the people who had elected him. Like them, he wanted change. A new Germany, a new Weimar. But without bloodshed. He was a moderate social democrat and had chosen to stay in the SPD rather than join its more radical 1917 offshoot, the USPD (Independent SPD). He believed in law and order and in reform over revolution.

Baudert got dressed and made his way to the SPD office. He was discussing his impressions from Berlin with his party colleague Hermann Leber when the doorbell rang. Two junior officers demanded to see him. 'The soldiers can no longer be held at bay,' one of them reported breathlessly. 'If we don't act quickly, there will be blood and thunder.'[49] Baudert saw only one way. If the fury couldn't be contained, perhaps it could be harnessed. He decided to join and lead the protests planned for the evening. Leber frowned. Was Baudert sure this was a good idea? As an MP, he was granting the planned unrest an air of legitimacy. It could all end in bloodshed if the military leadership, over which he had no control, responded with violence. Baudert had taken ownership of something that was to all intents and purposes a coup. He staked everything on his personal standing with all sides.

Baudert left his office and visited the police chief Bährede to urge restraint on the side of law enforcement. Then, he spoke to Oberst von Dalwigk, the leader of the Weimar barracks, and persuaded him to act as middleman between the angry soldiers and the Grand Duke. He was to be present at the Schloss to pass on their demands. Lastly, delegates of the soldiers gathered at the Volkshaus to elect a council and formulate these demands, chief among them: no more troop transports to the front, and the abdication of the Kaiser and all German dukes. The stage was set for Weimar's November Revolution.

In the evening hundreds of soldiers gathered at Karlsplatz behind Carl Weirich's shop. In front of the main post office, an imposing building in the style of the Italian Renaissance, a uniformed leader addressed the men, stressing the need for absolute discipline. No violence! Workers joined the soldiers, some waving red flags. Women made up a sizable proportion of the crowd. Mayor Martin Donndorf, a bespectacled man in his fifties with a well-groomed moustache, looked on in deep worry as he feared looting and vandalism might deface his beautiful town. The opera *Donna Diana* was on at the Court Theatre that night, but many of the pre-booked seats remained empty. 'At the theatre began a comedy, and in the harsh reality outside began a drama,' Baudert mused.[50]

The only problem was that none of the actors knew the script. How does one go about enacting a revolution? Weimar didn't have a well-established urban proletariat schooled in Leninist theory. The would-be revolutionaries didn't even know the lyrics of 'The Internationale', the anthem of world socialism. So the masses began their march in awkward silence, 'an indescribable gravity' hanging over them, as Baudert recalled.[51] Eventually someone attempted a well-known workers' song. Others joined in as Baudert led around 1,000 men and women to the Schloss.

When they arrived at the grand ducal residence, everything went to plan. Oberst von Dalwigk stood by as the soldiers' demands were read out. Then Baudert gave a speech in which he reinforced the demand for the abdication of the Kaiser and the Grand Duke. This was met with jubilation, but the anger that had built up over four years of misery also found its vents. At the mention of the royal names, boos, hisses and insults were hurled that gave Baudert the impression that 'the slightest trigger would have sufficed to instigate the storming of the Schloss'.[52]

Grand Duke Wilhelm Ernst had fled his palace and moved his family to the house of the Weimar lawyer Hermann Jöck. With no direct human target in sight, the revolution took a non-violent course. Von Dalwigk agreed to all demands. The Soldiers' Council freed peers who had been imprisoned for disciplinary offences. Then they occupied the post office, the train station, radio communication offices and printing presses without resistance. The nearby airfield of Nohra made its planes and cars available to the revolutionaries. Printers were put to work to spread the news: Weimar was in the hands of workers and soldiers.

Saturday 9 November 1918 was a memorable thirty-third birthday for Carl Weirich. His military life was over. So was Germany as he knew it. 'Having existed for only forty-seven years,' he reflected in his diary, his 'fatherland . . . in its form as the German Empire had collapsed'.[53] On the plus side, he would finally have time for his shop again once things settled. For now, the town around him changed rapidly in appearance and atmosphere. Planes dragging red banners dropped leaflets everywhere that spread the news:

> *Comrades and Soldiers!*
>
> *The revolution is marching. Our hour of fate has come. Military power is in our hands and political power will follow. Listen to us. Follow our instructions. The greatest calm and decisiveness is necessary. Looting and rough behaviour is undignified. Looting and other offences will be punished harshly, the death penalty is not ruled out.*

All workers are on our side and will elect a Workers' Council. Your
elected leaders will lead you to the goal.
    The goal is not far!
    Long live the socialist republic!
    The Soldiers' Council[54]

Many Weimarers were worried. Would the dramatic events spell
chaos and lawlessness? The Soldiers' Council had promised that
would not be the case. Public life was to continue as before. But
nothing felt as before. The majority of citizens complied with the
new regime, but a small number of rebels were rather enjoying
the momentary equilibrium. Some were joy-riding requisitioned
cars through Weimar's narrow streets. Others had taken horses
from the Marstall, the grand ducal mews, and were attempting to
ride through the town centre despite clearly lacking the skills to do
so. Once again August Baudert took control, quickly assembling
a Workers' Council to provide the revolutionaries with political
decision-making capacity. This rapidly assembled group didn't
take long to make its first decision: the Grand Duke must abdicate
immediately.

Wilhelm Ernst had returned to his residence in the night and felt
miserable. Around lunchtime, he summoned Baudert. When the
MP arrived, a door next to the main gate was immediately opened
for him. Inside, a servant took his coat and introduced him to Hugo
von Fritsch, a formal man with blond hair and moustache who
ran the grand ducal household. Von Fritsch asked him if he would
mind if the lawyer Hermann Jöck was present as a witness to his
conversation with Wilhelm Ernst. Baudert said he didn't care who
else was in the room. To his astonishment, von Fritsch promptly
burst into tears. It was all too close to his own heart, the man awk-
wardly apologized as he sniffed and tried to regain his composure.
Baudert told him that his tears honoured him as a servant of his
master but they wouldn't change the inevitable fate shared by all
German dukes. Still sniffling a little, von Fritsch showed the guest
up a flight of stairs to the reception room. The situation seemed

surreal to Baudert. 'Now, I was a guest at court!' mused the former textile worker.

The lawyer Jöck was already waiting in the room and von Fritsch left the two men alone while he notified Wilhelm Ernst. The Grand Duke finally entered the room dressed in a simple grey uniform without rank insignia or medals. His face was a stony mask behind which Baudert thought he saw a man whose 'soul was broken'.[55] 'Good afternoon, Herr Baudert,' Wilhelm Ernst began, 'you are a republican, I am a monarchist, but we are both humans.' Baudert conceded that the matter could be settled in a civilized manner but insisted that a full and immediate abdication was the only way. Wilhelm Ernst had no more strength to resist. Resigned, he agreed to end his ducal line. 'I have done what I could,' the last Grand Duke of Saxe-Weimar-Eisenach said quietly.[56]

Hanns Wagner knew nothing yet of the fact that his Grand Duke had abdicated. Nor that the Kaiser was forced to do the same, opening the way to the Armistice Germany would sign on 11 November. The young soldier had recovered from dysentery and then been moved out of Romania when the country was forced to pull out of the war and sign a treaty with the Central Powers in May 1918 following Russia's withdrawal the previous year. He was now in Lahr in Baden, southern Germany. Lahr itself was safe enough but Hanns saw no point in training further recruits for an unwinnable war. He decided to try his luck and apply for four weeks' leave. To his surprise, it was granted. He instantly made his way to the station and boarded a train that was so overcrowded that soldiers hung off the side 'like fat grapes'.[57] On 10 November 1918, after four years of war, Hanns was back home.

Arthur Schmidt also returned home, alive and with an Iron Cross on his chest. He was finally able to reunite with his wife Rosa and their two eldest children, now fourteen and eleven years old. His youngest son Ernst, who had been born thousands of kilometres away and seemingly a lifetime ago, was now nearly five years old. The baby

Arthur never knew was now a young boy who could walk and talk. The family would need time to recover from trauma and separation. Their wanderlust had evaporated. The world before 1914 had been one where one could travel to foreign lands, see the world and take risks. The world after 1918 was one in which death, suffering, economic collapse and political instability were ever present. What mattered now was that the family had time to heal. The Schmidts would build a new life right here, in Arthur's home town of Weimar.

PART I

Rebirth

From world domination to
spiritual greatness

1919

Catharina Lehmann was in a wistful mood as she put pen to paper on a cold winter's day in early January. 'It's a terrible shame,' she wrote. The demobilization of soldiers, the occupation of parts of western Germany by the victorious enemy and preliminary talks for a peace treaty – it all seemed deeply unfair to her. 'How they will oppress us,' she complained, 'yet we are powerless, a[nd] all protest is useless.'[1] Käte, as she was called by friends and family, was in her early forties and married to Gustav, a civil servant. A well-informed middle-class woman with a keen interest in politics, she had decided to keep a diary to leave her children a record of the tumultuous times she lived through.

The sight of Regiment 94 returning struck Käte as a pitiful mirror image of the scenes of August 1914 when soldiers in freshly tailored uniforms waved from the windows of departing trains. Now columns of the defeated shuffled home in tattered garments. They arrived in Weimar on 18 December, just in time for Christmas, but many found it difficult to resume family life. Nobody returned from the front lines unchanged. Some had debilitating injuries; others suffered from diseases. Many had seen misery, violence and death on an unimaginable scale.

Life in Weimar hadn't stood still either. Of its nearly 35,000 pre-war inhabitants, 4,000 had been sent to serve in the military. Regiment 94 had suffered an enormous casualty rate. Well over a quarter of the recruits perished at the front, compared to 15 per cent nationwide. Weimar mourned the military deaths of 1,338 men and three women.[2] Precarious levels of malnourishment had claimed many more civilian victims. Veterans often rejoined incomplete families. Careers had also been disrupted. Hanns Wagner, now twenty-one, resumed his book-printing apprenticeship from the same small room in Jena that he had last occupied in 1914 as a wide-eyed teenager who loved books and music. The scar on his foot was a permanent reminder that the terrible things he had seen and done were not the 'distant dream'[3] they began to seem.

Käte and Gustav watched the arrival of the 94ers from a window at the market square where they and other officials had been placed to give the soldiers a 'festive welcome'.[4] Weimarers had decorated their houses in the imperial colours, waved embroidered handkerchiefs and cheered the men as if they were victors. The soldiers marched in matching black, white and red. But Käte saw many 'deadly serious' expressions. Her own 'heart cramped given all the sad thoughts . . . Oh, how difficult it is to return to a vanquished country!'[5]

There was a life-threatening shortage of everything. Illegal 'hamster raids' drew Weimarers out into the countryside, where they foraged, bartered and stole what the authorities failed to provide. People descended on the manicured parks of the Schloss and the baroque Belvedere palace on the outskirts, chopping down trees for firewood. The Ettersberg hill just north of Weimar, where Goethe had loved to walk and work, had become a bald eyesore.

At the end of January, Weimar's gas plant stopped working, leaving 7,000 households without electricity.[6] Factories shut down and dismissed employees remained without pay. Schools shortened their lessons or closed altogether. For Jutta Hecker, who was now fourteen, this was painful. She wanted to go to university to become a scholar like her father Max, the much-acclaimed Goethe and Schiller archivist. But her Sophienstift school for girls had taken one blow after another. Just when lessons had resumed despite staff shortages, it lost its patron, the Grand Duchess Feodora, who'd left Weimar with her husband after the November Revolution. The new authorities commandeered the school building as temporary accommodation for returning soldiers, padding the classrooms with straw for the men to sleep on.[7] Soon 'coal holidays' closed all but two of Weimar's schools. Jutta now received only three lessons a day.[8]

The Spanish Flu seemed to have run its course with two intense waves in the spring and autumn of 1918, but other diseases like tuberculosis, typhus, cholera, dysentery and malaria remained rife. Friedel Weirich had suffered heavy bouts of pneumonia since October 1918. Occasionally, she recovered enough to go on a walk with Carl but she was not getting better.

In the midst of chaos, the country was preparing to hold the first fully democratic elections in its history on 19 January 1919. Germany's foreseeable future would be on the ballot paper. The electorate would choose 423 delegates for a National Assembly, a temporary parliament, tasked with drafting a new constitution for a new Germany. Far more people would get a say than before 1914. There were a staggering 20 million first-time voters. The voting age had been lowered from twenty-five to twenty, and women were eligible for the first time. This enlarged the electorate by 167 per cent.[9] There was much anxiety and hope over how these new voters envisioned the country's future.

Berlin, however, just wouldn't settle, and Weimar watched on anxiously. 'Terror in Berlin,' screamed the front page of the conservative local newspaper *Weimarische Zeitung* on 8 January. Its Berlin correspondent reported on extraordinary scenes. The German capital was a tinderbox ignited by the German Communist Party (KPD), newly formed by leaders Karl Liebknecht and Rosa Luxemburg, and other far-left activists. 'The scenes on Berlin's streets are marked by tempestuous demonstrations,' wrote the correspondent. The so-called Spartacist Uprising had been raging for three days. Interim Chancellor Friedrich Ebert of the SPD deployed soldiers and Freikorps, groups of veterans who hadn't disbanded. Largely right-wing and well-armed monarchists were hunting down badly organized far-left workers in order to protect the seeds of a democracy neither of them wanted. Ugly scenes ensued that would crush the uprising within a matter of days but not without killing over 150 people.

Observers in provincial Weimar were shocked by such bloodshed. Many worried that trouble in Berlin might spell trouble in Weimar. Curt Weiß, the fifty-seven-year-old headmaster of a local private school for girls, wrote in his diary on 7 January: 'Currently rumours are buzzing through the city. Fifty sailors are said to have arrived here from Berlin. Will they inflict harm on Baudert and transplant Berlin's "Spartacusiad" to Weimar? The things one fills one's diaries with!'[10] August Baudert followed the 'treacherous murders' in Berlin closely, as he later recalled.[11] But he judged that, with so few workers in disproportionately middle-class Weimar, the risk of revolutionary violence was low. Baudert allowed his thoughts to turn to building a new democracy. Right here in Weimar.

To August Baudert, the chaos in Berlin opened an opportunity for Weimar. Things had got so out of hand in the capital that Friedrich Ebert's provisional government no longer felt secure. They would need a safer place for the National Assembly to convene.

Weimar might be that place. It was competing with cities such as Nuremberg and Bayreuth to become the new government's temporary home. But when the Reichstag director Bernhard Jungheim paid Baudert a 'top-secret' visit, he was impressed. Weimar ticked all the boxes. It didn't have the explosive social upheaval of bigger cities. Compact and partially shielded by hills, it was defensible against would-be revolutionaries. It had a brand-new train station that was nearly finished and even a small airfield. The transfer of correspondence, supplies and people to and from Berlin wouldn't be a problem. The Court Theatre had plenty of seats. There was a big empty Schloss where people could sleep and meet. As a tourist town, Weimar had hotels to accommodate over 2,000 people, enough room for security personnel and journalists. Much smaller than Berlin, everything was so close together that people could walk between meetings, offices and accommodation. Weimar was perfect.

There were political advantages too. Weimar wasn't Berlin. The message to the Allies and the other parts of Germany was that the new Germany would not be another Prussian-dominated one. The German Empire, which had just been destroyed by war, had been set up under Prussian leadership in 1871 with the Prussian capital of Berlin as its capital. Creating a new Germany some-where else, somewhere that was neither Prussia nor Bavaria nor any of the other dominant German states, was a statement of intent. Weimar lay geographically almost in the centre of the country.[12] It would be the heart of a new Germany. And it would be its brains too. With its quaint houses, lush green spaces, its illus-trious history of poets, thinkers and dreamers, Weimar would lend the new democracy a new image. If the old Germany had been forged in war, the new Germany would be born out of idealism.

Weimar it was. The former Court Theatre would be the place where Germany's National Assembly would gather and where its new constitution would be written. Baudert shook hands with Jungheim and threw himself into the preparations for the exciting task ahead. The German Republic would be a Weimar Republic.

Weimarers didn't know yet that they would soon find themselves in the eye of the storm of German politics. But the prospect of the first fully democratic elections provided much excitement in itself. 'German men! German women!' the regional newspaper *Weimar-ische Landeszeitung* addressed its conservative readership. 'The day is nigh which will decide the fate of the German people, possibly for centuries to come . . . Never before, as long as the world has existed, has a people been confronted with a decision of such immense mag-nitude as you are now.'[13]

The urgency with which the paper appealed to readers to vote for the German National People's Party (DNVP) and its national conservative, pro-monarchy manifesto leapt off the page in every bold-printed letter. Leaning on the anxieties of the middle and upper classes in light of the attempted communist insurgency in Berlin and the speed of social change brought about by war and revolution, the paper warned of the SPD and the liberal German Democratic Party (DDP), whose manifesto it saw as a barely disguised 'copy of the socialist one'.[14] 'They will take most of your property as well as your fatherland, religion and freedom,' the *Weimarische Landes-zeitung* fretted, asking: 'Do you want things to get worse, much worse, than they already are?'[15]

Like many women, Käte Lehmann took her newly gained vote very seriously. But how could she be sure to make the right choice? A bewildering array of political parties had sprung from the fertile political soil of post-war confusion and opportunity. With the Kaiser gone, anything was possible and parties offered programmes ranging from socialism to the restoration of the monarchy.

'For weeks the public mood has been very excitable, the clash of the parties pulls this way and that, and it has transfixed us too,' Käte admitted in her diary.[16] All parties were acutely aware that, due to the enormous death toll of the war, around 2 million more women than men were eligible to vote. So they all appealed to these new voters directly. The SPD, for instance, promised women 'Equal rights – Equal Duties' on a striking election poster that showed a man and a woman side by side under the bright red banner of the workers' movement, a banner carried by her, not him.

Intrigued, Käte had attended an SPD event in the theatre, which she found 'interesting'. She never expected it to convince her, but saw it as her duty to consider all the options. Workshops offered to explain the very concept of democracy to female voters. In December, the Committee for the Political Education of the Woman hosted an 'Evening of Political Instruction' where for 20 pfennigs attendees were invited to a lecture by Herr Dr Schomberg on 'Germany's social legislation: social policy and social insurance'.[17]

There were women too who wanted to help others become confident voters. A prominent figure in female political education was Gertrud Bäumer, a forty-five-year-old women's rights activist. Gertrud was one of the founders of the liberal DDP. Making full use of her newly gained right to stand for election, she was one of the party's top candidates for the National Assembly in the Weimar constituency. She felt her campaigning was worthwhile, observing how 'women have matured to marvellous enthusiasm and political energy in the last few weeks'.[18] Curt Weiß attended one of Gertrud's events and was impressed with her 'erudite, meaningful and solid ways'. He predicted that she would 'probably be among the first women to enter the National Assembly'.[19]

Like Gertrud, the headteacher of a girls' school considered himself an enlightened educator and approved: 'she and other able women belong in parliament, too, like the wife and mother in the parliament of the home'.[20] Yet Curt couldn't get away from the idea that all these 'able women' had something in common. Considering the appearance of several of the 'leading women of the present', he thought, 'with very few exceptions, none of them is a lovable, alluring and likeable person! All celibate creatures, men whom nature had branded wrongly. Not made for love and marriage. And that's what women usually are.' Gertrud, who lived with a woman and would never marry or have children, was singled out as the 'pleasant exception: she stayed a woman and at the same time a person of genius, far above the average'.[21]

Käte too was impressed by Gertrud and her party, which she initially intended to vote for. But in the end, she reconsidered. Her main aim in this critical hour wasn't political idealism but keeping the social democrats out of power. She was not averse to drastic change per se, arguing that the total defeat of the German Empire might be a blessing in disguise. 'Maybe the old was rotten and had to fall,' she mused, 'a[nd] maybe our children and grandchildren will value this liberal movement that still seems so chaotic and strange to us.'[22]

Yet the thought that the Kaiser and his wife were now in exile in the Netherlands, 'shamed by their people', appalled Käte. 'So much of what was sacred to us, we now see trampled into the mud.' Whatever happened to the 'much-famed "German loyalty"'?, she wanted to know. Couldn't her compatriots see that the enemy shared blame for the war? 'People are often so unpatriotic,' she complained. In light of what she saw as her duty to her country, Käte couldn't bring herself to vote for Gertrud's DDP. After all, 'the party is always said to be internationalist, and Jewed-up'.[23] She would give the national conservative DNVP her vote and hoped the 'elections won't be disturbed by the Spartacists . . . With great anticipation, we look forward to the first election day on 19 January.'[24]

The Spartacists were thinking about ways to disturb the election. At 7 p.m. on 17 January, a twenty-five-year-old firebrand from Leipzig took the stage at Weimar's Volkshaus to speak to veterans. Despite the widespread fears in conservative circles of a 'Spartacist' rising, there was no sizable communist movement in Weimar. On 11 January, only twelve comrades, eight of them teenagers, had met in the library of the Volkshaus to form a local communist group. Weimar simply didn't have the numbers of politicized urban workers. Leipzig did. The revolutionary Independent SPD (USPD) would gain 42.8 per cent of the vote there in the upcoming elections compared to 7.6 per cent in the country overall and just 2.7 per cent in Weimar.[25] 'Leipzig is getting more Bolshevist by the day,' the *Weimarische Landeszeitung* warned.[26] So perhaps this Walter Ulbricht from Leipzig could win Weimar's veterans for the cause? Speaking in the great hall of the Volkshaus, he called on workers and soldiers to boycott the upcoming elections. Little did his audience know that the stout man with the brittle voice would one day realize his dream of establishing socialism on German soil. He would run East Germany as General Secretary of its ruling party for over twenty years. But that was another war away. For the moment, inspiring communist upheaval in Weimar proved impossible.

On 19 January, the much-anticipated election day had arrived. Gertrud Bäumer looked up from her desk in the polling station and let the magnitude of the moment sink in. 'Given all the inner exhaustion, the pressure mounted by all that's happened,' she wrote, 'one doesn't really have the mental capacity to consciously take it in: the first election day for women. Finishing line of a century – Beginning of a millennium.'[27] Käte Lehmann also felt overcome by a 'celebratory mood' as she dropped her ballot paper into the box.[28]

Gertrud watched women of all ages walk into her polling station. There were wives with their husbands, mothers with their daughters. 'Little children come along,' she wrote. 'They want to watch their mother vote. And mother says: they should remember this day their whole lives.'[29] There were elderly women too, escorted into the polling station by police officers who allowed them to skip the long queues. Gertrud was relieved to see that so many women had turned out. This had by no means been a foregone conclusion. In the build-up to the election, there had been much vocal opposition to female suffrage and not just from men.

In Weimar, Elisabeth Förster-Nietzsche was a powerful adversary to female voting. The sister of philosopher Friedrich Nietzsche was seventy-two years old and a staunch conservative. She ran the Nietzsche Archive, which she had founded in 1894 to control her famous brother's work. Friedrich had suffered a nervous breakdown five years earlier from which he was never to recover, yet at the same time his following began to soar in the early 1890s, making the publication of anything to do with him very lucrative. His younger sister, whom he had nicknamed 'the Llama' in saner days, comparing her to a stubborn animal that spat when angered, saw a golden opportunity and started selling edited versions of his writing as well as a Nietzsche biography she had written.

Weimar had seemed a suitably grand place for the archive, with its legendary literary tradition and many influential residents who

Elisabeth Förster-Nietzsche in the Nietzsche Archive in Weimar, 1910.

supported the venture, such as Rudolf Steiner, now best known for inspiring Waldorf education, and Meta von Salis, a Swiss historian who had exchanged frequent letters with both Nietzsche siblings. She had paid for the Villa Silberblick, a large, elegant house on a hill on the south-western outskirts of Weimar, so that Elisabeth had somewhere suitable to build the archive and care for her ailing brother until he died there in 1900.

Elisabeth depended on such generosity from others alongside the income she made from her brother's life work. She was on her own since her husband had died. Bernhard Förster had been a virulently antisemitic school teacher who had founded a settlement in Paraguay called 'Nueva Germania', which he intended to be a racially pure settlement where 'Aryans' would live without foreign or Jewish influence. Elisabeth had joined him in this endeavour, travelling to the New World in 1886. Three years later, the project had failed and Bernhard poisoned himself in a hotel room in San Bernardino. His widow returned to Germany dejected and penniless but found that her brother had become both incapacitated and famous. After Friedrich's death, she continued to edit and publish his work with considerable social and economic success. Fiercely guarding access to the original writings, Elisabeth had a monopoly on their interpretation, editing Friedrich's often fragmentary thoughts and scribblings into coherent works as she saw fit. This made her many enemies, but as an excellent networker, she also made many influential friends along the way. She was nominated for the Nobel Literature prize four times between 1908 and 1923.

Early in 1919, Elisabeth began to support the anti-feminist Emma Witte, who saw women primarily as mothers rather than as active members of society in any political sense. In one of her regular exchanges with her friend and benefactress early in 1919, Witte argued that there were 'millions [of] German women opposed to female suffrage' and these 'silent women' should join the call of the so far largely male-dominated anti-emancipation movement to oppose the 'degeneration of female and family life'.[30] Gertrud Bäumer had no idea how many such 'silent women' were really out there. Would they refuse to turn up on election day? Relieved to find that the majority of women were in fact excited to participate in the democratic process, she noted: 'the whole debate around female suffrage [now] appears blown out of proportion and artificial'.[31]

Everyone responded to the elections in their own way. Some Germans were more preoccupied with private matters than politics. Carl Weirich was focused on reviving his shop. He had only been released from military service in mid-December and there was so much to do, from ordering new stock to bookkeeping. The Christmas period had been so busy that there was hardly any time for anything and Friedel, while somewhat recovered, was still not fully back to work. Frau Straubel, the previous owner, was also less able to help as her husband lay on his deathbed. In the whirlwind of activity, Carl didn't even take the time to write about the elections in his diary.

Other Weimarers were very excited. At 8 a.m. on voting day, bells rang out over the town in celebration of this historic day and to call people to the polling stations. Local papers impressed on their readers: 'Yes, your one vote matters! It weighs no more and no less, it weighs just as heavily as that of every other German voter! . . . Vote! Vote! Vote!'[32] As more Germans than ever before went out to decide upon their country's future, long queues formed in front of the polling stations. Men in suits stood behind soldiers in uniform. Wounded comrades were carried by their peers. Entire families turned up together. By lunchtime over a third of votes had already been cast in Weimar with a second wave hitting Gertrud and the other people in the polling offices in the afternoon and early evening. The fear that Spartacists or other troublemakers might attempt to disrupt proceedings proved unfounded. Papers across the political spectrum reported the next day that the atmosphere in Weimar had remained calm, dignified and purposeful.

Of 24,807 eligible Weimar voters, 20,511 headed to the polls, a turnout of 83 per cent, which was exactly the same as the country overall and only slightly below the last election in 1912 – before the war and with a much smaller electorate. Germans elected 423 delegates, including the first thirty-seven female MPs – Gertrud was one of them and would remain so until 1932. Where Weimarers deviated from the German average wasn't the decision of whether to vote but how. In Weimar, Gertrud's liberal DDP carried the day with 36.7 per cent, edging it over the SPD, which came second with 35.5 per cent. Nationwide, the SPD won with 37.9 per cent of the vote, followed by the Catholic Centre Party with 19.7 per cent, which wasn't a political force in Protestant Weimar, where it only gained 2.7 per cent. Gertrud's DDP was in third place in the country overall. There was also a divergence on the conservative and antisemitic DNVP, which Käte Lehmann had opted for. More than one in five Weimarers had done the same while only one in ten Germans had.[33] The left-leaning newspaper *Weimarische Volkszeitung* jeered that the 'good, bourgeois society – it hasn't changed in Weimar, it is the same reactionary mass as ever'. It was particularly worried that a disproportionate number of new voters, young people and women like Käte, had flocked to the conservatives, putting this down to 'unscrupulous agitation, which did not hold back on lies and distortion'.[34]

Voting was drawing to a close when Ernst Hardt appeared on the stage of Weimar's theatre. The forty-two-year-old had just been appointed as its new director and had great plans for the place. The young Weimar-based intellectual with a cosmopolitan lifestyle, excellent connections and democratic politics had replaced the previous director Carl von Schirach. Schirach, whose father Karl was a German who had fought in the American Civil War and whose mother Elisabeth was American, was every bit as old-fashioned as Ernst Hardt appeared modern. He had been a cavalry officer and chamberlain at the court of Grand Duke Wilhelm Ernst. Running the latter's theatre from 1909 to 1919, he had put on a safe programme, picking plays and concerts from the standard canon. His dismissal in favour of the more liberal Hardt was contentious among Weimar's powerful conservative circles. In fact, Schirach took the state authorities to court and won the case, securing a generous pension at the rate of his full former salary. He also retained a private box at the theatre.

When he took the stage at the end of election day, Hardt was well aware that not everyone in the audience approved of his appointment. He needed to rally people behind the important role the town and his theatre would play in the rebirth of their country. He had put on a suitably stirring play: Friedrich Schiller's *William Tell*. The tale of the Swiss folk hero with its theme of national liberation from foreign oppression seemed the perfect backdrop. From now on, Hardt told the assembled Weimarers, their theatre would be known as the German National Theatre. This was where the first fully democratic German parliament would convene.

August Baudert had just over two weeks to transform sleepy Weimar into the hub of German politics. First and foremost, the main venue needed to be ready. Freshly minted theatre director Hardt was somewhat dismayed that he wouldn't be able to stage plays in his new place of work for quite some time, but a temporary venue of suitable grandeur was found. The Crossbow Society offered its grand clubhouse. The Crossbow was located at Schützengasse 14 in Weimar's old town, just a stone's throw from the theatre. It had a long tradition, counting illustrious figures such as Schiller and Liszt among its guests. Goethe had been an honorary member.[35] Members still practised shooting, but they were really there for networking. The Crossbow served as a kind of private club for the conservative elites. It charged the authorities over 1,000 marks a month for the use of its facilities as a theatre during the National Assembly.[36]

Other Weimar institutions offered their services for free. Weimar's florists donated lily-of-the-valley and carnations so that the theatre's auditorium could be decorated in vivid colours. 'Perhaps no parliament has ever been opened among such rich floral splendour,'[37] Baudert marvelled. But his 'pleasure over the successful work was significantly hampered by the many attacks' on him.[38] Not everyone in Weimar was happy with the upheaval caused by the National Assembly.

Given the political unrest in Berlin, Weimar was put on high alert. Friedrich Ebert had made an uneasy alliance with the German military, but many in the SPD, to which he and Baudert belonged, mistrusted the soldiers as reactionary and brutalized agents of the old regime who now listened to no one and were capable of extreme violence. Much of the sharp criticism Baudert faced for allowing soldiers into Weimar to protect the National Assembly came 'not least from within one's own ranks', he noted.[39]

Jutta Hecker had hoped to return to school once the Sophien-stift was no longer needed for returning soldiers. But now Baudert needed the building to house a telegraph office from where news could be sent to Berlin and the world. Around 10,000 metres of lead cabling were put into the ground in record time.[40] 'Now, a remarkable time began,' recorded the school chronicle, 'when telegraph machines clattered in the school hall.'[41]

Weimar pulled it off. On 6 February, the German National Theatre welcomed the republic's first parliament. Black motorcars carefully navigated the frosty streets, delivering deputies to the venue. Most arrived by special trains and found that everything had been organized to perfection. Each visitor received three cards: a pink one allowing access to Weimar and allocating a specific seat in the theatre; a grey one naming their accommodation; and a yellow one determining their restaurant.

A depiction of Theaterplatz on 6 February 1919. The view is from the theatre on to the square with its iconic statues of the poets Goethe and Schiller.

Despite rationing, the authorities had managed to procure plenty of food. While Carl Weirich continued to undertake 'hamster raids' into the countryside to feed himself and his desperately sick wife, the 3,000 visitors to the town were served 'a good choice of dishes and a fairly wide selection of luxuries', as the *New York Times* reported. 'The butter served is apparently the real article and marmalade and tea may be had,' the correspondent wrote in praise of what he regarded as 'a characteristic German system', which 'seems to work excellently except for the nuisance of keeping track of so many cards'. Weimar, he concluded, was 'a clean and attractive city as compared to the present Berlin'.[42]

In the square in front of the theatre, someone had brushed the snow off the statues of Goethe and Schiller. Rows of soldiers stood guard. More had been placed on the balconies of surrounding buildings, machine guns and rifles trained on the gathering below in case of trouble. Plain-clothes policemen from Berlin kept an eye on civilians. Six thousand more soldiers formed a protective 10-kilometre cordon around Weimar, preventing Spartacists from Leipzig and anybody else without a pink card from accessing what had become a fortress town. The fear of a communist attack was palpable, the atmosphere electric. Many Weimarers were keen to witness what they sensed was history in the making, and they had turned out in their droves to see the famous politicians arrive.

Inside the auditorium, men and women shuffled past one another in the narrow rows, pink cards in hand, to find their allocated number. It took forty-five minutes before everyone was seated. When Friedrich Ebert took the stage at 3.15 p.m. to open proceedings, the room was filled to the rafters. Around 400 of the 423 freshly elected deputies had come. Two thirds of them were first-time parliamentarians. Ebert, who would be elected as Germany's first President five days later, knew it fell to him to establish ground rules for the conduct of this new parliament.

Despite the momentous occasion, Ebert had not planned a bombastic speech. He was a down-to-earth pragmatist, and he looked the part: a portly man with thick brown hair and a bushy moustache streaked with grey. The forty-eight-year-old social democrat had never been a particularly powerful orator, but with his humble origins as a saddle-maker, he had proved a grounded compromise politician who was able and willing to work with most people to get things done. When he took his place behind a podium in the centre of the stage of the German National Theatre, there was no pathos, no rhetorical fireworks, just flatly delivered ground rules. He opened the Assembly with sober words: 'Through me, the Reich government welcomes the National Assembly which will provide the constitution. A particularly warm welcome to the women who appear in the Reich parliament with equal rights for the first time.'⁴³

The atmosphere was tense. In contrast to mature democracies, where there tends to be a consensus on the kind of state the delegates want to live in, regardless of their brand of politics, the fledgling German democracy had no established baseline. The Assembly had come to Weimar to establish one. The future of the nation hung in the balance. To Ebert's left sat socialist revolutionaries and democratic reformers. To his right staunch monarchists glared at him. In between liberals and Catholic centrists jostled for a say.⁴⁴

Ebert barely managed to string two sentences together without being interrupted. His confirmation that 'the old kings and dukes who ruled by divine right are gone forever' elicited a collective 'Bravo!' from the left and 'Objection!' from the right, a pattern that was repeated over and over, such as when Ebert announced that 'We have lost the war. This fact is not a consequence of the revolution.' There was only one thing everyone agreed on: that Germany's treatment at the hands of the victors was unfair. As Ebert listed one ignominy after the other – the retention of German prisoners of war, the occupation of lands in the east and west that had been German territory, the expulsion of Germans from those lands – there was booing and jeering from all directions. 'From such acts of the old policy of violence, no spirit of reconciliation speaks,' Ebert shouted over the roar of outrage and was rewarded with 'lively agreement'. 'The conditions of the Armistice were justified by being forced on to the old regime of the Hohenzollerns,' he continued. 'How can they justify making them constantly harsher for the young socialist republic even though we do all within our power to fulfil the heavy duties that have been forced upon us! We warn our enemies not to overdo it.' 'Too right!' came the chorus from the floor.[45]

But Ebert also had a positive message for his fellow deputies: 'The future may look at us in sorrow. But despite everything, we trust in the indestructible creative energy of the German nation.' And hadn't they come to a place that proved just that? A place where great Germans had created, written and argued? 'So here in Weimar we must achieve the transformation from imperialism to idealism, from world domination to spiritual greatness . . . Now the spirit of Weimar, the spirit of great thinkers and poets, must fill our lives again.'[46]

Some Weimarers were intrigued by the national drama in their theatre. Carl Weirich noted in his diary that 6 February was the day on which 'the new people presented themselves who would represent the fatherland headed by Fritz Ebert'. In the following weeks and months, he attended parliamentary sessions at the theatre and the Volkshaus with his wife 'in order to gain an impression of the contemporary leaders of the nation', naming Ebert, Baudert, the communist Clara Zetkin and Matthias Erzberger, who would soon be Vice Chancellor and Minister of Finance.[47] But like many other Weimarers, Carl was far more concerned with personal dramas at home. As Ebert struggled to make his voice heard over a raucous parliament, a few hundred metres from Carl's house, the bookbinder's predecessor Richard Straubel 'closed his eyes forever'. The old man had died 'a good German', Carl thought, and recorded more about Straubel's death than about the birth of the republic.[48]

Even many of those deeply invested in creating a stable German democracy found the proceedings in the theatre uninspiring. Harry Graf Kessler, an Anglo-German aristocrat and diplomat, had just returned to his estate in Weimar. The son of a Hamburg banker and an Anglo-Irish noblewoman, Harry was an elegant man in his fifties who led the eccentric lifestyle of a cosmopolitan dandy. A gay man at a time when homosexuality was illegal, he was careful not to draw too much attention to his relationships, but he flaunted his bachelordom nonetheless. A mythical aura surrounded him almost from birth. Kaiser Wilhelm I had been so smitten with his beautiful mother that he had fostered the Kesslers' swift rise and became godfather to Harry's younger sister Wilhelmina. There were even rumours that the German Emperor was the illegitimate father of either or both of the Kessler children, something Harry vehemently refuted. Multilingual, widely travelled and well-educated, the Count felt just as much at ease at court as he did in bars and ballrooms. He promoted art and moved to Weimar at the turn of the century to play an integral part in its thriving cultural scene. He befriended Elisabeth Förster-Nietzsche and helped her establish her brother's archive in Weimar. He also set up his own publishing house, the Cranach Press, named after the German Renaissance painter Lucas Cranach the Elder, who also gave his name to Harry's elegant Weimar villa at Cranachstraße 15. Then he took part in the First World War, both in the field and on diplomatic missions.

Now he had returned to Weimar to help steer the direction Germany would take at this critical juncture. But he found both the official proceedings and the backroom wranglings uninspiring. At a parliamentary session about the draft of the new constitution

Harry Graf Kessler in his apartment in Weimar, 1909.

Harry fell asleep during an 'exceedingly boring, colour- and passion-free, heavy and ponderous speech' by Hugo Preuß, one of the founders of the liberal DDP. '[N]ot a hint of the importance of the historical moment,' he complained in his diary.[49] When he visited his old friend Elisabeth Förster-Nietzsche in her Villa Silberblick, he found her deep in conversation with another liberal deputy, Hermann Pachnicke. Looking at the pair of them chatting, he saw something faintly ridiculous in the 'affected . . . "too-good-for-this-world" manner' in which Pachnicke spoke and the adoring posture with which she listened. Despite now being in her seventies, Elisabeth seemed to 'swoon' over the politician 'like a seventeen-year-old girl'.[50] With more than a pinch of aristocratic arrogance, Harry complained that most of the MPs gathered in Weimar came from middle-class backgrounds and lacked intellectual rigour as well as first-hand experience of the horrors others had lived through. 'The creatures wallow in their swamp of education, ignorant and happy, until the entire beautiful swamp world collapses in the catastrophe of world war and revolution!'[51] Harry was going through a socialist phase that earned him the nickname the 'Red Count'.

The spring of 1919 was a strange time. It was impossible to settle back into routines. A new era had begun whether it was welcome or not. The hustle and bustle of the National Assembly symbolized this for Weimarers. The Marie-Seebach-Stift, Germany's only old people's home specifically for retired actors and performers, had a ringside seat for events, perched on a hill to the east of the town centre. Now planes landed and took off from there several times a day, delivering mail and newspapers from Berlin. The German Air Shipping Company had set up the first regular civilian airline in the world, conducting two-hour flights between Berlin and Weimar from February until August, when it ran out of fuel. It was an exciting spectacle for the Seebach pensioners, watching the noisy planes swoop in and drop heavy, paper-wrapped parcels of 500 newspapers each so as to make the plane lighter for landing before touching down themselves. It was a difficult manoeuvre, especially at the beginning when snow covered the runway and only a single cross-shaped area had been cleared for landing.

Conscious of the worldwide press coverage, the authorities had employed famous First World War fighter aces like twenty-six-year-old Otto Könnecke, who had scored thirty-five victories in the war and been awarded Germany's highest decoration, the Pour le Mérite. Once they had dropped the newspapers and landed the planes, their cargo of 40 kilograms of airmail and 4,000 newspapers was loaded into motorcars, also still a novelty, and taken into the town centre. Berlin newspapers fresh from the printing press and embossed with a red 'delivered by airmail' stamp were now available in Weimar's streets, much 'to the astonishment of not just the Weimarers but also the Berliners, who ordinarily are never easily amused', one newspaper reported.[52] Urgent deliveries sent by train sometimes took up to five days to arrive due to strikes and lack of coal.

The National Assembly itself elicited a mixture of curiosity, ridicule and scorn from Weimarers. It was mostly old-age pensioners who had the time and the inclination to get hold of observer tickets for the National Theatre, 'taking up their post from 7 o'clock in the morning and the opportunity to visit the sessions from the rest of the audience', as the *Weimarische Landeszeitung* complained.[53] At the other end of the age spectrum, the beehive-like activity captured the imagination of children. Ilse-Sibylle Stapff, a bright seven-year-old girl, overheard how scornfully some of her family members talked about the deputies. The widow of a local school teacher had volunteered to host three MPs, and some of Ilse-Sibylle's relatives were outraged: 'How can this lady harbour *these* people? *These* people!'[54]

The girl also had a democratically minded aunt who worked as a stenographer for the Assembly. Wanting her niece to see democracy in action, she smuggled the child into the theatre one day. She had warned her niece that some deputies were very unruly, constantly shouting when others were trying to speak. But nothing could have prepared Ilse-Sibylle for the spectacle of seeing the argumentative socialist Luise Zietz in action. A passionate feminist and pacifist, she interrupted the speaker again and again until the President of the National Assembly Constantin Fehrenbach had had enough. He rang a loud bell and said in a strong south German accent that elongated every 'r' to rolling thunder: 'Frau Deputy Zietz, I call you to order!'

Ilse-Sibylle was spellbound. Back home, she assembled all her teddy bears, a toy dog, cat and elephant in her room. The biggest bear was Fehrenbach, who was placed in the middle. In front of him sat the deputies Gustav Stresemann (who would later be Chancellor and Foreign Minister), Luise Zietz, and the girl's favourite the liberal Gertrud Bäumer. The others were a changing cast of MPs. As one of the bears spoke, another would stand up and say 'Hear! Hear!' Then bear Zietz would make an angry intervention, which would cause big bear Fehrenbach to thunder, 'Frrrau Deputy Zietz, I call you to orrderr!' National Assembly became one of Ilse-Sibylle's favourite games.

Other Weimarers were less impressed. The right-wing press felt that the deputies inside the theatre were free to squabble and argue, 'yet the people outside had to shut their mouths'.[55] Headmaster Curt Weiß attended a session and was 'gripped by disgust in view of such behaviour from a group of ill-bred men whom this serious and urgent time has sent to rescue the fatherland. Should this tone become fashionable again in the German parliament . . . so help us God!'[56] Harry Graf Kessler was also underwhelmed by this 'assembly of excitable fuddy-duddies'.[57]

Many MPs enjoyed working in Weimar. At other times, the quaint and somewhat self-important town might have felt a little provincial but right then Weimar was safe, pretty and far away – an oasis of deceptive calm. When they weren't at the theatre, the Volkshaus or the Schloss working, the politicians continued debating in Weimar's cosy restaurants and pubs. The close proximity and inability to go anywhere but the allocated eating places meant that there was a far more intense exchange between people than there usually was in hectic Berlin. There were formal networking events too. Friedrich

Ebert hosted one at the Schloss, where he also had his office. The war and its aftermath had begun to chip away at old class boundaries, normalizing the idea that a former saddle-maker should host events for the great and good at the former Grand Duke's residence.

Throughout April, the Assembly made progress on drafting the new German constitution and remained blissfully ignorant of the peace treaty conditions that were being negotiated without their input in Paris. The entries in the guest books of Weimar's taverns were light-hearted. Even Matthias Erzberger, who had had the difficult task of heading the German delegation that signed the Armistice on 11 November 1918 just a few days after his only son Oskar had died of the Spanish Flu, began to feel more optimistic. At the Golden Eagle (Goldener Adler) tavern, he wrote one evening: 'Do your work first, then laugh and quench your thirst.'[58]

The world continued to rage outside Weimar's cordon of calm. The socialist People's State of Bavaria, which had replaced the Kingdom of Bavaria when it collapsed in the revolution of November 1918, was itself toppled and its leader Kurt Eisner assassinated on 21 February 1919. The Bavarian Soviet Republic was established in its place and in return overthrown in May by the army and paramilitary Freikorps units. There were bloody street battles in Berlin. General strikes shook Upper Silesia and the Ruhr. A Soviet Republic was established in Bremen. Halle, Leipzig, Erfurt, Eisenach and Gotha were also gripped by revolutionary unrest.

In Weimar, the fear of a communist insurrection remained strong while the significant military presence, ongoing strikes affecting train and mail traffic and the strict controls over who could leave and enter the town gave life a strange sense of surreal detachment. Käte Lehmann complained that 'we are now basically cut off from all the world . . . Every day we wait for the strike to break out here, too.'[59] Carl Weirich unhappily missed his mother's seventy-fifth birthday 'because Weimar had been locked down due to Spartacist activities outside'. When the restrictions were loosened, he and his wife took the difficult decision for Friedel to go away again for treatment since her health had deteriorated further and Carl couldn't care for her and run the shop at the same time. With 'great sadness' Carl saw her off to another sanatorium before returning to Weimar alone and worried.[60]

Rosa Schmidt was concerned too, although things could have been a lot worse. Unlike many other women, she had not lost her husband. Arthur had returned from the Western Front in one piece and with an Iron Cross on his chest. The family was together and Arthur finally got to know his youngest son Ernst. They settled in together in a flat at Breitenstraße 1 in Jakobsvorstadt, a quarter just north of the old town, dominated by small businesses, shops and tradespeople.[61] It was not the wealthiest part of town but pleasant. Their immediate neighbours were a couple of shop owners, a clerk, a paver and a carpenter.[62] The unusually wide cobbled streets of Am Viadukt and Breitenstraße met at their front door and just across the street lay an expansive park. Arthur's father Hermann also lived just a ten-minute walk away at Windischenstraße 20, right in the town centre.[63]

As the Schmidts made themselves at home in Weimar, they faced an uncertain economic future. There seemed to be no way to get back into their old business of running a hotel while all such establishments were requisitioned by the authorities for the National Assembly. They'd have to wait for normality to return to Weimar.

If there was one political event that cut through the daily struggle, it was the end of the peace negotiations. On 7 May, the German delegation in Paris received the conditions from the Allies. The French Prime Minister Georges Clemenceau told the German Foreign Minister Ulrich Graf Brockdorff-Rantzau that 'the hour of reckoning has come'. Upon seeing the terms, the German politician found it a harsh peace that 'would always trigger renewed objections against it. Nobody would be in a position to sign it in good conscience.'[64]

Alongside its colonies, Germany was to forfeit 13 per cent of its European territory, losing a tenth of its population. In addition it would have to disarm, reducing what had been one of the most powerful militaries on earth to a rump. Crucially, the 'War Guilt' clause, Article 231, forced Germany to accept all the blame for the war so that vast reparations could be demanded for decades to come. The German Foreign Minister told Clemenceau that such an admission of guilt 'would be a lie coming out of my mouth'. He explained that Germany didn't seek to avoid responsibility for the horrors that took place but 'we deny strongly that Germany, whose people were convinced that they were fighting a defensive war, is solely to blame for it'.[65]

Many Weimarers put their anger into less formal words. One local paper called the treaty a 'rape document'.[66] Käte Lehmann thought the conditions were even more 'shameful' than 'we could have imagined'. Curt Weiß called the Allied leaders 'executioners' who 'strangled Germany after it had stabbed the deadly dagger into its own body with both hands. The right hand: the arch-conservatives, the left one: the Social Democrats. Now proud Germany, that beautiful and venerable figure, lies on the floor and bleeds out.'[67]

Weimar's churches and other venues hosted talks and demonstrations against the 'shameful peace'. Mayor Martin Donndorf organized a rally on the market square. The town's high society was also outraged. Harry Graf Kessler wrote nothing in his diary for weeks after 7 May because he felt 'so depressed'.[68] Newspapers were speculating that he might replace Brockdorff-Rantzau as Foreign Minister. Perhaps the charismatic Count thought he could do a better job? It was a rumour Harry tried to dispel quickly with an interview in the New York Times. Any involvement with the peace treaty was a poisoned chalice. Strikes, communist agitation and right-wing threats of violence against any 'traitor' who might support the signing and fulfilment of the treaty created a tense atmosphere that often spilled over into unrest. Government control seemed brittle.

In Weimar, a criminal called Peter Schwärtz managed to break out of prison on the night of 18 June. Brandishing a pistol, he freed fifty-eight fellow prisoners, who armed themselves and then attempted to break into the Schloss where President Ebert and Defence Minister Gustav Noske were billeted. Security troops locked down the gates just in the nick of time. Noske and Ebert bumped into one another in the courtyard, both sleepy and pistol in hand. Frustrated that they couldn't get in, the criminals fired at the Schloss from the outside, nearly hitting Gustav Bauer, who would become Chancellor a couple of days later. As the gang roamed the town, they were engaged by security forces, and the ensuing shoot-out that involved machine-gun fire, grenades and rifles would have done nothing to calm the atmosphere in Weimar. It took until 8 a.m. before order was restored and most of the culprits were arrested. Schwärtz received a prison sentence of fifteen years but soon escaped again.

Many Germans were looking for scapegoats, someone to be angry with about the seemingly pointless suffering they had all endured. Many refused to believe that their army had lost on the battlefield. Elisabeth Förster-Nietzsche wasn't the only one who saw the present situation as 'Germ[an]y's suicide, for we have not been defeated!' as she wrote to Harry Graf Kessler. Reminiscing about the wars that had unified Germany in the nineteenth century, she mused, 'we old people, who have seen the proud, beautiful Germany and its rise, and have experienced nothing but victories . . . we cannot adapt to this terrible humiliation'.[69]

Public hatred for the newly elected people's representatives spiralled to new heights. Matthias Erzberger became a particular target, being the minister responsible for the peace negotiations. Now even the comment he had written in the guest book of Weimar's Golden Eagle became a source of ire. General Georg Maercker, who was in charge of the troops guarding the National Assembly, fumed: 'In these terrible days, Erzberger had the nerve to write into the guest book of a tavern in Weimar the words: "Do your work first, then laugh and quench your thirst." '[70] This was framed so that Erzberger appeared to have committed treason first and then laughed and toasted his deed.

Harry Graf Kessler described how 'an elderly, well-situated man' on the train to Weimar loudly declared that 'he would like to beat Erzberger to death, one would have to place a few hand grenades under the car'. The train was crowded, yet 'nobody raised even the slightest objection'.[71] Now even Weimar wasn't safe any more. Erzberger temporarily fled the town in a car to nearby Oßmannstedt where he boarded a train to Berlin.[72] Harry had little sympathy. He thought him a 'haughty figure' and concluded that 'Erzberger and his enemies approximately deserve one another.'[73] Even the thought that the politician might come to harm left him cold since 'it wouldn't be undeserved but brought upon himself by his disastrous activities'.[74] Two years later Erzberger was assassinated by right-wing terrorists.

Such murderous hostility heightened the government's dilemma. If they didn't sign the treaty, the war would resume and destroy Germany. If they did, public resentment might ignite a revolution. So the cabinet resigned, leaving the mess for others to sort out. The new government under Gustav Bauer had no choice but to sign the hated Treaty of Versailles on 28 June 1919. One local right-wing paper reacted with an emotional appeal: 'So we cry today, in this deeply painful hour of our history, words of deep sadness and greatest hope: Germany is dead! Germany shall live! Yes, Germany shall live!'[75]

There was a palpable sense of relief when it was time for the National Assembly to leave Weimar and move back to Berlin. Throughout July, the delegates had worked feverishly to finalize and pass the republic's legal foundation. On 31 July it was done. By a vote of 262 to 75, the new German constitution was passed and only the far-right, the far-left and the Bavarian Farmers' Party had voted against it. President Ebert signed it on 11 August and it became effective with its proclamation three days later. It was a momentous occasion: the first German republic in history, the first full German democracy with equality for the sexes, guaranteed fundamental rights for all and extensive welfare provision.

The new Germany came in new colours: black-red-gold, the colours of the liberal revolution of 1848 that had attempted and failed to create German unity under the banner of national liberalism. Despite all the aggravation and the division, the National Assembly had got there in the end. Out of the ashes of the German Empire rose the Weimar Republic.

★

The mood in Weimar was distinctly subdued. Even Gertrud Bäumer, who had been so excited to see women vote, was underwhelmed. 'Everyone knows in theory that we are living through an enormous watershed moment in German history right now . . . but none of this turns into feeling,' she wrote. The end of the National Assembly had felt 'sober, almost boring and conducted with relative indifference and obvious lack of enthusiasm'. There seemed to be no passion for the huge political project the nation had embarked on. 'Strangely, nobody seems to feel that this is the conclusion of a revolution.'[76]

It didn't help that the young republic had not yet developed its own rituals and pageantry. On the afternoon of the day the constitution was ratified, Weimarers and troops gathered in front of the National Theatre in the assumption that there would be some kind of declaration but by 8 p.m. nothing had happened. The crowds began to disperse and the military band left to play a paid gig in a Weimar restaurant. 'There was no jubilation, no address, no tribute, nothing,' a conservative newspaper complained. 'The Reich constitution shuffled out into the country like an indifferent guest.'[77]

Harry Graf Kessler was also disappointed at what he saw inside the theatre when Friedrich Ebert was sworn in as President on 21 August. The conservatives abstained in protest so their seats were filled by clerks to make the auditorium look full. At 5 p.m., Ebert appeared on stage, looking 'small and broad shouldered' to the aristocrat. Harry couldn't help but picture him in swimming trunks. The *Berliner Illustrierte Zeitung* had featured a photograph of Ebert and Defence Minister Noske standing side by side knee-deep in the Baltic Sea. Airmailed into Weimar, the image had been seen by almost everyone. It 'hung in the air above the frock coats during the celebratory proceedings', Harry thought.

It didn't get better from there. When it was time for Ebert to read the oath of office, nobody could find the manuscript. The organ stopped playing as planned and an awkward silence descended. Then finally someone shuffled through the crowded room towards the stage, piece of paper in hand. When Ebert finally took the oath in his 'likeable high voice', Harry thought the whole spectacle 'decent but without flair, like a confirmation in a respectable house'. He was embarrassed to observe 'petite-bourgeois theatre as the ending of the greatest war and of the revolution!' Having attended many pompous festivities in his life, the nobleman wasn't convinced the new Germany was ever going to pull it off. 'The republic should avoid ceremonies; this form of government doesn't lend itself to them. It's as if a governess is dancing ballet.'[78]

After the awkward ceremony was over, Ebert appeared on the balcony of the National Theatre. Despite scattered rain showers, many people had waited in the square since the morning: all age groups, men, women, a few soldiers. The atmosphere was jovial with music, drinks and street sellers. People had crowded on to balconies and roofs of the surrounding buildings to catch a last glimpse of the National Assembly.

Ebert began to speak.

> Weimarers! I will never forget this day and its meaning! But you, too, shall remember this hour! . . . Let us stand together in this hard struggle for the survival of our people, call with me on the vow of inseparable unity so that from here, from the heart of Germany, from the site of eternal spiritual greatness, it echoes into the entire German fatherland, into towns and villages, into factories and workshops: Our beloved German people, long may it live![79]

The crowds cheered and sang 'Deutschland, Deutschland über alles', the first verse of the 'Deutschlandlied' that would become the republic's anthem in 1922. Then Ebert climbed into a car and was driven away as women waved handkerchiefs and men raised their hats. He left behind a letter in which he thanked Weimar for its hospitality, expressing his hope that it would 'remain the centre of German culture and of the German patriotic and international spirit'.[80]

Almost unnoticed by the Weimar public at first, another revolution began. On 1 April 1919, the Grand Ducal Saxon Academy of Fine Art and the Grand Ducal Saxon School of Arts and Crafts were merged under the directorship of Walter Gropius, an architect in his mid-thirties. Gropius had already begun to make a name for himself before the war. When the then director of the Grand Ducal Saxon School of Arts and Crafts Henry van de Velde stepped down in 1915 due to his Belgian nationality, he'd suggested Gropius as his successor. But the promising young man from Berlin couldn't take the appointment, because he was drafted.

Shot out of the sky and buried under a pile of rubble and dead bodies for three days, he survived the war badly wounded and with two Iron Cross decorations. His reputation was beginning to build and it certainly didn't do it any harm that he had married the glamorous Alma Mahler in 1915 during a brief period of leave. She was the widow of the famous Austrian composer Gustav Mahler and widely regarded as one of the most beautiful and charismatic women of her age. But their tempestuous relationship didn't last, despite their daughter Manon, named after Gropius's mother, being born in 1916. By the time Gropius moved to Weimar, Alma was already having an affair with her future husband, Franz Werfel. Gropius's only solace was that the divorce settlement stipulated that he would be allowed to continue to see their daughter once a year.

Traumatized by war and heartbroken, the architect threw himself into his work in Weimar. His ambition for the new art school was nothing short of revolutionary: to combine traditional craftsmanship with art. To Gropius the idea that an artist couldn't physically make things was nonsense. To him, the process of building was integral to creativity. For that to work, the old generation of artists needed to be replaced by 'a new guild of craftsmen free from divisive class snobbery'.[81] His new art school would 'admit as apprentice any reputable person, regardless of age and gender, whose talent and prior education is regarded as sufficient by the masters' council'.[82] In the summer, eighty-four women and seventy-nine men enrolled as students in Weimar. The Bauhaus movement was born.

Distracted by hardship and turmoil, few Weimarers took note of the new art school and its ambitious director at first. But it wouldn't take long before the heady mix of classlessness, avant-garde culture and internationalism began to rile local conservatives who eyed the gregarious students and staff, many of whom were foreigners, Jewish or women, with suspicion. Many of the Bauhaus members in turn regarded Weimarers as provincial and reactionary, examples of the very culture they sought to smash. Just a few weeks after he had taken up his post, Gropius wrote to a friend in Berlin: 'A wasp nest has already woken out of its sleep here and is beginning to sting me. There will be an intense fight. But I'm not cut out to be defensive and will step forward.'[83] By December, Gropius referred to the local elite as 'idiotic fuddy-duddies', an 'all-German, reactionary clique which is rather big and fat around here'.[84] A group of forty-nine conservative Weimarers responded with an official notice to the authorities in which they accused the Bauhaus of 'treating everything of which Weimar had once been proud and which was highly admired far beyond the borders of our fatherland with artfully flaunted contempt'. Gropius was accused of 'onesidedly preferring foreign elements to the detriment of the majority of students of German descent' and of 'communist' tendencies.[85]

At Christmas, Gropius was in a good mood, personally serving food at one of the legendary Bauhaus parties. Students laughed, drank and played music together, 'and we improvised our Bauhaus dance', one of them remembered.[86] For its young members, the first Bauhaus year ended in boundless optimism, but Gropius knew they had made powerful enemies.

For many Weimarers, 1919 was a watershed moment. They hoped normality would return now that the troops had left, the cordon around the town was lifted and hotels and restaurants were back in use. Weimar's children could go back to school. Jutta Hecker's Sophienstift, which had housed the National Assembly's telegraph office, was cleared but it was in an awful state and needed renovating from the ground up. But at least the government paid 40,000 marks for this and the girls moved back into their old classrooms on 21 October. Jutta and her fellow students enjoyed a big reopening event with decorations, music and a song written by one of their teachers especially for the occasion:

Isn't it like a beautiful dream
That we're in the old room again?
That in the school, the old and the dear,
We can learn happy and without fear?
That there's no machine gun on the balcony,
That looks at us so threateningly?
And that no soldier demands to see
Our cards or some form of ID?
Now let us all be happy again,
Even if we sometimes think of the pain.[87]

Still, nothing was as before. Jutta's French and English teachers had not returned, and the ongoing coal shortages meant that only half the classrooms could be heated and used. Soon, even the soldiers would come back.

Many adult Weimarers tried to escape the bleakness of their day-to-day struggle by distracting themselves. Carl Weirich tried not to worry too much about his sick wife Friedel, whom he didn't see for months. There was nothing he could do. When he wasn't working to keep his shop going, he visited family members, went to the theatre or hiked in the mountains. Once, he shocked his seventy-five-year-old mother by taking her and a group of male friends to a performance of female wrestlers. The fight got so out of hand that 'in the end the hair of the female wrestlers flew about in the air as they fought one another', he noted gleefully.[88]

A dance craze swept through the country. Weimar did not suffer the shortage of young men the war had caused elsewhere since many soldiers had been posted in the town. 'Thuringian girls were happy with the billeting since they had plenty of dancers,' General Maercker wrote with a mixture of sympathy and scorn for his men who craved distraction from the trauma of war but also had a job to do protecting the National Assembly.[89] Even as hatred for the Allies intensified, young Germans began to adopt American dances like the Foxtrot, the Ragtime or the Onestep, a trend that many older residents saw as a foreign influence that 'in Weimar, in the heart of Germany, seems doubly shameful', as one teacher bemoaned.[90] General Maercker even petitioned for a dancing ban, which was denied with the explanation that it might cause another revolution.

The Weimar authorities tried to regain control over other vices that were seen as a threat to Weimar's reputation, particularly where they were visible to the many visitors to the town in 1919. The Hotel Hohenzollern by the train station was one such worry. During the war, it had lost its tourists. Then the military had stationed men like Carl Weirich there who had been deemed medically unfit for front-line service and were performing other duties. For this, the Hohenzollern received monthly rent from the authorities. Hotel manager Willy Wischeropp topped this up by other means. Professional gamblers and other 'persons of ill repute' met at the Hohenzollern to drink and play a notorious card game called 'Meine Tante, deine Tante' ('My Aunt, Your Aunt') with stakes of between 5 and 20 marks. Witnesses would later claim they had seen Weimar bankers and businessmen playing with up to 1,000 marks. Even the landlord himself wasn't impartial to a game or two, as he admitted to the police who investigated the matter in the summer of 1919. When officers questioned him on 4 August and told him that his hotel licence would be revoked if he continued tolerating such vices in his establishment, he decided that all was lost anyway and hosted another gambling night the next day.

To Willy it seemed a risk worth taking. According to the police files, his dubious clientele sometimes drank forty bottles of sparkling wine a night, spending up to 1,000 marks in the process. The 500-mark fine he received from a court in Weimar seemed a reasonable overhead. But the police had had enough. Interviewing witnesses such as head waiter Beck, they gathered enough evidence to revoke the licence Willy had held since 1907. On 25 November, the Hohenzollern lost its landlord.[91]

Carl Weirich felt optimistic in the second half of 1919. In mid-October, Friedel returned from the sanatorium for tuberculosis patients. Carl wrote that he was 'of course in a state of excitement in anticipation of a reunion after four months of separation'.[92] He had decorated their apartment with fresh flowers and hosted a little coffee gathering to welcome back his wife. Relatives, friends and neighbours came. Carl thought it was all 'rather touching'. But the joy didn't last. It was clear that Friedel had not recovered. If anything, her condition was worse. 'Christmas 1919 was a sad one,' Carl wrote dejectedly, 'because Friedel was confined to her bed.' The couple 'toasted a happy new year, but certainly didn't believe it would be'.[93]

1920

'The year began with grave concerns about the economic future,' August Baudert remembered.[1] He was now State Minister of the Free State of Saxe-Weimar-Eisenach that had replaced the Grand Duchy and deeply worried about the ongoing shortages. What effect would they have on the strained social fabric?

Carl Weirich was so shocked by the increasing food prices that they found their way into his diary. 'Inflation had arrived in the country,' he noted, '1lb bread cost 1.20 [mark]'.[2] This was twice what it had cost a year earlier and by May it would double yet again.[3] If this worried people like Carl, who had a regular if modest income, it was an existential problem for those who couldn't work. One in five Weimarers applied for state support because they were unemployed, suffered from war injuries, had been widowed or were retired. One pensioner wrote in a local paper: 'ill, of course, due to living off flour soup and potatoes . . . What's to become of me? Alone without help? Oh, it's frightful having to stare doom in the eye . . . I can only pay the doctor and the pharmacist by selling one piece after another from my cupboard and my home. It hurts.'[4]

Unprecedented levels of destitution drove many Weimarers to despair. According to police reports, Weimar's suicide rate was twice as high as the national average in 1919 and 1920, affecting men and women in equal numbers.[5] Almost every single case made the news. On 2 January, the 'depressed' wife of a civil servant vanished, leaving farewell letters. On 13 January, a young girl jumped into the River Ilm, and her body was found the next morning. On 20 January, a working-class veteran who had only just come home shot himself in the head and ran out into the street with blood streaming down his neck where police administered first aid and took him to the hospital. The next day, another man drank poison in a shop and only survived because someone called a doctor. At the beginning of February, newspapers reported that four people had killed themselves on the same day.[6]

Even the weather seemed abnormally violent. In early January, flooding blocked roads, ruined houses and disrupted the power supply because the electricity plant was under water. A storm ripped roofs off houses. Just when things seemed to calm down a little in February, a new wave of Spanish Flu hit a malnourished population. Recorded deaths stood at 4 per cent of those infected, but the real figure was likely higher.[7] The issue was exacerbated by the ongoing lack of coal. Headmaster Curt Weiß noted in his diary: 'I can barely write because I'm so cold!'[8] To save coal, one Weimar hospital decided to put all its patients into one building. When that too couldn't be heated any more, 192 sick people lay in their beds cheek by jowl in freezing temperatures.

Carl Weirich struggled to care for Friedel, whose lungs got worse and worse. He spent his days working in the shop, supporting his wife by night and getting what distraction he could by walking with visiting relatives or cycling. Everyone could see how Friedel was deteriorating. Neighbours, friends and family took it in turns to provide some solace. 'My dear wife lay on her bed like a holy woman,' Carl recalled.[9] As she wasted away, Friedel urged her husband to enjoy life and to gather courage for what was to come.

While Carl sought solace in nature, some of his fellow Weimarers took their despair to the street in 'Shortage Marches'. On 10 January, hundreds of angry citizens gathered on the market square, demanding coal and potatoes. Neither commodity had been provided by the authorities in the scheduled quantities. While some protesters had been admitted into the town hall for discussions with Mayor Martin Donndorf, those left outside became increasingly restless. Some attempted to storm the building, hammering on glass panes in the door with wooden poles. Security troops kept them at bay with difficulty.

One politician was sent outside to settle things. But he was attacked immediately. Even Baudert, who had proved so effective at calming angry protests during the revolution in 1918, faced 'insults and defamation such as people's traitor, scoundrel and similar niceties', as he recalled with indignation.[10] To prevent a storming of the town hall, Donndorf appeared on the balcony. Shouting over the jeering and insults hurled his way, he promised more supplies. Pacified, most people dispersed, but a hard core remained, roaming through the town and causing further damage to the Fürstenhaus, the parliamentary building, where they thought other politicians were hiding. Eight men were arrested, including two teenagers. Baudert felt 'more pity than hatred' for the angry young men.[11]

On Saturday 13 March, August Baudert led a State Council meeting at the Fürstenhaus to discuss the supply situation. After an hour, someone interrupted the session. There was a telephone call. It was Weimar's Police Chief Bährecke. Had Baudert heard what had happened in Berlin? The government had been toppled and had fled to Dresden. General Walther von Lüttwitz, the commanding officer of the army troops in and around Berlin, and Wolfgang Kapp, a right-wing political activist and civil servant, had taken charge.

This counter-revolution, later dubbed the Kapp Putsch, came in response to the fulfilment of the Treaty of Versailles, according to which Germany was only allowed to retain 100,000 of its 400,000 troops and none of the 120 Freikorps organizations. Lüttwitz and his supporters believed that hostility against the treaty was so wide-spread that they would inspire public support with their move against a government that had agreed to fulfil its demands. They certainly assumed they could count on local army and Freikorps leaders who might refuse to disband.

Baudert had no idea what the troops stationed in Weimar would do. Since it had hosted the National Assembly and then become the capital of the Free State, Weimar had been the headquarters of Brigade 16 of the newly formed Reichswehr. This had a contingent of the so-called Sicherheitspolizei (Security Police or SiPo), a militar-ized police force that could be used to suppress uprisings, and it had a citizens' militia. But how each would respond to Lüttwitz's call to arms was anyone's guess.

Baudert hung up and hurried back into the meeting, where he told the State Council what had happened. They were stunned. The first thing to do was to find out who was on the side of the legitimate government and who would join Kapp and Lüttwitz. As it turned out, the police sided with Baudert and the State Council. The militia stayed neutral. The Reichswehr and the SiPo declared for Kapp and immediately began to occupy strategic buildings. The stage was set for a civil war on the streets of Weimar.

At the Fürstenhaus, where the militia kept their weapons, the State Council prepared a message to be printed in the newspapers: 'In this hour we call on you for the protection of the democratic constitution and the legitimate government. The attempted Berlin military dictatorship must be prevented by all means.'[12] The exiled Berlin government had also called on workers to defend their 1918 revolution, and a large group of Weimarers appeared at the Fürstenhaus and demanded weapons to do so. Reluctantly, Baudert armed them with 300 of the 2,000 available rifles and they began to storm the buildings the SiPo had occupied. Chaos ensued, and they returned later to steal the remaining weapons.

Faced with the force and fury of the citizens' militia, only the SiPo in the post office resisted, and a few people were wounded in the ensuing shoot-out. Baudert meanwhile summoned his sons and kept them nearby for their security. He could hear gunfire and grenades booming in the distance, and then the tumult came closer until he heard orders being barked right outside his window. Someone shouted, 'Hands up!' Shortly after, footsteps hammered across the floor outside his office door. When he opened it, he found that SiPo members had been arrested by his security forces. Baudert sighed. Berlin's instability had caused Weimarers to turn on each other. The men in front of him weren't to blame. He ordered that they be made comfortable, disarmed and then let go. The grateful SiPo members admitted that they hadn't been keen to join in the putsch, a widespread sentiment, as the majority of Germans didn't think March 1920 was a good moment for a revolution.[13]

General Hagenberg, who commanded the local Reichswehr, didn't give up as easily. He ordered reinforcement units to Weimar the next day and set Baudert's government an ultimatum. When they didn't respond, he had the Fürstenhaus stormed and ministers detained. The lawyer Jöck, a member of the ultra-conservative DNVP, was appointed as Civil Commissar of the new government in Weimar. But Baudert was able to persuade him to step down the next day.

There was total chaos in Weimar. Jutta Hecker, who had just resumed her education, at least when coal supplies allowed, faced a week-long school closure once more. First, her school was occupied by SiPo troops, who were in turn dispersed by the militia. Shortly after, a forty-man machine-gun unit was set up in the building.[14] Not that it made any difference to Jutta. The streets of Weimar had become so unsafe that children weren't allowed to go anywhere.

On 15 March, workers joined the fray. They had followed a call by Ebert's beleaguered government for a nationwide general strike to oust the Kapp government. As in Berlin, in Weimar too, this forced things to a head. Faced with demonstrations in the streets and a town rendered dysfunctional by the strike, Reichswehr and SiPo units attempted to storm the Volkshaus, the headquarters of Weimar's workers' movement – not least to retrieve the weapons the militia had taken from the Fürstenhaus. Things escalated. Losing control, the putschists shot into the gathered workers. They killed five people immediately, among them Anna Braun, who was only twenty-six. Another thirty people were wounded and four of them died of their injuries shortly after.

Weimar was in deep shock over this bloodbath, and the public mood turned on General Hagenberg and his troops. The next day, on 16 March, they gave up. They declared their allegiance to the rightful government and fled into Prussian territory to evade punishment. On 17 March, Kapp fled to Sweden and an uneasy calm settled over Germany and Weimar – time to bury those who had died defending the fledgling democracy.

Alma Gropius, who was visiting her estranged husband in Weimar at the time, watched the scenes from his house: 'Today was the funeral of the workers who died in the fight. The procession walked past my window. A never-ending row of placards with messages: Long live Rosa Luxemburg! Long live Liebknecht! – the Bauhaus was represented in full.'[15] The following year, Walter Gropius would design a monument for the 'March Fallen' at Weimar cemetery.

In Weimar and Germany the Kapp Putsch had failed because there was no appetite for upheaval. Yet there was barely any punishment for those who had participated in an act of treason. This was partially an attempt to keep the fragile peace but also an expression of how sympathetic much of the judiciary were towards right-wing attempts to overthrow the new order. 'These crimes on our country, which would flare up in grave pangs for a long time afterwards, remained unpunished,' Baudert lamented three years later, in 1923, the year Adolf Hitler first attempted to overthrow Weimar democracy.[16]

Into this political chaos, the state of Thuringia was born on 1 May 1920. This region in the geographical centre of Germany had been notoriously divided for centuries. Prussian, Saxon, Hessian and Frankish influences had vied with smaller political entities for influence. In the November Revolution of 1918, when the six Thuringian dynastical rulers abdicated, separate republican regimes emerged. In the end, most merged to form the state of Thuringia. But the Prussian areas (notably Erfurt, today the state capital) stayed Prussian and the Free State of Coburg joined Bavaria. Unity was hard to come by in post-war Germany.

Nonetheless, there was still a degree of optimism in the air. On 1 May, a glorious spring day, workers proceeded through Weimar to whistles, music and drums. Around 6,000 people joined them in the old town, where the crowds celebrated a combination of May Day, spring and the foundation of Thuringia. At the Volkshaus, where people had been shot dead by soldiers just six weeks earlier, an entertainment programme drew people into the garden. It fell to Weimar as the new state's capital to lead the way into a better future.

In May 1920, the Hotel Hohenzollern also saw a new beginning. The tall white building was on the brink of being shut down due to the gambling scandal. Elisabeth Heydenreich, who ran the Ehringsdorfer brewery that owned the Hohenzollern, frantically looked for a new manager, desperate not to lose income.[17] Writing to the town authorities on 26 April in a note that was labelled with a thrice-underlined 'very urgent', she demanded to be given a temporary licence to run the Hohenzollern herself while she looked for 'a fitting and adequate replacement' for the disgraced former manager Willy Wischeropp.[18]

This was just the opportunity Arthur and Rosa Schmidt had been waiting for. Now that the restrictions imposed on Weimar's hospitality industry for the National Assembly had been lifted, they were ready to get back into their old business. With its modern amenities, handsome exterior and excellent location right next to the station, the Hohenzollern was just the stroke of luck the Schmidts needed to start their new life in Weimar. On 15 May, Arthur applied for a temporary licence to serve food and alcohol as the new manager, confirming that he understood that it was illegal to allow gambling to take place on the premises.[19] He paid a fee of 600 marks and received his confirmation by the end of the month. There was still a lot of work to do. The authorities demanded that the upstairs toilets be split into male and female, which required division walls from floor to ceiling. He had to have drawings done, indicating exactly which rooms would be used for drinking and eating. But Arthur jumped every hurdle and was handed his licence on 2 November 1920. The Schmidts were back in business.

Taking over a hotel may have been a risky proposition in such uncertain times, but it was also a way out of an increasingly difficult job market. Throughout 1920, unemployment spiralled upwards. In August 1919, only eighty-three Weimarers had received unemployment benefits – a stark contrast to the Reich overall where the number of people looking for work had doubled to nearly 3 million since the end of the war. Due to the largely middle-class nature of Weimar's job market and the work required for the National Assembly, the trend hit the town with some delay, but by July 1920 nearly 2,000 of its residents were also looking for jobs. For the working and lower middle classes this often meant absolute destitution since they had few savings.

The town council launched work-creation schemes that involved paying 170 people small wages to do largely meaningless work to keep them off the statistics.[20] A public building programme was also launched under the newly elected mayor, Walther Felix Mueller. Only forty years old, Mueller was dynamic and, together with his wife Hellen Mueller-Schlenkhoff, he harboured ambitious plans for Weimar. While Hellen launched social projects such as a support centre for newborn care and a medical institute for infants, earning her the title 'Mother of Weimar', Felix concentrated on solving two of Weimar's biggest social issues together: jobs and housing.

In 1920 alone, 224 one- and two-bedroom flats were built in the Landfried settlement north of the station. They provided cheap, if rather cramped and rudimentary homes, which meant most flats were rented by staff of Weimar's rail and tram wagon factory or by unemployed workers. This clientele with its far-left leanings and trade union links was so dominant at the Landfried that the settlement was soon nicknamed 'Little Moscow'.[21] Built largely from timber due to the lack of building materials, the houses ended up looking rather traditional, fitting in with Weimar's existing style. Lead architect and chief building officer August Lehrmann, who dominated Weimar's development for three decades from 1908 to 1937, was rather pleased with the way he'd made necessity a virtue. In light of a Germany-wide conflict between traditionalists and modernists like Walter Gropius and his burgeoning Bauhaus movement, it was Lehrmann's self-professed aim to 'steer Weimar's architectural development past the dangerous cliffs of modern art trends and influences without being seen as backwards'.[22]

Given that many less affluent Weimarers lived in flats without gardens, he also tried to ensure that there were plenty of public green spaces. Linking up existing parks and landscaped gardens north and north-west of the town centre, he created the Asbach Green Belt, which still exists today. Rosa Schmidt and her family had all this on their doorstep. The park lay across the street from their flat at Breitenstraße 1. Lehrmann's merging of the old and the new worked in lots of ways – the beautiful neoclassical station building was finished in 1922 and its tunnel, through which the platform on the other side could be reached, impressed many Weimarers. But the projects didn't go far enough. By October 1920, nearly 2,500 people were looking for a flat. Lehrmann and Mueller couldn't build houses as quickly as they were needed.

The infant republic was overwhelmed with enormous social and economic problems. Sensing mounting public disaffection, the federal government decided to bring forward the general election that had been planned for the autumn to replace the National Assembly with a regular parliament. Germans would go to the polls again on 6 June. For Weimarers, this spelled two elections in rapid succession, since the first-ever Thuringian state parliament also needed to be established and polling was scheduled to take place on 20 June.

Weimar saw another campaigning frenzy that topped the previous year's in nastiness. Headteacher Curt Weiß ranted: 'What humbug! What sin! What misfortune! . . . And this is what happens week after week: division, splintering, simplification, animosity, dilution, mass suggestion by the parties . . . This will have grave consequences.'[23]

Despite the sharp verbal attacks on the centrist parties from the political fringes, there was no actual political violence in Weimar. The atmosphere teetered somewhere between political apathy and simmering anger. Only 70 per cent of eligible Weimarers cast their vote at the federal elections on 6 June, down 13 per cent from the previous year. The press speculated that around 8,000 residents may have chosen not to vote because the weather was unseasonably cold and wet that Sunday. But 20 June, the Sunday of the Thuringian elections, was a sunny summer's day, and the number of visitors to the eighteen polling stations dropped further still, by over 2,800 people. The *Thüringer Tageszeitung* mused: 'Election fatigue has prevented many from carrying their ballot paper to the box. The novelty value had dissipated . . . Some people have even shunned their duty to vote with a resigned, "there is no point anyway!" and used the beautiful Sunday to be outside in the scenic countryside away from politics.'[24]

Fatigue with mainstream politics extended to those who voted. In the young republic's first regular elections, parties that supported the new democracy lost their majority, only gaining 43.6 per cent combined. Fringe parties gained over a quarter of the vote compared to 1919. In Weimar, the conservative – liberal German People's Party (DVP) became the most popular party with nearly a third of the vote. The Social Democratic Party came second with 20 per cent, having lost many voters to the more radical socialists of the USPD, and seventy-nine Weimarers even voted for the Communist Party. Gertrud Bäumer of the liberal German Democratic Party managed to keep her seat in parliament but her party convinced just one in six Weimarers – the same number that voted for the monarchist DNVP.

If the Weimar Coalition in Berlin had called early elections to stabilize its support before people drifted too far into apathy and resentment, the plan had backfired. The SPD, to which President Friedrich Ebert belonged, dropped out of government and was replaced by the conservative – liberal DVP. Constantin Fehrenbach of the Catholic Centre Party, who had chaired the National Assembly in Weimar the previous year, was made Chancellor of a minority government.

The Thuringian elections produced an even more radical parliament. The USPD socialists won with 28 per cent. On the right, the Thüringer Landbund (or Thuringian Agricultural League) won 21 per cent. So many Thuringians had opted for parties that openly opposed parliamentary democracy that the new state parliament had no mandate for anything. August Baudert noted with mild understatement in his diary that 'the formation of a government proved difficult'.[25]

Weimar may have been far from left wing, but even socialists were beguiled by its reputation as Germany's cultural heart. On Friday 27 August, a hot late summer's day, hundreds of young left-wingers arrived in the Thuringian capital from all over Germany. As train after train pulled in, the station and its large square filled with excited chatter. A greeting committee received every visitor with a loud 'Frei heil!' ('Free hail!') – the traditional phrase of the socialist gymnastics movement – before pointing them in the direction of the Volkshaus, a ten-minute walk away.[26]

In all, 2,000 members of the Young Workers' movement would convene for Reich Youth Day (*Reichsjugendtag*).[27] Their choice of Weimar had not been a coincidence. Almost exactly a year after Germany had received its republican constitution there from a National Assembly whose largest party was the Social Democratic Party with its deep roots in the German workers' movement, a new generation hoped to build on this achievement, creating a country for and by workers.

Having travelled far – itself an experience many young Germans found it difficult to come by in the bleak economic climate of the immediate post-war years – a large number of the excited youths dropped their bags and went exploring Weimar's most famous sights: Goethe's house, the National Theatre, Schiller's last residence. The next morning, some of the young men and women decided to take a refreshing dip in the Ilm. There was much singing and dancing in the streets. As German society struggled under the burdens of reparations, grief, disease, shortages, crime, humiliation and anger, the socialists gathered in Weimar and sang, 'Rain? Wind? We laugh about it: We're young, and that is wonderful!'

The convention had also not forgotten that it was Goethe's birthday. They flocked to the Goethe and Schiller memorial in front of the National Theatre where they placed a laurel wreath on Goethe's head. In the evening, the teenagers debated, sang and talked late into the night. 'The evening hours were the best,' one delegate reminisced, 'handshakes in the middle of the night sealed friendships for life.'[28] The next day, someone realized that the wreath had been stolen from Goethe's head. Outraged, the delegation held a mock trial against the 'wreath robbers' during which a swastika was burned – a symbol that was used by various right-wing and nationalist groups. The local press condemned this sharply because it left a black mark on the street.

When it was time to go home, a solemn mood settled over the group. Many delegates would return to cramped tenement houses in industrial cities, violent street battles with police, damaged families and cynical colleagues. Max Westphal, the twenty-five-year-old youth secretary of the SPD in Hamburg, sent the young men and women home with the appeal to live the way they wanted others to live, to infuse their communities all across Germany with 'the beautiful spirit of Weimar'.[29]

Weimar could draw on a proud local tradition of social democracy, as the grandeur of the Volkshaus demonstrated. Kurt Nehrling, a slight twenty-year-old with a narrow face and high forehead, was part of a new generation. He had joined the SPD in 1919 to help rebuild Germany. He was from Jakobsvorstadt, one of the oldest parts of Weimar, where his parents Max and Emma ran the Golden Star pub (Zum Goldenen Stern) at Jakobstraße 42, which was frequented by SPD members and activists. Exposed to beer-fuelled debates about socialism and workers' rights, Kurt grew up in a highly politicized enclave of Weimar society.[30]

In 1914, Kurt had been too young to go to war. He was fifteen, and one year into his apprenticeship as a metalworker. But he wanted to help. The moment he turned eighteen, he signed up to the Imperial Navy as a volunteer, despite the fact that, by then, the prospects of Germany winning the war were bleak. After just six months in the navy, he was dismissed, having been hit by the same disease that struck so many of his contemporaries: tuberculosis. For the teenager, not only did this spell the end of his efforts to help in the war, but the permanent damage to his lungs was so severe that he would never be able to do physical labour again. The young man returned to Weimar as a gaunt figure with deep-set eyes and hollow cheeks. But by 1920, there was light at the end of the tunnel. He had found a desk job as a district councillor, which allowed him to earn a living while his lungs recovered.[31]

Nothing could lift Carl Weirich's spirits for long. Helplessly, he watched Friedel slip away as he sat by her bed after long hours in the shop. Dr Hinrichs said that there was nothing he could do for her. On 27 September 1920, Friedel died surrounded by her mother and her husband, and 'many tears were shed for her at her deathbed'. Carl's young wife, only thirty years old, had been torn from him. 'W h y?' he asked his diary.[32] Carl spent the next week in an apathetic trance. Friedel's body was cremated at Weimar cemetery but he knew that she had never felt at home in Weimar. He saw to it that her ashes were buried in her home town of Oranienburg, next to their 'darling daughter Wilfriede'. How could he bear so much grief? His wife's words still rang in his ears. She had told him to live and to draw courage from nature, as he had always done.

Carl Weirich was not the only one to experience a great personal tragedy that autumn. On Saturday 9 October, the elegant villa at Berkaer Straße 11, just south of the old town, bore witness to a violent crime that shook Weimar to the core. In the early afternoon, a man broke into the basement of the house. Dressed in a field-grey army uniform and leather gloves, he carried a loaded handgun, thirty bullets and an open razor.

The man killed the maid, Frieda Steininger, before firing more bullets at the owner of the house, Emilie Scheer, and her youngest daughter Else. Then he shot himself. Else and her mother were rushed to the Sophienhaus hospital, which wasn't far from their house, but Emilie died on the way. Else was immediately operated upon and in critical condition but survived.[33]

Police established that the murderer had been the local unemployed decorator Karl Büchner but his motive remained unclear. According to the press, he hadn't slept at home for three days beforehand and had told his fiancée that he was going to get some money from the rich to fund their wedding. There were also wild rumours that the crime may have been political. 'The murderer himself was a communist,' wrote one local paper.[34] It's also possible that Büchner had sustained deep and lasting psychological damage during the war like so many young men. Police found out that he had required psychiatric treatment ever since he'd been buried in a collapsed dugout in 1914.

The botched burglary caught the imagination of Weimarers not just because of the gruesome details, but also because the victims had belonged to one of the town's most illustrious families. The Scheers had only moved to Weimar in early 1919. It had seemed an attractive proposition: calm and respectable, a great place for paterfamilias Reinhard Scheer to retire to. Unlike the man who had murdered his wife, he had returned from the war unscathed and celebrated. An admiral in the Imperial Navy, he had commanded the German fleet at the Battle of Jutland in 1916, the only full-scale clash with Britain's Grand Fleet. The result of the sea battle remains contested to this day, but both sides claimed victory. The German press dubbed Scheer the 'Victor of Skagerrak' after the German name for the battle. Many Weimarers were delighted to welcome the famous war hero as one of their own.

Scheer had no intention of retiring quietly. He wanted to set the record straight, especially regarding his strong advocacy of unrestricted submarine warfare in the Atlantic that drew the US into the conflict. It was also he who had envisioned a last big push against the British Grand Fleet. Though he occasionally wondered what 'might have happened if the order had not been given to the fleet in October 1918 and the outbreak of revolution had not been started through it', he burst back into public life with astonishing self-confidence.[35] His war memoirs justified the efforts of the Imperial Navy, the 'favourite creation of the nation', as honourable.

Real defeat, he claimed, came at home through the revolutionaries, not at sea or in the field.[36]

Like so many other men of the German military elite, Scheer played his part to breathe life into the embers of the stab-in-the-back myth, the potent idea that Germany was not defeated on the battlefield, but instead betrayed by communists and Jews at home. A staunch monarchist, he toyed with the idea of standing as a candidate for the DNVP and even put himself forward for the role of Navy Chief. In the end, both were too risky since Scheer was on the Allies' list of war criminals. So he turned his attention to getting involved in other ways, publishing articles, speaking and becoming a pillar of the Lutheran Church in Weimar.[37]

It was in the middle of this frenetic public activity that tragedy struck the Scheer family. In Weimar wild rumours circulated, claiming that communists or Jews had planned the attack. One local newspaper spoke for many when it bemoaned the 'spirit of decline and criminality, which is holding sway everywhere in our German people'.[38]

At Wörthstraße 49 on the western outskirts of Weimar, at one of its most prestigious boarding schools, a young woman had other concerns.

Marlene Dietrich was not yet a global movie icon. In October 1920, she was eighteen years old, a curious and lively teenager with wavy, strawberry-blonde hair and large blue eyes. A native Berliner from a well-to-do family, she had been sent to Weimar by her mother for education, in particular to take private music lessons so that she might fulfil her dream of becoming a concert violinist. Her teacher was Professor Robert Reitz, the thirty-six-year-old Swiss-born concert master of the Weimar State Orchestra. Marlene was looking forward to Weimar 'since almost all its inhabitants live under Goethe's spell', as she reminisced in her autobiography.[39] Looking back on those formative years, she speculated that her younger self longed for a male role model. Her biological father died when she was just six years old. Her mother married again, but then her stepfather fell on the Eastern Front in 1916 when she was just fourteen.

So she began to 'deify' Germany's most famous poet as a father sub-stitute. She couldn't wait to 'go to Weimar, the city of my idol'.[40]

While Marlene indulged her Goethe obsession in Weimar, boarding-school life under the strict, 'cold and unfriendly' regime of headmistress Helene Arnoldi was difficult to bear.[41] She became terribly homesick. On 10 October, the day after the double murder at the Scheer villa, her diary spoke not of shocking crimes but of 'Fräulein Arnoldi [who] wants to change me according to her wishes'.[42]

Marlene found refuge from the drudgery of boarding school life when visiting the 'shrines' of Goethe. 'His houses became my houses,' she recalled, 'the women he loved became rivals who made me mad with jealousy.'[43] While Marlene hated her maths lessons, she found 'some joy' in the violin lessons with Professor Reitz.[44] As a music student, she was also allowed to go to the opera three times a week, an experience that made her feel 'overcome by the magic, the lights, the *trompe l'oeil* in the auditorium, fascinated by the violins, by all the music'.[45] She always sat in the front row, right in the centre. As Marlene began to meet people, she immersed herself in Weimar's art scene. She would later remember this time as one of the happiest of her life.[46]

As 1920 drew to a close, Carl Weirich felt lonely and dejected. He was working harder than ever during the busy December weeks, with barely any time to grieve for his late wife. He travelled to his mother-in-law's home in Oranienburg for a Christmas 'without festive cheer'.[47] When he saw that his sister-in-law Hedwig looked terribly ill, he felt his own stifled grief well up. The coughing fits, the weakness of her body. He'd seen it all before. With great sadness he watched her children Helmut and Hilde sing Christmas carols. It was obvious that they too would soon 'not have a mother any more'.[48] Carl spent New Year's Eve back in Weimar alone. He'd lost too many of those he loved. 'Father, Arno, dear Friedel: DEAD.'[49]

1921

'What's missing in our time? A lot! Everything! Order, discipline, decency, coal and bread!'[1] With this gloomy message, the church of St Peter and Paul reminded Weimar's Protestant community in February 1921 to draw strength from a fundamental Christian value. 'We need love,' it told readers of its newsletter.[2]

Marlene Dietrich, who regularly attended church services in Weimar, appeared to heed this advice.[3] She reminisced in her diary about her remaining months in the Thuringian capital: 'I am eternally grateful for this time, and especially to the man who made it so beautiful for me.'[4] Now nineteen years old, she was engaged in an illicit affair with her violin teacher Robert Reitz, a thirty-seven-year-old married man whose wife was pregnant with their third child. The Swiss musician lived at Luisenstraße 55 on the southern outskirts of town, not far from the Nietzsche Archive and a twenty-minute walk away from Marlene, who regularly visited for violin lessons. Many years later, she would tell her daughter how in the spring of 1921 she 'offered up her virginity on the altar of a Handel sonata'.[5] She found the whole episode rather disappointing. 'He groaned, heaved, panted. Didn't even take his trousers off. I just lay there on that old settee, the red plush scratching my behind, my skirts over my head.'[6] Still, she continued the affair, recording this time in her diary as her 'happiest year in Weimar'.[7]

Carl Weirich also tried to combat loneliness with love in the spring of 1921. He found some distraction at the National Theatre, watching performances of *Hansel and Gretel* and the pantomime ballet *Die Puppenfee* (*The Fairy Doll*) in April, when Marlene Dietrich was also a frequent visitor. While she had a reserved seat in the front row of the stalls, he sat high above. Feeling a little guilty and hoping he could do so 'without damaging the memory of my dear Friedel', he rented a seat in the upper circle for the season.[8]

On an unusually cold day in early May, Carl took his cousin Frieda to see a performance of Richard Wagner's epic *Parsifal* at the National Theatre. Roused by the 'most noble' music, he stepped outside on the balcony of the foyer during the interval. To his astonishment, Weimar was covered in fresh snow. It was as if the town could start again from a blank canvas. Weimar looked 'wonderfully untouched' to Carl, no sign of the chaos and misery of recent years. His thoughts wandered to a time when he was free and without a care in the world, a time before war, before having a wife and a young daughter and before being plunged into dark grief.

As a seventeen-year-old, Carl had taken his first job with a company that made souvenirs in Nuremberg in Bavaria. Many of the other employees were teenagers like him. One in particular caught his eye, the typist Marie Müller. Like him, she was seventeen and they were quite taken with each other. But before long, it was time for Carl to move on to continue his apprenticeship in Deggendorf, 170 kilometres away. There, the young man began an affair with the kitchen maid Fanny Lindinger, and Fräulein Müller slipped from his mind. He eventually ended up working for a company in Oranienburg where he met another young typist by the name of Frieda Zemlin and the pair 'got on well from the first moment'.[9]

That now seemed a world away as Carl stared out into the snow. His life wasn't over. At thirty-five, he was young and had time to start another family. His thoughts turned to Nuremberg and to Marie Müller. On a whim, Carl decided to write to her.

Elsewhere in Weimar, Kurt Nehrling, SPD member and newly minted district councillor, had fallen in love with his co-worker Marie Prox. Marie was three years older than him and, like Kurt, she came from a left-leaning Weimar family. After a short courtship, the pair got married and Marie's family helped Kurt find his feet as he continued to recover from his debilitating lung disease. His new father-in-law took a particular shine to him. Emil Prox was the respected and well-read chairman of the Social Democratic People's Association in Weimar and a member of the town administration. He had collected a huge library and inducted Kurt into the theory and practice of social democracy.[10] The two spent hours talking about politics and society. The younger man became not only deeply attached to his father-in-law and political mentor but also developed an unshakeable belief that a better life for all was possible – a conviction that was to be severely tested in years to come.

On 10 July, Elisabeth Förster-Nietzsche celebrated her seventy-fifth birthday. Her tumultuous life now spanned three quarters of a century. She resolved to spend her remaining time securing the legacy of her brother. Her Nietzsche Archive sat timelessly on its hill on the outskirts of Weimar, looking down upon a town in the grip of troubles that didn't seem to concern it. The Villa Silberblick continued to be a gathering point for influential intellectuals and a pilgrimage site for admirers of her late brother. Elisabeth kept Friedrich Nietzsche's 'Death Room', the bedroom on the first floor of the archive in which he had died, in immaculate condition.

The Nietzsche cult, artfully fanned by a regular stream of new publications, continued to secure the archive the support of many powerful individuals. Between 1920 and 1929, a twenty-three-volume collection of Nietzsche's writings was published, much of it drawn from the philosopher's unfinished notes, which were edited, compiled and partially falsified by Elisabeth and others she worked with. Among this was a new edition of *The Will to Power*, a book of fragments assembled from Friedrich's literary remains. During his lifetime, the philosopher had considered writing a book with that title himself but eventually gave up on the idea, reusing the draft title page as a shopping list.

The concept of the will to power remained ill-defined and today many interpret it as the desire to exercise control over oneself and the way one sees the world. But there are many inherent contradictions and omissions in the way Nietzsche explores this across his published and unpublished writing, making the idea impossible to pin down. Elisabeth's version of *The Will to Power*, published under her brother's name as if he had written it, suggested rather more coherence than there really was. She had created the book by taking one of Friedrich's twenty-five draft outlines for it, one that happened to have just four clear chapter headings, and then scoured his notes for material that fitted each section.[11] When Friedrich Würzbach, Elisabeth's co-editor for a new edition of *The Will to Power*, asked for access to the original notes, he was told in no uncertain terms that the previous editions were definitive. Elisabeth's copy-and-paste creation has been published in different versions under Friedrich's name since 1901 and continues to be mistaken by many people as not just his own work but also his most important book.

Enhanced by Elisabeth's edits, Nietzsche's radical critique of conventional morality and his call on humanity not only to accept fate but to *love* it, no matter how much suffering it entailed, held a particular allure for those trying to make sense of the horrors of the First World War and the painful humiliation that followed for Germany. Richard Oehler, a cousin of the Nietzsche siblings and an influential librarian who, together with his brother Max and their cousin Adalbert Oehler, ran the archive in Weimar with Elisabeth, attempted to recontextualize Nietzsche's work in light of the post-war world. In an anthology of essays published in honour of Elisabeth's seventy-fifth birthday, he wrote: 'Despite all the ugliness, war also creates liberation . . . So Nietzsche did not await the upcoming age of war with shuddering anticipation, but with a keen interest to see what values it may bring. An eye such as his . . . does not flinch when it sees millions of people trickle into the sand.'[12]

Another famous contributor to Elisabeth's birthday anthology was the writer Thomas Mann, who also attended a colloquium in her honour at the Villa Silberblick on 10 July.[13] While he later became a prominent supporter of the Weimar Republic, he was much more sceptical of democracy in the early post-war years. Mann was fascinated by Nietzsche, sitting on the committee of the Munich-based Nietzsche Society together with Richard Oehler and others. He frequently visited Elisabeth in Weimar. In 1919, he was awarded the archive's Lassen Prize (named after a wealthy donor) for his *Reflections of a Nonpolitical Man*, which mirrors the nationalist leanings he held during the war.

Other famous well-wishers included the Norwegian artist Edvard Munch, best known for his 1893 painting *The Scream*. He had visited Weimar frequently between 1904 and 1906, painting portraits of Harry Graf Kessler, and Elisabeth and Friedrich Nietzsche. Munch suffered from bouts of depression and was often seen sitting alone, getting drunk, at the Hotel Russischer Hof in the town centre.[14] It is thought that his 1906 self-portrait shows him there. It depicts a dejected-looking man sitting at a table with a bottle of wine. Occasionally, Elisabeth's company at the Villa Silberblick had pulled Munch out of this malaise and the two remained in contact over the years. In 1921, Nietzsche's sister wrote the artist a letter thanking him for his contribution to her birthday present and expressing how happy it made her to hear 'of you and your great fame, which surrounds you like a glowing cloud now, and I am especially happy when I hear that you still think of me in old friendship'.[15]

Elisabeth also found academic recognition on her seventy-fifth birthday when the University of Jena awarded her an honorary doctorate for her 'preservation of the Nietzsche estate'.[16] She would use the letters 'Dr. phil. H.c.' to adorn her name for the rest of her life, having been the first woman to be bestowed with this honorific title by the university. She hoped this formal recognition of her work might finally help her win the Nobel Prize, following three failed nominations.[17] The prize money would certainly have been welcome.

Elisabeth had deftly taken control of the Nietzsche legacy but had no other income. From her powerbase in Weimar, she continued to manage a network of her late brother's admirers to fund the archive as well as herself. From the beginning, the backing of the Swedish art collector and financier Ernest Thiel was crucial. In 1919, when most Weimarers struggled to get by on a daily basis, Thiel had given her 100,000 marks as a Christmas present.[18] In December 1921, he sent another cheque for 30,000 marks to the archive, worrying that 'Germany's finances are in disarray and are getting worse, as far as I can see'.[19] It's no wonder she told Munch in the same year that 'Herr Ernest Thiel is a wonderful man.'[20]

But for the astute and ruthless management of her brother's writings and legacy, Elisabeth Förster-Nietzsche may well have ended up celebrating her birthday as a penniless widow, reliant on welfare from a state that had little to give. On 27 April, the Allies' Reparations Commission had told the German government that the final bill it would have to pay for the war came to 132 billion gold marks. This sum was deemed payable by Germany and, should it refuse, the French would occupy the industrial Ruhr region to extract coal and other resources.[21] Outraged at these terms, Chancellor Constantin Fehrenbach and his cabinet resigned.

A new government was quickly assembled under the former teacher Joseph Wirth, like his predecessor from the Catholic Centre Party. He believed only a 'policy of fulfilment' would create enough Allied goodwill over time to lighten the burden of reparations and eventually dismantle the Treaty of Versailles. His minority government held only 206 out of 459 seats in the Reichstag but managed to convince a majority – 221 to 175 – to vote to accept the terms since there was no other choice.[22]

The first payment of 1 billion gold marks was made on 30 May. But there was an even higher economic price to pay. National debt had already exceeded the state's annual income in 1918. The high social welfare costs and loss of revenue through the lost territories added to the mounting costs, causing the government to borrow and print more paper money, causing a massive devaluation of the currency. By October 1921, the mark was only worth a hundredth of what it had been against the US dollar in 1914.[23] Everything was in scant supply and therefore expensive. Butter had cost 1.30 marks per pound before the war. At the end of the war this had gone up to 5 marks and by mid-1921 Germans paid 26 marks for the same amount.[24]

In her letter to Edvard Munch, Elisabeth worried about how

'everything seems to become different and worse'. She told her friend that 'Weimar has changed a lot since you were here . . . Weimar used to be a pretty, clean little residential town with nice, ordered conditions, but now Social Democracy reigns here, and that lends Weimar a rather different look.'[25] For now, the strong support from her Nietzsche-admiring friends held out. Thiel sent enough parcels and money from Stockholm to continue serving coffee, tea and chocolate at the archive.

Politicians like August Baudert had a thankless task, dealing with 'strike unrests, bloody clashes on the borders of Thuringia, rising unemployment in the state'[26] and the stalemate between hostile political parties. How could they even begin to build back when there was no consensus? At the end of July, the Thuringian government resigned and dissolved parliament, hitting Baudert's plans 'like a bomb', as he put it. 'A state that stands on firmly built foundations can withstand such a shock a little more easily than one that is just being built up. Poor Thuringia!'[27] It wouldn't be the last time either. Only one of the Thuringian state parliaments during the Weimar Republic lasted a full term.[28]

Baudert's SPD won the next election in September, but it only got thirteen seats, just three more than the arch-conservative Thuringian Agricultural League and four more than the far-left USPD and the conservative – liberal German People's Party respectively. Over two thirds of the seats in the Thuringian parliament went to parties that didn't accept the political system they were supposed to build up.

Faced with an impossible job, Baudert and others were exposed to constant criticism. One article accused his government of astonishing 'carefreeness and inaction'.[29] Another time, he received an anonymous letter asking how much longer this 'ignorant, lame government will be taken for fools by criminals and scoundrels'.[30] One far-left paper hoped that the strict security measures around the state parliament wouldn't stop people from 'administering deserved and undeserved slaps to the faces of ministers'.[31] Baudert soon found out that these were no idle threats. One day, during a demonstration of unemployed workers, one man who 'sharply smelled of alcohol' and called the government a bunch of 'scumbags and people's traitors' walked straight into Baudert's office and hit him in the face. Baudert wryly noted: 'That punch didn't take away my belief in the victorious powers of socialism, but it did put me off my usual enthusiasm, love and flair.'[32]

Seemingly unaffected by the chaos and hardship around her, Marlene Dietrich continued to enjoy all the distractions Weimar had in store for a young single woman of the upper middle classes. She moved out of the strict boarding school and into her own rented room, one that couldn't have been more evocative for a Goethe devotee. The house in which she now lived had once been the home of the poet's friend Charlotte von Stein. Best of all, it granted her an independence she'd never had before. 'I was freer, and could divide my time as I saw fit,' Marlene reminisced later.[33] Soon, interesting neighbours moved in.

Bauhaus founder Walter Gropius had called the artist Lothar Schreyer to Weimar to run his school's stagecraft workshop. Schreyer was eccentric and experimented with new theatrical methods. From 17 September, he was Marlene's neighbour, renting rooms under the eaves of the house with his family. Residents often met at the communal dining room and Schreyer remembered later that 'at the end of the table sat a lovely, quiet, young girl whom we all liked, Marlene'.[34] She loved playing with the artist's young son, but was painfully shy with his parents. One day in October, she overheard them talking about a visit from Gropius's ex-wife, the famous Alma Mahler. 'Modestly, she said across the table to my wife,' Lothar Schreyer remembered, ' "Oh, I have such a strong wish: would you maybe introduce me to Frau Mahler?" ' The older woman suggested that Marlene might think of a way to draw attention to herself during the visit. The teenager nodded eagerly and hatched a plan.

Marlene's appearance that day was memorable, perhaps the first hint that her real talent lay in acting, not music. As Alma Mahler made her way down the stairs from the Schreyers' rooms, she was stopped in her tracks by a scene that could have come from a theatrical performance. It was dark outside and the lights in the hall had come on. In their spotlight stood a blonde girl in a simple but artfully cut dress. She was leaning against the white banister with a practised air of nonchalance, holding a violin in her left hand. The girl bent her knees into a deep curtsy, a gesture that seemed to Schreyer to belong to a time when Kaiser Franz Joseph still sat on the Austrian throne. Transfixed, Alma stood like a duchess receiving one of her ladies in waiting. She lifted her right hand for the blushing girl to kiss. Staring at Marlene's face, she said: 'What eyes this child has! What eyes!'[35]

Marlene Dietrich's eyes impressed many others in Weimar in the autumn of 1921 as the young woman began to refine her natural charisma. Before the theatre season commenced in October, she passed the time playing golf, sunbathing in the Ilm Park and making new friends at the 5 o'clock tea concerts at the Golden Eagle. There, she met people her own age like the baker Willy Michel or Johannes Michael Freiherr von Loën, a twenty-year-old aristocrat whom she called 'Hansi' and 'who dances rather well', she told a friend.[36] Marlene, whose bisexuality was later regarded as an open secret, also took her friend Marga to the Eagle, where the two girls danced together, 'which caused people to indulge in all sorts of talk', as she confided in a letter.[37]

Marlene seems to have been conscious of the fact that her behaviour typified the 'New Woman' all the magazines were writing about: confident and liberated from the conservatism of previous generations. But she didn't have much more opportunity to explore this before it was time to return to Berlin. 'Out of the blue my mother showed up in Weimar,' Marlene remembered.[38] When Marlene 'visited Goethe's Garden House for the last time' she was no longer the shy, homesick girl. She had discovered that her true talent was her charisma. 'I hear she has gone to the movies,' a Weimar actress wrote about Marlene in her diary on 28 May 1922.[39] It was true.

Following a tendon inflammation that stopped her from playing music, she resolved to become an actress. 'After my separation from Weimar came all the sadness of having to leave the violin,' Marlene noted in her diary, 'and then the other vocation.'[40]

Carl Weirich found new happiness at the end of 1921. Business picked up in the shop and there was the prospect of reuniting with his first love Marie Müller. The pair had exchanged letters for most of 1921 and Carl couldn't wait to see her again in Nuremberg in January. The year of 1922, he hoped, would be one of 'happy togetherness'.[41]

1922

Marie Müller wasn't entirely sure whether her future lay in Weimar with her teenage sweetheart Carl Weirich. Carl's frequent letters the previous year had made it clear that was his wish. After the tragic deaths of his first wife and their only child, he sought another chance to have a family of his own, 'to become happy again', as he put it. He thought that's what his late wife Friedel would have wanted too. After all, it was she who had told him to 'Live, love, laugh'.[1]

Marie felt she had only one chance to get this right for herself. She was thirty-five now, unmarried and childless. If she were to have a family of her own it would have to be soon. But was Carl the right choice? He visited her at her home in Nuremberg on 20 January and reiterated his proposal in person. Marie found that she still liked Carl. Of course, he wasn't the carefree seventeen-year-old boy she had fallen in love with so many years ago. But all the cycling and walking had kept him in good shape.

And yet, she had reservations and shared them frankly with Carl. Having lived with her mother her whole life, she was worried about moving to Weimar. Didn't Carl live in a completely different world? Also, while his shop seemed to be running well, he had no financial security. There were no guarantees that he could feed a family. Carl told her gently that Marie's mother would always be welcome in Weimar. As far as living in a different world went, Carl was very happy to be more flexible with Marie than he had been with Friedel. And money? 'Love and coin are two different things for me and I have managed to get by on just the former once before,' Carl told the woman he wanted to marry.[2] Marie kissed him and took him by the hand.

The next few months seemed to crawl by as Marie and Carl

eagerly awaited their church wedding in Nuremberg on 17 June. It had all seemed easy when they stood hand in hand in front of Marie's mother to ask for her blessing. Even Marie's little niece Getraude was so excited when she heard the news that she ran to fetch her musical box to play a love song for her aunt and future uncle. But Carl had to return to Weimar to tend to his shop. He passed the time by redecorating the rooms above that would be Marie's new home. Evenings spent at the National Theatre helped keep his longing at bay as he watched renditions of Shakespeare's *Hamlet* and Beethoven's *Fidelio*. He attended his neighbour Otto Krumbholz's wedding but found that 'such occasions awoke longing for my own bride'.[3]

Carl's pining found some relief when Marie came to visit him in Weimar to see if she might like the famous town. Carl showed her around and took her to Eisenach by train to meet his mother, who immediately took a shine to her son's Bavarian fiancée. Carl's nephew Willy accompanied the couple back to Weimar, where he was finishing his apprenticeship as a bookbinder. When the train stopped at Erfurt, the young man changed to a different compartment, leaving the two lovers alone in theirs.

Jutta Hecker's thoughts were far from love in the spring of 1922. She was now seventeen years old and attended a rigorous selective secondary school, the Wilhelm-Ernst-Gymnasium. Such schools had only been open to girls since 1920.[4]

The teenager continued to idolize her father Max and wanted to follow in his footsteps by receiving the best education possible. He still worked at the Goethe and Schiller Archive but had received almost no pay since 1920. With the financial support of the Grand Duke and Duchess gone, nobody felt responsible for the upkeep of the archive or the wages of its staff. The Goethe Society stepped in and paid Max Hecker some money but he struggled to feed his family. Nonetheless, his youngest daughter Jutta adored her father and wanted to spend her life with her nose in old German books, just like he did. For that she needed to read German Language and Literature at university. Her school work had to be excellent, empty stomach or not. Despite all the interruptions at the Sophienstift school for girls, she graduated in Easter 1921 with excellent grades and was deemed suitable to be one of the first girls to attend the selective former boys' school.[5]

Baldur von Schirach, the son of former theatre director Carl von Schirach, was two and a half years younger than Jutta and came from a much wealthier background but both Weimar teenagers would graduate from the Wilhelm-Ernst-Gymnasium. Carl was president of the Goethe Society that paid Jutta's father a pittance of a salary. But the Schirachs still felt some grievance about their social fall. Once the war was lost, Carl's military pension of 1,300 marks a year was scrapped and he relied on his monthly allowance of 695 marks alone.[6] And while the Heckers may have been poorer, they were a complete family. Baldur, on the other hand, had lost his older brother Karl, who had fallen into deep despair when his hopes of becoming an army officer were crushed as Germany lost the war and had to demilitarize. Just nineteen years old when this blow hit him in October 1919, the teenager took his own life. Baldur hardened his heart against the grief of this loss.

Carl and Emma von Schirach often visited the theatre with their son and moved in the town's elite conservative circles. Baldur received private tuition from Adolf Bartels, a well-known writer whose book *A History of German Literature* had become a classic. Like all his writing, it was steeped in antisemitism. His declared aim was to promote Germans' awareness of their ethnic or *völkisch* heritage. Even by the standards of a time rife with residual anti-semitism, Bartels was extreme, priding himself in being the 'best hated' literary figure of his day.[7] Yet he'd established a support base in Weimar from where he disseminated his writings and teachings to a dedicated following. Carl von Schirach moved in those circles and sent his son Baldur to Bartels to be educated in literary history. The antisemite became a mentor to the teenager.

Carl Weirich got married on 17 June 1922. In Nuremberg 'at 11.30 in the morning, my little bride stood in front of me all done up and festive', Carl wrote.[8] A lavishly decorated horse-drawn carriage took the couple to a medieval church. During the celebrations that followed, his new brother-in-law Gottlob compared life to a walk at high altitude. It could be exhilarating, demanding and dangerous all at once. And sometimes you may find a little luck. His wife Lydia had found a four-leaf clover just the other day. It had to be a good omen for Carl and Marie.

When the newlyweds arrived at Geleitstraße 10 in Weimar, Carl led his bride up to the flat above the shop, excited to see how she would react. She wasn't disappointed. The newly decorated place looked splendid. Friends and family had generously gifted all manner of items for their home. Frau Straubel, friends, customers and acquaintances in Weimar had helped or sent flowers, cards and gifts. The flat 'was like a rose garden', Carl wrote, 'and we wandered through the newly decorated rooms 4 or 5 times, delighted to call all this beauty our own. We lived joyously day by day and were perfectly happy and contented in our shared bliss!'[9]

The Weirichs knew they were very fortunate to have a decent place to live. Weimar was fighting a never-ending battle to provide enough housing not only for its existing population but also for the many bureaucrats and politicians who were moving to the town now that it had become the capital of Thuringia. August Baudert described the challenge of having to find places for civil servants to live and work as a 'particular bugbear for the Weimar government'. He'd tried to open the old palaces and manor houses of the aristocracy to make room available for flats but received complaints that this would leave too little room for office spaces. 'Whatever you do, it's wrong!' he fumed.[10]

Germany was a million houses short. Walter Gropius and his Bauhaus school saw this as an opportunity to try out some of their ideas of modern and affordable living. A lot of furniture and housing was still built in traditional ways, by hand and individually, one piece at a time. This was not only expensive but also impractical. People's lives had changed. Nearly half of women now worked in some capacity, while they were still expected to run the household and look after their children. So wouldn't it make sense to arrange kitchens in a way that saved time by putting everything within reach? Why not design new houses and everything in them in a purely practical style? If chairs and tables were stackable, small rooms could be adapted as needed. Utilizing new methods of mass production, everyone would be able to enjoy better living standards, the Bauhaus pioneers thought.

Bruno Adler, who taught Art History in Weimar and later emigrated to England, where he worked for the BBC during the Second World War, recalled that it seemed obvious that if 'modern technology had replaced craftsmanship, closing the gap to industry became more important'.[11] This didn't mean that the Bauhaus school taught that craftsmanship was obsolete. On the contrary, in their workshops, young men and women learned practical skills like weaving, woodcraft and pottery. But the designs they created aimed to be beautiful, practical, adaptable and mass-producible. Their 'form follows function' ideal became one of the most influential ideas of the twentieth century. It continues to inspire the way we live today, from IKEA flat-packs to typography, prefabricated housing and the cantilever chair.

Weimar's conservative elites sensed the explosive potential of Bauhaus ideas. They staunchly opposed its radical and somewhat arrogant assumption that it was time for the old to go, wholesale. This battle of ideas also played out when it came to building new homes. Gropius argued that the solution was 'the industrial production of housing in large numbers and for stockpiling, which won't be made at the construction site any more but in purpose-built factories where individual parts are produced that can be assembled . . . [and] put together to create different types of houses'.[12] They would have to show Weimar and the world that this could work.

The Bauhaus teacher Fred Forbát, who worked closely with Gropius, came up with the idea of having one large, square living room in the middle, which was surrounded by smaller, functional spaces such as bedrooms on three sides. This could then be extended by further rooms as needed – like a large model kit. They planned to build an estate of such houses in Weimar, where the Bauhaus community would live and breathe the concept while refining it further and designing furniture for it. When they presented their plans to the Weimar authorities, they hit a wall of outrage. In 1920, they had already mooted the idea of putting up temporary dwellings on the Hornberg, a hill on the eastern outskirts of Weimar, and had secured a lease for the land they wanted to build on, but vehement objections from nearby residents had scuppered their plans.

Political and financial concerns conspired against the Bauhaus from the beginning. Rampant inflation continued to devalue the movement's funds, control over which lay with a Thuringian parliament that was not only highly volatile but also full of political parties that viewed Bauhaus radicalism and the many foreigners associated with it with suspicion. With economic pressures bearing down on all its projects, Thuringia only paid the Bauhaus an absolute minimum, meaning staff and students relied on other forms of income. The students were supposed to sell the products and ideas they created but this didn't always turn out to be viable since Germans were so short of disposable income that new furniture, toys or dinner plates weren't high on their shopping list. The permanent shortage of coal and wood made it difficult to run even the workshops. In December 1921, Bauhaus master Gerhard Marcks, who was in charge of pottery, which he taught in Dornburg, outside of Weimar, came down with kidney inflammation because his workshop had frozen over.[13]

Political headwinds came from people like Emil Herfurth, a German, Latin and Greek teacher at Jutta Hecker's school. He was also a member of the Thuringian parliament, where he sat for the ultra-conservative DNVP, as well as a member of the board of the Goethe Society and the Society of Friends of the Nietzsche Archive. He became one of Gropius's many adversaries in Weimar. Opponents despised not only the art and architecture the Bauhaus school promoted but also the lifestyle of students and staff. Many wore eccentric clothing. In the summers, there was skinny-dipping in the Ilm, which appalled conservative sensibilities. Lydia Driesch-Foucar, who lived and worked in Marcks's pottery workshop in Dornburg, described what happened on hot summer days: 'after work it was down to the [River] Saale for communal swimming . . . Apart from Marcks and his family and the apprentices, guests from Weimar sometimes joined us. As if in paradise, the beautiful, strong men and women frolicked in the water, the sun and nature: truly Dionysian scenes and images.'[14]

No matter how much Weimar needed housing, it would not be built by Bauhaus students – for now. But there was a silver lining. The communists and socialists in the Thuringian parliament were sympathetic to Gropius's vision and pushed through a sizable public loan in June under one condition: the Bauhaus needed to prove that it was worth keeping and funding. Gropius agreed. His school would hold an exhibition the following year, complete with a concept house built to full scale as an example of the ideas that could be the solution to Germany's housing crisis. This *Musterwohnhaus* (model house) would be completely furnished and exemplify many other Bauhaus items and how they could be used in daily life. The town of Weimar refused to fund the project, but Gropius managed to convince the Jewish architect and investor Adolf Sommerfeld to support it. The Haus am Horn would be built whether Weimar liked it or not.

Among modernists, the Bauhaus movement was beginning to build such a strong reputation as the potential cradle of a new German culture that Gropius was able to draw famous and well-regarded artists to provincial Weimar. In June, the Russian painter Wassily Kandinsky, a pioneer of abstract art, had followed his call to teach at the Bauhaus. Other high-profile appointments included the German-American painter Lyonel Feininger, who was the master in charge of the printmaking workshop and a leading expressionist. The Swiss-born artist Paul Klee joined in January 1921 and ran two studios as master of bookbinding, stained glass and mural painting. The Dutch artist Theo van Doesburg also spent time in Weimar, teaching courses at the Bauhaus in 1921 and 1922 to promote his movement De

Stijl, which favoured abstract forms with essential lines and primary colours as well as black and white.

The calibre of creative thinking Gropius had brought to Weimar stoked a productive atmosphere of artistic competition. While the Bauhaus movement focused on the practical applicability of its work and the physical craft of its students, it also still contained many spiritual and Romantic elements. Early members had a tendency to glorify pre-industrial production methods. They lived and worked together in creative communes, much to the chagrin of conservative Weimarers. The Swiss expressionist painter Johannes Itten, who had been Gropius's first appointment as teacher at his new Bauhaus school in 1919, represented this strand of the movement's philosophy. Itten in turn invited Gertrud Grunow to Weimar to become the school's first female teacher. She ran a course on the 'theory of harmonization', which involved psychological and mental training to achieve a trance state. Grunow, Itten and Lothar Schreyer, Marlene Dietrich's former neighbour, were all part of an esoteric contingent within the Bauhaus movement.

Gropius had a hard time holding his Bauhaus together as his staff threatened to pull the movement in different directions. Newer recruits like Doesburg pushed for art to walk in lockstep with technology. The Dutchman gave projector presentations in Weimar, hoping to convince Bauhaus students and other interested parties that the future lay in well-designed mass production. Machines would make things in the future, not hands, and if art wanted a say in this, it needed to keep up. He saw no conflict between this conviction and being the main proponent of Dadaism in the Netherlands, a movement that rejected the cold logic of reason and capitalism that in its adherents' eyes had led to the war.

Werner Graeff, a twenty-one-year-old student, was fascinated with Doesburg, but he could also see why Gropius kept him at arm's length, not offering a permanent teaching position to this 'sensitive and overly aggressive man'.[15] In order to bring the conflict to a head, Doesburg convened a congress of Dadaist and constructivists in Weimar for 25 and 26 September 1922. It would be a small gathering, but explosive, a poke in the hornet's nest of modern art.

Aiming for maximum provocation, Doesburg invited the avant-garde Romanian poet Tristan Tzara to deliver a talk with the title 'Gegen Goethes Gebeine . . .' or 'Against Goethe's Bones . . .'.[16] But he was keen to keep politics out of it, arguing that prominent constructivists like the Hungarian painter László Moholy-Nagy were all about 'subjugating art to communism' while he wanted to establish an 'Internationale of Creativity' as an art community without politics.[17] Moholy-Nagy in turn saw Doesburg's Dadaism as 'a destructive and obsolete movement'.[18]

Against the odds, constructivist and Dadaist delegates got through a full programme together. They enjoyed a Dada soirée at the Hotel Russischer Hof for which Doesburg had designed the tickets. They listened to 'Wedding March for a Crocodile' by the young Italian composer Vittorio Rieti and to the recital of a poem by the influential German artist Kurt Schwitters about the letter W, 'a symphony of sounds, which took our breath away', one of the attendees remembered.[19] Tensions between Dadaists and constructivists remained palpable. Some events were interrupted by booing and hissing. In the end, constructivism carried the day. Gropius called Moholy-Nagy to teach at the Bauhaus from April 1923, swaying the movement away from its early Romantic tendencies and towards the idea that art and technology should work in unison. At the end of 1922, Doesburg concluded that Weimar provided 'fertile soil for a new productivity in Germany'.[20]

Rosa and Arthur Schmidt also felt productive in the autumn of 1922. It hadn't been easy, but their new business at Brennerstraße 42 by the station was up and running. The Hotel Hohenzollern remained open against the odds of rampant inflation and political uncertainty. Filling a hotel with over twenty rooms, a beer garden, a veranda, a large festive hall and a traditional barroom wasn't easy.[21] The pair needed to build up a base of regular customers. Weimar was a conference town, so that provided one stream of income. But local clubs and associations also needed somewhere to meet and this could become a solid backbone to their business. On Saturday 14 October 1922, they hosted a meeting of the East Thuringian branch of the Middle German Ball Games Association.[22] From 7.30 p.m. referees, organizers and linesmen discussed disputed and cancelled matches. As the men debated, Rosa and Arthur served them drinks and food. Their guests clearly enjoyed the service and returned to the Hotel Hohenzollern regularly for their future meetings. Keeping the place running was hard work. Now in their early forties, not only had Rosa and Arthur found a way back into the work they both loved, but they also had a fourth child, a baby boy named Horst. No matter how hard things got around them, the Schmidts had a future to build for themselves and their children.

1923

In the spring of 1923, Carl Weirich purchased a used bicycle for 2 million marks.[1] Had he waited until September, the same amount would have bought him a loaf of bread or an egg.[2] It was utterly pointless to save money and so Carl decided to spend it while he could. He was determined not to allow the desperate economic situation to crush his new happiness with Marie. Free Sundays, when his shop was closed, were for them. Hiking and cycling had kept him sane through so much grief before. So he had bought the 'precious bicycle' for his wife, even though she had never learned how to ride. Now nearly thirty-seven years old, Marie decided that it was not too late. She practised until she was ready to undertake long bike tours through the Thuringian mountains with her husband.

The Weirichs were fighting an exhausting and seemingly never-ending battle to keep the shop afloat amid rampant inflation. Marie would often travel to nearby Erfurt to get new stock directly from suppliers so that deals could be struck and middlemen cut out. Carl then offered his customers typewriters for '250,000,000 marks, pay cash and take home today'. Carl would later wonder how they even reported the 'shockingly long figures' to the tax authorities. All they could do is hold out and distract themselves from the prospect of economic ruin as best they could. So they cycled, read books or went to the cinema, where they watched some of the educational films that were popular at the time, such as the 1922 documentary 'The Fundamentals of the Einsteinian Relativity Theory'.[3]

In January, the Allies had met in Paris to discuss Germany's defaults on the agreed reparations payments. The outstanding amount may not have been huge – Germany had sent 11.7 million tons of coal in 1922 instead of 13.8 million.[4] But the French threatened to invade if the full amount wasn't forthcoming and they meant it. On 11 January, over 70,000 French and Belgian troops invaded Germany and occupied the industrial Ruhr region. While there was much international condemnation of this act from Britain, the US, the Soviet Union and even Poland and Czechoslovakia – both allies of France – the occupation went ahead and destroyed what little economic capability post-war Germany still had.

The Reichstag responded two days later with a rare display of unity. With 283 votes to 12, it decided to implement a policy of passive resistance.[5] The country wouldn't fight back – demilitarized such as it was, it couldn't – but it would boycott France's attempt to take coal by force. In order for German workers to stay at home and industry bosses to agree to this, the government had to step in to pay wages and compensation. And for this it needed to print more money. This was enthusiastically greeted by the population but it also proved to be the spark to the tinderbox of German economic trouble. The value of the mark was spiralling down at eye-watering speed. By June, a single dollar was worth 120,000 marks. By December, it would be 4.2 trillion marks.[6] Unable to buy what they needed any more, Carl and Marie used their bikes to go on 'hamster raids' into the countryside once again, gathering windfalls and other things one could get for free rather than in exchange for a wheelbarrow of banknotes.[7]

On Thursday 17 May, Rosa Schmidt was surrounded by complete chaos. The Hotel Hohenzollern brimmed with noise. Its hall and terrace were full of malnourished, disoriented children. As a trained childminder, Rosa was perhaps better placed to cope with this than some of the other adult volunteers who tried to help that night, but the situation was overwhelming nonetheless. A 'Kindertransport' of 1,000 children, aged between four and ten, had arrived at the train station outside her hotel. The authorities had decided that the situation in the occupied Ruhr had become so desperate that it was best to get at least the children out.

The French made it clear that they would not allow the adult population to go. After all, they needed people to mine the coal and as hostages to force Germany to pay up. The supply situation was already desperate at the beginning of 1923, exacerbated by a bad harvest the previous year. The German Health Ministry had warned in February that there wasn't adequate clothing for children. Every second child was malnourished.[8] In Weimar, Jutta Hecker's whole family was starving while she was trying to study.[9] As an industrial area, dominated by working-class communities, the Ruhr struggled even more with an estimated two thirds of schoolchildren not receiving adequate nutrition and the mortality rate of unweaned babies rising by somewhere between 15 and 33 per cent. One official warned that if nothing happened, a large number of the 6,000 children in his district just south of Dortmund might die.[10]

Around half a million families from all over unoccupied Germany volunteered to host the 'Ruhr children'.[11] A central agency in Berlin helped coordinate the efforts, and most of the evacuees were to go to rural areas where the food situation wasn't quite as desperate as in the cities. The Thuringian Farmers' League in Weimar agreed to take a few thousand children and to help find host families for them. Suspecting foul play, the French occupiers controlled the post and rail system, hardly letting any adults out of their occupation zone. This meant train schedules and communication between the Ruhr and the rest of Germany became irregular. The 1,000 children who arrived in Weimar were almost unaccompanied and they had not received the food and drink rations the Red Cross had intended to distribute. Only a minority had the identity cards pinned on them on which their home address, the station to which they were to be transported, and the name and address of their final destination were supposed to be written. Within a few hours, the authorities in Weimar had to reallocate 1,000 children to onward trains and host families. They did their level best to accommodate their 'little guests', as one local paper described.[12]

Weimar volunteers had decorated the waiting rooms at the station where some of the children were held until they could travel on. Members of the German Protestant Women's League tried to comfort them. But even simple logistical things that worked during the war were now a problem. Between 1914 and 1918, volunteer organizations and state-run institutions had run plenty of soup kitchens and other charitable organizations all over Germany for returning soldiers and people on the home front who had fallen into destitution. But the economic situation in the post-war years, particularly the rampant inflation, had caused many of them to sell up or trade their equipment. When 800 Ruhr children had arrived at Erfurt station a few days earlier, there were no cups to give them drinks in. In the end, the famous department store Römischer Kaiser (Roman Emperor) lent the volunteers around 300 clay mugs.[13]

Weimar didn't have big businesses that could help, but many smaller shops and organizations stepped in. Arno Schmidt, who had been the Grand Duke's official court baker and still carried this title with considerable pride, provided food while the authorities worked feverishly to sort the children into groups to travel on to thirty other stations where they would be picked up by the Farmers' League or directly by their host families. This wasn't always easy or orderly but 'the train administration were greatly accommodating in all aspects', as the local press reported.[14]

With the Hotel Hohenzollern directly adjacent to the station, Rosa Schmidt offered to accommodate the 'Green' group – children designated for train lines north out of Weimar. Whether they would get there as planned was anyone's guess. With few adults accompanying the children from Essen, they now relied entirely on the trains running as they should and on adults picking them up. In rural areas, host families often had to travel miles themselves to get to the nearest station only to find that the train would arrive a day later or their foster child had already been stranded there for hours. The Ruhr occupation was very nearly the straw that broke the young republic.

In the midst of all the chaos of 1923, the Bauhaus school presented itself to the public. From 15 August to 30 September, its first exhibition took place in Weimar and Walter Gropius had to make it a success to secure vital funding and recognition. His caution to stay politically neutral took nothing away from his radical motto: Art and Technology – A New Unit.

Poster for the 1923 Bauhaus Exhibition in Weimar, designed by Joost Schmidt.

Once again, Weimar was transformed with visitors from all over the world. This included the American architect Frank Lloyd Wright, the Russian composer Igor Stravinsky, the controversial Swiss-French architect Le Corbusier and journalists from across Europe. In all, around 15,000 people saw the exhibition. Among them was Erich Lissner, a twenty-year-old student at the Art Academy in Dresden for whom even getting to Weimar was an adventure. When the exhibition started, a pound of butter had cost around 1 million marks.[15] By the time it ended six weeks later, it was around 60 million. The value of money 'literally changed by the hour', Erich remembered.[16] He was only able to travel because he had managed to get hold of foreign currency in the form of Swedish crowns, which he exchanged into 'astronomical amounts of paper marks' at the exact moment he needed to pay for his train tickets.

Erich was hugely impressed by Weimar, which in his eyes now 'wasn't Goethe – but Bauhaus. The travel destination of thousands.'[17] He was a stranger yet felt instantly at home, wearing the same garb as Bauhaus students and masters: sandals and long, loose shirts referred to as 'Russenkittel' (Russian smocks) that were donned 'in protest at middle-class convention'.[18] The young man walked through the exhibition at the Thuringian State Museum, visited workshops and art studios across the town centre and discussed with Bauhaus students what they had been taught by their masters and whether their products could really be mass-produced with industrial methods. Erich left with a head full of ideas, impressed with the 'clear, pure form applied to everyday items' like lights, plates, chairs and coffee tables.[19]

He also visited the Haus am Horn – the first-ever building constructed on Bauhaus principles. To him this was just one manifestation of the Bauhaus spirit, not worthy of particular mention among the many things he'd seen and admired. But other visitors found the modernity of the detached family home extremely objectionable. The design was very simple. From the outside, it was a white, cubic, single-storey house with a flat roof. On the inside it contained a central living area surrounded by four bedrooms, a kitchen, a dining room and a bathroom. All the items in it were designed and made by Bauhaus staff and students, from furniture and lights to the built-in kitchen cabinets and children's toys.

From today's point of view, there was nothing particularly controversial about the house. Much of its design, such as the continuous kitchen worktops, the insulated walls or the multi-functional cupboards, later came into such widespread use that they now appear completely normal. But the ultra-modernity of the house riled many at a time when the battle for the German post-war soul seemed at its peak.

Modernists like the architect Le Corbusier admired its bold design. The liberal newspaper *Jenaer Volksblatt* praised the Haus am Horn as 'equipped with all modern, hygienic and practical technical installations while at the same time being built with the greatest economy regarding materials'.[20] The art critic and avant-garde writer Adolf Behne thought that 'the Weimar Bauhaus, the very fact that it exists and works, defends Germany's artistic honour in these difficult but important times'.[21] Still, even he was critical of some of the compromises that were made in the hectic schedule to get the house finished in time for the exhibition. Writing on 20 September, while the exhibition was still on, he called the Haus am Horn 'half luxurious, half primitive, half idealistic demand, half hard work, half craft, half industry, half type, half ideal – but in no aspect pure and convincing'.[22]

Like most architectural experiments, the house quickly drew a lot of nicknames, including 'coffee grinder', 'chocolate box', 'white cube' and 'North Pole station'. The *Berliner Tageblatt* newspaper said that 'as a house, the Haus is completely flawed' and the local *Jena-ische Zeitung* declared that it resembled 'the kind of house gentlemen and ladies can enter on the public squares of big cities for a small fee. Imagine a whole settlement in this "style" of building. Guests turn away, shuddering.'[23]

Baldur von Schirach also visited the Haus am Horn that summer and remembered later that he immediately had practical reserva-tions. He doubted in particular whether the average family could really afford to build or rent a four-bedroom bungalow. 'It was one of those typical German things,' he scoffed in an interview, 'an ideal-istic construct that couldn't withstand reality.'[24] Sixteen years old, he had just begun to take piano lessons at the State Music School, run by Bruno Hinze-Reinhold, who greatly admired Franz Liszt and emphasized the famous composer's contribution to culture during his time in Weimar. Baldur was surrounded by such conserva-tives who intended to defend the town's reputation as the spiritual heart of traditional German and European culture. Gropius's arch-enemy Emil Herfurth also belonged to these circles. In a pamphlet entitled 'Weimar and the State Bauhaus', he called it 'insufferable' that Gropius and his students had introduced such modern art to Weimar, a town he regarded as 'German in the best sense'. Gropius shot back by accusing Herfurth of belonging to a small 'clique of well-established culture mummies'.[25]

In the long run, the Bauhaus exhibition was a success. It laid the foundations for an international art and architecture movement that would revolutionize the way we live by disseminating its ideas across the world. Yet, it generated just 4,500 gold marks (which were infla-tion resistant) from the sales of the goods that had been produced by students and masters.[26] But this in itself was an important lesson. The focus on practicability and mass production was the way forward, not esoteric Romanticism. In the future, the Bauhaus would focus on things that were both beautiful and practical. While this concept would prove to be enormously successful, Gropius had not won over his enemies in Weimar. For now, the Thuringian parliament continued to support him. But soon his critics would rear their heads again.

On 9 November, Carl Weirich was celebrating his thirty-eighth birthday. It was a small party since that day was 'a little bit tumultuous', as the shopkeeper noted with wry understatement.[27] The previous day Reichswehr military units had been sent by the federal government in Berlin to occupy Weimar because of 'communist activities', as Carl put it. The Communist International, a Moscow-sponsored organization founded in 1919 to promote world communism, decided that German workers should try to launch an October Revolution in 1923. The conditions seemed similar to those in Russia in 1917 with high inflation, the misery of a lost war and widespread poverty providing the ingredients to cook up a storm. This 'German October' would be launched by the entry of KPD politicians into the state governments of Thuringia and Saxony, where they had made large gains during the last elections. The communists were to use their influence at government level to arm workers and then launch unrest that would in turn trigger Europe-wide outbreaks of upheaval.

In Weimar workers of the wagon factory followed the directive and demanded to be allowed to form paramilitary units called Hundertschaften as well as to set up councils in their workplace that would enable them to exercise more control. This was seen as a pre-revolutionary step in communist thinking, but the SPD-run minority government didn't dare to ban such activity outright, for fear of sparking further escalation. Such demands were made all over Thuringia and often amplified by strikes and general unrest.

The SPD, which had won the last state election in September 1921, decided to grant ministerial offices to KPD members, thereby forming a far-left government on 16 October in an effort to appease the angry workers. But the KPD had in turn made it a precondition for its participation in the Thuringian cabinet that some of the workers' demands be met. In neighbouring Saxony, communists had also entered the government. The participation of elected communists in state governments wasn't illegal, but in the heated atmosphere of 1923, even the hint of revolutionary activity was a red rag to a federal regime acutely conscious of its own fragility. Berlin had seen enough. The Reichswehr marched into Weimar.

The local KPD chapter responded to the occupation of Weimar by calling on workers to engage in a general strike. The SPD told its (more numerous) supporters not to resist the army. Since things had escalated in Saxony a few days earlier and President Friedrich Ebert had used the emergency Article 48 of the constitution to remove the elected government of Saxony by presidential decree, the Thuringian cabinet knew it didn't stand a chance. So its SPD ministers distanced themselves from the revolutionary activities of their KPD colleagues. Thuringia's far-left coalition collapsed.[28] The Berlin government banned the KPD nationwide until March 1924.

While Carl Weirich was having his small birthday party on 9 November amid the chaos in the streets surrounding his shop, another attack on state authority was launched 400 kilometres to the south. In Munich, a far-right Austrian firebrand attempted his own revolution that day and failed. Spearheaded by the Führer of the National Socialist German Workers' Party and the former First World War military leader Erich Ludendorff, around 2,000 Nazis went on a march through the Bavarian capital until they were confronted by soldiers and police. In their exchange of fire sixteen Nazis, four police officers and one bystander were killed. Nazi leader Adolf Hitler was arrested two days later. His attempt to seize power had failed, for now.

PART II

Struggle

They call it the heart of Germany

1924

Elisabeth Förster-Nietzsche was devastated. All the careful work she had put into stabilizing the Nietzsche Archive's funding had been razed by hyperinflation. The government's economic reset with a new emergency currency in the autumn of 1923 under the new Chancellor Gustav Stresemann had stopped the fiscal free fall but not before many German businesses had hit rock bottom. Elisabeth's fund of 800,000 marks had been swept away as if it were nothing. Her most generous donor, Ernest Thiel, had also fallen on hard times. He would soon have to sell his extensive art collection to the Swedish state to get by. He had little left to give to Elisabeth.

In January 1924, Friedrich Nietzsche's sister looked back on the disastrous year of 1923 with a good deal of political resentment. 'Has it ever happened in world history,' she asked the philosopher Rudolf Eucken, 'that the best social class of a people, those who work with their minds and the educated middle classes, has been ruined by the state just like that?'[1] Hyperinflation had been a disaster for middle-class Germans like her, whose wealth and standing depended on savings rather than physical assets.

Elisabeth resolved to roll up her sleeves and rebuild the archive's financial foundation. She still had her brother's writings and he still had plenty of admirers. And after all, wasn't there something quite Nietzschean in the situation? Shouldn't she try to embrace this terrible thing that had happened to her? Thiel certainly thought so. In a letter, he consoled her, arguing that 'Everything may look bleak, but it should be seen as a reward when life places great difficulties in one's path that have to be overcome.'[2] Elisabeth began to restore her empire in Weimar. Impressed, her old friend Harry Graf Kessler noted in his diary later: 'Admirable, the determination and courage of this 80-year-old woman, how she spoke about the loss of the entire accumulated wealth of the Nietzsche Foundation.'[3]

Nietzschean outlook or not, many of Weimar's small businesses were ruined or close to it. Carl Weirich had lost all his savings and was forced to start rebuilding his shop's finances from scratch. Still, it could have been worse, he thought. He and his wife Marie 'breathed a sigh of relief' when the financial chaos of the previous year ended. They had each other, the shop and a roof over their heads. So Carl took courage from the New Year's service he had attended at church. The priest, who happened to be his namesake, Karl Weirich, had told the congregation that they'd need 'courage to face all storms, including those that may engulf us in 1924, but with God's help they will be overcome'.[4] In February, Carl and Marie began to sell typewriters again. This time for their 'normal price'.[5]

In politics, nothing was back to normal. The anger and despair that dominated the public mood could not just be reset with a new currency. The young Thuringian state needed a new parliament and elections were scheduled for 10 February 1924. Given the tumult of the previous year, the middle and upper classes were deeply frightened of a communist takeover of parliament. So they formed an unlikely coalition called the Thüringer Ordnungsbund (Thuringian Union for Order), which consisted of conservative parties like the Thüringer Landbund, the DVP and the DNVP as well as the Catholic Centre Party, the liberal DDP and smaller lobby groups like the Association of House Owners, which met regularly at the Hotel Hohenzollern.

What held this broad melange together was their determination to prevent another left-wing coalition of social democrats, socialists and communists from running Thuringia. They presented themselves as the logical choice for anyone who had wealth or status to lose, running under the slogan 'The whole country went to the dogs, only the Ordnungsbund can now save us'.

The strategy worked. With a staggering turnout of nearly 90 per cent, the Ordnungsbund got 48.02 per cent or thirty-five out of seventy-two seats, almost an outright majority. Almost. It was two seats short. Turning to the left for help was out of the question after an aggressive campaign that had likened the coalition of the SPD and KPD to a 'Tree of Sins' that had to be eradicated root and branch.[6] So the Ordnungsbund turned right, to the seven MPs of the Vereinigte Völkische Liste – the list of *völkisch* candidates. They were part of a movement that began in the nineteenth century and defined members of communities and nations by ethnicity rather than culture, language or political boundaries. They regarded Jews as a foreign race who could never become German by assimilation or conversion to Christianity. Adolf Hitler's National Socialist German Workers' Party or Nazi Party (NSDAP) was built on *völkisch* ideology, right down to adopting the symbol that had already been widely used in *völkisch*-nationalist circles: the swastika.

The NSDAP wasn't on the ballot paper on 10 February 1924. Hitler's trial for the Munich Putsch began just over two weeks later and his party was banned across Germany. But nobody could stop his followers from standing as independent candidates. In this way, seven *völkisch* men made it into the Thuringian parliament, three of them NSDAP members – a small number but they held all the cards.[7] Without their say-so, the Ordnungsbund would not be able to pass any laws. This band of antisemitic extremists was led by Artur Dinter, who knew exactly what he wanted in exchange for enabling the Ordnungsbund to run a functioning government.

Dinter was forty-three when he moved to Weimar in 1919 to work as a freelance writer. During the war, he had turned to the influential texts of the British-German writer Houston Stewart Chamberlain, whose rabid antisemitism and pseudo-scientific racism provided the inspiration for his own virulent tracts. Dinter's 1917 bestseller *The Sin against the Blood*, published before he settled in Weimar, had already made him notorious. Among other things, it purported that a single act of sexual intercourse between a non-Jewish woman and a Jewish man would damage the genetic material she would pass on to any future children. By 1934, the novel had sold over 260,000 copies.

In the Thuringian parliament, Dinter pinned the collaboration of his parliamentary group to the demand that the new government consist only of 'non-Marxist men of German blood'.[8] In other words, he wanted all Jews removed from parties and positions of power. Pressing for the dismissal of the Jewish head of the Thuringian State Bank, Walter Loeb, Dinter's *völkisch* faction declared openly in a parliamentary session: 'We don't tolerate any civil servants in government who are Jewish. If the government doesn't remove the Jew Loeb, we'll pass a motion of no-confidence. If we don't get a majority for that, the *völkisch* faction will deny their parliamentary cooperation.'[9]

There was significant public outrage and the case was discussed well beyond Thuringian borders. But few were as clear in their defence of Loeb as an SPD member of the opposition, who called out Dinter's seething antisemitism for what it was, old hatred in a new form: 'Because we're no longer in the Middle Ages and Jews can't be burned any more, one searches for a rope to hang them with.'[10] It was a cry in the wilderness. *Völkisch* and conservative publications everywhere ranted against German Jews, blaming them for defeat in the war, the revolution that followed and the economic and political crises since 1918.

Antisemitism had long become an acceptable outlook in conservative circles. This was especially true in Weimar even though the town only counted 100 Jews among its 35,000 inhabitants. Only twenty-five of them were active members of the religious community, among them Professor Julius Wahle, who had become the director of the Goethe and Schiller Archive in 1921, where he worked with Jutta Hecker's father Max on the Weimar Edition, a complete collection of Goethe's writing.

Many of the other Jewish Weimarers were well-respected business owners like Kurt Sachs, a decorated war veteran who ran a textile business in town.[11] Their prominent positions in public life made them vulnerable. Dinter's electoral list of *völkisch* candidates for the Thuringian parliament had received 9.3 per cent of the vote overall. In Weimar, where he was based and regularly gave public speeches, they gained twice as much.[12] Among elite conservative circles, antisemitism had become so normalized that Loeb was eventually forced to resign and few people with power or influence did anything about it.

Not everyone in the broad coalition of the Ordnungsbund thought that caving in to right-wing extremism was a legitimate price for staying in power. The Nazi MPs may not have campaigned under the banner of their party, but everyone knew how hostile they were to democracy and how they had tried to destroy it by violence in the Munich Putsch not four months earlier. While a formal coalition was not on the cards, many moderate politicians in the Ordnungsbund felt that any kind of agreement with Nazi representatives would lend Hitler's movement a dangerous amount of respectability. Besides, there were Jewish politicians in the Ordnungsbund, like Eduard Rosenthal, the top candidate of the liberal DDP. A professor of Law at the University of Jena, he had penned the Thuringian constitution. His status as a founding father of the modern Thuringian state didn't protect him. It was a sign of things to come that the *völkisch* faction was successful in lobbying for his resignation despite vocal opposition.

Internal discussions over the ethics of working with extremists notwithstanding, the Ordnungsbund was keen to avoid new elections. Soon, it would give in to more of Dinter's demands to stay in power. While the Nazi Party remained illegal in the rest of Germany until February 1925, Thuringia would lift the ban in March 1924, granting Hitler's party a political sanctuary from which to rebuild his movement. As an SPD politician put it, 'Thuringia has replaced Bavaria as marching territory for anti-republican and war-mongering organizations.'[13]

Jutta Hecker, now nineteen years old, was preparing to move to Munich, where her older brother Wolfgang, a professional soldier, had joined Hitler's putsch attempt in Munich the previous year. He praised the Führer's passion often and at length, recounting how he (Wolfgang) had shed many tears when the coup ended in defeat.

But Jutta wasn't going to Munich for politics. She graduated from the Wilhelm-Ernst-Gymnasium on 12 March 1924 with a diploma that attested her capability to 'leave this institution to read German Studies'.[14] She would enrol at Munich's Ludwig Maximilian University, which had admitted women since 1903. By now, almost a fifth of all students were female. Jutta went to fulfil her dream of stepping into her father's footsteps at the Goethe and Schiller Archive in Weimar one day. But she was to find that other ideas had begun to seep on to the campus. The majority of staff and students despised the republic and democracy. *Völkisch* groups clashed with communists and socialists. Jutta's copy of the lecture register contained adverts for books about race hygiene.[15]

On 20 April, a strange birthday party took place at Hotel Hohenzollern. The man who turned thirty-five that day hadn't been able to make it in person. Adolf Hitler was in jail in Landsberg, 60 kilometres west of Munich. He had been convicted of high treason less than three weeks earlier, sentenced to five years in prison and fined 200 gold marks. He would only serve 264 days of that sentence under rather comfortable conditions that allowed him to receive visitors, write his book *Mein Kampf* and change the strategy of his Nazi movement from violent revolution to strategic electioneering. For the time being, however, he was indisposed and his well-wishers met without him at the Schmidts' hotel in Weimar.

The most famous guest that day was Erich Ludendorff. Many Germans regarded him as a war hero for achieving early victories in the First World War. Ludendorff had been the lead policymaker in Paul von Hindenburg's military dictatorship that directed German politics and economics during the war. Despite having supported Hitler's putsch attempt in Munich, he had got off scot-free. His freedom allowed him to travel when Hitler couldn't, giving him a chance to galvanize the many *völkisch* and nationalist movements into one political force – maybe still under Hitler's spell, but ideally increasingly under Ludendorff's leadership. And where better to do this than in Weimar with its long tradition of German culture and its current political conditions that were far more sympathetic or at least tolerant towards far-right agitation than elsewhere in the country.

Other guests at the Hohenzollern had also taken part in Hitler's putsch. There was Alfred Rosenberg, who, according to his own recollections, had listened to Hitler for just fifteen minutes before he was convinced that this was the man to follow.[16] His antisemitism was obsessive. In the previous four years alone, he had published seven books and thirteen articles with titles such as 'The Traces of the Jews across the Changing Times'.[17]

A fellow traveller also staying at the Hohenzollern was Julius Streicher. The founder of the Nuremberg chapter of the Nazi Party was a vegetarian and a teetotaller like Hitler.[18] Like Rosenberg, he considered serving Nazism as 'the greatest summons of my life'.[19] He also helped spread the movement's virulent antisemitism through a magazine that he'd founded: *Der Stürmer* (*The Stormer*), which printed graphic, often sexually explicit propaganda against Jews.

Neither Rosenberg nor Streicher nor any of their numerous fellow Nazis assembled at the Hotel Hohenzollern that day had any idea that they drank, ate and slept in an establishment run by a Jewish woman and her husband. Rosa and Arthur led largely secular, 'explicitly German' lives, as their granddaughter later recalled.[20] Even if they had had reservations, the Schmidts simply couldn't afford to be picky about their guests. After a year of devastating hyperinflation, large gatherings were a blessing.

So Rosa and Arthur looked after their guests as they would with any other group. Rosa mostly worked in the kitchen.[21] Her husband with his experience as head waiter ensured the smooth running front of house. They prepared and served food and drinks while their raucous guests hammered out the ideological foundation for the reestablishment of the Nazi Party.

There were many differing opinions among the men but all agreed that whatever else their movement was, it would act 'against the current world and state order and for Adolf Hitler'. Alfred Rosenberg insisted that loyalty to the Führer was non-negotiable. So the gathering sent warm birthday greetings to their absent leader and resolved to 'fight for a new German state'. This fight would start in August in Weimar, at a large meeting of all *völkisch* and nationalist groups determined to bring about a 'national rebirth'.[22] The Schmidts would have a front-row seat.

'It's a crying shame that one has to fight again now instead of work,' architect Walter Gropius complained to his new wife Ise in the spring of 1924.[23] The pair had met the previous year during one of Gropius's lectures. Ise, in her mid-twenties and fourteen years his junior, fell head over heels for the charismatic Bauhaus director. She promptly left her fiancé, moved to Weimar and married him, throwing herself wholeheartedly into the Bauhaus movement as her husband's secretary, organizer and partner.

While Gropius's private life may have taken a turn for the better, his professional one had not. The change in the Thuringian government from left-wing to conservative with far-right support was a nightmare for his movement, which relied on state funding. Now, a government ruled Thuringia that was hostile to modernity, despised the alternative lifestyle that many Bauhaus staff and students embodied and viewed the widespread left-leaning sentiments within the movement with considerable suspicion. Gropius knew that the political winds had changed, and so did his enemies.

In late April, a fifty-page booklet entitled 'The State Bauhaus and its Director' was widely circulated. Many local politicians received a copy. Soon simply referred to as the 'yellow brochure', it spread its hateful diatribe well beyond Weimar. Officially, the Weimar craftsman Arno Müller masqueraded as the author, but in reality, it had been penned by Hans Beyer, who had once worked for the Bauhaus but had been sacked in 1922 for dilettantism and disloyalty.[24] Bitter and equipped with inside knowledge, he did his worst. His treatise insinuated that Gropius's school was infused with 'art communism' and that this was why it had enjoyed the support of the SPD and KPD as the 'favourite child of the socialist government'.[25] It claimed the whole institution was subversive and also chaotically run with accounting irregularities, corruption and nepotism baked into its very foundation. Beyer directly challenged the new Thuringian government with the accusation that the Bauhaus was bad for Weimar's reputation. 'It absolutely cannot be the responsibility of our impoverished state,' the yellow brochure posited, 'to maintain art schools with such inadequate organization on tax monies paid by a people fighting for its existence.'[26]

Gropius was furious, ranting that this 'filthy brochure'[27] was 'degrading' his great and ambitious Bauhaus school 'to a party-political punching bag'.[28] Once again the architect's fighting spirit kicked into gear. When he found out in the press that the government intended not to extend his contract as Bauhaus director, he told Ise that it was time 'to go on the offensive'.[29] He published his own brochure, justifying his institution's economic and artistic record. But an inquiry, initiated by the far-right faction in the Thuringian parliament, revealed that the school's finances were indeed in disarray, which provided plenty of political ammunition for Gropius's political enemies to argue for state funding cuts. The architect tried to raise private money to become independent of the political whims of the day. He tried to gather influential supporters. A 'Circle of Friends of the Bauhaus' was founded with prominent backers such as Albert Einstein.

Gropius soon found that the times had irrevocably changed. Fear of socialist subversion at the heart of the Bauhaus sat so deep that during Weimar's occupation by Reichswehr troops the previous autumn, soldiers had raided not only the school building but also Gropius's private flat, expecting to find incriminating material but finding none. With a right-wing government in place, all the school's enemies felt free to unleash their vitriol. Students of the traditionalist State School for Fine Arts, with which the Bauhaus shared its building, had begun to vandalize changes the Bauhaus students had made to the foyer and staircase for the 1923 exhibition. Eventually, the Thuringian Ministry of Education and Justice got involved and ordered Gropius to remove the artwork, light fittings and ornaments before restoring the original wall plaster and glass panes.[30]

Soon, the government halved the annual budget of the Bauhaus from 100,000 to 50,000 marks, knowing full well that this wouldn't be enough to run the institution. As the downward spiral continued, potential private investors were put off by the political uncertainty. Finally, the government told all staff that their contracts would run out on 1 April 1925. Six days after Erich Ludendorff and Hitler's inner circle had met at the Hotel Hohenzollern, a Bauhaus official complained bitterly about Weimar's 'helplessly encrusted Babbittry' that allowed 'a plebeian, *völkisch* circus to poison the atmosphere'.[31] It was time for Gropius to cut his losses: the Bauhaus had no future in Weimar.

On 20 July, *völkisch* representatives met again at the Hotel Hohenzollern to make last-minute preparations for their impending national gathering in Weimar.[32] Rosa and Arthur Schmidt were catering to a full house, and Erich Ludendorff paid a flying visit. In Hitler's absence, Ludendorff spearheaded the National Socialist Freedom Movement (NSFB), a loose alliance that served as a placeholder for the banned Nazi Party in the federal elections in May 1924, in which it had won 6.5 per cent of the vote or thirty-two seats in the Reichstag, including one for Ludendorff himself.

The antisemitic DNVP gained nearly a fifth of the vote, coming in second, just one percentage point behind President Ebert's SPD. The communists gained 13 per cent – about the same as the Catholic Centre Party. The rest of the vote spread across splinter parties. It was a damning indictment of the state of mainstream politics, and Ludendorff was delighted: 'I felt how what had happened on 9 November had stirred feelings everywhere,' he recorded in his memoirs. 'I was happy to see the warm jubilation with which the *völkisch* movement was met.'[33]

As much as discontent had created political headroom for far-right sentiment, far-right groups were deeply divided. New organizations appeared everywhere, only loosely connected by their shared sense of disillusionment, ethnic concept of Germanness and visceral antisemitism. Some of their leaders were deeply cynical about the Churches, like Ludendorff, who had adopted a form of esoteric neo-paganism. Others were more tactical, like Hitler himself, who believed Christianity still had a role to play.

Such differences were reflected in the confusing array of newly founded groups that often disappeared as quickly as they arose. There were political parties like Ludendorff's as well as veterans' groups like the League of German Officers, or Stahlhelm (League of Front-Line Soldiers). There were plenty of youth organizations too. Baldur von Schirach, who was now seventeen and thoroughly under the spell of his antisemitic tutors, had joined the Prussian League, which pressed for the restoration of the monarchy. Since this was an openly anti-constitutional aim, the youth wing had been banned in 1922 by the Ministry of the Interior, but it continued to exist in Thuringia as a subsidiary of the Young German Order, another anti-semitic organization, whose aim was to unify young Germans in the spirit of front-line camaraderie.

In Hitler's absence, Ludendorff attempted to unite these groups, but the four hours he spent in Weimar in the afternoon of 20 July suggested that he didn't have the magnetic appeal of his imprisoned rival. His flying visit to the Hotel Hohenzollern did nothing to recon-cile Hitler's Nazis with the *völkisch* delegates of the gathering. When he left, the arguments over the direction and leadership continued to be as raucous as when he arrived. The once-imposing general didn't even have the power to impress those who craved to be impressed. When Baldur von Schirach and his comrades in the Knappschaft, the youth wing of the Prussian League, lined up on Weimar's airfield to be inspected by their idol, they tried their best to look smart in their makeshift uniforms, which Baldur recalled as consisting of 'grey wind jackets and breeches, ski caps made from grey canvas, which were called "Hitler caps" '.[34] Ludendorff radiated indifference, even disdain, regarding the formation coldly. He walked up and down, his 'enormous, square double chin grim, rigid, austere, the corners of his mouth drooping', Baldur observed.[35] Feeling that their military discipline was substandard, Ludendorff didn't address the boys. The great general had nothing to say to the armies of young men in search of a leader.

Kurt Nehrling found it difficult to sit still as his fatherland sunk into chaos and thuggery. He was now twenty-five and wanted a better future for his young family. His wife Marie was heavily pregnant with their second child. Their daughter Ursula was two years old. He wanted his children to grow up in a democratic, social and fair Germany. But far-right and far-left paramilitary groups waited in the wings for an opportunity to deal the teetering republic the last blow. Democracy would need its own army if it were to survive. So the paramilitary Reichsbanner Schwarz-Rot-Gold was formed in February 1924. Named after the black-red-gold tricolour of the republic, it sought to defend democracy against its many enemies and in time became one of the largest organizations in the country. It was closely affiliated with the SPD and, as a party member, Kurt joined it right away, determined to fight for democracy.

But as Ludendorff readied the Nazi troops at the Hohenzollern, a personal catastrophe knocked the fighting spirit out of Kurt. When Marie went into labour, something went terribly wrong. Both she and the baby died. Now a bereaved single father of a toddler, Kurt had to juggle raising little Ursula with his work as a civil servant in the Thuringian government. There was no time for grief or political idealism.

'They starved and bled, they lay in trenches day and night; they were killed or died after painful suffering. How can we forget that?' asked the pastor in Weimar's church of St Peter and Paul.[36] It was 3 August 1924, the ten-year anniversary of the day Germany declared war on France. The Weimar Republic called upon people to mark the date. It would be the state's first and only official memorial event in honour of the 'victims of the World War'.

While the young republic found it awkward to honour the dead and veterans of a lost war, grief and solemnity proved powerful unifiers. Weimar's town church was filled to the rafters with people who would normally be at each other's throats. All the local military organizations were represented, right-wing ones hostile to the state as well as the Reichsbanner, which swore to protect it. 'All the different attitudes and opinions shan't stop us from our one great vision,' promised the pastor and quoted the first line from the national anthem that called on people to forget their differences: '"Germany, Germany above everything!"'[37]

Ten days later, Rosa Schmidt could see trains pulling into Weimar from the window of the Hotel Hohenzollern, each one spilling more passengers into streets bubbling with noise and colour. She had been busy preparing for the spectacle for weeks. Here was a chance to anchor the family business firmly in Weimar's re-emerging conference industry.

Over the next few days, thousands of members of paramilitary organizations as well as 25,000 spectators would come to hail 'His Excellency Erich Ludendorff' and affirm their allegiance to 'German culture, for which Weimar is a symbol and a home' as the official event programme put it.[38] Rosa's hotel was fully booked and also served as a first port of call for all arrivals. Here they would be told where to sleep, eat and line up for parades. It had all been prepared with military precision. In Weimar, Germany's right-wing groups would learn to march in lockstep.

Local newspapers had encouraged everyone to decorate monuments and hang black-white-red banners from their windows in homage to a Reich that had long gone. Weimarers had responded in their droves. Marching bands hammered out pulsating rhythms as they weaved their way through streets lined with onlookers and flags. 'People of Weimar!' one paper exalted from its pages, 'The Commander of the World Wars, General Ludendorff, will set foot in your town!'[39] Since the abdication of Kaiser Wilhelm II, many Germans had craved a new leader and Ludendorff was keen to fill that void.

The 'Conference of the National Socialist Freedom Movement' was about to begin. Throughout the weekend of 16 and 17 August, shouts of 'Heil!' merged with the 'singing of patriotic songs from thousands of mouths', the local press reported. 'Young and old people were up on their feet.'[40] Devout Catholics and Protestants mixed with neo-pagans. Workers and tradesmen marched with aristocrats. The town was filled to bursting with nationalists, Nazis and *völkisch* activists. 'An inseparable bond holds them all together,' one local paper wrote, 'the bond of loyal German camaraderie until death.'[41]

Despite the best efforts of the nationalist press, the much-vaunted unity of the assembled far-right activists proved illusory. Fuelled by alcohol, Nazis clashed with spiritualists and war veterans with armchair generals, over competing visions and strategies for new Germany. Arguments broke out everywhere, from street brawls to formal lectures. Ludendorff wrote in his memoirs that he had been keen to introduce issues of culture and religion alongside 'the usual lecture themes . . . such as organization, politics, the economy, press and marketing'.[42] His companion Mathilde von Kemnitz, a doctor, philosopher and fellow ideologue who was soon to become his second wife (while he would be her third husband), also delivered a lecture on her *völkisch* philosophy entitled 'The Power of the Pure Idea'. She reflected afterwards that there had been 'much ugliness' in Weimar, 'though I didn't let that dampen my happiness'.[43]

There was indeed much ugliness during an event that had been billed as being 'without party-political undertones'.[44] SPD delegates in the Thuringian parliament complained the following week that the right-wing state 'government neglected to provide sufficient police protection', while the visitors had 'taken it upon themselves to make a racket in the streets late at night, undertake assaults and robbery of republicans and the Volkshaus and attack non-Nazis with firearms and bladed weapons. In some cases republicans were beaten and assaulted until they broke down unconscious and covered in blood; others were badly injured through knife attacks and one was robbed; one raid-commando fired shots at visitors of the guest room in the Volkshaus.' The SPD suspected the government had not only tolerated this anti-republican gathering but 'even supported it according to one Nazi leader'.[45]

The town's mayor, forty-four-year-old Walther Felix Mueller, appeared alongside his star guest Ludendorff and provided police protection for him when there was none for SPD politicians. Mueller was sitting in the German National Theatre – with many other public dignitaries and journalists from across Germany – when ardent Nazis like Artur Dinter took to the stage. Flanked by crimson flags embossed with swastikas, Dinter ranted against the 'Jewish republic'[46] and preached retribution. 'Here, side by side with the greatest German commander, I accuse the current government of the Reich of high treason and treason against the people! They deserve the gallows!' Some clapped and jeered. Others stayed silent. Then he asked the audience to raise their right hands and swear an oath. Some did and their chorus filled the theatre with solemn menace: 'We swear to follow our Führer Ludendorff into death when he calls upon us, and we will not rest until the November criminals have received their punishment.'[47]

Only a few days earlier, on 11 August, Mayor Mueller and many fellow Weimar dignitaries had sat in the same seats, clapping the people Dinter wanted hanged. Among the representatives of the Berlin federal government visiting the town were prominent social democrats like Paul Löbe. Löbe had been vice president of the Weimar National Assembly in July 1919, when it met in the very same theatre to draft the new German constitution that Reich President Ebert signed into law on 11 August of that year. Löbe and many others were in town to celebrate the fifth anniversary of the Weimar Republic, re-pledging their allegiance to its democratic values and swearing to protect it from the 'worshippers of the swastika'.[48]

Assessments of Ludendorff's attempt to unify the nationalist right in Weimar varied. Aristocrat Harry Graf Kessler, who happened to be in town, wasn't particularly impressed. He was in the theatre when Dinter asked his audience to swear an oath of allegiance to Ludendorff and noted in his diary: 'The speaker looks around expectantly. The followers of the swastika raise their hand; the "people" with insignificant exceptions *do not*.'[49] Ludendorff himself seemed 'careful, non-committal, harmless and empty' to

Harry, the entire event 'without atmosphere'. At the military parade that followed, Harry estimated he saw fewer than 10,000 men rather than the 60,000 that had been expected. He saw many '12 to 16 year old children walking along like sheep' and 'quite a lot of old gentlemen with shouldered umbrellas'. He got the feeling the spectators were no more impressed than he was, 'they even laughed at the many comically fat or skinny figures and wrong commandos . . . The indifference of the population despite military music, uniform kitsch a[nd] Ludendorff was very noticeable . . . The "German Day" in Weimar is barely worth mentioning, almost a fiasco.'[50]

Carl Weirich didn't mention the German Day in his diary. His brother- and sister-in-law Karl and Hedwig came over that week and the two couples went hiking. The visitors were impressed by Bratwurst, grilled Thuringian sausages, but there is no talk of Ludendorff in Carl's notes.[51]

Ludendorff's lover Mathilde, on the other hand, was so taken with the charged atmosphere that she found it hard to let go. She wrote in her memoirs how 'Just in the nick of time, I rushed with my suitcase and flowers to the train and – as the last days had echoed constantly with shouts of "heil" – I called "heil" instead of "halt" to the train driver. This was my luck. He was so baffled that he indeed only signalled for departure a moment later, when I already stood on the running board.'[52]

Other attendees were equally enthused. One twenty-six-year-old man, an aimless and unsuccessful writer with a doctorate in philology, had travelled all the way from his home town of Rheydt, 400 kilometres to the west. He hadn't initially wanted to go, noting in his diary on 15 August when many like-minded friends were already in Weimar: 'I believe such party conferences are terrible things. The crowds, masses of people, who all want to have the chance to talk. And all the fervour. Oh dear!'[53] But in the end he was glad he had attended. On 19 August, he wrote:

Weimar is Goethe. A town of disciplined unity and of full, round harmony. I find all my expectations completely met. Yes, this glorious

Weimar. A place of the blessed culture of a more beautiful time. And then this festival life in the town today. All of these young people who fight with me. My heart is lifted! Oh, our blessed youth! We enthusiasts, we fanatics! Holy flame ignite! At the National Theatre there is great tumult. 卐 . . . I see Ludendorff for the first time . . . Ludendorff eradicated many sceptical thoughts in me. He gave me firm, final belief.[54]

Joseph Goebbels had found his calling.

In the medium term, Ludendorff couldn't galvanize warring nationalist factions. While his National Socialist Freedom Movement prepared for another election when the German parliament collapsed again in the autumn of 1924, he became increasingly erratic, even accusing some fellow MPs of belonging to a subversive Druid movement. Eventually, he abstained from parliamentary sessions altogether. From prison, Hitler distanced himself from Ludendorff and his NSFB party. He correctly anticipated that division and the general's waning star would make it an unattractive option on election day on 7 December. In addition, the government had stabilized the economy by ending hyperinflation and by agreeing a more manageable reparations solution with the Western Allies, including a staggered payment schedule and large American-backed loans under the Dawes Plan. The NSFB lost over half its vote share, gaining just 3 per cent or fourteen seats.

The electoral results, in which the fringes lost ground and the SPD made the biggest gains, reflected an atmosphere of cautious optimism at the end of 1924. The year is often seen as marking the beginning of the so-called Golden Twenties. Even if this was achieved on borrowed money and therefore on borrowed time, it ripped the country out of its doom spiral. The uplift in the general mood did not lead to an alleviation of moral angst, however. The acceleration of modernity continued to move at dizzying speed, represented by cultural icons like the scandalous cabaret star Anita Berber, a drug-taking, androgynous nude dancer who courted outrage with her boundary-breaking persona. Associated with German high culture,

Weimar was a natural powerbase for those who saw themselves as guardians of tradition and moral discipline. Under the leadership of the right-wing Thuringian government, pressure mounted on Weimar's institutions to remove modern, foreign and Jewish influence irrespective of the economic upwinds.

One by one, the town's modernist experiments ended and its institutions were brought to the national-conservative heel. The liberal director of the National Theatre Ernst Hardt faced increasingly personal attacks from conservative opponents and the press. He let his contract run out in 1924 and moved to Cologne. The theatre was handed over to Franz Ulbrich, who, while a proponent of expressionist theatre, was more willing to bend to pressure to return to a more traditional programme.

The year 1924 also marked the end of the Bauhaus in Weimar. The Thuringian Ministry of Education announced in September that all the school's staff and teachers would be dismissed effective from 1 April the following year. On 26 December, Gropius and his colleagues pre-empted their sacking and dissolved the Weimar Bauhaus themselves.[55] They had received several offers for relocation and opted for Dessau, the capital of the Free State of Anhalt. 'We regret that it was allowed to happen,' the Bauhaus masters wrote in

Bauhaus party at the restaurant Ilmschlösschen near Weimar on 29 November 1924.

a declaration as they left, 'and, further, that the objective and always non-political cultural work of the Bauhaus has been disturbed by party-political intrigue.'[56] Students and staff had one more wild party in Weimar, their 'Last Dance', before painter and Bauhaus master Lyonel Feininger declared: 'Gentlemen, we're done weimaring, now it's time to dessau!'

Carl Weirich spent Christmas 1924 unperturbed by the seismic historical shifts underneath the surface of German society. Business in the stationery shop was brimming right up to Christmas Eve. He and Marie exchanged presents in their flat above before venturing out on to the market square, where Pastor Wessel had put up Weimar's customary 'Christmas Tree for Everyone'.[57] This long-standing tradition began in 1815, the year Napoleon had been defeated for good. A generous Weimar bookseller had placed his Christmas tree outside, so that all of Weimar's children, be they rich or poor, had the joy of gathering around a tree with friends and family. It was the first public Christmas tree in Germany and launched a tradition that was soon picked up by many other towns and cities. Over a century later, Carl and Marie stood on the cold market square with their neighbours and sang Christmas carols, blissfully unaware that the release from prison of one Adolf Hitler four days earlier would soon change their lives forever.

1925

On the afternoon of 22 March 1925, Baldur von Schirach was standing to attention with the other boys of his paramilitary youth group. It was the ninety-third anniversary of Goethe's death. But that wasn't what he was here for. The teenager stood rigid, his hair parted neatly on the left, blue eyes staring intently down the road in front of Weimar's imposing Schießhaus. The elegant, early-nineteenth-century clubhouse with its colonnaded front ran behind the young guards in a C-shape, overlooking the town from its elevated position to the north-east of the centre. It was filled with people who had taken their seats hours earlier to secure a space.[1] It would be the site of Adolf Hitler's first speech outside of Bavaria.[2]

The arrival of the Führer or leader, as Hitler styled himself, had been hotly anticipated in Weimar. Since his release from prison, he had been busy rebuilding his splintered movement under the auspices of the Nazi Party, which he refounded on 27 February 1925. Having failed to seize power by revolutionary means, Hitler decided it was time to try a different strategy: getting elected. For this, he needed a local party infrastructure, so he divided the country into administrative units called Gau.

Gau Thuringia had only just been founded and was headed by Artur Dinter as Gauleiter or Gau leader. His deputy was Hans Severus Ziegler, a journalist and writer in his early thirties. He'd worked as a secretary for the writer Adolf Bartels, and Bartels had in turn helped him achieve his PhD in German literature. Bartels and Dinter, who were both significantly older than him, had become Ziegler's mentors. Like Baldur, he had German-American roots. His mother came from the New York Schirmer family of classical music publishers.[3] Ziegler now ran a newspaper called *Der Nationalsozialist*

(The National Socialist). The business side of Gau Thuringia would be run by Fritz Sauckel, a former merchant mariner who had thrown himself into far-right activism full time after failing to complete an engineering course at a technical school in the Thuringian town of Ilmenau.[4] He joined the NSDAP in 1923 as member 1,395, founded a local party chapter in Ilmenau, enrolled in Hitler's Sturmabteilung (Stormtroopers; SA) paramilitary organization and even planned a 'March on Berlin' simultaneously with Hitler's Munich Putsch, for which he was briefly detained before it could take place. Hitler never forgot this fervent loyalty.[5]

With such committed followers in the region, it's hardly surprising that Hitler considered moving the Nazi Party headquarters to Weimar. There were other benefits too. It was geographically in the centre of Germany. It had a state government that tolerated Nazi activism. Bavaria had allowed the Nazi Party to re-form but imposed a speaking ban on Hitler at the beginning of March and other states had followed. He was only allowed to speak publicly in four states now and Thuringia was one of them.[6] And then, of course, there was Weimar's symbolic appeal as the heart of German culture. Could the spirit of Weimar breathe life back into the dormant Nazi movement? While reluctant to give up his considerable powerbase in Munich, the Führer wanted to take a look at the Thuringian capital himself.

Hitler's introduction to Weimar had been impeccably prepared. 'And then came Hitler,' Baldur von Schirach remembered. 'Actually, I didn't notice him at first. For suddenly a car appeared of a type I had previously only seen in pictures, a Mercedes Kompressor, a six-seater with spoked wheels. All the rage! I was so fascinated that I hardly paid any attention to the men who got out of this marvel.'[7] One of the men who got out was Dinter. Anticipating that there might be trouble if Hitler arrived by public transport, the Gauleiter had made alternative plans. This turned out to be prescient as 200 communists had gathered at Weimar station hours before the Nazi leader's scheduled arrival.[8] He had picked Hitler up at Jena, where he'd arrived by train from Munich. With him were Ernst Röhm, founder of the Stormtroopers, and Julius Streicher, publisher of the antisemitic newspaper *Der Stürmer* and soon-to-be Gauleiter of Nordbayern.[9]

Hitler walked past Baldur and into the Schießhaus to frenetic applause and shouts of 'Heil!' But as he took his place on the stage, the division that had taken seed during his absence was audible. 'Compromiser!' someone shouted, displeased that the Nazi Party had forsaken the path of violent revolution. 'Dinter out!' called another, showing how controversial a figure the Gauleiter was, not least because of the intense religiosity that laced his Nazism. Banking solely on his charisma and reputation, Hitler threatened to leave should the audience not calm down. That had the desired effect and he appealed to the movement to 'let the past be the past, look to the future, shake hands and unite'.[10]

Baldur would remember few details from this speech, but 'I still know,' he wrote later, 'that I listened up at the sound of his voice. It was a completely different voice compared to speakers I'd heard previously – teachers, priests, officers or politicians. This voice was deep and raw, resonant like a cello. The accent, which we assumed to be Austrian but which in reality was Lower Bavarian, sounded strange here in central Germany and because of that it forced one to listen.'[11] Not everyone was swept away. As Hitler spoke about his usual topics – lost German greatness, his burning love for the fatherland and the Nazi movement – it took an hour before he even earned his first applause, Baldur later recalled.[12] At the end, Hitler demanded that the Nazi leader in the town of Gotha, Paul Hennicke, shake hands with Dinter. But as Dinter held out his hand, Hennicke left him hanging, embarrassing both Gauleiter and Führer.[13]

Hitler needed a break. He was taken to the house of Hans Severus Ziegler at Luisenstraße 10 in the leafy southern part of town, near the Nietzsche Archive and Harry Graf Kessler's Weimar villa.[14] Ziegler had only just joined the party, but Hitler trusted the worldly young man instinctively. He came from an upper-class background far removed from Hitler's own much humbler origins, making him ideally placed to induct the Führer into the circles of Weimar's haughty elite. Ziegler asked Baldur and his friend Hans Donndorf to stand guard outside the house while he took Hitler inside. When the two men re-emerged an hour later, Baldur suddenly found himself face-to-face with the infamous demagogue. Hitler's intense blue eyes bored into his as he took the boy's hand and shook it firmly. The teenager was beside himself, and rushed home to compose a poem about the experience:

> Behind me are thousands of you,
> And you are me, and I am you.
> I have never lived a thought,
> That hasn't been by your hearts wrought.
>
> And when I form words, I don't know any,
> That isn't one with your destiny,
> For you are me and I am you,
> And we all believe, Germany, in you.[15]

Baldur would later be embarrassed by the literary quality of this output, calling it one of 'many bad poems'.[16] But at the time, he proudly showed it to Ziegler, who published it in *Der Nationalsozialist*. Hitler was touched and saw to it that his young fan was sent a note: 'Herr Hitler has read your poem in the Gau newspaper and sends you his photograph with a personal dedication attached in thanks.'[17] Baldur put the picture into a silver frame and placed it on his desk. For the star-struck teenager, things would never be the same again.

Having enjoyed a bit of a break at Ziegler's house, Hitler spoke at three more events in Weimar: at the clubhouse Erholung (Respite), at the Hotel Germania and again at the Schießhaus in the evening. The next morning, he visited Adolf Bartels' more modest flat at Lisztstraße 13, followed by brief drop-ins at the houses of Goethe and Schiller. Then Hitler left Weimar in the afternoon. Not everyone was impressed but some Weimarers were deeply touched by the experience. Ziegler founded a Weimar Nazi Party group on 6 April.[18]

Run by Fritz Sauckel, it became one of the busiest NSDAP chapters in Thuringia, hosting events almost weekly.[19]

In the spring of 1925, Weimar's cultural landscape changed forever. The Bauhaus moved to Dessau, where it would soon erect a distinct school building designed by Walter Gropius. The architect also protected the Bauhaus name, so that people who remained in Weimar could no longer use it. Gropius's successor in Weimar was the architect Otto Bartning, who, less confrontational than his predecessor, managed to retain many Bauhaus elements if not its radical zeal. He'd worked closely with Gropius and is often counted among the initiators of the Bauhaus but found better working conditions in Weimar than Gropius had. He was granted more funding, and could focus entirely on architecture because the artists at the Academy of Fine Arts were glad to be fully independent again after the Bauhaus departure.

Bartning began to build a new venture that opened a year later, in April 1926, and was called the 'Staatliche Bauhochschule Weimar' or 'State Building Academy Weimar', usually just referred to as the 'Bauhochschule'. It focused entirely on modern building and architectural techniques. Students were asked, for instance, to spontaneously draft ideas according to the demands set out by the teacher so that repetition of established patterns would be avoided and students were forced to come up with their own responses to problems and challenges. Course director Ernst Neufert, who had previously worked in Gropius's private architecture firm, collated the students' designs in a freely accessible database.[20] A town-planning course was run by Cornelis van Eesteren, who belonged to the Dutch De Stijl movement.

The Bauhochschule constituted less of a break with the Bauhaus than one would expect given the hostility Gropius had encountered. Bartning even took over some of the Bauhaus branches as they were. Carpentry stayed under the same leadership and in the same workshops. Many of the new staff had previously been connected to the Bauhaus movement in some way.[21] The Bauhochschule did well commercially. It sold items and designs from its workshops through its own company both domestically and internationally. It was more progressive and modern than it usually gets credit for since its development was cut short by the ascent of Nazism in Thuringia.[22]

But that lay in the future. For now, it seemed the Bauhaus idea could live on in Weimar even without its founder or its name. Some, like the sculptor Oskar Schlemmer, who had been appointed Master of Form at the Bauhaus theatre workshop in 1923 under Gropius, were even optimistic about the new opportunities under Bartning. 'In Weimar itself, the real father of the Bauhaus idea has been appointed,' Schlemmer wrote, hoping to retain his position and convinced by Bartning's ability to create something great in Weimar, 'at least if the Thuringian government will give him the opportunity'.[23]

On the afternoon of 20 April, Harry Graf Kessler walked up the hill to visit Elisabeth Förster-Nietzsche in her villa. 'As ever,' he noted in his diary that evening, 'she received me in the spirit of deepest friendship.'[24] Elisabeth was in serious financial trouble, yet over coffee she told him how happy she had been to have received 1,200 marks from Munich beneficiaries the previous Christmas. Generous as this was, it was a drop in the ocean. Harry was impressed by her fighting talk, 'which in such situations is always utterly remarkable in her and bordering on the heroic, forcing one to admire Nietzsche's sister'.[25]

Had he met Elisabeth just a few months earlier, he would have encountered a very different woman. In January, the state of German politics had kept her awake at night. 'I often can't sleep out of sadness over the fact that we, a great, strong people, are exposed to such humiliation,' she wrote. 'But maybe this too will change in my lifetime. I'm always a little impatient because I can't hope to wander this world for too many more years, and I would yet like to see Germany in its old strength and glory. The other day, someone replied: "then you'll of course have to live to at least 90", and under this condition . . . I would object less to such a long lifespan than my usual feelings on the matter.'[26]

Four weeks after she wrote those words, Reich President Friedrich Ebert died of septic shock, aged fifty-four. Like many conservatives, Elisabeth rejoiced at the death of the Weimar Republic's staunchest defender. A new President might usher in a new Germany and he would be chosen directly by the people. It was a sign of how divided Germany was that no fewer than seven candidates ran for President in the first round of voting on 29 March, ranging from the communist Ernst Thälmann to Erich Ludendorff. None of the candidates received the required absolute majority. The second round was scheduled to take place on 26 April, six days after Elisabeth and Harry had coffee together. She was optimistic because the right-wing parties had decided to field Paul von Hindenburg as their collective candidate. In his late seventies, the former Chief of the Great General Staff had retired and been reluctant to become head of the republican system he despised. But he'd been won over by the argument that he wouldn't be running for parties but for the fatherland and agreed to stand against Wilhelm Marx from the Catholic Centre Party and Thälmann from the KPD.

Elisabeth fervently believed in the stab-in-the-back myth peddled by Hindenburg and yearned for the pre-war times that he embodied. The tall, broad-shouldered man with the iconic square-shaped head and bushy moustache was a walking, talking emblem of the pre-1914 world. He was regarded as an *Ersatzkaiser*, a Kaiser substitute, and Elisabeth was among the nostalgics who found that comforting. In a 'Letter for German Women' she urged fellow female voters to choose Hindenburg as the only candidate who stood 'above all the party rancour'.[27] She was delighted when he won the election, narrowly beating Marx with 48.3 per cent to 45.3 per cent of the vote. The republic was now headed by a monarchist.

Harry Graf Kessler found this development dangerous and unsavoury. 'All the philistines are happy about Hindenburg,' he ranted after another visit at Elisabeth's villa in May, 'he is the God of all those who long for a return to philistinism . . . Adieu progress, adieu vision of a new world which was supposed to be the ransom of humanity for the criminal war; finally one can live like a fat ram or a fattened goose again in comfort until the butcher comes along and demands his blood.'[28]

Elisabeth was a dear friend, but Harry found her hankering for anachronistic splinters of pre-war Germany difficult to bear. While he was visiting her, a general who had just been stationed in Weimar appeared at the villa. 'Frau Förster nearly flung her arms around his neck,' Harry scoffed, adding that he found it even more 'irritating' that the old lady had attended the general's ceremonial march into Weimar the previous day and allowed her young great-nephew to ride on the driver's seat of her car with a military steel helmet on his head and a drum on his lap – 'in other words playing soldiers in the most stupid, infantile way'.[29]

Elisabeth talked about all this excitedly, oblivious to Harry's simmering resentment. 'The disgusting impression left by the inter-twining of "cottage"-militarism and narrow-minded officiousness at Frau Förster-Nietzsche's this afternoon continues to linger,' he wrote in the evening.[30] By June, he tried to avoid political topics with Elisabeth altogether, as he told the artist Henry van de Velde, a former fellow Weimar celebrity, in a letter: 'Our old friend Frau Förster is still very nice and brave, but unfortunately she's become increasingly nationalistic. It is completely impossible to discuss politics with her. One risks awkward situations. That's why I don't meet anyone in Weimar any more.'[31]

In the summer of 1925, Carl Weirich was meeting plenty of people, enjoying a social life like he hadn't had in years. Happily married to Marie, who also became a much-cherished help in the shop, Carl finally had some stability in his life. Business was steady, both he and his wife enjoyed good health and there was even enough time and money for a holiday in July together with his mother and brother in the Bavarian mountains. He also often managed to combine work and pleasure when he attended conventions and professional training courses across the country. He had a great time in Munich at the conference of the Federal Association of Bookbinders, which finished in the early afternoon each day and allowed him and others some time for sightseeing.

Carl visited a transport exhibition with 'great objects from steam and electric trains to ships as well as motorized cars and radio technology'.[32] He went to an amusement park and climbed the Zugspitze, the highest mountain in Germany. The increasingly military atmosphere in the Bavarian capital didn't bother him. With a colleague, he visited the famous Löwenbräukeller beer hall one night where he enjoyed an evening of military music played by a Reichswehr band. He also thought about politics at times. After all, a 'quarter of a century had unfolded in a pretty subdued mood for us Germans', he mused. 'The lost war and the vexatiousness of our enemies weigh heavy on anyone who earnestly contemplates the future. But faced with the great developments of world history the individual is powerless . . . We act in our small world and labour in our shop and are happy if our work is success-ful over the years.'[33]

Rosa and Arthur Schmidt's hotel was doing well. Not only was it recovering from the hyperinflation but it was also beginning to build a reputation. It was no longer a gambling den but a well-run and respectable conference venue. On Sunday 12 July, the Schmidts hosted a special visitor, one who had gained great notoriety in recent years. This radical had the power to unleash such anger with words that most of Germany wouldn't let him speak. Now he had come to Weimar again and checked in with them. Rosa and Arthur managed to impress their guest so much that he would make their hotel his choice of residence for his next few visits. Adolf Hitler liked the Hotel Hohenzollern.

The Nazi leader had come to Weimar in his ongoing quest to galvanize his disjointed movement. He'd called around 250 people to an invitation-only event at the Erholung. Among the crowd were twenty Gauleiters and eighty local group leaders as well as Joseph Goebbels, who met in Weimar the man whom he'd follow into darkness and death.[34] Goebbels had joined the Nazi Party as soon as it had re-formed earlier in the year. He'd proved an able propagandist and ran the business side of his Gau of Rhineland North.

Hitler spoke for two hours before retreating with leaders to a more intimate setting in the evening.[35] Some were still deeply critical on points where their views diverged from the Führer's. This included Goebbels, who wished for a stronger anti-capitalist emphasis in the Nazi programme. The more people Hitler met in person, the fewer questioned his leadership. Goebbels was among those entirely enthralled with Hitler, as he captured in his diary: 'these large blue eyes. Like stars . . . With wit, irony, humour, sarcasm, with seriousness, with burning, with passion. This man has everything it takes to be a king. A born leader of the people. The future dictator.'[36]

On 29 August, Baldur von Schirach walked into 'one of the cheapest residential areas' in Weimar.[37] He was looking for the office of the local Nazi Party and found it to be a rather modest affair. But the young aristocrat wasn't put off by that. He was now eighteen. It was time to forge his own path in life. He resolved to fight for Germany like his older brother had wanted to. Baldur agreed to pay 80 pfennigs a month and hand out leaflets when required as he became Nazi Party member 17,251.

Hitler had appreciated the unassuming but neat Hotel Hohenzollern. So he decided to stay at Rosa and Arthur Schmidt's establishment again for his third Weimar visit that year.

The local NSDAP chapter that was organizing the itinerary had no problem getting the approval from the Thuringian Ministry of the Interior. After all, there hadn't been any trouble during Hitler's last visit. But the local Nazis were warned that the event on 28 October would be monitored carefully. If Hitler 'overstepped the boundaries of reasonable criticism or attacked the government in his utterances in a way that was unconscionable', police would shut down the event.[38] The authorities' sympathies in Weimar and Thuringia now lay openly with the right. Despite being a member of parliament, Artur Dinter had got away with leading a group of men as they intimidated the delegates of the Women's International League for Peace and Freedom, who held a congress in Weimar on 5 October.[39] Hitler knew he had nothing to fear in Weimar. In July, he'd bragged that he now had 'more supporters in formerly red Saxony and Thuringia than I have in nationalistic Bavaria'.[40] Hans Severus Ziegler's newspaper *Der Nationalsozialist* had also hoped it was 'satisfying for Adolf Hitler that the state of Thuringia itself gladly admitted him as a guest'.[41]

This time the Führer came from Nuremberg by car. His first appointment in Weimar was again at the Erholung, where he was supposed to speak in the evening in front of 800 people. When he arrived with Ziegler half an hour late, the atmosphere was already crackling with nervous energy. The hall was overcrowded and several hundred people had been turned away at the doors. Paramilitary formations guarded the entrances and the surrounding streets against potential disruption from communists and socialists. Deafening shouts of 'Heil!' greeted Hitler, who spoke for nearly three hours. It was almost midnight when he returned to his room at the Hohenzollern.[42]

The next day, Ziegler took him to the National Theatre, where he met ex-director Carl von Schirach. Normally extremely class-conscious to the point of arrogance, Carl von Schirach warmed to the Austrian former lance corporal and invited him back to the family villa at Gartenstraße 37 for tea. Hitler seemed to say and do all the right things. Wearing a blue suit, white shirt and black tie, he looked formal enough as he sauntered around, admiring the family's colonial-style furniture. He lightly kissed Emma Schirach's hand and gave her flowers.[43] The American was delighted. 'How well behaved, what good manners,' she gushed in English. 'At last a [G]erman patriot.'[44] This was in no small part a hurtful jibe at her son, who never seemed to be good enough at music, the arts or in his education to please his mother.

There was also genuine admiration for Hitler in Frau Schirach's remark. An opera enthusiast, Hitler found it easy to charm the musical family, letting them do most of the talking but adding insightful comments when he could. Hitler made a lasting impression that day. Carl told his son afterwards, 'I've actually never met anyone in all my life who, as a layman, knows so much about music, especially about Wagner, like this, your Hitler.'[45] Baldur later remembered the occasion as 'a completely casual tea hour'.[46] By now a party member as well as a fully fledged Stormtrooper, he was determined to hitch his fate to that of the Führer. But was that what Hitler wanted? The Austrian asked the teenager what his plans were. 'I still had one and a half years before graduating from school,' Baldur remembered later, 'and then I wanted to go to university. Hitler said: "If you go to university, join me in Munich." '[47]

On 13 December, the Hotel Hohenzollern was brimming with people. The Schmidts had agreed to host 120 well-heeled guests for an evening event. The Thuringian chapter of the Nazi Party had invited potential donors for a fundraising dinner. The star speaker was none other than Adolf Hitler himself, who would once again stay overnight.

As Rosa cooked and Arthur topped up empty glasses, Hitler struck a calmer tone than usual. He stressed the necessity of propaganda in his struggle to overturn the current system and seize power in Germany. Newspapers, leaflets, posters and new media like the radio would all need to play their part. All of this cost money and relied on substantial support from wealthy citizens willing to chip in for the kind of future they wanted to see for Germany. *Der National-sozialist* was happy to report that the evening was 'an extraordinarily pleasing practical success'.[48]

Hitler had by now given up on the idea of moving the NSDAP offices to Weimar. Munich was the uncontested 'capital of the movement' and it would only be a question of time until the speaking ban would be lifted there. But there were crucial people in Weimar, where Nazi ideology had long ceased to be a taboo among the upper classes. Even Carl von Schirach was sympathetic, despite the fact that Nazism attacked the pillars of Germany's encrusted class system. In 1926, he would join the NSDAP as member 48,505.

By the end of 1925, the Thuringian NSDAP had 600 members, organized across nearly 100 tiny but well-distributed chapters.[49] The Nazi Party wasn't a major force but it was building the infrastructure to become one. The capital of Thuringia in the centre of Germany had played a large role in this and Hitler knew it. At the end of 1925, he proclaimed: 'I love Weimar!'[50]

Elisabeth Förster-Nietzsche wrapped up a very special Christmas present for a man she greatly admired. It was a copy of 'Nietzsche's Words about States and People', a 1922 publication of assembled scraps of Friedrich Nietzsche's writings edited by her. She hoped the Italian dictator Benito Mussolini would like it. Since his March on Rome in 1922, she had followed his rise and the establishment of fascism in Italy. Mussolini's propaganda spoke of lost glories, of humiliation, military catastrophes and liberal politicians who offered no solutions. It was a message that resonated in Germany. Cosima Wagner, the composer Richard Wagner's influential widow, was also among the many Mussolini fans, considering him a 'statesmanly personality'.[51]

Elisabeth became fascinated with the Italian dictator when he described her philosopher brother as his 'spiritual master'. In an interview in July 1924 published in the *New York Times* and the *Deutsche Allgemeine Zeitung*, Mussolini said: 'I have been influenced by Nietzsche . . . I came across his books. I have read them without exception. They made the deepest impression upon me. They cured me of my socialism . . . I was also deeply impressed by Nietzsche's wonderful precept: "Live dangerously." I have lived up to that, I think.'[52]

Elisabeth was enthralled. Germany hadn't found its Nietzsche-inspired saviour yet but Italy had. She sent her Christmas gift to Mussolini with her best seasonal greetings and was delighted to receive a telegram from Rome in response. Mussolini thanked her and promised a 'letter to follow'.[53]

*

Carl and Marie Weirich spent a very happy Christmas together. The pair had caught a train to her home town of Nuremberg on Christmas Eve. When they arrived they found the old city was a picture-perfect winter landscape. Snow had fallen on the timber-framed houses and the couple wandered through the ancient cobbled streets feeling lucky to be among loved ones.[54] Best of all, Marie was pregnant. The Weirichs looked forward to 1926, the year they would start a family together.

1926

For Elisabeth Förster-Nietzsche, 1926 began with grave concerns. Having taken out a large loan of 32,000 marks the previous year to buy the plot below her villa, her financial situation was as precarious as ever. She wrote to Harry Graf Kessler to ask for advice. Harry warned that 'liquid funds are so scarce at the moment that it probably won't be easy to find a mortgage at low interest rates'. He loaned his friend 3,000 marks for now, and tried to reassure her: 'I don't doubt that the matter can be resolved in some way.'[1]

In private, the aristocrat was deeply worried about the financial situation of the archive and Elisabeth's personal fortunes. Meeting with her cousin Max Oehler, whom Harry considered a 'likeable, burly but cultivated man who'd seen the world', he confessed that he thought it might be best to merge the Nietzsche Archive with the Goethe and Schiller Archive after Elisabeth's death.[2] Seeking support from foreign dictators was a very bad idea, as far as he was concerned. When she proudly told him over coffee that she had struck up a friendship with Mussolini, Harry lost his patience. 'I told her that . . . Mussolini is tainting her brother. He is a danger for Europe, for the Europe that her brother especially had longed for, a Europe of good Europeans. The poor old lady became rather "agitated" [English word], but then changed the topic and the rest of the conversation unfolded amicably. She is nearly eighty and it is beginning to show.'[3]

Elisabeth was indeed beginning to feel her age. She suffered from severe bouts of head colds and fevers. She also noticed her physical and mental capacities dwindle. One day she thought her garden had changed an awful lot overnight only to find that she had confused her reading glasses with her distance ones. But 'Mussolini is the pleasure of my high age,' she admitted.[4]

Arthur and Rosa Schmidt's future was looking up. Their eldest child Alexandra had finished school and was now working at the Hotel Hohenzollern alongside her parents, who appreciated the extra pair of hands. The business ran well enough for the family to support their teenage boys Arthur and Ernst as well as little Horst, who was only four. One of the things that helped the Schmidts book up their twenty-three rooms and fill the large restaurant and café spaces in their establishment with paying guests were the innumerable new clubs and military groups that popped up after the war. As Germany's political, economic and social future hung in the balance everyone seemed to have something to fight for or against. That suited the Schmidts just fine. Organizations were always welcome to hold meetings at the Hohenzollern.

The year 1926 turned out to be a particularly busy one for such gatherings in Weimar. In April, two mortal enemies of Weimar democracy gathered in town. On 4 April, the Thuringian chapter of the Roter Frontkämpferbund (Red Front Fighters' League or RFB) summoned 2,000 of its members to Weimar for a congress. The town itself had over 200 members, mostly workers from the wagon factory.[5] The rest came from further afield by train. The RFB was the paramilitary wing of the Communist Party and saw it as their role to protect KPD gatherings from Nazi organizations like the SA and far-right and nationalist formations like the Stahlhelm, all of which also found Weimar an evocative meeting place.

Barely a week after the gathering of communist paramilitaries in Weimar, Rosa and Arthur were hosting a particularly rowdy gathering of their mortal enemies, the Stahlhelm, at the Hotel Hohenzollern. Their troops were closely affiliated with the monarchist DNVP and often deployed to protect their gatherings from socialist and communist paramilitaries like the RFB. Many of its members believed in the stab-in-the-back myth and denied Jewish-German veterans admission to their organization. Ignorant of Rosa

Schmidt's Jewish background, which few people outside the family knew about, the Weimar chapter of the Stahlhelm gathered at her hotel on 10 April.

As the men ate and drank, their raucous gathering continued into the small hours of the morning. The Schmidts knew they were in trouble. By police order, they were supposed to stop serving at 3 a.m. But how do you tell dozens of boisterous, battle-hardened and alcohol-fuelled men to quietly leave your establishment? Weimar police officers Rissmann and Gramens were not amused to find that the Hotel Hohenzollern seemed to be drifting back into its wartime excess and decided to crack down on such goings-on immediately. They issued Arthur with a fine of 10 marks plus a 1-mark administration fee or two days in prison. Arthur cut his losses and paid up.[6]

A month later, Carl Weirich witnessed a larger political gathering. 'Reich President Hindenburg in Weimar for short visit,' his diary entry for 10 May 1926 records.[7] This 'short visit' sent the town into a frenzy. People started gathering in the streets from the morning to catch a glimpse of the famous general and head of state. The streets were closed to regular traffic and lined by paramilitary troops. The black-white-red of imperial Germany was everywhere in recognition of the fact that Hindenburg was more celebrated for his service to the old Reich than his leadership of the new black-red-gold republic.

The President arrived by special train at noon and was greeted by cheering crowds on the square outside the station and the Hotel Hohenzollern. There, he inspected police troops and spoke to veterans before boarding a horse-drawn carriage that would parade him through Weimar's streets. Crowds cheered, bands played, men saluted their war hero. A plane whizzed overhead dropping carnations. Young girls handed flowers to the President. Visibly touched, Hindenburg called Weimar 'a German national shrine . . . which symbolizes for us the highest state of German literature and spiritual development'. State Minister Richard

Leutheußer thanked him for coming to the place 'they call the heart of Germany'.[8]

At 1 o'clock on the afternoon of 24 June 1926 cries rang through the flat above Carl Weirich's shop at Geleitstraße 10. Marie Weirich was panting, exhausted and covered in blood. She had given birth to a healthy baby boy. Dr Seiß and Midwife Krause were relieved. Marie was just over a week away from her fortieth birthday and hers was considered a comparatively late and risky pregnancy. But Wilhelm Otto Emil Weirich was a perfect boy, weighing over 4 kilograms, and Marie was able to breastfeed him immediately.

Baby Wilhelm was showered with gifts. He received two blankets from Granny Weirich. Carl's neighbour Frau Straubel gave him a little cape adorned with *Heinzelmännchen*, mythical, gnome-like creatures. Aunt Frieda sent Wilhelm a musical box. Other well-wishers gave toys, rattles, socks, child-sized crockery and night clothes. Carl was beside himself with joy and pride. He had been blessed with a second chance to start a family. Carl bought a baby book for Wilhelm in which he planned to record every detail of the boy's development. This time, he wasn't going to miss a moment of his child's life.[9]

Marie Weirich's fortieth birthday on Saturday 3 July was a joyful affair. Wilhelm was nine days old and his proud parents welcomed many neighbours into their small flat to introduce their son to them. More gifts arrived for the boy, but Carl had also bought something for his wife. To mark the occasion, he had spent 135 marks on a fine porcelain crockery set.[10] Together with friends and family, the Weirichs celebrated that their flat at Geleitstraße 10 had become a family home once more.

Next door, at Geleitstraße 12A, Joseph Goebbels was having a nap. He'd arrived in Weimar that morning after a long train journey and checked into the Hotel Chemnitius to rest a little before the other Nazis arrived. He'd made a name for himself in the movement and would soon be appointed Gauleiter of Berlin. He was expected to shake hands and be on top form. The first Nazi rally since the party's relaunch was taking place in Weimar that weekend. It would set the tone for the movement and all its institutions. 'Weimar!' Goebbels scribbled in his diary. 'One of the most important milestones on our journey.'[11]

Rosa Schmidt had no time for a nap. The Hotel Hohenzollern was fully booked for the weekend, and it housed the Nazi Party's organization office.[12] The NSDAP was expecting up to 20,000 people from all over Germany for its Weimar rally. Some would soon arrive on organized buses and lorries. At Goebbels' hotel, 200 men from the western German industrial town of Essen checked in at 2 a.m. after a thirty-five-hour drive.[13] But most would get to Weimar by train and the Hohenzollern acted as a first port of call.

Hitler himself required more central and private accommodation this time. He was booked into the prestigious, if somewhat old-fashioned, Hotel Elephant in the town centre. The Elephant had seen some famous visitors in its time. It had been run under that name since the seventeenth century and counted illustrious figures such as Goethe, Schiller, Liszt and Wagner among its guests. More recently, Walter Gropius and many of his Bauhaus colleagues and authors had met, slept, eaten and drunk at the Elephant. Now, Adolf Hitler checked in, naming his profession as 'Schriftsteller' or 'author' upon registration.

The Elephant was an ideal base for the Nazi leader. Paul Leutert, who had run the hotel since 1893, was sympathetic towards the movement. He would soon ban Jews from the premises.[14] Thuringia's Deputy Gauleiter Hans Severus Ziegler described Hitler's accommodation there as 'simple and plain . . . in the early years, one room, which served as both living room and bedroom'.[15] But crucially, the set-up gave Hitler privacy with windows facing the garden to the back while also being located directly at the busy market square, allowing the Führer to appear right in the centre of Weimar for public speeches or to greet his followers. Ziegler regarded Hitler's room at the Elephant as his 'headquarters in the centre of Germany'.[16]

When Hitler arrived at the Elephant by car in the afternoon, the market square right in front of the entrance was already a hive of activity. Stormtroopers had gathered there to greet their leader with frenetic shouts of 'Heil!' According to Goebbels, the Berlin contingent started chanting 'One day, Hitler will lead us out of this misery!'[17] As the Führer settled into his room, Goebbels spent the afternoon cruising through Weimar on a motorbike together with Heinrich Himmler, who had joined the Nazi Party in 1923 as member 14,303. Himmler, an effective Nazi Party activist in Bavaria, had also joined the Schutzstaffel or SS the previous year, which was then still a branch of the much larger SA. In a few years' time, he would take it over and turn it into one of the most powerful and murderous organizations of the Nazi state.

There were other Nazi functionaries too, including the ideologue Alfred Rosenberg, the future Deputy Führer Rudolf Hess and Philipp Bouhler, who was to run the Aktion T4 euthanasia programme in which more than a quarter of a million people with disabilities would be murdered. Hitler had also invited the fourth son of former German Kaiser Wilhelm II, Prince August Wilhelm of Prussia, also known as 'Auwi'. He was not yet a member of the Nazi Party but was in the Stahlhelm. A few years later, he would officially join the NSDAP as well as the SA, supporting Hitler so enthusiastically that the left-wing press ridiculed him as 'Auwi the Little Brown Shirt'.

For all the celebrity attendees, Hitler fretted over the absolute numbers of supporters that had gathered in Weimar. According to Baldur von Schirach, who was running errands on his bicycle all day, picking up Nazis from the station and showing them to their hotels, Hitler worried that there might not be enough people to fill the market square in front of the Elephant where he planned to appear at the key event the following day. He ordered Gauleiter Artur Dinter to summon more Thuringian NSDAP members to Weimar.[18] In the end, the local police counted 7,000–8,000 attendees, of whom 3,600 were Stormtroopers.[19] The liberal *Jenaer Volksblatt* scoffed the following Monday: 'The Weimar population, which two years ago had participated in high numbers, held back this time. The sea of flags seen back then became a puddle.'[20]

This hadn't been for a lack of advertisement. Weimarers were well aware that the Nazis were holding their party conference in their town. Hitler himself had sent a letter to the Thuringian government asking for permission to use the German National Theatre, which was duly granted against objections from the SPD faction, who thought it politically tasteless to 'hand over the site where the Weimar German republican constitution was created to people who have been convicted for attempted high treason against this constitution', as they put it in their parliamentary intervention.[21]

As late as Friday 2 July, a large, swastika-framed newspaper advert encouraged Weimarers to join the Reich Party Conference of the National Socialists. It invited everyone, old supporters as well as curious newcomers. But Jews were already explicitly excluded.[22] With Julius Streicher, Gauleiter of Nordbayern and publisher of *Der Stürmer*, and Artur Dinter, the programme contained two speakers whose verbal attacks on Jews were so aggressive that even fellow Nazis found them extreme. Goebbels noted in his diary: 'Dinter and Streicher spew bile.'[23] Baldur von Schirach attended Streicher's speech and remembered it as an 'embarrassing incident' that caused much headshaking from the 'alienated' audience. It wasn't enough to deter the young Nazi activist. Baldur concluded that such incidents were mere 'blemishes'. For him the movement was about 'Hitler, the camaraderie of like-minded people, the equality of high and low, rich and poor'.[24]

Sunday began with a meeting in the German National Theatre led by Hitler himself. This was strictly for party members and friends who could purchase a limited amount of tickets for 3 marks each.[25] Notably, Mayor Walter Felix Mueller stayed away from the ceremony. In the cradle of Germany's post-war democracy, Hitler performed a ceremony to sanctify a movement intent on killing the young republic. Artur Dinter was delighted: 'Where Ebert once sat, today Adolf Hitler sits and stands . . . This is the beginning of a new era!'[26]

Standard bearers of newly formed SA units, by now mostly clad in the distinctive brown shirts that gave the movement its colour and nickname, marched across the stage, one by one. Each touched their new flag to the so-called Blood Flag to consecrate it. The Blood Flag had been carried during the Munich Putsch in 1923 and allegedly became soaked in the blood of a killed SA man. At the National Theatre in Weimar, Hitler introduced this quasi-religious ceremony for the first time. Thereafter this flag consecration was often performed in public, including at the Nuremberg rallies after 1933 where other Nazi banners were 'sanctified'. Baldur watched the first of these rituals in Weimar with a sense of awe: 'For us young people this was a sacred act,' he remembered later, 'Hitler appeared to us at that moment to be more than a politician.'[27]

There were many other firsts that Sunday in Weimar. At the great hall of the Crossbow Society, the youth wing of the movement received its name: Hitler-Jugend or Hitler Youth. At another meeting, Rosenberg suggested using just one standard symbol for all Nazi publications: an eagle holding an oak wreath with a swastika in the middle. This would later become the official emblem of the Nazi state.[28] Hitler established another central ritual in the afternoon. Standing in an open-top car in front of the entrance of the Hotel Elephant, he greeted the SA troops with an extended right arm and they responded in kind. The Hitler salute had been used within the movement for a few years but this was the first time it had been presented in public.[29] Local reporters recognized it as a copy of Benito Mussolini's Roman salute. The *Jenaer Volksblatt* wrote: 'Hitler inspected a so-called parade there. He was greeted in the fascist way and responded in kind with a half-raised arm. Then he climbed on to a platform to be looked at for just under an hour.'[30]

This was another public first: having failed with his illegal attempt to seize power, Hitler now wanted to be seen to stick to the rules. Mayor Mueller had issued a speaking ban on Hitler, who was after all still forbidden from public speaking in most other places in Germany. He stuck to this, only addressing invited audiences indoors. While his followers encouraged him again and again to break Mueller's rule on the market square, Hitler stood in silence as his troops marched past.[31]

The thin veneer of discipline didn't fool anybody in Weimar. The Nazis were only in town for two days but managed to leave a trail of blood and disruption. Confrontations had already started on the trains to Weimar on Saturday. The Berlin delegation stopped the train conductor from continuing his onward journey because he'd allegedly called the Nazis 'nationalist pigs'. On their way down the hill and into the town centre, the men repeatedly clashed with police. In the afternoon on Saturday, a mass brawl in the station building had to be broken up by police, who confiscated several daggers and clubs. Later that night, communist and socialist paramilitaries were gathered in the Volkshaus when 300 Stormtroopers tried and failed to break in several times with the intention of burning the place down.[32]

Ordinary citizens were also harassed by the visitors. The Nazi delegates attacked public figures like Weimar's Jewish opera star Emil Fischer, who reported their exact words to the police later: 'We shit on the Jew Republic!', 'Beat the Jewish gang out of our German fatherland!', 'We need no Jew Republic, boo, boo, Jew Republic!' and 'We were born for the putsch, for the *coup d'état*, that's what we swore to Adolf Hitler!'[33]

Nazis broke into cars and vandalized buildings. Beatings and knife attacks led to countless injuries.[34] They insulted women who wore the fashionable bob haircut and beat up two students of the Bauhaus successor school. According to a police report, Julius Streicher was one of the perpetrators, showing that thuggery and a propensity for violence were baked into the movement right from the start and reached all the way to the top. Roland Freisler, who would later become the most infamous judge of the Nazis' murderous legal system, was among those involved in the mass brawl at the station, where he was egging on SA troops with the same sharp tongue he would later use to humiliate defendants in his 'people's court' before sentencing many of them to death.[35]

Hitler got involved personally to paper over the cracks in the

facade of respectability. When a group of his followers beat up a
worker on the market square, Gregor Strasser, a leading Nazi on the
left wing of the party, appeared at the police station shortly after and
apologized on behalf of Hitler, who had either been told about it or
witnessed the incident from a window at the Elephant.[36]

The worst incident occurred right in front of the Hotel Hohenzollern. At 3 a.m. between Sunday and Monday, loud shouting rang
through Paulinenstraße, which ran between the hotel and the train
tracks. Drunken SA troops had got into an argument and a violent
brawl broke out. Police officer Paul Schmidt, who'd been on duty
in the station, rushed to the scene but found that the situation had
already calmed down when he got there. Satisfied that the crowds
had dispersed, he turned around to walk back to his post, when shots
rang out.[37]

Schmidt collapsed. A pool of dark blood gathered on the cobbled
street beneath his body as he gasped for air. Someone had shot him
from behind with a pistol, piercing his left lung. Police immediately
searched all known places where SA men had taken accommodation. While they found a worrying number of firearms, daggers and
clubs, they couldn't identify the shooter, described as a young man,
around twenty, with a crimson swastika armband on his left arm.[38]
Schmidt was rushed to hospital. He was in critical condition but
alive. He would never work again and had to live off a pension of
160 marks a month – 66 per cent of his previous salary.[39]

'In the town there is intense embitterment about the conduct
of the swastika troops,' one local newspaper reported the Monday
after the Nazi rally.[40] Shellshocked by the violence, a meeting of the
town council accepted an SPD motion to never again allow Nazi
Party rallies to take place in Weimar. Mayor Mueller testified to the
atrocious behaviour he had witnessed: 'If you enjoy the right to be
somewhere as a guest, then it should be a given that you behave with
decency. But the National Socialists aren't good at that.'[41]

The leadership of the German National Theatre wrote to the
authorities to demand that the building would never again be
abused for political purposes. In the Thuringian parliament a heated

exchange ensued between the left-wing opposition and the conservatives whose majority continued to depend on the seven Nazi MPs. Their leader Dinter relished this. When an SPD delegate lambasted the conservatives for sanctioning the NSDAP rally, Dinter got up and claimed that police officer Paul Schmidt who was then still fighting for his life in hospital had actually been shot by a communist. That was too much for the KPD delegates. One of them picked up an ink pot and threw it at Dinter's head.[42]

The town council fretted about Weimar's reputation as the ugly scenes were reported in national newspapers. 'The conduct of the swastika gangs kept the Weimar police busy for the last few days and nights,' wrote the *Frankfurter Zeitung*. 'The *völkisch* men tried to act as though they owned the town,' declared another paper. The *Berliner Tageblatt* described how 'the town can breathe again now that only a few of Hitler's people remain here'. This is 'how the National Socialists behave if they are allowed even a little bit of leverage', the paper warned. It also criticized the Thuringian state government for being so lenient, which it saw as a 'very dangerous gamble of state authority, which, after all, is treated with contempt already from the National Socialists, especially in Thuringia'.[43]

The Nazis considered their first big rally a resounding success. Goebbels wrote in his diary: 'The Third Reich is coming.'[44]

On 10 July 1926, the Villa Silberblick was full of lively chatter. It was Elisabeth Förster-Nietzsche's eightieth birthday, and fifty-two people had gathered at her house for a celebratory lunch. For the afternoon reception nearly three times as many turned up to congratulate her.[45] Elisabeth had received so many flowers that the 'house had become a marvel of botanical art, so much so that the town's gardeners came to see the whole thing'.[46] She appeared to have reached the height of her powers.

Harry Graf Kessler couldn't make it to her party. In fact, he hadn't even sent her a note. He was gravely ill. What had begun as pneumonia quickly spread through his body, causing intestinal bleeding. His sister Wilma was looking after him in London. Wilma reassured Elisabeth that 'in all his severe suffering and never-ending weakness, his thoughts are with you at this time'. A cheque was enclosed for the 'betterment of the Nietzsche Archive'.[47]

The day brought more good financial news for Elisabeth. Reich President Paul von Hindenburg was granting Nietzsche's sister a special fund. Supporters had applied for this on the basis that 'Nietzsche's main work, *Thus Spoke Zarathustra*, was the book that was, alongside the Bible and Goethe's *Faust*, the one that was taken to the front the most by German soldiers' as 'it underlines the value of such soldierly virtues as toughness, obedience, discipline. By helping to spread these ideas, Nietzsche's sister has enabled the ethical impact of her brother's writings.'[48] Elisabeth was handed a letter from the Finance Minister, informing her of a personal monthly stipend of 150 marks from the President. The state itself would provide another 300 marks for the archive. 'So the worst of the emergency is averted,' she wrote to Harry.[49]

Events in Weimar were also keeping her in good spirits. As the cradle of the new post-war Germany, the town wanted to expand its place on the cultural landscape of the country, perhaps even rival the Bavarian town of Bayreuth as the place where the German elite flocked to celebrate the composer Richard Wagner. There was the annual Bayreuth Festival, so why shouldn't there be a Weimar Festival? No, Weimar had national ambitions. Only a 'German Festival' would do. The first one was to be held in the summer of 1926 to coincide with the fiftieth anniversary of the opening of the Bayreuth Festival Theatre in 1876. Conservatives like the composer Otto Daube had high hopes for it. 'It is the German spirit,' Daube argued, 'that we have preserved in Weimar and Bayreuth. If we stand by the two pillars of our German culture, we stand by ourselves.'[50]

Elisabeth thought she could help build bridges between the festival and Bayreuth. Her brother had had an intense and complex relationship with Wagner, who was thirty-one years his senior. Wagner and his wife Cosima, who was closer to Nietzsche's age than that of her husband, treated him like a son, but the two men fell out. Nietzsche became so obsessed with their feud that he continued it after Wagner's death. His last completed pieces before his mental breakdown included *The Case of Wagner*, a book in which he critiqued Wagner's music, and an essay entitled 'Nietzsche contra Wagner'. Elisabeth took it upon herself to take on this strand of her brother's legacy along with all the others. She invited the Wagner clan to the Nietzsche Archive for breakfast while they were in town for the German Festival. She wrote to Harry that this 'ended with some general soul fraternization without either party making any concessions to the other'.[51] Her friend found the whole episode rather distasteful, noting in his diary: 'And so the great, world-shaking feud Richard Wagner–Nietzsche, "The Case of Wagner", fizzles out at the coffee table . . . It's all so infinitely affected'.[52] The German Festival itself didn't take off either, making a loss of 30,000 marks. It would never happen again in this format.[53]

Despite her exciting summer, Elisabeth was under no illusion as to how frail she was. A few days after her birthday, the strain of the celebrations caught up with her. Attempting to write 'about 600 thank-you notes', she began to feel weak and 'a time of great depression began'.[54] Her friend Rudolf Eucken and the University of Jena rector Professor Gutbier both died in short succession after her party. 'Both had delivered such wonderful, truly friendly speeches at my birthday,' she wrote to Harry in disbelief. Eucken 'had spoken so refreshingly, youthfully and enthusiastically and we were both delighted to be 80 years old . . . a singular feeling of loneliness came over me, as if I were a relic from a world which nobody understands any more.'[55]

On 20 October, Hitler checked in at the Hotel Elephant. This was to be a short visit but an important one. Thuringia was a key battleground in the fight for Germany, and Hitler wanted to rally far-right groups behind his Nazi Party for the upcoming state elections, which were to be held in January 1927. His party now had close to 50,000 members, nearly twice as many as the previous year. In Weimar, he gathered the leaders of organizations like the Stahlhelm and the Association of Front Warriors in one room and lectured them for over three hours, impressing on them how important it was that they fought the campaign together. When Hitler left Weimar the next day, he was confident that he had aligned his political foot soldiers.[56]

At Christmas 1926, dark thoughts troubled Carl Weirich's mind. Baby Wilhelm was doing well but it was by no means certain that the boy would grow up at Geleitstraße 10. Carl's neighbour Frau Straubel owned the house, but she was getting old and her daughter wanted to sell up. Carl was given the option to buy it for 38,000 marks so long as he could put a deposit down immediately. This 'bitter pill' was hard to swallow.[57] If he couldn't find the money quickly, they could lose everything: their home and the shop. Soon, Frau Straubel's son-in-law returned and told Carl that he had found a buyer who was willing to pay 41,000 marks.

Now Carl and Marie sat with Wilhelm in their newly refurbished flat wondering if this was their last Christmas there. Marie's brothers Wilhelm and Anton came over and the family undertook a bracing winter walk together up the Ettersberg hill where they talked things through. Both of Wilhelm's uncles tried to be reassuring. They could help a little. Carl resolved to talk to the bank to see if he could get a loan.

By 30 December, the Weirichs had made a decision. Scraping together everything they had and what Marie's brothers were able to give, they took out a mortgage to cover the rest. They paid the 41,000 marks and nearly 3,000 marks in legal costs. It was hugely worrying but also exciting. It was the Weirichs' wish for the New Year that 'we might continue to live together peacefully under one roof with our future tenants and share joy and grief with one another as we have done since 1914'.[58]

1927

Adolf Hitler felt the Thuringian state elections on 30 January 1927 were important. The last ones in 1924 had led to the lifting of restrictions on the Nazi Party. Munich would always be the 'capital of the movement', but Thuringia was the 'heart' of the country. So the Führer campaigned for nearly two weeks, including two stops in Weimar.[1] But to no avail. The elections ended in great disappointment for the Nazis. The NSDAP won just two seats in the newly elected state parliament. They were filled by Artur Dinter and Willy Marschler, who had both been among the seven *völkisch* MPs in the previous term. Overall, the election produced no clear winner. The conservative bloc suffered drastic losses and formed a minority government with three smaller parties. The two Nazi MPs went into opposition, no longer able to pull political levers.

With the economy propped up by American loans, tourism flourished again in Weimar. Between 1927 and 1928, overnight stays increased by over 60 per cent from 77,000 to 125,478, giving Rosa and Arthur Schmidt the confidence to invest.[2] The Hotel Hohenzollern already provided several income streams. Apart from the rooms and restaurant, it had a café, a festive hall that was rented out for events and smaller club rooms where many associations met on a regular basis. Now Arthur had an idea how unused space in the basement could be monetized. At the moment, it just provided spaces to store wood and coal, a stable for six horses, the laundry and the beer cellar. There were two spare rooms.

Arthur wrote to the town council manager for his alcohol licence to be extended to the cellar, soon dubbed the 'Beer Tunnel'.[3] He made a compelling case, arguing that he wouldn't be competing with the 'better places' in the area. The windowless space wasn't nice enough for that. Arthur and Rosa intended to cater to 'less wealthy travellers', 'people travelling for business' and the many 'coach drivers and chauffeurs' that hung around the station waiting for punters. Arthur even promised to install an extra telephone, which would make the rooms a great alternative to the station waiting room, where there was always trouble. The Schmidts would serve these hard-working people 'beer and other fortifying, spiriting drinks as well as food at cheap prices'.[4]

The authorities consulted the police, who were supportive. As it happened, a group of drivers had recently petitioned to be provided with a room in the train station where they could wait during inclement weather. Ideally, they said, it should have a telephone to arrange their pickups. This had been turned down since the drunken and at times rowdy behaviour of some of the drivers had been a nuisance around the station. 'So if the landlord of the Hohenzollern Schmidt can provide waiting rooms for these people (that is in close proximity to their vehicles) with a telephone and serving food and drinks, then this enterprise can only be supported,' wrote a police official. 'That way, most of the chauffeurs and coach drivers are off the street while they are waiting.'[5]

The landlords of the other hotels near the station were also happy with the Schmidts' proposal – an indication of how well respected they and their business had become in the area. When one official raised the concern that Arthur's 'Beer Tunnel' may encourage rowdiness, Otto Jacob, owner of the Preußischer Hof (Prussian Court), argued that this was nonsense. After all, 'it was in his own interest to keep his premises calm and orderly'. Besides, added Jacob, he also catered to drivers and in his view most of them were 'sensible people, who advocate to eradicate drunken colleagues'.[6]

After months of anxious waiting, on 4 June the Schmidts finally received formal permission to establish their Beer Tunnel. What seemed a small step on paper marked a new chapter in the Schmidts' life as a family. The Hotel Hohenzollern hadn't just survived the difficult years of hyperinflation but was beginning to thrive. The couple had a new project to sink their teeth into. Their eldest son Arthur, who was now twenty years old, had moved out. Taking after both his parents, he wanted to see the world and found employment on a cruise ship. His older sister Alexandra was still helping at the Hohenzollern but it was just a question of time before she would marry and move out. Ernst was thirteen now and Horst five. The Schmidts had established themselves in Weimar – unstable politics or not.

Kurt Nehrling was steadily building back from times of hardship. The social democrat was grateful to have retained his position as a civil servant in the Thuringian Ministry of Economics despite ongoing health issues and being a single father to five-year-old Ursula. The shock of losing his wife and second child still sat deep, but Kurt was only twenty-eight and determined not to give up on life and happiness. Despite all he had endured, he never stopped wanting to learn, read and discuss, to find a way to make a difference. In 1925, he'd joined a group of fellow intellectuals in the Weimar branch of the German Association of Monists who argued for a science-based, freethinking world view. Through SPD circles, he met fellow party member Hedwig, or Heddy, as her friends called her. They got married in December 1926.[7] Kurt's idealism had got him through the deepest crisis. Now, it was time to settle and build a new family home.

Kurt didn't find it easy to build or buy accommodation on the Weimar Republic's overheated housing market. He was a member of a not-for-profit housing cooperative for war veterans, which was building a new settlement north of Röhrstraße, a thoroughfare north-east of the town centre. Kurt and Heddy wanted to join this project, building a semi-detached house with two floors, a basement and an attic. The newbuild was set to cost 11,440 marks, but even with a 5,000-mark loan from his employer Kurt could only raise 6,100 marks. For the remaining sum he wrote to the state authorities, who were able to loan people up to 3,500 marks by law. That still wouldn't have been enough, but Kurt argued that an exception ought to be made for disabled veterans.

Kurt's debilitating tuberculosis classified him as '60% disabled by war'. In the end no exception was made and he had to top up the shortfall with a mortgage from a private bank. He may have owed his employer, the state and the bank eye-watering amounts of money but eventually all loans were granted and the Nehrlings were building their own home in Weimar. On 7 September 1927, it was ready for them to move in.[8] Their road was called Heimstätten-Weg after the name of the housing cooperative. Today, it is the Kurt-Nehrling-Straße.

Wilhelm Weirich said his first word on 27 March and it was 'Papa'. Or did his proud father imagine that? No, Wilhelm definitely said 'Papa', Carl decided, and proudly recorded it in the baby book. Things weren't always easy at Geleitstraße 10. Wilhelm was teething and going through the usual childhood illnesses, including a heavy case of mumps. But he was a strong boy and took his first steps at Carl's hand by August.[9] Wilhelm's first birthday on 24 June was a highlight for his parents. The baby was showered with gifts, receiving a tiny pair of leather boots, a silver spoon and clothes. At the exact hour of Wilhelm's birth, Carl lit a candle on a slice of cherry cake that he carried to his cot. The 'boy didn't have anything to say about that!' his father joked.[10]

A family photograph of Carl, Marie and Wilhelm Weirich, taken on 11 November 1927 by Carl's brother Otto.

Despite the daunting mortgage the Weirichs had taken out to buy Geleitstraße 10, they were recovering financially. Carl had secured a middle-ranking position within the Thuringian State Association of Bookbinders and Paper Merchants. For one thing, this made him a linchpin for textbook production in the area. It was his job to organize the distribution of printing paper to the bookbinders, and when they had produced the school books, they were stored in his shop until they were picked up by the paper merchants who sold them to customers. Carl made a fair bit of additional income in the process, which was 'very much needed for this year and the next few, given the dearly purchased business premises', he noted.[11]

Another perk of his new role was that it allowed him to travel for conferences and training courses. This was exhilaratingly glamorous. When the State Association held a conference in the town of Sonneberg in southern Thuringia, he was flown in from Weimar. 'My first-ever aeroplane flight,' he noted with real awe. Air travel was still a futuristic novelty and here Carl was, soaring over the dark green mountains of Thuringia. At the conference, he made a new friend, Theo Rüdiger, who invited him to Bayreuth for the Wagner Festival, where the two men received their tickets from Winifred Wagner.

Richard Wagner's thirty-year-old daughter-in-law was now a fully paid-up member of the Nazi Party. She was so close with Hitler that she was one of the very few people who addressed him with the informal 'Du', and her four young children called the Führer 'Unkel Wolf'. Goebbels was utterly infatuated with Winifred. 'A vivacious woman,' he gushed in his diary. 'They should all be like that. And fanatically on our side.'[12]

The Nazis relied on fervent supporters like Winifred Wagner to carry the movement through the so-called Golden Years of the Weimar Republic. The young democracy was by no means out of the woods, but most Germans had lost their appetite for extreme politics. As in Thuringia, NSDAP support fell nationally. Hitler used those meagre years to grow a solid party base. Between 1926 and

1928, membership of the NSDAP doubled to over 100,000 despite the poor results at the ballot box.

Hitler's early followers weren't opportunists riding the tides of extremism. They were fanatics swimming against the currents of moderation. Baldur von Schirach continued to be one of them. Now twenty and a recent graduate of the prestigious Realgymnasium in Weimar, he was convinced that a new life awaited him in Munich. He had never forgotten that Hitler himself had invited him there, and how good that had felt. He enrolled as a student of German, English and Art History at the Ludwig Maximilian University on 30 April 1927.[13] Defending this choice to his father, he declared: 'I want to be near Hitler.'[14]

The Führer may have called his young admirer to Bavaria but he wasn't exactly waiting for him. At first, Schirach just couldn't get hold of him in Munich, which he found intensely frustrating. He knew he could play a role in exploring a new target group for the Nazis: university students. They had so far preferred their old, conservative organizations and fraternities. Schirach believed Hitler's charisma could win them over to Nazism. In the end, it was sheer luck that provided him with the opportunity to talk to Hitler when he spotted him walking his German shepherd dog. Hitler immediately recognized the young man from Weimar and invited him back to the small room he rented in Munich. They drank tea as Schirach explained how the Nazi student movement needed a spark, a speech from Hitler.

Hitler was sceptical. He believed that a largely upper-class audience like Schirach's fellow students wouldn't be susceptible to the trance-like state he induced in beer halls. He didn't want to risk being heckled or, worse, face a half-empty venue. Schirach offered Hitler a deal: he'd book the Hofbräuhaus beer hall and ensure a room full of students. That would grant Hitler the tried and tested environment of a packed beer hall – any unfilled seats or any problems and Schirach would speak to the students himself.[15] The evening of 21 November 1927 was a complete success for Schirach. The room was 'so packed out that students sat on the tiled stoves', as he recalled.[16] Hitler had clearly underestimated how much political anger there was among the student body. Their parents had lost status and wealth in recent years, leaving many of the students fearing for their own future. Many were also deeply antisemitic, sentiments further inflamed by the arrival of Jewish students from states in central and eastern Europe where access to university had been restricted for them. Hitler was surprised by the wave of resentment he was able to whip up that night.[17] The event would prove to be his breakthrough at German universities, where he would gain some of his most fervent supporters. Hitler was deeply impressed by the man who had opened the ranks of young intellectuals to his movement. He appointed Schirach Reich Führer of the National Socialist German Students' League in July 1928.

Soon after Baldur von Schirach had departed for Munich, a delegation of Thuringian Nazis arrived there. Fritz Sauckel, Deputy Gauleiter of Thuringia since February, and Hans Severus Ziegler, who had held that same position since 1925, had come to present their grievances about their boss, Gauleiter Artur Dinter. Dinter wasn't committed to the party, they complained, he'd lost touch with ordinary members and he was a religious zealot whose erratic leadership had caused permanent rifts within the Thuringian chapter of the NSDAP.[18]

The Deputy Gauleiters didn't have to make this up. Dinter shared the Nazis' racism, and specifically their antisemitism, but for him the movement was about the religious redemption of the German people. Earlier in the year, he had founded the Religious Community of Spiritual Christianity, in which his own role was that of a 'perfector of the Reformation'.[19] By that he meant that German Christians should abandon all traces of the older religion of Judaism from their faith, for instance by dismissing the Old Testament as Jewish. This was not only quite far removed from Hitler's more neutral approach to religion but also challenged the Führer's authority over the ideological direction of Nazism.

Hitler gave way to Sauckel and Ziegler, dismissing Dinter as

Gauleiter on 28 September 1927 and appointing them as Gauleiter and Deputy respectively. The path was clear for Sauckel to take over the Thuringian NSDAP at a time when the role of Gauleiter had not yet been clearly defined. He proved to be an effective Gauleiter with an instinct for identifying useful people. The twenty-seven-year-old Martin Bormann, for instance, had just moved back to his mother in Oberweimar on the south-eastern outskirts of Weimar and joined the Nazi Party as member 60,508 when both he and Ziegler took him under their wing.

Bormann was a disoriented young man who came from a humble background and had lost both his father and a brother at a young age. After the war, he'd become radicalized and joined a Freikorps paramilitary unit that got him involved in far-right political activity and violence. In 1924, he and his friend Rudolf Höss, the later commandant of Auschwitz, committed a murder in which the victim was brutally beaten before his throat was cut. Höss received a ten-year-sentence, and Bormann one year for acting as his accomplice.

Ziegler and Sauckel recognized the ruthlessness, organizational talent and ideological fanaticism in the young man. Bormann began to work for Ziegler, helping him produce and distribute his paper *Der Nationalsozialist*.[20] For Sauckel he worked as a driver. They had briefly tried him as a press officer but his unpolished mannerisms and lack of public-speaking experience made him unsuited to this role. It became clear, however, that Bormann's previous experience as a farm manager made him an efficient business leader for the Gau.

Bormann moved to Munich the following year where he began a steep career trajectory that was to lead him all the way to the top. He would one day become Hitler's private secretary and head of the Nazi Party Chancellery. It worked for all sides. Hitler had received a man he trusted to become one of his closest aides while Sauckel and Ziegler had proved that they were capable of running the crucial Gau Thuringia with a finely attuned sense for loyal party soldiers.

Sauckel also proved that unlike Dinter he was a hard-working campaigner for the Nazi Party. He travelled around the eighty-two local group offices tirelessly, speaking to everyone in the movement and making his presence known. He absorbed people's anger and amplified it. There was no trace of the detached intellectualism of Dinter about him. With the mix of populism, ruthlessness and sympathy that he had so admired in Hitler, Sauckel moved around his Gau and either won people over or expelled them. It worked. Membership in the Gau had risen under Dinter too, from 600 in 1925 to 720 in 1927, but under Sauckel it doubled within his first year in office.[21] Hitler was satisfied.

Carl Weirich knew nothing of the wranglings within the Nazi Party, nor would he have cared if he had. He had other concerns. On 11 October, he received an urgent telephone call from his brothers in Eisenach. His mother had suffered a stroke. The news hit him with blunt force. Marie Weirich was nearly eighty-four years old, and had visibly declined throughout the year. Carl had sensed that she was getting frail. But he loved his mother dearly, and nothing could have prepared him for the shock.

Marie Weirich passed away the next morning. 'She isn't there any more,' her devastated son wrote in his diary, 'she who has given me, her youngest, everything: life, a happy childhood, appreciation for nature and, from both father and mother: care for my economic existence! Thank you for that! Support during the difficult war years, when I lost my child and my wife Friedel and then renewed joy and happiness through the beginning of my second marriage. Support during the birth of my son and heir. Trust when we bought our house. Grandmotherly devotion to our little Wilhelm! For all that, eternal gratitude!'[22]

As Carl Weirich grieved for his mother, Harry Graf Kessler was wrestling with a very different problem. He was still frail from his protracted illness but well enough to visit Weimar. Unfortunately, this coincided with an event he was expected to attend but would rather have avoided. Polite as he was, he had no idea how to get out of this social obligation.

Elisabeth Förster-Nietzsche was hosting a Nietzsche Conference from 15 to 17 October, which would have been the philosopher's eighty-third birthday. The star speaker was Oswald Spengler, a conservative nationalist whose book *The Decline of the West* was immensely popular among German intellectuals, having sold hundreds of thousands of copies. In it, he argued that cultures developed like organisms, growing and flourishing before they invariably decline and die. According to Spengler, the West was in its 'evening' and would soon collapse, just like the Roman Empire.

The reception of *The Decline of the West* was deeply divided. Many scholars thought the book was shoddy. Others, including Hitler, who had read it in prison, despised its pessimism. Yet others became fervent Spengler fans because his work hit a raw nerve in the post-war era when a sense of crisis was all-pervasive, giving the impression that humanity in general and Western culture in particular had reached a catastrophic end point. Elisabeth was one of Spengler's admirers, especially as he based much of his writing on her brother's philosophy. Spengler sat on the board of the Nietzsche Archive and was a frequent visitor at the Villa Silberblick, giving keynote addresses like the one on 15 October with the title 'Nietzsche and the Twentieth Century'.[23] Elisabeth couldn't wait to introduce him to Harry Graf Kessler.[24]

For his part, Harry had no desire to meet the anti-democratic activist. For Spengler the Weimar Republic was weak because it was limited in its actions by the will of the masses. For him, the way forward lay in the destruction of the republic by a dictator. Spengler didn't believe this was Hitler, because he found Nazi ideology barbaric and crude. He'd declined offers to write for Nazi publications. Much like his host Elisabeth, he admired Mussolini.

Harry found it difficult enough to contain his contempt for Elisabeth's admiration of the Italian dictator. 'I stayed silent out of politeness,' Harry told his diary.[25] But Elisabeth was an old friend, no matter how far her political views diverged from his. Spengler was a different matter. He couldn't stand the man and tried to make an excuse for not going to Elisabeth's Nietzsche Conference. But her 'sad face'[26] persuaded him to attend Spengler's lecture for their friendship's sake. Nonetheless, he was frank with her. 'To be completely honest and between us: I wouldn't feel comfortable meeting Herr Oswald Spengler in an intimate setting. I don't hold anyone's views against them and am in regular contact with people from the far right to the far left; but there are forms of political agitation and of intellectual arrogance that are so unpalatable that one should rather avoid those who espouse them . . . I ask you not to take it badly if I judge a man so harshly whom you clearly regard as wonderful.'[27]

Their ideological worlds were drifting apart inexorably, barely held together by a thin strand of personal affection. Harry noted that Elisabeth was 'as kind and friendly as ever; but sadly one gets the feeling that everything is steeped in petite-bourgeois affectations that stand in contrast to Nietzsche. Like when she always repeats how she was a "German émigré" (she hasn't made it out of the country in thirty years), and that that's why she couldn't be anything but a German nationalist . . . It is painful to hear such nonsense from Nietzsche's sister in the Nietzsche Archive!'[28]

Spengler's lecture on 15 October did nothing to dispel Harry's contempt. The Nietzsche Archive didn't have room for such an event, and so the great hall at the Erholung had been booked. It was already overcrowded when Harry arrived. There was no way he could stand for the whole talk. Someone got him an extra chair. It didn't take long before Harry regretted coming at all. The whole thing was a 'debacle', he fumed in his diary. Not mincing his words, he described Spengler as a 'fat priest with a fat chin and brutal mouth' who 'for an hour presented the most hackneyed, trivial stuff . . . Yes, Spengler somehow managed to make Nietzsche boring.'[29] Harry left Weimar the next day with an ominous feeling hanging over him. The Nietzsche Archive was beginning to take a very dark turn.

Rosa and Arthur Schmidt had a busy night on 27 November. Adolf Hitler was due to speak at the Hotel Hohenzollern and the whole place was brimming with Nazis from all over the country. The

Führer had summoned anyone who held political office for a strategy meeting ahead of the federal election scheduled for the next year. While Hitler now preferred to stay at the upmarket Hotel Elephant, he continued to use the more reasonably priced Hohenzollern and its larger spaces for talks and gatherings. This time Sauckel had booked it for Hitler to speak to the other Gauleiters, Reichstag MPs and Nazi members of state parliaments. Hitler stressed that he'd decided to shift the campaign focus away from working-class voters. He felt that they had taken as many of those from the KPD and the SPD as they were ever going to and that there was much more to be gained by focusing on 'small retailers, who are threatened by competition through department stores, and clerks, many of whom are antisemitic already'.[30] He had no idea that he spoke those words in a hotel run by a Jewish woman.

That night, Hitler held another event, a 'Welcome Evening' at the Hohenzollern. This time, he focused more on defining Nazi opinions on German culture. *Der Nationalsozialist* reported later: 'In sharp words he decried the soul poisoners of the German people, who commit their mischief in Weimar too, that town of the highest cultural traditions, and who defile this site of awe-inspiring art reprehensibly with nigger and jazz music.'[31] As Hitler ranted about modern art and the threats he thought it posed to what he regarded as German culture, Arthur and Rosa served beer and made sure the Nazi delegation had a good time. It was a full and raucous evening at the Hohenzollern and that was good for business.

Late on Christmas Eve 1927, as families across Weimar sat in their houses exchanging presents by candlelight, Carl Weirich was alone in his shop. The place was a mess, and, Christmas or not, he wanted to finish putting everything in order before he could enjoy the festivities and take some time off. The last few months had been a whirlwind of activity, never giving him enough room to focus on one thing at a time. In his new role as industry captain for the regional paper and book sector, he had sat in on board meetings on things like hymn-book production and communal paper acquisition strategies for Thuringian government ministries. It was satisfying work but demanding all the same.

It hadn't been enough to dull the aching loss of his mother. As Carl pottered around his shop on Christmas Eve feelings of bitterness crept into his grief. The reverence for their mother's memory had lasted barely a month before he and his siblings had fallen out over her inheritance. On 13 November, they had all met together with their spouses at his brother Emil's house and tried to be rational about it. But soon an argument broke out over the value of individual items since it was difficult to compare the prices his parents had paid for them before 1914 to what they would be worth now. The war, hyperinflation and a new currency didn't make these calculations straightforward. Heated words were exchanged at a family meeting. Carl grabbed his hat, about to storm out on his siblings, when Emil urged everyone to calm down and put their differences aside. Carl reluctantly agreed to stay, but the matter remained unresolved.

Carl felt miserable about the whole affair. Why did his brother Otto think it was worth losing his family over a bit of extra cash? He thought of the family he had lost and the one he had gained. He was downstairs in his shop when he should have been upstairs with Marie and Wilhelm. He would make sure to spend Christmas Day with them, 'unwrapping presents underneath the Christmas tree with little Wilhelm, now 18 months old'.[32]

1928

Elisabeth Förster-Nietzsche's long friendship with Harry Graf Kessler was threatening to break apart. She couldn't understand why a cultured man like him couldn't see that democracy and republicanism were a peril to German culture. As a member of the monarchist DNVP, she'd initially favoured a return of the Kaiser. Wilhelm II was now sixty-nine years old and continued to live in exile in the Netherlands, barred from re-entering Germany. His second wife Hermine, who was nearly thirty years his junior and styled herself 'Empress' or 'Kaiserin' despite having married Wilhelm four years after his abdication, visited Elisabeth regularly at the Nietzsche Archive for tea and discussions. However, a restoration of the monarchy appeared unlikely, and Elisabeth was more and more convinced that a dictator was the answer, someone who would restore German honour with an iron fist, someone like Mussolini.

Elisabeth began to host the first public lectures supporting Italian fascism in 1928.[1] She believed this was the right thing to do, but it came at a heavy personal price. The politicization of the Nietzsche Archive was a tragedy as far as Harry was concerned and her friend found it increasingly unbearable to see her, even for coffee, under the circumstances. On his last visit at the beginning of March, the pair had clashed so vehemently that they didn't talk or write to each other for weeks. Harry had no time to resolve the matter as he was feverishly working on a biography of the murdered former Foreign Minister Walther Rathenau. So Elisabeth had all the more time to ponder what had happened to their friendship.

Given the deafening silence from Harry, she resolved to write him a farewell letter. With her customary self-aggrandizement, she likened the rift between them to the complex relationship between her brother and Richard Wagner. So she intended to begin her letter to Harry with the same words Friedrich Nietzsche had sent to the famous composer: 'We don't want to hide the fact that we have become estranged.' Just as she was about to put pen to paper, her eyesight suddenly deteriorated. Eye specialist Dr Meyer-Steineg advised spending some time in health clinics. So that's what she did, at first in Weimar and then a fortnight at the hospital in Jena. 'Much good it did,' she grumbled, 'but I had time to think about a lot of things.'[2]

The silence was finally broken when Harry sent a bouquet of flowers up to the Villa Silberblick for Easter. They drove Elisabeth to tears and she immediately responded with a letter. At the health clinic, she had reminisced about happier times, when, at the turn of the century, she, Harry, the painters Henry van de Velde and Ludwig von Hofmann and a few others had worked towards creating a *Neues Weimar*, a New Weimar that could be a cultural cradle for a new Germany. But even then, she now reflected, there had been a gulf between her and the others, a gulf that came from the heavy burden of her brother's legacy.[3]

In her high age Elisabeth felt more than ever that it fell to her to ensure that the visions of her brother, such as she saw them, were realized. Nietzsche had written: 'I want to create a new class: an order of higher humans with whom those of troubled spirit and conscience can take counsel; who like me know not only how to live beyond political and religious doctrines, but have also overcome morality.'[4] Elizabeth enclosed a new, one-volume version of *The Will to Power* in which she'd underlined the passage in red ink. She confided in Harry that she had always hoped that he 'would create the order of those higher humans of whom my brother had dreamed'. She could now see, however, 'that it may still be too early to think about that . . . Now take this Easter present in friendly reciprocation, my dear friend, and perhaps you can understand . . . that I have the right to see things in this world a little differently from other people.'[5]

Harry wrote back the next day, saying he'd found both pain and solace in Elisabeth's words. They reflected how far the two had drifted apart but also what connected them still on a 'higher level'. Day-to-day politics, he suggested, did not belong on that higher level. Hadn't Nietzsche looked for people who knew 'how to live beyond political and religious doctrines'? 'I have strived my whole life to, yes, take politics seriously since it belongs to those things on which our daily life and work depend, but to bar it from entering into my relationships with higher humans as a matter of principle,' he wrote in an effort at reconciliation.[6]

Harry Graf Kessler's liberalism inoculated him against the moral angst that beset many of his peers despite the relative recovery of the economy. Many sensed that the veneer of stability was paper thin. Culture in the Weimar Republic fed on impermanence, trauma and uncertainty. The result was a dizzying kind of hedonism. The urban middle classes danced, filmed, viewed, painted, listened and built as they got swept away by an intense tide of creativity. Berlin in particular became a hotbed of experimentation. In the summer of 1928, Bertolt Brecht's *The Threepenny Opera* had its debut, offering an evocative critique of capitalism. Fritz Lang's dystopian film *Metropolis* was released the previous year. Cabaret and nightclubs offered entertainment everywhere. Marlene Dietrich was beginning to forge a career on stage and in film. But all this seemed far away from Weimar. Only a third of Germans lived in large cities. The frantic innovation that was happening there with strong influences from America alienated and unsettled many people in rural and small-town Germany. To the conservative elites in Weimar, the new culture seemed detached, foreign and subversive.

The prolific local architect Paul Schultze-Naumburg became so radicalized by his objections to modern culture that he turned into one of its most vocal critics. Like many of the interwar period's most visceral anti-modernists, he hadn't always been staunchly conservative. Born in Naumburg, around 45 kilometres north-east of Weimar, he had been immersed in art from a young age. His father was a portrait painter who counted many other artists and thinkers among his friends. Among those who frequented the Schultze-Naumburg home was the young Friedrich Nietzsche, whom Paul got to know as a child. The boy thrived in an environment surrounded by philosophers, poets and painters and showed immense talent from an early age. It came as no surprise that his parents decided to send him to art school.

After graduation, as a young man in the 1890s, he'd founded art schools himself in Munich and Berlin and joined groups of progressives in both cities that wanted to break away from traditional, state-funded art. Schultze-Naumburg travelled to France and Italy to broaden his horizons, and, like many other artists of this era, he firmly believed that art had the power to change the way people lived. Slowly moving away from fine art, he began to take an interest in architecture, design and clothing. At the turn of the century, he argued that modern women should be liberated from restrictive dress, especially from corsets, and he designed comfortable and practical clothing for women. While never a fan of urban life, he was keenly interested in technological progress, embracing innovations such as cars and cameras as they became more widely available.[7] But he also developed a profound scepticism towards modern cultural trends, which he perceived as cold, abstract and out of sync with tradition and life in Germany.

The houses Schultze-Naumburg designed before and during the First World War picked up local traditions but didn't aim to copy historical styles with all their flourish and opulence. He was a proponent of the so-called *Heimatschutz* or 'Home Protection' architecture, which sought to modernize and rationalize housebuilding but also preserve tradition by ensuring new buildings would blend into their environment. Schultze-Naumburg built himself an estate in Saaleck, south-west of Naumburg, according to this style, using timber, gabled roofs and other architectural features that blended this new structure into the quaint village. His Saaleck mansion became a hub for like-minded artists and a training centre for students of house and furniture building.

Schultze-Naumburg became a fashionable architect with wealthy clients who commissioned him to design villas for them in the leafy suburbs of Berlin and other large cities. Many of his customers were Jewish. Grand Duke Wilhelm Ernst also supported the local star architect and even the imperial family admired his work. During the war, he built Cecilienhof Palace for Crown Prince Wilhelm and his wife Cecilie in Potsdam. Amid the splendour of the Hohenzollerns' summer residences this last palace of theirs was built in the style of an English Tudor manor house. In 1945, it would be the location of the Potsdam Conference where Germany's post-war future was to be decided.

By the end of the First World War, Schultze-Naumburg had become a staunch conservative and opposed to the inherent modernism of the new era. Like Elisabeth Förster-Nietzsche, he joined the monarchist DNVP. Like her, he became more and more concerned about the state of German art and culture, vehemently opposing the Bauhaus movement – especially the flat roofs it favoured. He argued that gabled roofs were not only more practical and economic, but that they were also the natural and traditional way to build houses. An effective writer, capable of reaching wide audiences, he argued in a brochure on this topic in 1927 that 'the way the roof fits on a Nordic house' was the way most Germans naturally wanted their homes built.[8] As his fears and hopes for German architecture radicalized in the mid-1920s, the celebrated architect frequented the fashionable salons in Munich where Baldur von Schirach was also a regular guest. There, Schultze-Naumburg was introduced to Hitler. At Bayreuth, he also met Winifred Wagner and other far-right and völkisch thinkers. Joseph Goebbels and Heinrich Himmler visited him at his Saaleck home.

One of Schultze-Naumburg's protégés at this time was the racist author Hans F. K. Günther, whose thoughts on eugenics were to become such a prominent influence on Nazi race policy that people called him the 'Rassenpapst' or 'Race Pope'. The Saaleck Circle also included Hans Severus Ziegler and Wilhelm Frick. Frick had joined the NSDAP in 1925 as member 10, and in 1928 he became the leader of the parliamentary Nazi faction in the Reichstag.

It wasn't long before Schultze-Naumburg's angst about the state of German culture became one with his fears for Germany's ethnic purity. In 1928, his book *Kunst und Rasse* ('Art and Race') described modern art as 'degenerate'. The architect argued that the ugliness of its form was a mirror of the ugliness of the bodies and souls of those who produced it. He used photography to underline his point, juxtaposing images of expressionist art with images of people with physical and mental disabilities. This later became the basis for an exhibition the Nazis hosted in 1937 on 'Degenerate Art'. Schultze-Naumburg and his associates formed a group at Saaleck with the aim of protecting German culture from supposedly foreign and corrosive influences.

The Nazis saw political potential in the widespread moral panic. Hitler charged his ideologue Alfred Rosenberg with the formation of a *völkisch* and antisemitic 'National Socialist Society for German Culture'. This was founded on 4 January 1928 with Rosenberg as its Führer and Gotthard Urban in charge of finances. Urban was another Weimarer who had gone to school with Baldur von Schirach and Martin Bormann. It was Schirach who had introduced him to Rosenberg and he became one of the ideologue's closest associates.

By December the new organization had been renamed Kampfbund für deutsche Kultur (Militant League for German Culture) or KfdK and attracted support from influential people all over the Reich. When it presented itself to the public in January 1929, the KfdK could name Adolf Bartels, Carl von Schirach, Winifred Wagner and Paul Schultze-Naumburg among its many sponsors. Elisabeth Förster-Nietzsche had also attended the inaugural meeting of the Weimar chapter, which Hans Severus Ziegler held at the Hotel Elephant in March.[9] Asking for 12 marks in annual membership, the League promised to save 'that which is today deeply threatened: the German soul and its expression in creative life, in art and knowledge, law and education'. Like Schultze-Naumburg, the KfdK saw a connection between art and biology and took it upon itself to 'educate the German people about the links between race, art and science, decent and determined values'.[10]

The Nazis realized they would never reach everyone through mass rallies. It's hard to imagine people like Elisabeth Förster-Nietzsche standing outside for hours surrounded by tens of thousands of people. The all-important conservative elites had to be wooed in other ways and giving them a role in the KfdK proved remarkably effective. When the writer Adolf Bartels co-founded the Weimar branch, it immediately drew powerful support from the Nietzsche Archive. Bartels' influential co-founder was the scholar Hans Wahl, who was director of the Goethe and Schiller Archive and of the Goethe Museum (the poet's old house in the old town). Wahl had personally shown Hitler around on his visit in 1925, though he would later deny that the Führer had ever set foot in his hallowed halls. Goethe was to play a key role in the supposed rediscovery and defence of German *Kultur*. In his lifetime, the poet was a complex man with Jewish friends who nonetheless believed in some of the contemporary stereotypes about Jews. There was enough ambiguity there to remodel the legacy of the country's national poet into a new 'German Goethe' in the 1920s and 1930s.[11]

Baldur von Schirach was enthralled by the idea that, in contributing to Nazism, he was making history. His privileged upbringing in Weimar afforded him the opportunity to do whatever he wanted with his life. In 1928, he paused his political activism in Munich for a while to accompany his mother Emma on a trip to her home in the USA. While her husband was descended from German nobility, Emma came from a dynasty that was the closest thing America had to an aristocracy. She could trace her lineage back to Arthur Middleton, a Founding Father of the United States and signatory of the Declaration of Independence.

Her son was introduced to lofty company on their trip to Philadelphia and New York. Schirach's uncle Alfred E. Norris offered him a position in his bank in Manhattan.[12] Many might have deemed this preferable to peddling student politics for a political party that languished at 3 per cent of the vote nationally. But not Schirach, who politely declined the invitation and returned home to Hitler. In July, he was elected as Reich Führer of the National Socialist German Students' League.[13] Now leading the battle for the hearts and minds of Germany's future intellectual elite, he was just where he wanted to be, by Hitler's side.

Muted cheers rang through the Volkshaus in the early morning hours of Monday 21 May where social democrats, socialists and communists anxiously awaited the results of the German federal election. Weimar's left-wingers had high hopes that the papers might proclaim a 'Red Thuringia' based on an upswing in votes for the SPD and KPD in their state. The Thuringian results were in by 1.45 a.m. and announced on the radio as the first in all of Germany.[14] The KPD remained largely stable at 13 per cent of the vote; the SPD went up to 35 per cent from 30 per cent. Nearly half of the state had voted for left-wing politics, enough for one local paper to declare 'Lurch to the Left – Red Thuringia' on its front page. But in light of the fact that a narrow majority had voted for non-socialist politics, the same paper ended its analysis by asserting: 'In any case one can, now that the entire result is in, oppose the expected claim that Thuringia was now majority "red" again.'[15]

The Nazis had made no electoral headway in Thuringia despite a rise in party membership. They only achieved 3.7 per cent, down from 5.4 per cent in 1924. It was a huge disappointment for their supporters and activists given the enthusiastic reception they received wherever they went. In the Reich overall, the NSDAP also only managed to get 2.6 per cent. What happened in Thuringia more or less reflected the picture across Germany: the winners of the election were parties on the left and splinter parties that catered to very specific demographics, such as the middle-class Economic Party or Wirtschaftspartei (WP), which roughly doubled its vote to 4.5 per cent overall and 8 per cent in Thuringia.

The splintering of the middle-class vote was a reflection of the fact that many people in that income bracket were beginning to feel politically homeless as the parties they had previously voted for were hopelessly divided. The monarchist DNVP had become too radical for many voters under the influence of one of its founders and would-be leader Alfred Hugenberg. As Germany's most prominent media mogul, Hugenberg controlled around half of the press in the country, giving him enormous wealth and influence. He used this to push the party further to the right. This radicalization and internal division made the DNVP the biggest loser of the 1928 election. At Reich level it plummeted by 6.2 per cent to 14.3 per cent. In Thuringia it only got 5.4 per cent, down from 8.8 per cent. The pro-democracy parties benefited and received nearly half of the vote – the best result for them since the first election for the National Assembly in 1919.

Still, the political mobility of the middle classes pointed to simmering disaffection. For the time being, this found no vent because the economy was at its most stable since the pre-war era. With the exception of a looming agricultural crisis caused by overproduction, most sectors were busy building back from hyperinflation and chaos. Carl Weirich didn't even mention the elections in his diary, instead noting theatre visits, work trips and even a Bratwurst sausage he was particularly impressed with. Yet, beneath the surface of economic relief, an undercurrent of political malaise began to gather pace. At 76 per cent, the turnout of the federal elections was at the lowest in the young Weimar Republic's history. In Thuringia this was very noticeable. 'Polling day passed quietly in the entire constituency,' one paper reported, 'by 4 o'clock it was already obvious that the listlessness of the election campaign extended to the election itself.'[16]

Weimar itself reflected this listlessness in turnout and results. But in their support for one party, Weimarers stood out: 11 per cent of them – three times as many as their fellow Thuringians and four times as many as their fellow Germans overall – had voted for the Nazi Party.

For many Weimarers something far more exciting than elections was happening on 20 May. It was an unseasonably cold and overcast Sunday, but, undeterred by the inclement weather, many people flocked to the public lido known as the Schwanseewiesen (Swan

Lake Meadows).[17] Perhaps surprisingly for a town landlocked in the middle of Germany, Weimar had a lively and competitive swimming scene, producing many successful athletes in the field. But its facilities had long been too small for the size of the local population, and the professionalization of competitive sports in the early twentieth century also meant that it was increasingly unsuited to training athletes properly, never mind hosting competitions in Weimar.[18]

In 1926, the town council had agreed a plan to build not only a new, state-of-the-art lido that could compete with any in Germany, but also an entire sports complex around it. The Wimaria-Stadion, a multi-use stadium with capacity for 12,000 spectators, was nearly finished. The Weimarhalle, an event venue that would become the biggest in town, was also in the planning stages.[19] On 20 May, the Swan Lake lido was officially opened, providing a perfect opportunity for the townspeople to see the beginning of their impressive sporting landscape emerge. Many locals decided to take the plunge on the cold election Sunday in May.

The building of the modern sports park in Weimar was proof of the fact that the town had ambitions beyond the usual tourism and conference traffic. This suited Rosa and Arthur Schmidt just fine. Under their careful leadership, the Hotel Hohenzollern had cultivated a reputation as a meeting place for sports committees. With its location right by the station and a mere ten-minute stroll away from the Weimarhalle Park, it was an ideal venue for these kinds of gatherings, as it would be for athletes and officials in the future.

To put the Hotel Hohenzollern firmly on Weimar's sporting events map, the Schmidts ensured that they were involved in the preparations for the grand opening of the new Wimaria-Stadion, scheduled for 28 October. Football was still in its infancy as a spectator sport. But the English game had experienced a boom in Germany after the First World War, and Weimar wanted to be a part of that trend, opening the Wimaria-Stadion with an unforgettable football spectacle. The German Federal Football Convention was to be held in Weimar on 28 October accompanied by several high-profile games in the brand-new stadium. An all-star team consisting of the best players from the clubs of the Central German Football Association would play the official German Olympic team. There was a lot to organize at the preparatory meeting on 22 September that Rosa and Arthur hosted at the Hohenzollern.[20]

In the end, all went to plan. Weimar muscled in on the increasingly lucrative market of spectator sports. From 1928 onwards, competitions such as the German Swimming Championships in 1933 were held in its cutting-edge facilities. Rosa and Arthur Schmidt were once again right at the heart of developments in Weimar. On 17 December, the 'HOTEL HOHENZOLLERN Arthur Schmidt' became an officially registered business with an annual value of 11,000 marks.[21] The Schmidts proudly announced on letterheads that they were the 'best recommended house in the square'.[22]

The opening of the Wimaria-Stadion also turned out to be a great success. Around 10,000 spectators turned up to watch football on 28 October 1928, a record the stadium has never broken since. Political malaise notwithstanding, 1928 was a year of optimism for Weimar.

The 1928 election had produced such a fractured federal parliament that a majority could only be constructed by having no fewer than five parties together in a coalition that ranged from the left-wing SPD to the conservative – liberal German People's Party (DVP). As far as the conservative elites were concerned, the only silver lining was a safety net in the form of *Ersatzkaiser* Paul von Hindenburg. As head of state, he could influence coalition talks, ministerial appointments and the legislative process. His extensive emergency powers could also be used to rule by decree should the Reichstag become dysfunctional. But Hindenburg had turned eighty the previous year and was getting frailer by the day. The search for a suitable successor gathered pace.

The Reich President was directly elected by the people, but conservatives hoped that what they wanted was the same as many ordinary Germans: a well-respected representative of the pre-war era. Such a man could be presented as a tower of strength amid the chaos of parliamentary democracy. But who might be suitable? Erich Ludendorff, Hindenburg's deputy during the war, had withdrawn from politics. He now believed in wild conspiracy theories that bordered on paranoia. But there was another famous military leader of the First World War who appeared a credible option for a new leader to steer the German ship through the political storm.

In mid-November 1928, Admiral Reinhard Scheer was summoned from his home in Weimar to see Reich President Hindenburg. Scheer was now a sixty-five-year-old retiree, mostly concerned with writing books and cultivating the memory of his leadership of the fleet at the Battle of Jutland. But the 'Victor of Skagerrak' also campaigned relentlessly to rebuild the German Navy, which had been severely limited by the Treaty of Versailles, and to 'restore for us the place among the peoples of the world that we deserve'.[23]

Following failed forays into politics, first in the DNVP and later the DVP, he had largely retreated from political life. Many potential conservative allies were appalled by his lifestyle and views. Following the murder of his wife by a burglar in Weimar in 1920, he was rumoured to be having an affair with the politician and campaigner Katharina von Oheimb. She was an influential *salonnière* in Berlin with powerful contacts but lived a scandalous life by the standards of the time. She was married four times, enjoyed hunting and had a Zeppelin licence. Between 1920 and 1924, von Oheimb had been an MP for the DVP but also harboured socialist and progressive views, working towards the political emancipation of women. She seemed to be the one who convinced Scheer to join the DVP in 1921 but stay within its left wing, which argued for a collaboration with the SPD.[24]

Scheer had faced harsh criticism from the inner circle of the old military elites. His former Chief of Staff of the Naval Command Magnus von Levetzow complained bitterly of 'how easy would it have been for Scheer; all he had to do was sit tight on the plinth of Skagerrak that had been erected for him, the laurel wreath on his head would have become ever more golden, furthering the fame of his fatherland and the desire of future generations to emulate him. Instead he jumped off the plinth and revealed his stumbling mediocrity to all the world and – even worse – [he proved himself to be] an un-German man, a reed stick in the wind.'[25] But there simply was no other war-hero figure on which the military elites could pin their hopes for the presidency. According to von Levetzow, Scheer had been summoned to Hindenburg in November so that the ageing President could show him his testament, in which he 'recommended Admiral Scheer to the German people as his successor'.[26]

An essay Scheer wrote around this time showed that he had political ambitions. 'What Germany had been through decades of greatness, the home of peace in Europe, it can only become again when it has restored its right and might.' But he also made it clear that he thought there was a place for the SPD in this process – if the party could 'give up its toxic idea of the class struggle and its undignified and delusional internationalism'.[27] Scheer was a complex man full of contradictory ideas. But for the time being he seemed the conservatives' best bet to replace Hindenburg with a figure that Germans might trust and look up to.

There was only one problem. On 26 November 1928, days after he had visited Hindenburg, Reinhard Scheer suffered a stroke and died unexpectedly. Three days later, his body lay in state in the church of St Peter and Paul in Weimar. Flags were flying at half mast across the town and thousands of people had come to pay the dead admiral their last respects. For the service in the church, 600 tickets had been issued, but one local newspaper estimated that around 2,500 people squeezed in before the authorities decided to shut the doors for safety reasons.[28] His ashes were interred next to his beloved wife Emilie's in Weimar cemetery. The simple tombstone features the flag of the Imperial German Navy and underneath it just one word: 'Skagerrak'.

Bereft of one of their last war heroes, German conservatives clung on to the frail Hindenburg in their efforts to undermine the republic that they so despised. But they knew they were playing for time. Soon, the old man would retire or die. They would have to keep their eyes open for a younger man to lead Germany out of chaos and decline – a new kind of Führer.

PART III

Crisis

A mix of Hitlerism and Goethe

1929

Carl Weirich couldn't believe how cold the winter was. As a native Thuringian, he was used to snow-covered mountains in February, but this was something else. One Sunday in February at 10 a.m., he was meeting up with three friends to go for a long hike and enjoy the crisp, fresh air. As the men stepped off the narrow-gauge railway that had taken them to Kranichfeld, about 20 kilometres south of Weimar, it was −23°C. It would prove to be Thuringia's coldest winter in the twentieth century.

Undeterred, the friends set off from the station and hiked the 7 kilometres up the Riechheimer hill. A keen amateur photographer, Carl took beautiful images of the pristine landscape. When the men arrived at their destination, they stepped into the cosy restaurant at the top. It was busy. Skiers and hikers from Erfurt mixed with the locals as the timber-framed walls held in the warmth provided by a tiled stove in the corner. A vending machine offered postcards, chocolates and boiled sweets.

Blissfully ignorant of the troubles 1929 would bring, Carl gazed out of the window and marvelled at the dying light of a 'blood-red sunset'.[1]

Elisabeth Förster-Nietzsche went very quiet. Had she sent her two letters to Italy yet, or were they still on her desk? She couldn't remember. But what she'd just heard made her want to read them again, perhaps change a few things.[2] She snapped back into the room when Harry Graf Kessler stood up to leave. It was a late July afternoon when he had dropped by with his friend Helene von Nostitz, Paul von Hindenburg's elegant niece and a highly respected intellectual and *salonnière* in Berlin.[3]

Elisabeth was worried she'd offended them with her pensive mood. Had she ended a fascinating and highly pertinent discussion prematurely? She hadn't seen Harry since the pair nearly fell out over their political differences the previous year. Yet here they were, amicably discussing the effects of great historical figures on the 'higher human beings' her brother Friedrich Nietzsche had described, those 'free spirits' who rise to excellence by realizing their full potential. Could they flourish in a system dominated by a great and overbearing person?[4]

They had used Napoleon and Otto von Bismarck as examples. Both men were dominant figures with huge impact. Yet they allowed room for human creativity and excellence to flourish. As far as Harry was concerned, the same could not be said about Benito Mussolini. Straining to keep his tone 'purely factual', he conceded that the Italian dictator was an 'important man and statesman'. But he was 'no blessing for Italy and the world . . . and not the person to realize the ideals of your brother, either', Harry told Elisabeth firmly. Nietzsche had envisioned a world in which extraordinary, self-determined people had room to develop. Mussolini's Italy was 'the exact opposite: namely a form of state which by design suppresses the development of strong and free personalities'.[5]

Fascist Italy used 'police and military power' to suppress human growth on purpose. What's more, Harry elaborated, 'Mussolini fundamentally embodies the most dangerous tendency of democracy because he leans on his rule by . . . majority (however this may have been achieved) to cut off the existence of individual free people by law. What is slowly developing in the United States as the worst side of democracy, the rule of the stupid will of the masses over the will of the individual, fascist Italy enshrines in its fascist constitution. Mussolini is basically the most sublime embodiment of democratic herdthink . . . the thing your brother fought against most vigorously.'[6] This stopped Elisabeth in her tracks. She had pinned all her hopes on Mussolini as a role model for Germany. To her, it was obvious that the fatherland was inexorably marching towards the abyss unless a strong man stopped the madness.

Now eighty-two years old, Elisabeth was acutely aware that she didn't have many years left. She'd felt so severely ill at times that summer that she 'believed this could be the end of me soon', as she confessed to Harry a few months later.[7] A spell of ill health shook her so badly that she wanted to bring her affairs in order. She re-arranged the entire Villa Silberblick, 'thousands of books, boxes and folders had to be carried upstairs and downstairs. The whole thing greatly exhausted me, but I thought it was necessary,' she admitted. Personal effects were separated from archival files. She turned what had been a large dining room into a 'marvellous library and study for the gentlemen scholars, so the whole ground floor is now the archive. I moved into the upper floor near the rooms my beloved brother occupied. Those, too, have turned out very nice, and I have now sorted everything out that I needed to.'[8]

Financially, however, there were still many open questions. Some income for Elisabeth's projects suddenly appeared in the form of a mysterious donation of 20,000 marks that she was informed would now be an annual occurrence, but the generous donor insisted on complete anonymity.[9] She had no idea if this would continue after her death. The archive was supposed to outlast Elisabeth yet it relied on personal favours and grants to her. When she died, most of these might cease. Even worse, the next year, her brother would be dead thirty years, which meant his work would go out of copyright and she would lose control over its publication. This was a huge concern regarding royalty payments. Damocles' sword dangled over Elisabeth's life's work.

So what to do about Mussolini? Harry's comments about the Italian dictator being the opposite of what her brother would have wanted made her doubt her previous interest in promoting his regime. For the first time since the end of the First World War, she wondered: should she be 'glad that there isn't an exceptional, great man in Germany at the moment leading and guiding us'?[10]

In July, Carl Weirich was glad to spend a few days on a work trip to Danzig (now Gdańsk), where the Federal Association of Bookbinders held its annual conference. He needed a break from the headaches in Weimar. First, the cold winter had caused problems at Geleitstraße 10, creating costs for Carl on top of the high mortgage. Days after his scenic winter walk, temperatures had plummeted further, down to −38°C. Weimar's fountains and water pumps froze, as did the pipes and drainage in Carl's house, and he spent 150 marks on emergency plumbing.

But worse was to come. Carrying heavy piles of freshly printed school books, he suffered a painful hernia. It was the last thing he needed in the busy spring period, but the doctor insisted he needed surgery at the Sophienhaus hospital, just down the road from the Nietzsche Archive. His stay there wasn't too bad. Carl felt he was in good hands with the surgeon Dr Daumann. His fellow patients proved good company, and Marie and Wilhelm came to visit. Fifteen days' enforced rest wasn't the worst thing in the world. He even had time to read and devoured the novel *Gösta Berling's Saga* by the Swedish Nobel Prize-winning author Selma Lagerlöf. It had been made into a film a few years earlier, featuring a young Greta Garbo.

Carl had only been out of hospital for two days when more bad health news befell the Weirichs. The family doctor was very concerned about a cough Wilhelm had developed. Carl's heart sank.

Carl and Wilhelm Weirich walking near the spa town of Thal, Thuringian Forest, 20 May 1929.

He'd lost his first wife to lung disease, followed by many more loved ones over the last few years. He and Marie were too old to have more children. Wilhelm meant everything to them. So when the doctor suspected whooping cough and advised them to take the boy to the caves in the spa town of Thal, 70 kilometres west of Weimar, they did so. Wilhelm returned home to Weimar at the end of June, thankfully recovered.

Two weeks later, Carl was off to Gdańsk, determined to take time out for himself on his work trip. He knew the old port city by its German name Danzig, and 95 per cent of the population spoke German. But Danzig was no longer in Germany as it had been before the First World War. It was now a Free City with special rights for the newly independent Poland under the protection of the League of Nations, the new global peacekeeping organization. Carl wasn't resentful as such about this situation during his visit, but he nevertheless felt that the natural map of Europe had been artificially altered by the victors of the war. He noted in his diary how strange it felt to travel on a German train, surrounded by German passengers and with German food served in the dining car while the sealed carriages stopped nowhere as it passed through the 'so-called German corridor under Polish occupation as a result of the Treaty of Versailles'.[11]

Jutta Hecker's summer was as hectic as Carl Weirich's. Now twenty-four years old, she'd become a confident, well-educated woman since she'd left 'this Weimar with its Goethe' behind and moved to Munich.[12] 'As if out of opposition against [Weimar] Classicism' she chose to write her doctoral dissertation about a different topic: the blue flower as a symbol of Romanticism. Jutta never finished this project in Munich. She got engaged but shortly before the big day the relationship fell apart and with it Jutta's happiness.[13] 'Life led me through many catastrophes caused by personal blows of fate and by circumstances of the times,' she later mused, looking back on these years.[14] Disillusioned and disoriented, she packed her bags and returned home to Weimar without finishing her degree. She resolved never to talk about what happened, instead focusing fully on her old dream of becoming a renowned literary scholar like her father.[15] Max Hecker helped his daughter build on the work she had already done for the Goethe and Schiller Archive in her summer holidays. She became a freelancer for the institution, work she found satisfying and meaningful.

Every day in the archive, she walked past the bust of Princess Sophie of the Netherlands, who had also been the Grand Duchess of Saxe-Weimar-Eisenach. Sophie had inherited the entire Goethe estate in 1885 when the last grandson and descendant of Germany's national poet died, and she had worked to ensure that this legacy would be passed down responsibly from one generation to the next. So she had funded the building of the Goethe and Schiller Archive, completed in 1896, out of her own pocket.

The 'image of this lonesome brave woman' who worked so self-lessly to preserve Goethe's 'precious legacy' spoke to Jutta.[16] She would never marry, never have children. She would dedicate her entire life to the preservation and protection of the German cultural heritage that her father and the other Goethe scholars fretted over in these uncertain times. Before long, Jutta, like many of the staff at the archive, was part of circles that obsessed over the legacy of German literature. She began to frequent Elisabeth Förster-Nietzsche's events and discussions at the Villa Silberblick as she worked on cataloguing Goethe's extensive correspondence.[17] She also began writing and publishing, picking up her Munich dissertation again, this time working on it from Weimar.

In the summer of 1929, another Weimarer dropped out of Munich's Ludwig Maximilian University. Baldur von Schirach had never been particularly interested in academic study, but he'd found something he was passionate about: Nazism. He established himself as a speaker with encouragement from Hitler. In June and July alone, Schirach spoke in nineteen different cities across Germany. His audiences grew larger, not least due to support from powerful benefactors like Joseph Goebbels, who appeared with his protégé in Hamburg in front of 3,000 people on 1 July.[18] This hectic schedule proved incompatible with studying for a degree. 'I was one of the few Germans who were in the lucky position not to have to train for a particular profession,' he mused later.[19] Hitler agreed. 'Schirach,' he told him, 'you're studying with me!'[20]

All over Thuringia, people pored over maps in the morning of 12 September. One question was on everyone's lips 'in businesses, in offices and in workshops, even in schools', as a local paper reported: Would *Graf Zeppelin* come this way today?[21] Nobody could be sure which path the famous airship would take, but 'Zeppelin fever' spread far and wide. Many Weimarers flocked out in the afternoon hoping to catch a glimpse of the glamorous future of travel.

LZ 127 *Graf Zeppelin* wasn't the first rigid airship ever built but it captured the imagination of millions. It had just completed the first circumnavigation of the world by airship. This 'deutsche Weltfahrt' or 'German world tour', as the press soon dubbed it, was a source of pride and hope to many Germans. According to the Treaty of Versailles, Germany wasn't allowed to have an air force. But the rules had been relaxed in 1925 and Hugo Eckener, the chairman of the Luftschiffbau Zeppelin company, had taken advantage. He not only built and commanded *Graf Zeppelin* but also managed to get many powerful people from former enemy nations on board. For the round-the-world flight in August, American publisher William Randolph Hearst's company had raised half the funds. In exchange, Eckener had agreed to make Lakehurst, New Jersey the start and end point of the journey and allow four of Hearst's staff on board. This included the only female passenger, British journalist Lady Grace Drummond-Hay, who became the first woman to travel around the world by air. If she'd paid for her ticket, it would have cost almost $3,000 (equivalent to over $50,000 today). The journey took twenty-one days and was a sensation. Eckener, who had a psychology degree, played his cards well. People could send souvenir mail around the world on the *Graf Zeppelin*. Its journey was covered globally with dramatic images and footage. Eckener was even received by US President Herbert Hoover. Germany was beginning to gain self-confidence.

The world tour had only been completed a week before Weimarers gathered on 12 September to see if a silver shape might appear on the horizon. At 3 p.m. there was much pointing and anxious shouts of 'there it is' when the long, silver shape of the *Graf Zeppelin* appeared in the sky. The roar of its five Maybach combustion engines reached people's ears with surprising delay. Then the cacophony was amplified by bells ringing all over the town and whoops and shouts as people waved their hands enthusiastically. Carl Weirich was as awed as his fellow citizens. A world-travelling airship was flying over Weimar. What a time to be alive![22]

Three weeks later, on 3 October, Harry Graf Kessler was sitting in a barber's chair in Paris shifting nervously from side to side. Did he hear that right? 'Stresemann est mort.' Gustav Stresemann couldn't be dead. Germany's Foreign Minister had overseen not just the recovery from hyperinflation in 1924 but had since fought tooth and nail to give Germany a good name again. The situation was so fragile. Germany relied heavily on American loans to steer its economy through the choppy waters of reparations and post-war crisis. It simply needed someone like Stresemann, who was both a proud nationalist and a persuasive diplomat, to walk the tightrope of domestic and international tensions. If he really was dead, Germany was in trouble.

As soon as he was out of his chair, Harry got hold of a copy of the *Paris-Midi* newspaper. There it was in black and white: Stresemann had died of a stroke at 5.30 a.m. 'This is an irreplaceable loss with unknowable consequences,' Harry thought. A feeling of dread befell him. 'So this terrible year of 1929 is continuing its harvest,' he wrote in his diary, 'piece by piece the world as it was for me and my generation is vanishing. Truly an "année terrible"... The general feeling is not just consternation but also disquiet about what may happen now. I fear Stresemann's death will mainly have serious domestic consequences, the lurch to the right of [his German] People's Party, a break of the coalition, an easier path for dictatorial ambitions.'[23]

*

Three weeks later, on 25 October, a small notice appeared in a Thuringian newspaper with the headline: 'Black Day in Wall Street'. It informed readers that Thursday 24 October had been a 'great day of struggle' on the New York stock market. 'Panic-like sales caused share prices to fluctuate by up to 50 dollars during the course of the trading day. Due to the calming explanations of the leading banker things settled down in the hours of the afternoon.'[24]

Arthur and Rosa Schmidt were too busy to take much note of American news in the autumn of 1929. New elections for the Thuringian state parliament had been scheduled for 8 December and this meant it was a busy time for political organizations and parties to meet up. By now, the Hotel Hohenzollern was well set up for hosting such conferences, providing quieter rooms for private discussions or its large hall for briefings. The Nazis may have felt that they were beginning to outgrow the modest venue by the station, but other political parties continued to appreciate the convenient location, reasonable prices and excellent service.

On 3 November, the Hohenzollern hosted the Economic Party or Wirtschaftspartei (WP), which had done well in the 1927 elections. It had come from nowhere to gain nearly 10 per cent of the vote then. There was room for the WP to poach more conservative votes in an increasingly fractured political landscape. Now the Thuringian branch of the WP sat around the Schmidts' tables in Weimar discussing how best to do that.[25]

Kurt Nehrling didn't have the energy to help the SPD prepare for elections. Violent coughing fits and constant fatigue were sapping away his strength. He was losing weight at an alarming speed. His eyes now sat deep in an increasingly gaunt face. With his hairline receding prematurely, he looked drawn and haggard, much older than his thirty years. His tuberculosis was back with a vengeance.[26]

That was incredibly bad timing. His young family relied on him to pay off the loans they had taken out to build their house. Heddy looked after her step-daughter Ursula from Kurt's first marriage, who was now six, and Ursula's little half-brother Heinz, who was not yet two. Kurt had just been promoted to a senior civil service position as secretary of state in the Thuringian government. Now he was unable to work just as dark clouds of economic trouble began to gather on the horizon.

On 8 December, Thuringians flocked to the polls. It had been a strange election campaign, dominated by malaise and pessimism. The Wall Street Crash at the end of October had at first seemed sideline news. Now it was beginning to affect the German economy. As American investment was withdrawn from Germany and confidence in recovery crumbled, companies hired fewer workers, people spent less and the downward spiral gathered speed.

Unemployment was heading towards 10 per cent, higher than at any other time in living memory. Weimar wasn't hit quite as hard at first with its largely middle-class economy and many state employees and civil servants. While unemployed workers were getting restless and desperate, wealthier Weimarers fretted about the political implications of their misery. Unemployed voters were seen as low-hanging fruit for communists.

The political fringes had lost electoral traction in the 'Golden Years' since 1924 but they hadn't been idle, using the time to consolidate their grassroots organizations. Now there was a sizable vocal minority of radicals at both ends of the political spectrum, able to mobilize hundreds of thousands of people. This applied especially to young men who had grown up in broken families and known little but upheaval. Many wouldn't accept the idea of growing old in a country shackled to debts their generation had not accrued. This generational clash suited the Nazi Party.

The middle-aged Thuringian Minister of the Interior, Karl Riedel of the DVP, could only shake his head as he watched his nephew become a fervent Nazi supporter. The young man attended countless NSDAP meetings and became obsessed with Wilhelm Frick, the leader of the Nazis' group of twelve deputies in the federal parliament. When Riedel asked his nephew how the extensive programme of national renewal that the Nazis propagated should be funded given the dire economic situation, he replied: from Jewish bank accounts whose 'slumbering gold could be used for the German people's community'.[27]

The vast majority of Germans had no time or enthusiasm for political activism. They focused on getting by, no longer believing that politics was relevant to them. In this atmosphere of apathy, most parties found it difficult to mobilize voters, particularly the many middle-class parties. Whom to cast your vote for if all the parties that potentially represent your interests don't stand a chance of getting much more than 10 per cent? 'All hands on deck!' pleaded one liberal-democratic journalist on the eve of the elections. 'The Social Democrats and Communists on the one side, the National Socialists and the Agricultural Leaguers on the other side are on fire for this election. Only in the middle lukewarm indifference reigns . . . So the question of turnout is crucial this time. Not taking part in the election is akin to aiding fatalistic politics.'[28]

This prediction turned out to be correct, at least as far as right-wing extremism was concerned. Turnout did slump across Thuringia to 75 per cent – three points lower than in 1927 and way off the record set in 1924 of nearly 90 per cent. But the left didn't benefit from this. The SPD stayed on 32 per cent, winning the election, while the KPD lost four points and ended up with just 11 per cent. As predicted, the malaise hit the middle-class parties the most. The Economic Party stagnated at just under 10 per cent, the nationalist DVP got 9 per cent, the arch-conservative DNVP got 4 per cent and the liberal-democratic DDP just 3 per cent. The Thuringian Agricultural League came second with 16 per cent.

The Nazis managed to mobilize their voters more effectively. They jumped from just 3.5 per cent in 1927 to over 11 per cent in 1929.[29] In Weimar, this trend was even clearer. There, the Agricultural League wasn't an outlet for far-right sentiments in the way it was for many people in rural areas. It also didn't have enough workers for a sizable KPD vote. So most of Weimar's yearning for radical change led to the Nazi Party, which became the main beneficiary of the very low turnout of 67 per cent. Just two percentage points behind the

SPD, the NSDAP came second in Weimar, gathering an astonishing 24 per cent.[30]

In Thuringia overall, the Nazi Party had come third and would be hard to ignore. The pessimistic journalist who'd predicted chaos if centrist voters didn't turn out was in an even gloomier mood the day after the election. If the social democrats weren't ready to participate in a coalition 'that would have to range from the Agricultural League or the Economic Party to the German People's Party and the Democrats', if despite the gravity of the situation 'they continue to sulk and exclude themselves from cooperation' then, he concluded with bitter sarcasm, 'the Thuringian parliament will be run by the six Nazis. And so we look towards a bright future!'[31] Hitler's Gauleiter Fritz Sauckel took up one of those six Nazi seats in the Thuringian parliament. If he played his cards right, a government couldn't be formed without his party.

When coalition talks began on 17 December in Weimar, everyone knew they would be tough. The two left-wing parties held twenty-four seats between them. The five conservative and right-wing parties had twenty-three seats together, excluding the six Nazis, without whom they could not get a majority. There was a lot of bad blood between the left and the right. Even if the election-winning SPD agreed to work with some of the conservative parties, it would place demands on them that they couldn't fulfil without alienating even more of their voters and vice versa. Georg Witzmann of the conservative – liberal DVP recalled later that 'a coalition with the Social Democrats in any form' had been out of the question, not least because among the conservative parties 'there had been a great lurch towards the NSDAP'.[32]

Hitler was acutely aware of the power dynamics in Thuringia and decided to gamble. In 1924, the Nazi deputies had tolerated a conservative minority government and lent it its votes in exchange for concessions. This time, there was real power to be had as an integral part of the Thuringian government. Hitler made it known that he would consider a coalition but only if the two most important ministries came under Nazi control: Interior Affairs and Education. The

Ministry of the Interior could hire and fire civil servants like Kurt Nehrling and it controlled policing. The Ministry of Education was not only responsible for schools and the University of Jena but also state funding for cultural institutions like theatres, operas, cinemas, concerts and events.

Hitler was demanding nothing less than control over security, culture and education in Thuringia. 'He who owns those two ministries,' he reflected, 'and ruthlessly and consistently makes use of his power within them, can achieve extraordinary things.'[33] But he'd have to get there first. Not everyone in the other parties was happy to work with the Nazis at all, never mind let them have the two central ministries. The DVP politician and Reichstag member Siegfried von Kardorff warned his Thuringian colleagues: 'It pains my soul to see you in such company.'[34] Perhaps he sensed the danger behind the Nazi's strategy. Nobody needed a crystal ball for that. Gauleiter Fritz Sauckel spelled it out in a public speech in December, before the coalition talks had even begun in earnest: 'With our mandate we do not wish to serve the current state – on the contrary, we want to destroy it.'[35]

Wilhelm Weirich couldn't wait for Christmas. Now three and a half years old, he was a cheerful boy whose affectionate nature made his father laugh even during the most stressful periods in the shop. 'He is so funny now,' Carl wrote in his diary, 'early in the morning he pops over to us, and asks us to make a hill in the bed, and when he sits on top of it, he lets himself drop down and rubs his nose against ours.'[36]

On Christmas Eve 1929, the toddler could barely contain his excitement. Together with his parents and his aunt and uncle, he sat in the flat above his father's shop, eyes glowing in the candlelight. The air smelled of pine from the Christmas tree that stood in the corner and of home-cooked food. Finally, it was time to open his presents. There was a new cage for his pets, a wooden sledge and, best of all, a model train set. Carl had pushed aside his financial worries for a moment and bought the present for 119.50 marks. Money well spent, he thought as he watched his son's face light up with unbridled delight.[37]

1930

Adolf Hitler was having tea at the Hotel Elephant on the afternoon of 10 January 1930. His calm voice effortlessly cut through the clinking of cutlery on porcelain and the general chatter of the twenty or so men around him. Gradually, conversations at the other tables faded as guests turned one by one to listen to the leader of the Nazi Party. He spoke with passion but in a rational tone very different from his beer-hall tenor. What Thuringia needed, Hitler said, was a stable government, strong enough to withstand the political and economic storms engulfing the country.

Otto Wagener, who was sitting at one of the other two tables, was astonished to see the effect his boss had on the room. The portly, middle-aged man was the operating chief of the SA and one of Hitler's closest confidants. More used to seeing Hitler whip crowds into a frenzy, he was surprised at the amount of goodwill he was able to conjure among sceptical politicians.[1]

Hitler was in Weimar to negotiate the NSDAP's participation for the first time in government in Germany. Wagener and Gauleiter Fritz Sauckel arranged a 'political tea' where Hitler could speak to 'important representatives of the right-wing parties, the state and the economy of Thuringia'.[2] But they certainly didn't expect this to be a piece of cake. In exchange for its necessary participation in a coalition, not only did the NSDAP demand control over the two most important ministries, but Hitler insisted on filling them both with a specific candidate: Wilhelm Frick.

Frick was an incendiary choice and Hitler knew it. A slender man with short-cropped grey hair, Frick had a calm manner about him that belied his fanaticism. He had a doctorate in law and worked as a senior civil servant in police administration in Munich during and after the war. It was in this capacity that he supported Hitler's putsch attempt in 1923 by delaying the police response. He'd been convicted for aiding and abetting high treason, but the sentence of fifteen months had been suspended and so Frick got himself elected as a Reichstag deputy in the election of May 1924. He'd been in parliament ever since, making a name for himself with antisemitic and anti-constitutional rants.

Hitler had brought Frick along to introduce him to his potential coalition partners. He was from south-west Germany so most people only knew him by his reputation as an unsavoury agitator. As the Führer captivated the room with his monologues, Frick sat quietly at the table next to him. Hitler believed him to be the right man for this crucial job, reasoning that 'he is a former administrator, knows policing, is calm, clear and determined and probably won't make any tactical mistakes'.[3] But the representatives of the other parties remained unconvinced.

Joseph Goebbels, who had arrived in Weimar by train a couple of hours before his boss, was getting bored with all the 'back and forth. Then the argument over the political offices. Terrible. I've had it up to here,' he complained in his diary. 'Frick is supposed to become Minister of the Interior, but the G[erman] People's Party doesn't want to swallow him.'[4] Still, Hitler held all the cards. Without him, the right-wing parties couldn't rule and new elections would have to be called. So he set the other parties an ultimatum: accept Frick within the next three days or the Nazis will withdraw from the coalition talks. With that, he allowed himself to be whisked away from the stunned tea party, leaving Sauckel to tie things up. The Gauleiter later told Wagener that the mood among the men had shifted immediately. Frick's appointment was a certainty.

This lifted Goebbels' mood. He followed Hitler to the Hotel Kaiserin Augusta opposite the station, just a stone's throw from the Hotel Hohenzollern but considerably bigger and more upmarket. There, he watched him talk to 300 'bigwigs', politicians and businessmen. 'It reeks of poshness,' the working-class propagandist wrote resentfully in his diary. But 'Hitler speaks fabulously. I rarely see him like this.'⁵ After the talk, he sat with Hitler and the other senior Nazis long into the night. 'We had much cause for laughter,' Goebbels wrote.⁶ The next day, he and Hitler made time to go to the German National Theatre together to watch *Madama Butterfly*. They were both in excellent spirits. The first Nazi minister in Germany would be sworn in just a few days later in Weimar.

August Frölich was fuming as he walked into the Fürstenhaus, the home of the Thuringian parliament in Weimar. In his early fifties, the balding SPD politician, whose distinctive round glasses framed lively, deep-set eyes, looked back on a long political career that culminated when he was head of the Thuringian government from 1921 to 1924. Then he'd had to look on as his coalition with the KPD was dissolved by military intervention from Berlin. Since then he'd led the SPD group in opposition as one right-wing coalition after another took over while the SPD remained the single largest party. This had been frustrating, but what Frölich witnessed on the morning of 23 January was in a different league.

He'd noticed it on his way in. The black-red-gold tricolour of the Weimar Republic was no longer flying from the top of the Fürstenhaus. Why was that? Frölich asked the representatives of the five right-wing parties that were about to formally elect Germany's first state government with Nazi participation. What's more, Frölich thundered, by supporting Wilhelm Frick, they would elect a 'traitor as a constitutional minister'. So perhaps then, he mused, it was rather fitting that they had taken down the flag of German democracy from this roof so 'that the colours of the Third Reich under Hitler–Frick can replace the colours of country and state'.⁷

Frölich reminded his fellow parliamentarians that Frick had made the case as a Reichstag deputy to let the murderers of high-profile politicians like Walther Rathenau and Matthias Erzberger go unpunished. Raising his voice above the heckling from the six Nazi MPs, he addressed the DVP deputies who had had the biggest qualms over enabling Frick's appointment. Did it not bother them that Frick had decried their party founder Gustav Stresemann as a paid foreign agent for doing his best to reintegrate Germany into the international community?

That hit a sore spot with the five DVP members but they saw no way out of their predicament. Their parliamentary group leader Georg Witzmann countered that his party did have grave concerns about Frick but that it was important for Thuringia to have a government. The NSDAP had assured the DVP that they wanted 'to serve the good of the state with their work' and Frick had promised to swear an oath to the constitution and abide by it. Besides, the only other option would be to work with the SPD, and that was no option at all for the DVP. For all their radicalism, Witzmann argued, the Nazis were 'ideologically and politically closer' to his party than socialists and communists. And with that, he and everyone else who wasn't in the SPD, the KPD or the liberal-democratic DDP elected the new government with twenty-eight votes to twenty-two. Frölich was devastated. He was convinced that 'with the election of Herr Frick, today becomes a day of political and cultural shame for Thuringia'.[8]

Ten days later, Adolf Hitler made some last corrections by hand to a letter he had just dictated. He wasn't a big letter writer. He knew that his words needed the rolling thunder of his voice and the collective hysteria of a beer hall to come to full effect. His grammatical style that bent sentences out of shape in order to deliver their shot at the end appeared awkward and exposed in the still black-and-white world of ink and paper.[9] But needs must. He had news to impart to a friend and generous financial supporter who was living overseas.

Hitler had dictated the letter in Munich, but his thoughts were still in Weimar. 'There,' he told his émigré friend, 'we really are the decisive party now.'[10] Within an astonishingly short time, Hitler mused, 'the arrogant, conceited or stupid rejection of the party that had been the norm a few years ago has turned into apprehensive hope'.[11] He'd shown 'the party politicians that any attempt to take the National Socialist movement for fools is ridiculous'.[12] Hitler recognized that there were risks in participating in a chaotic coalition.

He was sure that it took a very particular character and skill set to survive being a minister without disappointing voters or being played by more experienced parties and politicians. Only a 'dyed-in-the-wool National Socialist' would do, and Wilhelm Frick fitted that description 'to the utmost degree'. Hitler thought his loyal comrade was an 'energetic, keen and responsible administrator with extraordinarily great ability and a fanatical National Socialist' to boot.[13]

'However, now begins a struggle that won't be easy,' Hitler admitted. 'Our task in Thuringia consists of two areas. As Minister of the Interior, Dr Frick will execute a slow purge of the administration and the civil service of red revolutionary elements . . . The second big task for Dr Frick as Education Minister will be to nationalize the education system. In Thuringia, we will now make the entire school system serve the education of Germans to become fanatical Nationalists. We will purge the teaching body of Marxist-democratic tendencies and, in turn, adapt the curriculum to our National Socialist tendencies and ideology. The first step is the implementation of a Chair for Race Questions and Race Studies at the University of Jena.'[14]

'I don't believe that any political party in Germany has ever been met with more infernal hatred than us,' Hitler wrote.[15] But 'Thuringia, from which great spiritual renewal has emanated more than once in German history, will again be the starting point of a spiritual revolution.' It was just a question of time. 'If fate keeps me in good health and bar any unforeseen catastrophes, the German people will have left the nadir of its humiliation in two and a half to three years. I believe that in that time, the victory of our movement will come.'[16] Hitler's prediction would prove disturbingly accurate.

Elisabeth Förster-Nietzsche wasn't sure what to make of Wilhelm Frick. There was no denying the man's power. As Education Minister he was responsible for cultural affairs. The permanently cash-strapped Nietzsche Archive couldn't afford not to be on good terms with the Thuringian government. There was also the existential issue of the copyright on Friedrich Nietzsche's work expiring. 'If we don't achieve an extension this year,' she told her friend Harry Graf Kessler, 'then we are lost.'[17]

The problem was that Elisabeth disliked the Nazis. Hitler and his thuggish band of revolutionaries were clearly masters of propaganda and mass mobilization but they seemed crude and uncouth to her, not the sort of people you invited for tea to talk about philosophy.[18] There was also the matter that the Nazis demanded absolute commitment from everyone and tolerated no independence of thought or deed. Elisabeth still felt closest to the monarchist DNVP and had no desire to join the Nazi Party or shackle her brother's legacy to their fortunes. Yet Frick demanded exactly that. Elisabeth had sent him a formal letter of congratulations upon his election and invited him to 'do me the great honour to come to me every now and then for a chat'.[19] But Frick wanted more, writing back that 'I will not lose hope that you too, dear Madam, will pledge allegiance to the freedom movement of the German people in the spirit of your highly esteemed brother, the fighter Nietzsche.'[20]

Elisabeth resisted the passive aggression with which the minister tried to coerce her to join or at least endorse the Nazi Party but she knew she needed to keep him on her side for funding and support.[21] Relying on the charity of politicians 'weighs heavy on me', she confided to Harry. 'I have been an independent person from youth and so now it will be difficult for me in my high age to wait for help from others.'[22] She would just have to grin and bear it. Frick became a regular guest at the Villa Silberblick.

Dark clouds hung over the Weirich family. Carl was deeply concerned about the state of the economy and the implications for his livelihood. The impact of the Wall Street Crash in America hadn't been immediately obvious, but it became very noticeable now that the brief illusion of economic recovery had gone up in smoke.

Weimar's workers felt the crisis most acutely. In a town full of small business owners, civil servants and moderately wealthy retirees, they only made up around 28 per cent of the population.[23] But they were hit hard when the export-oriented German economic

213

model was imploding in light of the global crisis. Weimar's biggest employer, the wagon factory, ground to a near halt. Smaller workplaces producing anything from pianos to shoes also had to close or were dissolved to merge with bigger companies. Before long, the majority of Weimar's workers were either unemployed or working on severely reduced hours and wages. Those who still had work soon earned on average around half of what they had in 1928.[24]

The plight at one end of the job market in turn reduced the customer base for small businesses like Carl's stationery shop or Rosa Schmidt's hotel. Fewer people could afford to buy typewriters or souvenirs at Geleitstraße or go for a drink after work at the Hotel Hohenzollern, where the Beer Tunnel, in particular, had been set up to cater to workers and people on lower pay. The number of overnight visitors to Weimar had already fallen to below 1924 levels in 1929. Now it was plummeting further.[25] The Schmidts' eldest son Arthur, who was twenty-three, had just decided to seek his fortune in America, settling in the land where all this trouble seemed to come from.[26]

Carl worried that the increasing misery in Weimar would sooner or later become 'a concern for our existence, too, with the mortgage on the house', he confided in his diary.[27] As the family lived above the shop, losing the house would leave them homeless. Carl knew this was happening to plenty of people in Weimar. In the spring of 1930, 2,506 Weimarers were looking for a new home. The number of evictions went up as people simply couldn't pay the rent. The town council tried to respond by building 125 emergency flats in 1930, but this was nowhere near enough, and the state of those flats was pitiful: one or two rooms without kitchens or sanitary facilities.[28] Homelessness was a terrifyingly real threat even for moderately comfortable people like Carl. He tried to secure the family finances by signing a contract with a building society to stabilize mortgage payments for the next five years. But there was no getting away from the reality of rapid economic decline. When he attended a conference of the bookbinders' guild in the Hotel Chemnitius next door to his house, what was billed as a 'festive meal' had turned out to be a 'washout because money had to be saved'.[29]

Carl ploughed on regardless, working hard to feed his family and keep the business going. His position within the Thuringian branch of the bookbinders' association came with a lot of additional responsibility but also some perks. He was given a large delivery car with which to distribute 10,000 school textbooks across the region. He started in Weimar at 8 o'clock in the morning and then drove around all day, visiting nine towns and villages before returning to Weimar at 6 o'clock in the evening. Carl was fascinated by the technology, taking the opportunity to travel by car whenever he could. One time, he even took little Wilhelm. The late 1920s should have been a time of technological marvels and innovation – cars, planes, Zeppelins, radio and moving pictures – in other words, a time of optimism and progress. But the ever-increasing misery made that difficult to buy into. In 1930, Carl wrote in his diary: 'The economic decline . . . threatens to suffocate our fatherland.'[30]

Kurt Nehrling was also struggling. Like Carl Weirich, he'd overstretched financially for his mortgage. But he couldn't try to outrun the economic collapse by working longer hours. There was no cure for his tuberculosis. All Kurt could do was hope for another spell of dormancy. In the meantime, he simply couldn't work.[31] Weimar spent a staggering 2 million marks in 1930 on social welfare, which it tried to finance with cuts elsewhere (paradoxically also in social housing), making more debt and raising taxes. A new 'citizen tax' was introduced and then raised continually. This kept Weimar's tax income artificially stable despite high unemployment and low wages.[32] But it hit contributors like Carl Weirich hard and did very little to help recipients like Kurt Nehrling.

Kurt's problems didn't end there. Both he and Heddy were vocal members of the SPD in Weimar. Now, the Thuringian government had an Interior Minister who saw them as mortal enemies to be expunged from public life. Vulnerable, ill and financially in an extremely precarious situation, the father-of-two had no idea if he'd ever be able to return to work. Like many politicians before him, Frick extolled the 'spirit' of Weimar in his first speech to ministerial staff. His version would bring terror and deprivation to many social democrats, communists and Jews in Thuringia.[33]

Hitler was keen to ensure intimidation spread throughout Thuringia, reaching the Nazis' coalition partners too. There was significant friction between Frick and the DVP. He had insulted the party repeatedly and the resulting tensions threatened to break the fragile coalition. Hitler promptly appeared in Weimar, where a packed hall at the Erholung clubhouse 'greeted him fanatically', according to an attending journalist.[34] The Nazi leader defended Frick's behaviour and confirmed that he didn't expect his party to play by the normal rule book. Violence, intimidation and insults weren't occasional aberrations of Nazi politics but a feature. If anyone expected his party to moderate its course once in power, they were mistaken.

The Nazi Party may not have been the largest in the Thuringian parliament but it had the biggest impact on the young state. Frick made sure of that. Weeks after taking office, he proposed an Enabling Act that all but suspended parliamentary control over the executive for six months. Given that the newly formed coalition had a majority, it passed without problems on 20 March, and Frick began his task of removing opponents from public office immediately. Claiming that he was taking a chainsaw to an overgrown public sector, Frick replaced pro-democracy, left-leaning and Jewish civil servants with people loyal to the Nazi cause. His Enabling Act had stipulated that 'in light of the emergency situation of the country and people, the entire state administration and the entire civil service structure will be reformed to make it simpler and smaller'.[35] In reality, people like Kurt Nehrling came under enormous pressure for wearing the wrong party badge.

Frick extended his control far beyond the realms of government. When a local hospital needed a new doctor, he ensured a Nazi candidate got the job. He appointed men he trusted as police directors.[36] Walter Ortlepp, who now ran the police from his office in Weimar, in turn brutally cracked down on attempts by Kurt's fellow social democrats and by the communists to mount resistance. He told the police to stand by when Nazi troops ambushed left-wing events and street protests. Sometimes SA and police attacked such gatherings together. Nonetheless, workers continued to take to the streets of Weimar in protest throughout 1930 and 1931.[37] Ortlepp, who never tired of trying to intimidate and harass them, was rewarded for his services in 1936 when Hitler made him State Secretary.[38]

Shocked by the changes in Thuringia, the central government in Berlin tried to curtail Frick's doings by temporarily blocking federal funding for Thuringian police services, but the state government went to court and won. Berlin had to lift the sanctions in exchange for a promise from the Thuringian government to 'definitely assure the non-political behaviour' of police and other civil servants.[39] Frick had no intention of sticking to this order and brazenly said so in public. Police, his administration argued, could never be 'non-political' but always had to be an instrument of the government.[40]

Not only did Frick not stop replacing left-leaning people with Nazi sympathizers, but he hired a team of special advisors and enforcers who were paid by the state, yet operated outside its checks and balances. Among these men was Deputy Gauleiter Hans Severus Ziegler. Goebbels delighted in Frick's belligerent and uncompromising style in Thuringia. 'A German minister indeed,' he wrote, adding that Frick was 'brave, has enormous courage and is brazen against the bigwigs in Berlin'.[41] It seemed nobody could or would stop a man whose party had six MPs in a regional parliament. Hitler was learning valuable lessons from Frick's regime in Weimar.

On 6 April, Goethe scholar Max Hecker celebrated his sixtieth birthday. Completely bald with bushy eyebrows and a strong nose, he was a striking man whose jovial disposition betrayed his Rhenish origins. He was proud that his daughter Jutta had just completed her doctoral dissertation and had dedicated it 'to the archivist of the Goethe and Schiller Archive, Prof. Dr Max Hecker, my father, as a festive gift for his 60th birthday'. But when he received the collection of essays his colleagues had assembled in honour of his birthday, it brought home just how desperate the situation was. The book would ordinarily have been substantial, perhaps 500 pages thick. Now, there had only been funds for a sorry seventy-five-page edition.

Leafing through the booklet, Max also noted with a heavy heart the absence of his friend and colleague Julius Wahle from the pages of well-wishers. Wahle had been director of the archive from 1921 to 1928. He'd worked closely with Max on the Weimar Edition or 'Sophie Edition' of Goethe's writings, at the time the only complete collection of the national poet's work. When Wahle had retired after forty-eight years of service to the institution, his colleagues declared 'that the Goethe and Schiller Archive owes him infinite gratitude'.[42] Two years later, this former giant of Goethe scholarship couldn't even contribute an essay to his colleague's birthday book. 'My dear, honoured friend,' he wrote to Max, 'pressing circumstances, with which you are familiar, disallow me, to my greatest regret, to make a scholarly contribution.'[43] Max knew what 'pressing circumstances' his friend was referring to. Julius Wahle was Jewish and suddenly that mattered.

Frick argued that 'forces alien to our race and people' had long tried to 'destroy the spiritual, traditional and religious foundations of our German thoughts and emotions in order to uproot the German people and thus dominate it more easily'. He ranted openly in parliament against the 'deception' perpetrated 'against the German people by Marxism and the Jews'.[44] Strident antisemitism was becoming mainstream. Frick's words, however crudely delivered, met little resistance. The coalition carried Nazi legislation through the Thuringian parliament. Most teachers, theatre directors, actors and university staff carried them out in practice.

The Goethe and Schiller Archive was no exception. It was now run by Hans Wahl, who not only described himself as a 'long-term and fervent opponent of the Jews' but had also been one of the founding members of the Weimar chapter of the Militant League for German Culture, whose declared aim it was to cleanse cultural life in Germany of Jewish and foreign influences.[45] His predecessor Wahle knew which way the wind was blowing and began to be cautious about public writing and appearances – not least because he didn't want to damage the work he had done at the archive. Julius Wahle had been a huge asset to Goethe scholarship, but academic life in Weimar moved on without him with remarkable indifference.

With the same mix of indifference, approval and unease, Thuringia adapted to Frick's other reforms. His first act on 7 February had been to ask Thuringian school officials to compile a list of libraries that stocked Erich Maria Remarque's recently published anti-war novel *All Quiet on the Western Front*. The Nazis and many conservatives were alarmed by the speed at which the book had become a bestseller, selling over 600,000 copies within just a few months.[46] With its graphic depictions of violence, trauma and nationalist indoctrination, it presented war as futile.

Frick demanded to know who promoted such views at Thuringian schools and once he had a survey he promptly banned the book's use in the classroom. When an American film adaptation was released in December, Nazi Stormtroopers provoked a mass brawl at the Berlin premiere. Berlin Gauleiter Goebbels sent his men into the cinema, where they let loose live white mice into the auditorium and set off stink and smoke bombs. 'Already after 10 minutes, the cinema is like a lunatic asylum,' Goebbels gushed in his diary. 'The police are powerless. The angry crowd assaults the Jews. The first dent in the West. "Jews out!" "Hitler stands at the gate!" The police are on our side. The Jews are small and ugly. Outside a storm on the ticket office. Glass shatters. Thousands of people enjoy the show with pleasure. This showing is cancelled, and the next one. We have won.'[47] A few days later, the film was banned Germany wide. Not for the last time, Frick had tried something in Thuringia that was later rolled out across the Reich.

In April, Frick's ministry reintroduced compulsory school prayers and suggested five texts for daily use, three of which were openly hostile to Weimar democracy.[48] Some politicians felt this went too far, but prioritized the survival of their coalition over resistance. Schools largely went along with Frick's reforms. SPD deputy Hermann Brill would later bemoan the 'cultural apathy and moral cowardice of the movement of teaching associations, who did nothing against the undignified hate prayers'.[49] In the end, the federal Interior Minister, Joseph Wirth, from the Catholic Centre Party, stepped in and took Frick to court over the matter. Three prayers were deemed anti-constitutional and removed.

This small setback didn't stop Frick. He'd already set in motion another invasive strategy to change the culture in Thuringia, enacting a decree called 'Against the Negro Culture for German Folkdom'. This argued that 'for years, in almost all cultural areas, influences of alien races have increased'. As examples, it named 'jazz band and drum set music, negro dancing, negro singing, negro pieces', which 'amount to a glorification of negrodom and a slap in the face to German cultural sensibilities'.[50] Frick's regime now set about controlling the cultural output in Thuringia.

Due to the general moral panic over modern culture, Frick's zealotry met little resistance. The far-reaching measures in his decree dictated everything from the plays that could be staged in Thuringian theatres to who was allowed to act in them. Police were given powers to 'step in with all severity' if they deemed a performance indecent or harmful. 'Weimar,' Frick declared, 'must be trendsetting for this and become a centre of German culture. Thuringian state theatres, especially the National Theatre in Weimar, will in light of their great traditions become the nurseries of the German spirit.'[51] If this was the new spirit of Weimar, mused the SPD deputy Max Greil, who'd been in Frick's job of Education Minister between 1921 and 1924, then 'this was the spirit of nationalist small-mindedness'.[52]

Elisabeth Förster-Nietzsche took a sip of tea and looked at her visitor. He was a neat, slender man with middle-class manners that matched his high-collared shirt and suit. Yet there was also a raw energy about him. He spoke with an intense, surprisingly high voice as his deep-set eyes challenged interlocutors to react. His angular face was dominated by bushy eyebrows, a prominent nose and a wide, thin-lipped mouth. Unusual for male fashion of the day, he wore his grey hair cropped very short all over.

Elisabeth hadn't been sure what to expect when she invited Wilhelm Frick for tea on 22 May. He'd sent her a copy of the new school prayers but she had mixed feelings about his programme. When the coalition had first taken power she had confessed to a friend that 'this government in Thuringia is not for me at all, and, from what I hear, people say it won't last long'.[53] Some of Elisabeth's closest friends were subjected to Frick's repressions, like the sculptor Richard Engelmann, who had been a professor at various incarnations of Weimar's schools of art and architecture since 1913. His Jewish background now made him a target.

Frick had begun the culture purges by sacking Otto Bartning, the director of the Bauhaus successor, and replacing him with the ultra-conservative architect Paul Schultze-Naumburg, who had promptly joined the Nazi Party and promised to cleanse art and architecture in Weimar of Jewish, socialist and modernist elements. Reinhard Buchwald, an art historian who worked as a civil servant in the Thuringian Education Ministry until Frick sacked him, thought that 'the wheel of history was turned back by generations of art, but the same applied to everything in 1930, in Weimar and elsewhere'.[54]

Schultze-Naumburg immediately set about destroying what was left of the Bauhaus legacy in Weimar. He unified the different art and architecture schools into one, had the wall frescoes of the Bauhaus artist Oskar Schlemmer painted over and pieces of modern art removed from the museum of the Weimar palace, arguing that they had 'nothing in common with the Nordic-German character' but represented 'the subhumanity of eastern and other races of lesser worth'. While liberals in Berlin declared Schultze-Naumburg's iconoclasm 'a scandal in a state of culture', there was little resistance in Weimar.[55]

Schultze-Naumburg and Frick spent so much time together at the former's Saaleck mansion, that this had given Frick an opportunity to befriend the architect's wife, Margarethe. Watching the pair in Berlin one day in June, Goebbels gleefully wrote in his diary: 'Frick is in love with her.'[56] He wasn't wrong. In 1934, both the Fricks and the Schultze-Naumburgs would get divorced so that Frick could marry Margarethe. For now, both men were focused on purging the Thuringian art scene of people they considered undesirables. As a German Jew, Elisabeth's friend Engelmann was one of them. Schultze-Naumburg not only wanted him forcibly retired but his academic chair dissolved to ensure that his legacy would be eradicated. Elisabeth was devastated. She tried to help and even wrote a letter to Mayor Walther Felix Mueller to urge him to intervene.[57] But it was in vain. Neither she nor Mueller had that kind of power.

Frick took a hammer to a cultural landscape in Weimar that Elisabeth felt she had helped build. Frick wasn't local. This radical Nazi had been parachuted in by Hitler and here he was destroying things people had nurtured for decades. And yet Elisabeth found she was getting annoyed when the left-wing parties criticized Frick, particularly when that criticism came from the establishment in Berlin, a city she despised. 'I've become a very patriotic Thuringian even though I used to feel Prussian,' she admitted to a friend, adding, 'Herr Frick is on his best way to becoming the people's darling, and he has supporters in all parties apart from the Social Democrats.'[58]

Therein lay the problem. Whether Elisabeth liked Frick or not, she needed him and he needed her. She was struggling financially and the archive had come under attack for dodgy academic practices. So Elisabeth had hoped to affiliate her archive with the University of Jena by appointing a scholar who was also a professor there. They had even found a candidate in the young philosopher Hans Leisegang. But now Frick controlled such appointments. Frick in turn wooed Elisabeth for her political support. The woman seemed to know everyone in Weimar and beyond. Local connections were one thing Frick didn't have. More importantly, the Nazis had by now changed their view on Friedrich Nietzsche and saw how concepts like the 'will to power' and 'super humans' could be moulded to give their radical new ideology philosophical roots. If Elisabeth were to publicly endorse Frick's policies, that would lend them respectability. So it was that the two found themselves having tea at the Villa Silberblick on 22 May.

Frick was making every effort to charm the old lady, and Elisabeth began to warm to him – at least enough to maintain regular contact and make it known to friends and influential contacts that she was on good terms with the new minister. In a letter to Friedrich Stier, the civil servant in the Thuringian Ministry of Education responsible for the University of Jena and therefore important to Elisabeth's plans, she wrote: 'Meanwhile, I have become acquainted with Herr Minister Frick and I can tell you that I admire him greatly. He certainly is a noble and excellent man.'[59] This may have been less down to Frick's charm offensive than the fact that he had agreed to appoint her favoured candidate to the vacant chair in Jena.

Nonetheless, she found the Nazi intense and pushy. In exchange for his new role as a political benefactor of the Nietzsche Archive, Frick demanded nothing less than her public endorsement of his repressive reforms. Once again Nietzsche's sister firmly told the minister that, while she was happy to be seen to be on friendly terms with him, she had no intention of joining the Nazi Party or endorsing its ideology. She urged Frick 'warmly to leave me be in my party-political independence, but do me the pleasure of coming to me for a chat every once in a while'.[60]

On a sunny summer day, Wilhelm Weirich was enjoying a party for his fourth birthday with many relatives and neighbours. The boy forgot about all of his other presents and the cake with its four candles when he spotted the brand-new scooter. His eyes lit up as he

Wilhelm Weirich on his fourth birthday, 1930.

wrapped his hands around the handles. Before either of his parents could say anything, he was whizzing around the lounge, grinning from ear to ear. Carl reminded his son that it was a lovely summer's day. Wouldn't it be much more fun to try the new scooter outside? So the family went downstairs together and on to the scorching hot Geleitstraße. Carl fetched his camera from the flat upstairs to capture this happy moment of family life.

When they all went back upstairs, Wilhelm was exhausted. He proclaimed he didn't need any dinner, and fell asleep on the sofa. Carl watched his son breathe quietly, two fingers in his mouth and a cushion hugged tightly to his chest.[61] In just under three weeks' time, Carl had an appointment to remortgage the very roof over his head and the family business below.[62]

Had it really been thirty years? Elisabeth Förster-Nietzsche could remember her brother's death with vivid clarity. Friedrich Nietzsche was buried in the small village of Röcken about 70 kilometres north-east of Weimar, close to Leipzig. It was where he and Elisabeth had been born and spent their early childhood. Looking down on his grave on 25 August 1930, Elisabeth understood that it wouldn't be long before she would be laid to rest beside it. She was eighty-four years old and felt particularly frail on this day. When she arrived by the medieval stone church with a small party of people to honour Friedrich Nietzsche on the thirtieth anniversary of his death, Elisabeth asked for help from her 'oldest friend', Harry Graf Kessler.[63] With her arm hooked through his, she looked at her brother's name engraved in stone and wondered what would happen to his writings. 'We were on the brink of financial collapse,' she explained later, admitting that she 'cried and sobbed all day and couldn't sleep at night any more'.[64]

There was some hope. Hans Leisegang, the young academic who had recently taken up a position at the University of Jena, had repaid Elisabeth's efforts to help him into his new post by assembling a dossier that showed that The Will to Power – an enduring bestseller for the Nietzsche Archive – was in its essence a product created by

Elisabeth and her co-editor. Leisegang proved that the book was a subjectively assembled collection of Friedrich Nietzsche's aphorisms and notes rather than being the intellectual property of the philosopher. Elisabeth could keep the copyright for it. It was ironic that the work she'd claimed so long was her brother's magnum opus helped save the archive by being proved to be inauthentic.[65]

But it wouldn't provide enough income, especially not in times of economic crisis. Elisabeth petitioned the federal parliament in Berlin to extend her general copyright on Nietzsche's work. With a fractured parliament that couldn't even agree on how to solve the urgent economic crisis, none of the requests to support the Nietzsche Archive found a majority. Resistance had come especially from left-leaning parties.[66] So when President Hindenburg had dissolved the unwieldy Reichstag on 18 July 1930 and scheduled new elections for 14 September, Elisabeth felt a flicker of hope. Perhaps the next parliament would shift to the right and provide a political climate more appreciative of Nietzsche.

'A black day for Germany,' Harry Graf Kessler gloomily noted in his diary on 15 September.[67] He was spending a few days in the Swiss mountain resort of Kandersteg. Even surrounded by spectacular Alpine scenery, it was impossible to forget the political chaos that reigned in Germany.

The atmosphere during the election campaign had been tense. 'It was especially the extremist parties that tried by all means to whip up the public mood at the eleventh hour with demonstrations, chanting etc.,' complained the liberal *Jenaer Volksblatt*. 'From lorries, bicycles and on foot, often led by marching bands, their supporters moved through the streets and threw massive amounts of leaflets into the crowds of spectators. There was no shortage of assaults on those who disagreed with them.' There had also been many injured and two dead when Nazis clashed with communists in bloody street brawls.[68]

All this seemed a world away from Harry's mountain sanctuary. But when his assistant Fritz Guseck telegraphed him the election results, his heart sank. They could only be described as an 'advance of the radical parties of the fringes', as the *Jenaer Volksblatt* put it.[69] The SPD still came first with a quarter of the votes, but the Nazis were second with 18.3 per cent – a huge upturn from 2.6 per cent just two years earlier. In Berlin, Joseph Goebbels was beside himself. 'Fantastic,' he wrote in his diary that day, 'I didn't expect that. Our people are over the moon. Jubilation like 1914.'[70] The other winner of the election was the KPD, which got 13.1 per cent, an increase of 2.5 per cent from the last election. All moderate parties had made losses, as Goebbels noted with glee. 'The communists also gained. But we are the second-largest party. Now onward. Never tire, never slow. Fight is the motto. Opposition or government, we will struggle for a new Germany.'[71]

Harry felt sick. 'The Nazis have increased their seat share nearly tenfold,' he wrote in his diary. He saw this as a 'political crisis which can only be overcome through the strict collaboration of all forces that support the republic or at least tolerate it *if* these forces are furthermore able to summon the talent to improve the economic and fiscal situation by the next dissolution of the Reichstag'.[72]

To Harry, the rapid rise of the Nazis was a 'fever dream of the dying German lower middle classes; but the poison of its disease can harm Germany and Europe for decades. This class can't be saved; but in its death struggle it can bring horrific new misery down on Europe.'[73] The middle classes felt the impact of the crisis acutely and they also worried about their employees and other workers turning to communism. Weimar was full of such people. At 19.5 per cent, the overall rate of the NSDAP vote in Thuringia was only marginally higher than the national average. In Weimar, a staggering 28.2 per cent of people voted for the Nazi Party.[74]

Elisabeth Förster-Nietzsche spent Christmas worried for the future. It had been a tough year and the autumn had brought more bad news. Wilhelm Frick had been unable to secure an extension of the copyright on the Nietzsche estate despite now heading a Nazi Reichstag delegation of 107 members in Berlin.[75] She'd also fallen out with

Professor Leisegang, who wanted full access to the philosopher's notes, which would have broken her monopoly and exposed how much liberty she'd taken in her editing. Much ugly mud-slinging ensued against the academic, in which Frick happily participated, knowing the professor was no Nazi supporter. 'Next they'll claim I'm a Jew despite my blond hair and blue eyes,' Leisegang complained.[76] The university sided with him and distanced itself from Elisabeth.

But then suddenly things fell into place in December. The federal government sent the archive 5,000 marks despite the post-election chaos.[77] Frick topped this up from the Thuringian budget. The Nietzsche Archive also won a lawsuit against the Kröner Publishing House, which had to pay it 20,000 marks for the right to print *The Will to Power*. Her anonymous donor, who soon turned out to be Philipp Reemtsma, a cigarette manufacturer from Hamburg, sent the next annual instalment of 20,000 marks as promised.[78] Elisabeth had even found another Jena professor: the legal philosopher Carl August Emge, who was less wilful than Leisegang and a Nazi Party member. He agreed to work with limited access to the Nietzsche originals.[79]

Elisabeth duly congratulated Frick when his party made landslide gains in Berlin and told him that he was 'the best and most glowing representative of National Socialism' and that his efforts to support her would secure him 'the honour for all time that he had stood up for the last great German philosopher and his house, the Nietzsche Archive'.[80] As the Nazis began to embrace Nietzsche as part of their ideological foundation, Elisabeth extended her contacts to them and local supporters like Lisbeth Staupendahl. Staupendahl was a Weimar businesswoman who ran a successful removals company that had once worked for the grand ducal court but had also helped move Bauhaus founder Walter Gropius from Weimar to Dessau. She'd joined the NSDAP in 1925 and urged Elisabeth to do the same, arguing that Friedrich Nietzsche would have regarded the Nazis as the realization of his philosophy.[81]

Elisabeth made an effort to appear enthusiastic. She even asked for tickets for Hitler's next speech in Weimar in the German National

Theatre on 12 October. Deputy Gauleiter Hans Severus Ziegler sent her two VIP tickets, delighted that Nietzsche's sister was 'taking a keen interest in the development of our movement' and had asked to be introduced to Adolf Hitler. Elisabeth agreed to attend but there is nothing in her letters or notes to suggest that she met Hitler that day.[82]

Elisabeth's relationship with the Nazis remained ambivalent. On the one hand, she understood that they were gaining power at breakneck speed. She also agreed with them on fighting democracy and communism. But she harboured deep misgivings about the violence that surrounded them as well as their virulent antisemitism. She didn't want the new world Hitler offered but a return to the old world of her youth. When the banker Pilder asked her about her relationship with the Nazis in November, she'd told him that she wasn't part of the movement because 'I stayed loyal to the conservative creed my whole life.' This meant 'loyalty to the imperial dynasty'. She was a child of 'Germany's great past and that great period when our dear old dukes, under Bismarck's leadership, turned the small German states into a wonderful, great, powerful Reich'.[83] At Christmas 1930, she saw no conflict in thanking both the Nazi Frick and the democrat Harry for their help in sustaining her brother's legacy.

For his part, Harry was a lot more pessimistic about the future and Weimar's part in it. What he'd heard about Frick's reforms in Thuringia had shocked him deeply. In December, he wrote in a newspaper article:

If Weimar, which for one and a half centuries had been a centre of German culture, allows itself to be forcibly turned into an insignificant small town, then this is regrettable but not a matter that is life-threatening to the rest of Germany. After all, Germany has other cultural centres that can replace Weimar. But it is a German matter of the first order if the spirit that empties museums in Weimar and allows its once flourishing art school to wither due to a narrow-minded and crude ideology spreads over the entire German cultural field . . .

Against this small town spectre that threatens not just German economics and politics now but also already German culture, we must appeal to German cultural determination and one can't phrase this appeal any better than in the words of Herr Frick himself and of his friends: Germany wake up![84]

1931

Early in 1931, Rosa Schmidt's hotel was in the news because of an old crime. Five years earlier, police officer Paul Schmidt had been shot in front of the Hohenzollern during the first Nazi Party rally in 1926. Now the case was being reinvestigated. Due to the involvement of one particularly notorious Nazi, the story had never really gone away.

When Wilhelm Frick had first got his ministerial job, the social democrat August Frölich reminded him in parliament that, while the shooter had never been found, he suspected that the NSDAP had something to do with it. After all, Frölich mused, it happened after an incendiary speech 'delivered at the station by your party comrade, the lawyer Freyse from Kassel'.[1] This 'Freyse' was Roland Freisler, who had joined the Nazi Party a year before the incident and used his legal training to help violent SA offenders get mild sentences. He gained notoriety as an impulsive agitator, shouting at colleagues and judges in court as he pleased. By now he was a national figure in the party and didn't like the way this old Weimar case continued to resurface.

The town of Weimar also found it uncomfortable, particularly as the victim just wouldn't stay silent. Paul Schmidt had survived but with life-changing injuries that rendered him unable to work. He wasn't happy with the fact that he'd been fobbed off with just two thirds of his old pay as an early pension, demanding 80 per cent of his old salary.

Now, he faced an ugly campaign. Weimar officials insinuated that he had shot himself in order to retire early. Schmidt was interrogated for three hours, during which the prosecution claimed his wound looked 'strange' and that 'burn wounds' and 'black powder marks' weren't in the right places. Five professional witnesses, two medical and three ballistic experts, dismissed these claims and the retrial found nothing new. In the end, as one local paper mused, the whole thing was 'a pointless and expensive court case'.[2]

For many Weimarers, Paul Schmidt's case was at best a small distraction from their own daily struggles. Unemployment was spiralling out of control. In 1930, over 3 million Germans had been looking for work. In 1931, that figure spiked to 4.5 million – more than twice the pre-Wall Street Crash record of 2 million in 1926.[3] In Thuringia, 158,986 people were unemployed, an unprecedented number that amounted to an unemployment rate even higher than that of the Reich overall.[4] In Weimar, 3,240 people were registered as unemployed on 1 January 1931, up from 1,773 just a year earlier. The effects were visible at every level. People travelled less. The tram noted a reduction of 21 per cent in passengers in 1931. Passenger use of local trains and buses had fallen by half and services were reduced accordingly. Most worryingly for Rosa, all of this meant that far fewer people came to Weimar. At times visitor numbers dropped by over 70 per cent from the already low levels of 1929.[5] Things were looking bleak for the Hotel Hohenzollern.

Carl Weirich was also worried. One of his mortgage payments was due and he had no idea how he was supposed to meet it.[6] Nobody seemed to be doing anything to get the economy back on track. Chancellor Heinrich Brüning, who through President Hindenburg passed more laws by presidential emergency decree in 1931 than by parliamentary vote, told the public to accept their predicament. In a radio address on 25 January he said: 'It is not only through reparations burdens that we have fallen into financial misfortune, but to a very large measure by letting ourselves imagine that despite a lost war, despite huge sacrifices in blood and treasure, both state and individuals could live better than in pre-war times.'[7]

Brüning drove a hard austerity programme but found out when he toured Germany in January just how much hostility it faced. He was greeted by scores of angry farmers in Silesia. In Breslau, he was booed by 40,000 Nazi activists. In Chemnitz, unemployed workers threw stones at his motorcade. At the end of his tour, he concluded that it was easier to believe in parliamentary democracy when things were going well.[8] Now he saw a tide of extremism sweep through the country. He implored the Reichstag deputies to respond by pulling themselves together in a show of strength and unity. But the Nazis and communists in parliament had no intention of shoring up democracy.

Carl didn't believe that austerity was the answer. He wrote in his diary that it was obvious to 'all the world that a Germany in its death throes pulls the victorious states into misery with it'. After all, 'America and England were in crisis, too'.[9] Why didn't they ease the burden of reparations? In reality, they tried. In June, Brüning met with British Prime Minister Ramsay MacDonald, with whom he issued a joint statement that stressed 'the difficulties of the existing position in Germany and the need for alleviation'.[10] US President Herbert Hoover agreed and proposed a one-year moratorium for all war debts – Germany's to the Allies and the Allies' to one another. This was a generous offer that was eventually accepted and practically marked the end of German repayments for the First World War.

However, there was strong French resistance that took weeks to overcome. In the meantime, several major banks in Austria and Germany collapsed, escalating the economic free fall and whipping up revanchist sentiment all over the country. Even the usually mild-mannered Carl fumed in his diary that 'France is probably supposed to drown in gold.'[11] He was grateful for measures taken by 'our President Hindenburg' through emergency decrees to protect indebted middle-class people like him. Interest payments on some loans were suspended and creditors couldn't enforce cancellations for the time being. The Weirich family could stay in their house and keep their shop. But for how much longer?

In the winter and spring of 1931, the Nazis were busy fanning the widespread frustration. They held a national strategy meeting in Weimar, which, according to the organizers, had 'under the leadership of Dr Frick become a haven for endangered Germanness'.[12] Held on the weekend of 7 and 8 February, the conference focused on agriculture. Hitler's public event at the National Theatre was sold

Adolf Hitler, Wilhelm Frick, Fritz Sauckel and Wilhelm Brückner in front of the Goethe and Schiller Monument in Weimar in February 1931.

out with people spilling over into the foyer and other rooms where they could hear him through loudspeakers.[13]

Hitler entered the stage to frenetic applause and Beethoven.[14] He talked for one hour, describing agriculture as the 'life source of all the life of a nation' before connecting this to more general grievances. The crisis, he said, was not caused in Germany, as Brüning had argued in his radio speech, but by the globalized economy. 'The future lies in our own soil,' Hitler argued. 'The flood of terms like "world economy", "export and import", "world market" and "revenue" has derooted and devalued humans.'[15] 'Nothing new,' mused a critical journalist in his dispatch, 'but if Hitler says it, then it will of course be gospel to certain people.'[16]

Not everyone in Weimar was happy with the way Hitler used the town as a base from which to launch his campaign against democracy. In parliament, the left-leaning parties argued fervently against his repeated use of Weimar in general and the National Theatre in particular. Other organizations also complained, like Thüringer Volksbühnen (Thuringian People's Theatres), which voiced 'loud protest against the party-political misuse of the Goethe stage and against all attempts to politicize the theatre to further narrow-minded, anti-classical party ideology. Such measures harm Weimar's reputation as a place of classical culture, they profane the dignity of the theatre and so damage Weimar's name in front of the entire cultural world.'[17] The Thuringian government paid lip service to such demands, decreeing on 27 March that all state theatres must from now on only be used for artistic events. Just over two weeks later, Hitler held his next convention on the 'Goethe stage' in Weimar.

It was entirely possible to stop Wilhelm Frick's abuses of power, as his fall in Thuringia proved. The SPD and KPD tried to bring the government down through a vote of no confidence but failed repeatedly, lacking the necessary majority. It was remarkable how long the other parties tolerated the Nazi terror. Their thuggery was right in front of them, even in the debating chamber itself.

The Gauleiter and head of the parliamentary group of the NSDAP in Thuringia, Fritz Sauckel, was particularly aggressive. He was keen to step out of Frick's shadow and catch Hitler's attention by creating as much outrage as possible. Building an image as a radical bruiser, his rhetoric was repetitive and crude but often quite effective.[18] He crossed the line in a lead article for *Der Nationalsozialist* in which he described the Nazis' coalition partners of the national-liberal DVP as 'bourgeois wimps' and as 'idiotic geriatrics, traitors and cheats'.[19]

The fragile coalition of right-wing parties had been under strain right from the beginning, and the DVP had always been the most fragile link. Sauckel's remarks broke that link. On 1 April, the DVP voted with the opposition parties on a motion of no confidence against Frick and fellow Nazi Willy Marschler, who had served as Councillor of State for Weimar. Hitler rushed in to 'try to negotiate given the great importance the National Socialists place on their position in Weimar', as the local press reported.[20] To no avail. The DVP deputies had made up their minds to bring down Frick's regime. The liberal *Jenaer Volksblatt* hoped that the whole episode would trigger an 'awakening and specifically the increasing awareness of the Thuringian people . . . as to what National Socialism is [and] what's behind the phrases of Hitlerism'.[21]

Frick had done lasting damage. His regime had altered the composition of administrative, educational and cultural bodies across Thuringia. Law enforcement was now infused with Nazi sympathizers, including in the capital, Weimar. Perhaps most toxic of all had been the corruption of Thuringia's young parliamentary culture.

A minority government now ruled the state, barely tolerated by the largest parliamentary party, the SPD. This deeply divided assembly now tried to cope with the worst economic and social crisis in living memory. Thuringia was in big trouble, given its many small, export-oriented businesses that produced things like toys, hunting rifles, garden gnomes and glass ornaments. Yet its parliament had lost the capacity for civilized debate and decision-making.

This problem didn't go away just because Frick was no longer a minister. On the contrary, the Nazi deputies increased their efforts to disrupt. On 19 May, Sauckel challenged an SPD deputy from the stage: 'Herr Gründler, would you like to step outside with me for a little while? After you.'[22] He then walked towards Gründler while other Nazi MPs also got up. Paul Papenbroock, a fellow NSDAP deputy, hit the SPD man on the head from behind. Now all SPD and Nazi members were on their feet facing each other in the debating chamber. The parliamentary president tried to cancel the rest of the session but people had already grabbed chairs and a brawl ensued.[23] It was a mirror image of what was happening on streets and squares, in assemblies, pubs and bars across the state – and in the Reichstag.

Philipp Kallenbach, the one remaining deputy of the liberal-democratic DDP in the Thuringian parliament, called what Frick had done to political culture 'positively devastating'. He lamented that 'hatred and bigotry against broad swathes of society were the fuel behind the administrative measures. All areas of public life are, as far as this was possible in such a short time, politicized according to the NSDAP's ideology.'[24] On the day the government fell, Sauckel proved the point by promising his former coalition partners of the DVP: 'We will be back . . . and the German people will walk over the dead body of your party.'[25]

Hitler had every reason to thank Frick despite the collapse of his regime. Praising his man for 'putting Thuringia in the centre of the national, political and economic restoration of Germany', he added: 'We all believe with unshakeable conviction that the hour will come in which you will be recalled to serve our people in a position of responsibility – and next time it will be forever.'[26]

On 10 July, Elisabeth Förster-Nietzsche turned eighty-five. She was delighted with the flood of congratulatory cards, flowers and presents she had received but she was missing letters from some of her closest friends. The difficult economic situation was now engulfing everyone's lives, even those of some of her wealthiest benefactors. Her old friend and generous donor, the Swedish financier Ernest Thiel, was in trouble again and increasingly depressed about it. Harry Graf Kessler was another struggling friend. He was accumulating high debts and had to sell some of his art. When a buyer came to collect a large stone statue, he looked on broken-hearted as workers built scaffolding outside his Berlin home before heaving the piece out for transport. 'At five minutes past 2 o'clock, she floated out of the window,' Harry wrote in his diary, 'covered by a large cloth as if she was sad too and had veiled her head . . . I felt a pain that I will never quite overcome.'[27]

Worse was to come. His livelihood and printing business were at risk. He wrote to his sister (in English and French): 'At the worst I would sell the house in Weimar . . . but the last thing I shall do, is to give up my press. For then je n'aurais plus qu'à me faire enterrer [they might as well bury me now].'[28] But at the end of October, he sold his press in Weimar too. Harry didn't write to Elisabeth about this. He barely wrote anything at all in 1931. He was too ill with repeated bouts of pneumonia and pleurisy. When he was well enough to write, he let Elisabeth know that, as she celebrated her eighty-fifth birthday, he'd been in hospital in Berlin. Elisabeth was 'truly shocked'. 'I hadn't imagined it to be this bad,' she wrote back, and 'I can't express to you how intensely I feel for you in your illness, a[nd] how painful it is to me that you had to be ill in Berlin of all places, that place which I loathe so deeply.'[29]

Elisabeth enjoyed her birthday regardless of the absences. There had been a speech in her honour by Werner Deetjen, director of the Weimar Library, president of the German Shakespeare Society (founded in Weimar in 1864) and a member of the Nazis' Militant League for German Culture. Addressing Elisabeth directly, he praised how 'out of your own strength and with keen understanding for his high importance you have set your world-famous brother a monument in sisterly love . . . May you get certainty soon, despite the difficult situation of our fatherland, that that which you have created is maintained securely in economic terms for all times.'[30]

Elisabeth was hopeful. Unfortunately, she wrote to her cousin Richard Oehler, 'our excellent Dr Frick' had been pushed from power. Hitler's man in Thuringia had just begun to win her over, even if the Nazi Party itself had not. On the contrary, Elisabeth believed it was their radicalism that had caused Frick's fall. 'Frick with his fine manners can't stand up against this party,' she complained. She admitted that his departure made her 'indescribably sad', not least because Frick had lobbied for continuing state subsidies for the Nietzsche Archive.[31]

Mentally, Elisabeth was already preparing for a world beyond Frick in Thuringia. She had other powerful friends, even if some of them were struggling a little. Her eighty-fifth birthday, 'on which an abundance of recognition, praise and admiration was poured over me despite my protestations', had been balm for her soul, she told Harry.[32] What she didn't tell him because she knew he'd disapprove was that among her birthday telegrams had been a friendly message from Italy and 20,000 lira. Benito Mussolini sent his regards.[33]

Baldur von Schirach was sitting in his flat in Munich, looking into the pale blue eyes of Adolf Hitler. The Nazi leader looked tired, but he was clearly enjoying the noodle soup he loudly slurped from a spoon. Hitler had just rushed back from Berlin, where he'd had acrimonious

discussions about his party entering into a coalition. The talks had
failed and he'd returned to Munich, exhausted. He'd sent Schirach
a message inviting himself to dinner. Schirach had grown close to
Hitler over the last few months. The young aristocrat had found a
way into Hitler's private orbit through Heinrich Hoffmann, Hitler's
photographer and friend. Schirach had been more interested in Hoffmann's daughter Henriette or Henny, a bright and lively teenager
with wavy, chestnut brown hair cut in a fashionable bob. He'd first
met her when he was twenty-three and she was seventeen years old
and was fascinated.[34] Henny had helped out printing and distributing propaganda in Munich in 1930 when 'One day,' she recalled later,
'a young man in a light suit came running up the stairs, whistling
the Yankee Doodle; he'd just returned from America.'[35] Henny was
immediately intrigued by Schirach, and they soon started dating.
Through Henny and her father, Schirach built a close relationship
with Hitler, getting a glimpse behind the mask of the Führer.[36]

As the two men sat in Schirach's flat with a steaming bowl of
noodle soup between them, they realized they each had a problem
to which the other held the answer. Schirach was having an identity
crisis. He was now twenty-four years old and the one thing he
knew about himself was that he was not an academic. So what was
he doing being a student leader? Soon he'd be too old for the job
anyway and then what? Perhaps he could be a poet? He was still
writing for the party and was getting praise for it. But that wasn't a
proper job, he mused.[37] Besides, the thrill of politics had him firmly
in its grip. He still had no other plan, no other goal in life than to
serve Hitler.

Hitler's thoughts revolved around where to take the Nazi
movement from here. The electoral success the previous year had
been spectacular but it hadn't led to government participation in
Berlin. Frick's regime in Thuringia had imploded and activism was
also making much slower progress than expected. There was also
massive infighting in the NSDAP. The Führer was dowsing fires left,
right and centre while the movement appeared to stand still.

The Hitler Youth worried him especially. Since its official

foundation in 1926 in Weimar it had been in the hands of Kurt Gruber, a capable enough leader from Saxony. But Gruber's working-class outlook meant that he envisioned the Hitler Youth as a proletarian movement in direct competition with the communists, a 'labouring German working-class youth which, under the blood-red banner of the swastika . . . stands ready to break the rule of subhumanity on the street'.[38] For Hitler that was all well and good ideologically but restricting intake to one social class meant capping numbers. The Hitler Youth had grown to a sizable movement of 40,000 members under Gruber's leadership but in the context of Germany's youth club culture that was nothing. Sports and church organizations counted hundreds of thousands of children as their members.[39] Hitler believed that, like the Nazi Party itself, its youth wing needed to address all social milieus, all confessions, all regions, boys and girls. Hitler wasn't sure Gruber was the man for this. Perhaps Schirach had advice.

'Herr Hitler, I would like to do this myself,' Schirach recalled saying to his boss. 'Schirach, don't joke about this,' came the reply. 'After all, you built up this great university movement and now you want to look after children?' He did, promising Hitler: 'I will build you the largest youth movement Germany has ever seen.' Two weeks later, Baldur von Schirach was appointed Reich Youth Führer.[40]

A difficult year drew to a close for many Weimarers. SPD man Kurt Nehrling had no idea how he was supposed to feed his family. At the end of February, Frick's regime had seen to it that he lost his job in the ministry permanently. At school, his nine-year-old daughter Ursula was exposed to Frick's education reforms replete with hateful school prayers and censored libraries and there was nothing he could do about that. The Nehrlings struggled so badly financially that they feared losing everything, from the roof over their heads to the food on their table. With their long-standing SPD affiliation, neither Kurt nor Heddy would get a position anywhere in the public sector. Frick may have been gone, but his appointments in the civil service had not. The couple resolved to make themselves independent of politics by establishing their own business. Heddy and Kurt would run a textile and wool shop from their home at Heimstättenweg.[41] People always needed cloth and fabrics. There was hope to cling on to at Christmas for the Nehrlings.

Carl Weirich shielded his young son from his own existential fears. As every year, the family sat together in their flat above the shop at Geleitstraße 10. Despite their worries, Wilhelm received a wonderful present: a miniature mountain around which a model train whizzed on its serpentine track. On top sat a little replica of Lichtenstein Castle, which people called the 'Fairy Tale Castle of Württemberg'.[42] The magic of their family Christmas was enough for the Weirichs to forget about the world outside for a while.

Harry Graf Kessler also tried to put on a brave face. The day before Christmas Eve, he wrote to Elisabeth Förster-Nietzsche to tell her that 'I'm still feeling so-so, and I will try to gather strength over the next few weeks in order to get through the rest of the winter without new misfortune.' He finished with an upbeat message for his old friend: 'As sad as these times may be, as much as black clouds appear to gather on the horizon, one thing is certain still: that somewhere behind these black clouds Nietzsche's sun is shining, heralding a new spring.'[43]

But Harry's health and personal finances were on the brink of collapse, and he felt the same was true for Germany. Just a few days earlier, he'd met with Eduard von der Heydt, a banker to whom he owed vast sums of money. The two men were having breakfast together at Berlin's luxurious Hotel Esplanade. Movie stars like Charlie Chaplin had been where Harry was sitting now listening to one of the most powerful financiers in the country ponder whether a Nazi government would really be such a bad thing. Heydt was extremely well connected. He was ex-Kaiser Wilhelm II's personal financial advisor. Now he was pondering whether to link the Nazis up with useful people. He was no antisemite himself, he insisted. He had way too many Jewish friends and even his young ex-wife Vera von Schwabach hailed from a Jewish family. But as far as he could see, democracy had come to the end of the line. To him, the choice was now between a Nazi government or a military dictatorship, and in that case he preferred the Nazis. For one thing, Heydt argued, the NSDAP accepted expert help. He told Harry that the former president of the Reichsbank Hjalmar Schacht was already 'entirely their man'. 'Generals were generals,' on the other hand, they 'knew everything better'. Besides, Heydt continued, 'the Nazis weren't as bad as they looked'. He was going to meet Hitler in confidence the next day.[44]

Harry was shocked, writing in his diary on New Year's Eve: what an 'end to a catastrophic year and beginning to one that will probably be even more catastrophic'.[45]

1932

Those eyes! It was as if they looked right into you. Elisabeth Förster-Nietzsche was fascinated by Adolf Hitler's striking looks. He'd appeared in her box at Weimar's German National Theatre. A slender man of medium height and build, there was nothing particularly impressive about him as such. But those pale eyes sparkled with intensity. Elisabeth thought he looked manic, more priest than politician.[1]

It was the evening of 30 January 1932, and they were both attending the German premier of Benito Mussolini's play *Campo di Maggio* about the downfall of Napoleon.[2] A *New York Times* journalist in the audience wasn't particularly impressed, writing home that the play 'represents Napoleon as a shining, blameless hero who goes down to defeat through his own tragic error of divesting himself of absolute power and granting a Constitution to France'. He noted, however, that 'the performance was attended by Adolf Hitler, a number of his lieutenants and representatives of the Italian Embassy'.[3] This was interesting company for Elisabeth, who still admired Mussolini but hadn't made up her mind about Hitler. There wasn't time for anything more than pleasantries during the fifteen-minute interval so she invited the Nazi leader and the Italian diplomats up to the Nietzsche Archive the following day.

Hitler accepted the invitation. Wilhelm Frick had clearly done a good job in building the first bridges to Friedrich Nietzsche's sister but she still hadn't become a Nazi. Nazism, on the other hand, was beginning to embrace Nietzsche. Hitler, who had studied the philosopher's writings in prison, wasn't overly taken by them himself, but he understood that handpicked and distorted aphorisms could lend his own ideology roots and legitimacy. 'Was Nietzsche an antisemite?' asked the Nazi newspaper *Völkischer Beobachter* (People's Observer), and answered the question without giving a single quote from Nietzsche's work: 'He was. He was one in the actual, purest and holiest sense of the word: out of a belief in the greatness of the German character.'[4]

As the philosopher's sister was key to appropriating Nietzsche for Nazism, Hitler turned on the charm. He bought an elaborate bouquet of flowers and made his way up to the Villa Silberblick. When Elisabeth's servant Paul Tiedemann opened the door, he was in awe. A cobbler by trade and a Nazi Party member, here he was opening the door to the Führer himself.[5] The mistress of the house would later tell her friend Harry Graf Kessler that everybody in the house was now a Nazi. Her cousin Max Oehler had joined the previous year. Her other cousin Richard Oehler would soon follow. Her scientific director Carl August Emge was a Nazi too, and even her servant was 'brown'. Harry was appalled. So many of the people he'd once considered friends were besotted with Nazism. 'In short, the entire class representing intellectual Germany, which has its roots in the period of Goethe and the Romantics, is Nazi-infested without knowing why,' he complained in his diary.[6] What did everyone see in the Nazi leader? To him 'the weak, extremely effeminate character of Hitler and his associates, in which they weren't unlike Wilhelm II', belied that he was 'all mouth and no trousers when it came to it'.[7]

Elisabeth's benefactor Ernest Thiel thought he had an explanation. Watching the situation from his native Sweden, he wrote to her: 'I'm not surprised you've all been taken in by Hitler . . . As I see it, the infatuation with Hitler is on the one hand the expression of a suffering people and on the other that of a humiliated people. By the first I mean people the majority of whom can't earn their daily bread and by the latter I mean a people whose pride has been mortally wounded by the Versailles Peace.'[8] Harry could see another reason too, musing that 'at least the Nietzsche Archive gains a material advantage from its fascism'. But he still wanted to 'cry at what Nietzsche and the Nietzsche Archive had come to'. At the Villa Silberblick, the only person who was not a Nazi Party member was now Elisabeth herself, who assured Harry that she remained 'a German nationalist'.[9]

Hitler had arrived at the Villa Silberblick to see if he could change that. When Paul brought the guest into the room, Hitler was still holding his giant bouquet of flowers. He was flanked by some of his men, including the director of the Weimar art school and prominent architect Paul Schultze-Naumburg. Elisabeth introduced the group to the Italian diplomats who were having tea with her, and a lively discussion ensued in which Hitler spoke about the theoretical possibility of an Anschluss, a unification of Germany and Austria. While he tried to reassure the Italians that he had no desire to annex Austria when he came into power, Elisabeth thought it unwise and insensitive to speak about such topics in front of foreign diplomats. Perhaps this Hitler was more zealot than statesman. She told Harry later she 'didn't have the impression he was a great politician'.[10]

Gaining the open endorsement of Friedrich Nietzsche's sister was clearly an ongoing project, but Hitler had more pressing concerns in early 1932. Paul von Hindenburg's seven-year term was coming to an end and presidential elections were to take place on 13 March. The Nazi leader wanted to run as a candidate. This was a unique opportunity. Nazi support was soaring and as German President, Hitler could rule by decree, suspend the Reichstag, appoint his own Chancellor and ultimately dismantle the whole democratic system from within. He had never been so close to power. There was just one problem: he was not a German citizen and therefore not eligible to become President.

Hitler saw himself as a German, but he had been born in Austria. Living there as a young man, he bitterly complained to friends how all Austria ever knew was to 'suppress talent out of competition, envy and bureaucracy'. He planned to emigrate to Munich, that 'most German of German cities'.[11] Hitler served in the Bavarian army and was wounded in the First World War, which he felt made him deserving of German citizenship. Instead, the Bavarian authorities tried to deport him to Austria after his failed coup in 1923. His home country promptly refused to take him back, on the grounds that Hitler clearly considered himself German. He retorted in a public statement that 'The loss of my Austrian citizenship is not painful to me, as I never felt as an Austrian citizen but always as a German only.'[12] In 1925, he applied to be released from Austrian citizenship, which was duly granted. Since then, he'd been stateless.

Anticipating that being stateless might one day be an issue for someone who'd made it his life's mission to run a state, Hitler's associates had undertaken several unsuccessful attempts to get him German citizenship. The easiest route appeared to be through appointing him as a civil servant, who were all citizens by legal default. Hitler's men were falling over themselves to try to achieve this for their Führer, but few were in a position to get a convicted traitor a job in the public sector.

The first Nazi minister in Germany, Wilhelm Frick, had the power to appoint civil servants when he was in charge of Thuringian culture and education in 1930. He tried to give Hitler a position at the Bauhaus successor. Unsurprisingly, there was resistance against appointing to an academic post someone who'd dropped out of school without any form of higher qualification, and the attempt failed. Under the leadership of Erwin Baum from the Thuringian Agricultural League, the Thuringian cabinet declared that it had no intention to 'enable Adolf Hitler to acquire Thuringian citizenship by employing him as a Thuringian civil servant in name only'.[13] Hermann Brill, SPD deputy, and a vocal opponent of Frick's regime, later mused, full of bitter irony: 'The world might have been spared a lot if Hitler had been able to follow his artistic inclinations at the Weimar School of Art to design wallpaper patterns or porcelain vases.'[14]

When the worst of the public outrage had subsided and Baum was on summer holiday, Frick tried again. In July 1930, he appointed Hitler as gendarmerie commissioner in the south Thuringian town of Hildburghausen. Hitler reluctantly accepted the commission but later tore the document to shreds when he realized this wouldn't work – it was an ignominious way to become a German citizen through the back door. It would only make him vulnerable to press scrutiny and ridicule later.

This was exactly the problem he was facing now that he wanted to become German President. Not only was he still stateless but, as Joseph Goebbels bemoaned in his diary, 'hacks have found out that Frick suggested in the year of 1930 to appoint the Führer to a minor post in Hildburghausen in order to get him citizenship. A feast for those distorters . . . This question is yet to be solved and quickly. After all, the Führer must be a citizen to be a candidate.'[15] In the end, the problem was solved not in Thuringia but in the Free State of Brunswick, where Nazis were part of the government. They appointed Hitler as a Brunswick legate to the Upper House in Berlin. This made him a citizen of Brunswick and Germany as of 1 March 1932 – just in time for the first round of the presidential elections.

The citizenship scandal refused to go away. In mid-February the KPD had initiated an inquiry into the Hildburghausen affair in the Thuringian parliament. A parliamentary committee, headed by the SPD's Hermann Brill, was established to look into the matter from 14 March. They were determined not to spare Hitler the public embarrassment. Perhaps they could even damage his chances of becoming President. It was now or never. Every attempt had to be undertaken to keep the Nazis out of power. In Thuringia, they had seen a glimpse of what Nazi rule meant.

The newly minted German citizen Hitler arrived in Weimar on 5 March as part of his nationwide election campaign in twelve towns and cities. Many residents didn't seem to care about the unsavoury revelations. Nearly 8,000 people gathered on the market square to hear Hitler speak about how special Weimar was to his mission: 'I've come here to this square, on which in 1926 the movement showed itself to the public for the first time, to offer you my gratitude for your belief, your trust and your willingness to sacrifice,' he told them. 'I believe that you will see in a few weeks or months how rightly you acted in the face of German history.'[16] The local Nazi Party was so sure Hitler would win the upcoming presidential elections that they booked the sleek, newly finished Weimarhalle (Weimar Hall) for 1,000 marks for an event on 15 March entitled 'Our Victory!'[17]

When Hitler travelled to Weimar on 15 March, he hadn't won the first round of the presidential elections. He'd come second with 30 per cent of the vote behind Paul von Hindenburg, who had narrowly missed an absolute majority, gaining 49.5 per cent. A second round was scheduled for 10 April, giving Hitler an opportunity to use the expensive booking at the Weimarhalle for more campaigning rather than a victory speech. But first, he had another matter to attend to.

Hitler and Frick had been summoned to appear in front of Brill's parliamentary commission that was conducting the inquiry into the Hildburghausen affair. The social democrat questioned Hitler so effectively that his mask of respectability slipped. Goebbels, who'd accompanied Frick and Hitler, felt the 'Führer is excessively provoked by the red deputies and throws his retort back in their faces in a fit of rage'.[18] Others saw it too. 'Herr Hitler was exceptionally nervous,' one liberal journalist reported. 'Soon the great tribune of the people fell into rolling pathos and bloated phrases and always in moments when it was the most embarrassing to him.' Frick and Hitler 'appeared as they were, small and ugly'.[19]

Hitler's spirits lifted when the questioning was over and he stepped outside. 'In Weimar itself the mood is brilliant,' wrote Goebbels. 'The party has already partially overcome its first momentary depression. Fight! Attack! Fanfare! In the evening, we all talk in the new hall.'[20] Many Weimarers didn't seem to care that Hitler had just been exposed and humiliated like a 'prima donna without make-up', as the social democratic newspaper *Das Volk* put it.[21] They flocked to the Weimarhalle in their droves. The brand-new events venue had only just been finished to the north-west of the town centre, not far from the Schwanseebad lido. As a prestige project, the Weimar administration had built it in a record time of just fifteen months despite the economic crisis that had slowed down its housebuilding programmes. The 2,300-seat hall had not even been officially inaugurated when the Nazis overcrowded it with 4,000 spectators on the evening of 15 March.[22] To frenetic applause, Hitler, Goebbels and Frick admitted the 'victory' they had come here to celebrate hadn't happened yet.

Hitler wouldn't become President in the second round of the elections on 10 April either. Germans now had a choice between three candidates who all hated democracy: communist Ernst Thälmann, monarchist Paul von Hindenburg and fascist Adolf Hitler. Social democrats and liberals threw their support behind Hindenburg as the least bad option and this was enough for him to win, with 53 per cent of the vote. Hitler received 37 per cent.

For the Nazis, the struggle would have to go on. And there was no better place to fight than Weimar. Had it been for Thuringia only, Hitler would now be President. He got 45 per cent of the votes there, narrowly beating Hindenburg's 41 per cent. While Weimar still preferred Hindenburg, with 50 per cent voting for the ageing incumbent, Hitler's vote was above average there too, with 43 per cent.[23] Sensing that much of the public mood was on their side in the Weimarhalle on 15 March, Hitler, Frick and Goebbels announced that, in 'true Goethe spirit', they would 'defy all force, stay the course'.[24]

One week later, Carl Weirich was sitting in the Weimarhalle. He was impressed. It was only a five-minute walk from his home but it seemed a world away. It was vast and modern but somehow blended into a town that prided itself on its history. The final design had been influenced by Paul Schultze-Naumburg, who had demanded in September 1930 that the new building must neither disrupt nor alter the town's historical appeal 'due to the sacred soil that Weimar is to the whole world'.[25]

Weimar had pulled off an incredible feat. It had built the largest conference hall in Thuringia in just fifteen months at the height of the Great Depression. The Weimarhalle was finished just in time for its intended deadline, the Goethe centenary on 22 March. Carl was there to witness that moment, which became the highlight of 1932 for him, 'the year of the one hundredth anniversary of the death of our great poet prince Wolfgang von Goethe'.[26] It seemed the whole world had descended on Weimar. The top political brass had come down from Berlin, as had ambassadors, journalists and many public figures. When the hour of Goethe's death approached at 11.30 a.m., the whole town erupted with the sound of bells being rung in unison. This launched a solemn procession to Goethe's tomb in the burial chapel of the Dukes of Saxe-Weimar-Eisenach in Weimar's Historical Cemetery. In a rare display of the old and the new regime side by side, Chancellor Brüning laid a wreath together with Feodora, the former Grand Duchess of Saxe-Weimar-Eisenach.

While there were Goethe celebrations all over the country in 1932, nobody claimed Goethe like Weimar. This had been his home. It was where he'd lived and written the works that would define the German literary canon. This is where he'd died and where he continued to be worshipped by tourists flocking to Weimar. 'Take your shoes off, for the soil on which you walk is holy land,' Julius Petersen, president of the Goethe Society, proclaimed in the Weimarhalle, likening Weimar to Bethlehem. The Weimar Republic, baptized in this haven of high culture, had returned here for one more celebration of a democracy in its death throes.

Hotels like the Hohenzollern were booked out for days. Rosa and Arthur Schmidt needed the business. Not only had they suffered from the sharp reduction in visitor numbers, but they had also lost their eldest daughter Alexandra as an invaluable helper in the hotel. She was getting married to Artur Greulich, a grocer from Lehnstedt, just outside of Weimar. The pair were moving into a flat at Zeppelinplatz – only a ten-minute stroll away from the hotel – but they were looking forward to having their own young family.[27] Alexandra and Artur were now neighbours of the Nehrlings. The couple had finally given up on regaining a position for SPD man Kurt in a civil service staffed with Frick's men and decided to turn their temporary textile venture into a proper shop located on Zeppelinplatz. Having just opened the new business, they too appreciated the extra footfall.

Carl took advantage of the event by selling souvenirs and

postcards in his stationery shop. The whole town went Goethe crazy. Visitors could buy Goethe busts and Goethe cake. They could eat like Goethe. They could watch Goethe plays at Goethe's theatre. Carl loved it. He visited many more Goethe events that spring, including *Goethe lebt . . . !*, a film about the poet featuring local actress Emmy Sonnemann. He attended a Goethe Fest in Tiefurt, just outside of Weimar, where there was a procession with actors all dressed up in period costumes. He was most grateful not for the spectacle itself but for the distraction it afforded, because 'it was in the days of the weeks honouring Goethe, of all times, that . . . our second mortgage of 11,000 [marks] was cancelled'. This was a huge blow and a time of 'particular anxiety' for the Weirichs as they stared down the abyss of losing their home and their livelihood.[28] No bank would lend them money in this time of crisis. There was only one way: go cap in hand to friends and family to see if anyone could help. In the end, they scraped the funds together from a cousin and little Wilhelm's favourite uncle and namesake. Carl agreed to pay the money back with 6 and 5 per cent interest respectively, despite having no idea if he would be able to do that or when. The Goethe spectacle helped many other Weimarers take the edge off personal catastrophes. The 'poet prince' was venerated by vast swathes of the population. He had the potential to be a rare unifying figure in a minefield of contested history and culture. President Hindenburg said the man's name 'stands next to Homer and Dante and Shakespeare among the princes of European thought'.[29] The Goethe Society told Germans that the 'spirit of Goethe' called for a 'harmonious end to self-destructive strife'.[30]

The Goethe celebrations in Weimar had the opposite effect, exposing the polarization of society. The Nazi newspaper *Der Angriff* (The Attack) had called for a boycott of the event to avoid any 'commensality with the organizers' and encouraged their supporters to 'give special expression to their own views of Goethe and his German humanity'. The poet had become contested. The Nazis argued that their Goethe wasn't a 'cosmopolitan and citizen of the world, good European, freemason and humanitarian apostle'.

Theirs was a Goethe who 'was in his being explicitly German [and] openly endorsed Germanness'.[31] The culture wars of the day played out in Weimar, clear for all to see. While only official buildings were to be flagged on 22 March, Gauleiter Fritz Sauckel ordered all Nazi Party members and sympathizers to hang swastika flags from their windows, which many did.[32]

The Nobel laureate Thomas Mann, who was awarded one of Hindenburg's special Goethe Medals in Weimar, found the town's 'mix of Hitlerism and Goethe' deeply disturbing. 'Weimar is a centre of Hitlerdom,' he observed, adding that 'the type of young person who roams the town with unguided certainty and greets one another with the Roman salute dominates the town'. But it was not only the young who had radicalized. While Mann praised Goethe as a citizen of the world who would have looked upon the new German conservatism 'coldly, even with contempt', Goethe archivist Max Hecker called his idol the 'most German of Germans' whose poetic art came to him from the 'inscrutable depths of his Germanness'.[33] Hecker, a convivial Rhinelander who'd come to Weimar to study Goethe, had begun to drift off to ethnic nationalism amid the existential crisis engulfing the republic.

Like her father, Jutta Hecker was excited about the Goethe anniversary. She was at the parental home when her father received a visitor from Italy. The man introduced himself as a professor of German Studies at the University of Turin. He had come to tell Max Hecker that he had been selected as one of three German scholars to attend the Goethe festivities in Rome, where the poet had spent some formative months during his 'Italian Journey' in the 1780s. It was a personal invitation from the Italian king, Victor Emmanuel III. The Heckers were awestruck. They often struggled to feed their children and now they had a royal invitation to Italy. Max Hecker immediately accepted. Then the Italian professor turned to Max's daughter and asked: 'You, too?' Jutta couldn't believe her luck.[34]

At the end of March, the Heckers found themselves in a taxi in Rome, escorted by impressive men in uniform to the house that

Goethe had occupied. When they arrived, the room was buzzing with eminent Goethe scholars from all over Europe. Most spoke German but there were fragments of other languages too. Then a door opened and the room went quiet. In walked a stout man with dark, blazing eyes and a prominent jawline. He was almost completely bald and his strutting walk may have looked comical in a different context. Yet he commanded the room. Everyone rose and there was complete silence during his ten-minute speech about Goethe, which he delivered in heavily accented German. Jutta was completely in awe of Benito Mussolini, finding the 'Duce' even more impressive than the king. Years later she admitted how much she had fallen for his 'clever, cunning deception'.[35]

Emmy Sonnemann didn't think of herself as a political person. She lived for the theatre. She'd been twelve years old when she saw Shakespeare's *The Merchant of Venice* and knew she'd found her vocation. Her father, the wealthy owner of a chocolate factory, wasn't keen on the idea of his daughter becoming an actress. But her mother supported her, and Emmy began taking lessons in her home town of Hamburg, followed by engagements in Munich, Vienna, Stuttgart and finally at the German National Theatre in Weimar, where she arrived in 1922. She had married fellow actor Karl Köstlin, but in 1920 the couple decided that they 'were no more than good friends' and had had an amicable divorce.[36]

Emmy loved the freedom she enjoyed as a single woman in Weimar. She regularly got leading roles and felt taken seriously as an actress. She earned enough to live in a three-bedroom apartment and even the abject misery that the Great Depression brought to so many around her left her largely untouched. One day, when she strolled through the large Goethe Park on a sunny spring day, she was confused why all the benches were taken up by 'idle young men'. 'Some of them had sticks and were drawing circles in the ground,' she observed. She sat down and listened to their conversations. Only then did she realize that the men were unemployed. How had she missed how bad things had got around her? The world outside acting tended to pass Emmy by as she worked or met friends at the Kaiser Café to peruse newspapers for theatre reviews.[37]

One day in April, a group of men walked into the café. 'Isn't that a famous politician?' Emmy's friend whispered, pointing at a man with a 'small, short moustache'. Emmy had seen his face in the papers. 'That's Adolf Hitler.' The women stood up and made to leave, but one of Hitler's men stopped them and introduced the women to his boss. Hitler kissed their hands and said: 'I hear you're members of the German National Theatre. I would be devastated if I was to chase you out. Please stay and do me the pleasure to tell me about the theatre. You couldn't do me a greater favour.'[38] Emmy found the Nazi leader surprisingly easy to talk to. He could be charming when talking to women. She regaled him with amusing episodes from her life as an actress in Weimar and 'Hitler cried tears of laughter.'[39]

A few weeks later she met him again, on the day she saw the unemployed men on the park benches. Hitler was strolling through the same park, as was his wont whenever he had any time to spare in Weimar. He spotted Emmy and asked her why she looked so upset. She told him about the misery she'd just witnessed. 'His large blue eyes rested on mine for a while,' she remembered. He responded: 'I can reassure you. It won't be long and we National Socialists will be in charge. We won't take more than three or four years and then there won't be a single unemployed person in Germany any more.'[40] Now Emmy's interest was piqued and she attended one of Hitler's speeches at her workplace, the National Theatre, a couple of days later. There were no spare seats, so she listened with a few of her colleagues from the backstage area. She couldn't hear much beyond occasional fragments. But the 'thunderous applause' made an impression on her. 'Theatre people have a special sense for such moments,' she mused.[41]

If Emmy was impressed by Hitler, she was even more struck by one of his closest lieutenants. 'Say, is that Göring or Goebbels?' she whispered to a friend at the Kaiser Café a few days later. The two women had been hiding behind a newspaper in their usual corner at the back of the café, trying to stay inconspicuous while tuning into the conversations around them. 'Göring, of course,' Emmy's friend whispered back. Suddenly, Hermann Göring and his right-hand man Paul Körner stood in front of the women and asked if they might sit with them for a while. They were immediately engrossed in conversation and later went on a long walk together.

'For the first time in my life I forgot my roles, the theatre and everything,' Emmy remembered. She was completely enamoured with Göring. He was the same age as her but a world-weary sadness seemed to emanate from him. He told her that he'd lost his Swedish wife Carin just a few months earlier to tuberculosis. Emmy was fascinated. She'd seen the couple in the audience at one of her performances the previous year. She didn't take much note of Göring at the time, instantly forgetting his face, but his wife had 'enchanted me irresistibly', she recalled.[42] Now Göring spoke of Carin with 'unending love and such deep grief that I warmed to him more with every word'. Emmy had just lost her mother and her companion's sadness resonated with her own.

Göring returned to Weimar a couple of weeks later to give a speech. Emmy had seen it advertised on posters all around town but didn't dare attend, because the man 'had made such a strong impression on me as a human that I now feared the politician and speaker Göring might destroy this impression again'. The pair met up afterwards for a 'thrillingly exciting' evening at the Golden Eagle tavern. Emmy had been so nervous that she changed her mind about what to wear three times. In the end it didn't matter. When she walked home with him later that night, Emmy realized: 'It was only a short walk but in that time my future life was decided.'[43]

Baldur von Schirach and Henny Hoffmann got married on 31 March. Despite their privileged backgrounds, even they struggled a little under the pressures of the global economic crisis. Much of the Schirach family fortunes were tied up in the US, where the stock market had collapsed. So the couple got married in Hitler's Munich flat, with the Führer himself serving as best man. Hitler sponsored an extravagant feast, complete with roast beef, but being a vegetarian and a teetotaller, he stuck to spaghetti with tomato sauce and mineral water himself.

The newly-weds had a short honeymoon in the Tyrolean mountains for a few days before Baldur had to get back to work. There was much to do. The SA and the Hitler Youth had been banned for the spree of street violence they'd embarked on following Hindenburg's re-election, which meant Schirach had to reorganize events, training and other plans to go ahead illegally and undercover for a while. And then there were yet more elections. Under the strain of rapidly escalating economic misery and political fragmentation, the German and the Thuringian governments collapsed and new elections for both parliaments were scheduled for 31 July.

This gave Schirach an opportunity to show how useful he could be to Hitler. Working together with his photographer father-in-law Heinrich Hoffmann, he produced an illustrated book entitled *The Hitler No One Knows: 100 Photographs of the Life of the Führer*. The images showed Hitler in settings ranging from political rallies to beach walks, reading a newspaper in an armchair or relaxing in a sun lounger with his favourite German shepherd dog. This proved to be one of the most successful image campaigns to shape Hitler's personality cult. By 1935, 420,000 copies of the book had been printed.[44] It's impossible to tell what role Schirach's efforts played in the electoral campaign. In the Reichstag, the NSDAP became the largest party for the first time, getting 37.3 per cent of the vote, ahead of the SPD, which came second with just 21.6 per cent. Nearly half the votes in Weimar went to the Nazis for the federal election.[45]

It still wasn't enough for a majority. Hindenburg had also made it clear that he had no intention of appointing Hitler as Chancellor. So the Reichstag collapsed immediately and new elections were scheduled for 6 November. This gave the Nazis some time to put changes in place. They filled the Reichstag seats with loyal party soldiers who could draw their 800-mark salaries as MPs and therefore reduce the burden on the party purse. Baldur von Schirach became one of 230 Nazi deputies and at twenty-five also the youngest member of the

Reichstag. Henny was delighted. She was pregnant with their first child and could now be sure that her husband wouldn't go to prison for his illegal political activities, since the prosecution of a Reichstag MP required the ascent of a parliament that was currently paralysed. Schirach's parents in Weimar were astonished. His father thought this was all happening a bit too fast, but his mother was proud and now claimed she'd always known her son would one day be a great politician.[46] Schirach himself thought of this election as 'just the beginning. The real goal is: the National Socialist dictatorship.'[47]

In Schirach's native Thuringia, the state parliament elections had gone even better for the NSDAP. The party wasn't far off an absolute majority, getting 42.5 per cent of the vote – in Weimar it was even slightly higher at 44 per cent.[48] Clearly, all the efforts of the social democrats, communists and others to expose the doings of Wilhelm Frick's regime had been ignored by many Weimarers who saw little but their own economic, political and cultural anxieties and craved the quick and extreme solutions that the Nazis promised.

Occupying twenty-six out of sixty-one seats, the NSDAP no longer had to wrangle with other parties for political offices and control. Supported by the six deputies from the Thuringian Agricultural League, it formed a Nazi government in Thuringia months before Hitler was to become Chancellor of Germany. Gauleiter Fritz Sauckel's hour had come. He took over as the new Leading Minister of State. A Nazi playbook unfolded in Thuringia that was to prove useful for Hitler's strategy in Berlin. Sauckel was completely open about his plans in parliament: 'Of course we will abuse the power the Thuringian people have given us in the last election in every way.'[49]

Once again, the 'spirit of Weimar' was conjured. The late Friedrich Ebert had used the same term in 1919 to dream up a liberal and democratic Germany. Now Sauckel evoked 'Nietzsche, Goethe, Schiller, Bach, Wagner and Liszt and all the masters of the fine arts who worked in Weimar in the last century' to underpin a very different regime.[50] Like Frick, Sauckel would start by changing young minds, requiring all high school students to finish the last lesson of each week with a new ritual. One lead student or the teacher was to read Article 231 of the Treaty of Versailles that declared Germany responsible for the war. Then the class was to answer as one: 'The German shame shall burn in our souls until the day that brings honour and freedom.'[51]

Elisabeth Förster-Nietzsche adapted nimbly to the political changes that came over Thuringia. She immediately made contact with the new leadership, and the Nazi members at the Villa Silberblick were increasingly brazen in using the archive to advertise for the party. The last pretences of neutrality were rapidly dissolving. The Nietzsche Archive and its ageing figurehead gained a reputation as a Nazi stronghold.[52] Elisabeth herself still harboured mixed feelings. She'd do whatever it took to secure backing for Friedrich Nietzsche's legacy, and she had no objection in principle to Germany being turned into a far-right dictatorship. But she still found the Nazi leadership undignified and lacking in taste, manners and education.

She told Harry Graf Kessler that she was horrified at Hitler's conduct with Hindenburg. The Nazi leader had met with the new Chancellor Franz von Papen and President Paul von Hindenburg on 13 August to negotiate a possible Nazi participation in government. Papen had offered him to become Vice Chancellor and appoint a few other Nazis as ministers. Hitler had declined, demanding the chancellorship for himself as the leader of the biggest party. This was something Hindenburg rejected vehemently. He'd made it clear that he had no respect for Hitler, whom he habitually referred to as the 'Bohemian lance corporal', and who seemed to exercise no control over his drunken thugs in the SA who were busy unleashing a horrendous wave of violence on the streets. Hitler retorted by making disparaging remarks about Hindenburg's age and declining mental faculties.

Elisabeth thought this was outrageous. 'How different had Mussolini behaved when, after his March on Rome, he left everything as it was and didn't dismiss the King,' she commented to Harry. Hitler's disrespectful remarks about Hindenburg 'would cost him millions of votes', she predicted. Now 'seriously worried', she asked Harry whether he thought Hitler might still somehow come to power. She thought this would be a 'misfortune' for Germany given what she was witnessing in Thuringia where he'd installed 'unsuited and uneducated people'. She pointed to Sauckel as an example, 'a former sailor and metalworker apprentice', who had been made 'a minister here in Weimar'. She told Harry she'd stick with the national-conservative DNVP.[53]

But Elisabeth knew that this made her part of a tiny minority. The DNVP had only been voted for by 6 per cent of the population. She increasingly felt like a dinosaur in a rapidly changing world she no longer understood. She tried to flee back into the aristocratic hier-archies she'd known as a child. An afternoon tea meeting with the ex-Kaiser's wife, 'Empress Hermine', was a highlight of 1932 for her. Perhaps one day 'an old wise Kaiser' might spring from Germany's mythical Kyffhäuser mountains, uniting the quarrelling Germans and leading them to better times, she fantasized. 'Poor old lady!' Harry mused, pitying his friend for failing to understand that a monarchist restoration was 'unthinkable under any circumstances'.[54] In her heart, Elisabeth knew this and it was making her depressed. Now eighty-six years old, she was in constant pain, particularly in her lower back, where it was often excruciating. During Harry's visit she broke down in tears. Why was she still here? Doing his best to console her, Harry told her that 'she mustn't think of death just yet'.[55]

A week after his visit to Weimar, Harry reported to Elisabeth from the German capital. With four days to go before voters were asked to head to the polls again, he observed that the 'election campaign is surprisingly calm in Berlin this time, which is a welcome contrast to the immense turmoil and civil-war-like mood of the previous one. Maybe we'll get through the looming winter without larger disruptions after all.'[56] He didn't know how misplaced this hope would be, and that he'd never see Elisabeth again.

In Thuringia, the Nazi government wanted to use its first few months to try to showcase what it could do once in power in Berlin.

For that to work, it needed to be seen to tackle the abject poverty that was tearing through communities, especially in the mountainous Thuringian Forest. Sauckel promised to make it a governmental priority to end the misery for 'workers, farmers, the middle classes and freelancers'. This is what made the Nazis unique and their electoral potential enormous. Instead of emphasizing the class struggle like communists and socialists or trying to cut rights and help for workers like conservatives, they emphasized that everyone was affected by this crisis. Their propaganda bridged class divides with Sauckel arguing that the way out of this 'deepest political, cultural and economic crisis' was 'a true and social people's and fate community'. What made this idea seductive to those who were looking for someone to blame is that it defined this 'people's community' or *Volksgemeinschaft* sharply against supposed outsiders. Sauckel emphasized that it encompassed only 'valuable forces . . . in terms of race and ethnicity'.[57]

Even before he took office, Sauckel had repeatedly incited violence against Jews, especially in Weimar. During the Goethe festivities he'd called on Nazi supporters to ensure that 'Jews and Jew comrades who arrive here for the Goethe week get the right impression of Weimar'.[58] In December, Thuringian NSDAP activists launched a boycott campaign under the slogan 'Don't Buy from Jews'. Jewish organizations tried to fight back by legal means. In 1930, they'd won a court order that declared such boycotts illegal and they were now reporting the Nazi Party to the police. But many Jews preferred to emphasize their role as assimilated, German citizens rather than escalate a fight they knew they could not win.[59] In Weimar, Rosa Schmidt was one of them. She considered herself German and was married to a decorated war veteran. It made no sense to her to draw attention to her Jewish roots. She had enough on her hands to keep the Hotel Hohenzollern afloat. Now wasn't the time for political activism.

Sauckel's antisemitic actions did little to fix the economic emergency that engulfed the majority of Thuringians. Neither did measures like work-creation schemes or show visits to the most impoverished parts of Thuringia. All of these were symbolic acts intended not to make a difference but, as Sauckel's Finance Minister and Deputy Gauleiter Willy Marschler put it, to 'usher our state over into the Reich that the Führer wants, the Third Reich'.[60]

Sauckel carefully aligned his messaging with Hitler's. He announced that he'd halve ministerial salaries in Thuringia before Hitler, during another sold-out appearance at the Weimarhalle on 23 October, promised never to draw any kind of state salary for himself, claiming that his 'best reward would be the victory of the movement'.[61] Hitler was still attracting huge audiences. His speech at the Weimarhalle was so in demand that it had to be broadcast live into several other venues. Elsewhere, his appearances often caused street brawls between supporters and opponents. In other Thuringian towns like Jena, Ronneburg and Gera, his car had been spat at and attacked with bricks. But not in Weimar, where thousands of people flocked to see or at least hear the Nazi leaders speak and the streets remained quiet.[62]

Overall, the atmosphere was different in November compared to the frenzy in July. Harry Graf Kessler had been right, things seemed to have calmed down a little. But the calm stemmed from apathy, not recovery. This meant that the many non-voters the Nazis had been able to mobilize previously didn't bother going to the polling stations on 6 November. Turnout across Germany dropped. Some voters were also appalled at the brutality enacted by boisterous SA hordes. There had been hundreds of horrific acts of political violence around the previous election, and this was not how Germans envisioned the restoration of law and order that Hitler promised. So the Nazis came out of the November election as the largest party but having taken a heavy hit. They fell to 33 per cent of the vote, having lost four points in three months. In Weimar they also fell, to 39 per cent – still a lot but not the upward trend the Nazis were hoping for.

Nonetheless, Weimar remained a retreat for Hitler. Thuringia was a battleground he had won in his war for Germany. When, in late November, he was summoned to Berlin to engage in new coalition negotiations, he boarded the night train from Munich to Berlin but then changed his mind along the way and got off in Jena to travel on to Weimar instead. He wasn't going to accept anything less than the chancellorship, and the government could come to him when they were ready to give it to him.

'Bravo!' gushed Goebbels, who was waiting for him at the Hotel Elephant. 'Press has gone mad . . . Now we just need to hold our nerve!'[63] The tactic worked. The government sent an envoy to Weimar. It didn't offer anything new: the vice chancellorship for Hitler and a few ministerial positions for the NSDAP. The Führer turned this down as before and Goebbels approved. 'No accommodation with reactionaries. The crisis will lift us to the top,' he wrote. Sitting with his boss at the Elephant late into the night, Goebbels was sure of it: 'Hitler's hour will come.'[64]

Christmas 1932 was a miserable one for many Weimarers. So it was for Carl Weirich. He took comfort from a 'particularly beautiful Christmas Day service' at church, but the weather was downcast, 'as was the mood among the population', he noted in his diary. 'The economic crisis in Germany has affected my shop, too, through less revenue.'[65] Things were desperate. If another mortgage was called in or the economy didn't get better soon, he might lose everything. He needed to secure a future for his family, especially for little Wilhelm, who was going to start school in 1933. One government after another had failed to make things better. Now Carl was pinning all his hopes on one 'young man, the Führer of the National Socialist Party A. Hitler'.[66]

PART IV

Decisions

A New Weimar

1933

Emmy Sonnemann bowed and walked off the stage. The actress had played the German National Theatre for years. Her life in Weimar followed enjoyable routines. But today was not like any other day. It was 29 January and Emmy's life was about to change forever.

Her boyfriend Hermann Göring had called from Berlin in the late afternoon. They had been seeing each other for a few months now but it was a long-distance relationship. 'I was an actress who saw her job as a real vocation,' she wrote in her memoirs, 'and so I needed the freedom to lead my own life.'[1] As one of Hitler's closest lieutenants, Göring kept his flat in Berlin, where an entire room was dedicated to his late wife Carin. Emmy found this 'a little creepy . . . Hundreds of little objects which reminded him of her were displayed as if in a museum.' But she was also touched by Göring's devotion.[2]

When Göring had called her that afternoon, he sounded excited. 'Tomorrow is the day,' he'd said breathlessly. 'Adolf Hitler will become Reich Chancellor. You absolutely have to come to Berlin. I'll send you a car.' Emmy barely had time to pack, rushing back from her stage performance in the evening and getting ready as quickly as she could. When she arrived in Berlin after a long drive, it was the middle of the night, but Göring had a favour to ask before they went to bed: 'Go to Adolf Hitler tomorrow morning and bring him some flowers. He'll like that.' The next day, Emmy did as she was told. She bought the florist's last available bouquet and was taken to Hitler's room at the luxurious Hotel Kaiserhof. When she entered, Hitler was standing by the window with his back turned to her, staring out, as if 'he'd escaped his surroundings', it seemed to Emmy. Finally, he turned and looked at her. 'These are my first flowers,' he said and took them in a solemn gesture. 'And you are the first woman to congratulate me.' After a pause, he fell into one of his monologues, lecturing no one in particular on how he had proved his doubters wrong. Emmy sensed she had no role to play here, 'this man had to be alone now'. She slowly walked out as Hitler continued to mumble to himself.[3]

For a moment, the magnitude of how her own life was about to change came crashing down on Emmy. Göring would have a place in Hitler's government as Reichsminister without portfolio, Reichskommissar of Aviation and head of the Prussian state. Would she 'have given him a wide berth if I'd known what he'd become?' she pondered. 'But I only knew one answer to this question: "I love him." '[4] When she saw her boyfriend again in the afternoon, he was a 'major leading personality of the Reich'.[5] However apolitical she told herself she was, she felt proud to be the woman by this man's side. She decided then that she could live with his politics.

Göring told Emmy that there would be a huge torch procession celebrating Hitler's chancellorship and that he'd booked her a room at the Kaiserhof from where she could watch. Expecting trouble, possibly from the army or communists, he gave her a pistol 'in case something happens'. Emmy looked at the weapon in horror. It 'certainly didn't help me feel calmer'. As she sat in her room in the evening, she heard drum beats and singing in the distance. She rushed to the window and stared down as endless columns of men marched by in lockstep. Emmy took in the 'unforgettable, gigantic spectacle' as the flames danced in her eyes. She'd later tell herself that she'd 'had no bad premonition whatsoever that night'.[6]

A few floors below Emmy Sonnemann, Harry Graf Kessler was attending an event of the SeSiSo Club, a group of influential politicians, intellectuals and public figures who regularly met at the Kaiserhof. He saw what Emmy saw: men in uniform marching through Berlin, but he loathed 'that carnival'. 'When we came out from our lecture,' he wrote in his diary, 'an endless SA column goose-stepped past some bigwigs . . . The whole square is full of gawpers.' Harry had seen enough. He needed a drink. Preferably somewhere else.

Together with Hans von Seeckt, one of the three founders of the SeSiSo Club, he went to the Fürstenberg Bräu beer hall at Potsdamer Platz to escape, but 'the carnival mood was reaching its zenith' there. With Stormtroopers everywhere, an atmosphere of rowdy jubilance engulfed the city. The men had just ordered drinks when two young women appeared by their table. Seeckt was enjoying this, ordering them drinks and food. But it soon dawned on him that they were prostitutes and had no intention of leaving the table, 'so that we ended up spending the rest of the night until 2 o'clock with those two blonde children', Harry wrote. A gay man, he found it intensely amusing to watch an 'increasingly awkward' Seeckt struggle to politely send the giggling women away. The man was nearly seventy, a former Chief of the German General Staff and soon-to-be military advisor to Chinese leader Chiang Kai-shek. Yet here he was, with two sex workers who called him their 'little grandpa'. Really, Harry mused with all the gallows humour he could muster on the evening Hitler had come to power, the undignified spectacle seemed a 'fitting and all-round appropriate end to this "historic" day'.[7]

While Harry was getting drunk in a noisy bar in Berlin, Carl Weirich listened to the 'jubilation and euphoria of the people' in Weimar.[8] He was sitting in his flat with Marie, following a live broadcast from the capital. He'd forked out on a Seibt radio for Christmas 1932, thinking it would be good for Wilhelm to be able to listen to the many 'good educational features and musical programmes' that were being broadcast. At 200 marks, it hadn't been cheap. Carl and Marie had to give up their music lessons, but it was worth it. On New Year's Day, they had listened to the church bells in Naumburg, a religious service in Nuremberg and a Bach cantata in Leipzig.

The new technology was awe-inspiring, and soon became the centrepiece of the family home. Friends would gather to listen to particular programmes or big events happening far away. Wilhelm's first two pencil drawings were of the house at Geleitstraße 10 and the family radio.[9] His father liked 'being able to stay up to date with politics'.[10] And so the Weirich family sat up until late into the night on 'the day the office of the Reich Chancellor was assumed by Adolf Hitler'.[11]

Elisabeth Förster-Nietzsche saw Hitler a few days later. They were both attending a performance of Richard Wagner's musical drama *Tristan and Isolde*, played at the German National Theatre in Weimar in honour of the fiftieth anniversary of the composer's death. When the Nazi leader visited Nietzsche's sister in her box, she assured him he would always be welcome at the Villa Silberblick. She later even offered to arrange for a vegetarian breakfast.[12] Hitler would visit Elisabeth on every one of his Weimar visits between 1933 and 1935.[13]

Whatever reservations she may have had, Elisabeth knew that power now lay with Hitler. There would be no more haggling with local intermediaries. The Thuringian parliament was to hold its last ever session just two weeks later, on 14 February. In deference to Hitler's regime, the Thuringian Nazis read out a statement of subordination. In protest, the SPD and KPD deputies walked out and the remaining MPs voted to adjourn the state parliament 'indefinitely'.[14]

Rapid and ruthless change was afoot. Following the same reforms Hermann Göring was enacting in Prussia, Thuringia ordered the enlistment of SA, SS and Stahlhelm men as Hilfspolizei or 'auxiliary police' from 22 February. Under Sauckel's leadership, they proceeded to beat, imprison, torture and kill political opponents. After a communist arson attack on the Reichstag in Berlin on 27 February, President Hindenburg used his emergency powers to suspend civil liberties, in effect untethering Nazi thugs and police from the law. The escalation was immediately palpable, including in Weimar, where Harry Graf Kessler arrived by train on the evening of the day after the Reichstag Fire. He'd come to negotiate the remortgaging of his villa, and what he found was a town he no longer wanted to call home. 'In Weimar at the station,' he wrote in his diary that night, 'the old luggage carrier was waiting for me with a very timid look on his face. Here in Weimar things were terrible, "auxiliary police" (SA) everywhere, one didn't dare say a word.'[15]

Within days, hundreds of people were arrested in Thuringia and taken into 'protective custody'.[16] Weimar's jail had a capacity of 102 inmates. Now it housed 117 people, of whom fifty-four were political prisoners, including four women. Fearing the situation might escalate, the chief prosecutor of the Thuringian state court asked the Justice Ministry to 'house some of the political prisoners elsewhere; the current situation is unsustainable'.[17] That 'elsewhere' was quickly found. On 3 March, Sauckel ordered prisoners to be taken to a school building located on an airfield in Nohra on the outskirts of Weimar. He inspected the facilities on Sunday 5 March, by which time around 200 people had been taken there, including five of the ten KPD deputies in the Thuringian parliament. He was shown three large rooms with straw on the floor for the prisoners to sleep on and a few blankets. The hygienic conditions were poor since there weren't enough toilets and washing facilities. Inmates were regularly assaulted and had no way to contact relatives or friends. From 8 March, newspapers began to call the makeshift prison in Weimar-Nohra a 'concentration camp' – the first in Nazi Germany.[18]

In Weimar, there was no doubt that the Nazis intended their rule to be permanent. There was a huge torch procession ushering in the new era on the first day of Hitler's chancellorship. It was led by SA, SS and Hitler Youth troops and the street through which the main march took place – a broad boulevard south-east of the town centre – would soon be called Straße der SA or SA Street. When the throngs reached the market square, they were greeted by Fritz Sauckel, who declared that in the future they'd be free to 'exercise the kind of intolerance that accepted nothing and permitted nothing that is against the ideas of Germany'.[19] SA troops took down the Bauhaus-designed plaque from the facade of the German National Theatre that commemorated the National Assembly of 1919.

The *Weimarische Zeitung* exuberantly announced: 'Political parties are now a sideshow!'[20] But this wasn't quite true yet. Hitler wanted a parliamentary majority as a legal veneer to the process of turning democracy into dictatorship. So a federal election was scheduled for 5 March. Fierce violence against political opponents skewed the results of the country's last multi-party election in a generation. The Nazis increased their vote share to 43.9 per cent but this still wasn't a majority. As ever, the number was higher in Weimar but with 49.7 per cent still just shy of the target. Notably, in the Thuringian capital 11.9 per cent of voters stuck with the KPD despite the incarceration of a number of communist deputies.[21]

Weimar may have looked and felt different, but life went on. Rosa and Arthur Schmidt hosted Carl Weirich and his friends at the Hotel Hohenzollern on Saturday 4 March, the day before the election. Their guests had not come to discuss politics, organize resistance or decide what to do next. They'd rented the room to celebrate the anniversary of the Zither Association. Carl had played the string instrument for years but had had to scrap his regular lessons to save money. He still loved playing and socializing with other zither enthusiasts. Rosa and Arthur had a business to run. Nazi government or not, they continued to host social evenings as well as more formal gatherings like that of the Thuringian Teachers' Association, which met to elect a new board in April.[22]

Carl's interest in politics soared now that his radio kept him abreast of developments. On 21 March, he tuned in as the Reichstag was reopened in a ceremony in Potsdam, the former power centre of the Kings of Prussia. Hitler used the opportunity to associate himself with older German regimes. Crown Prince Wilhelm was present, as was the still popular President Hindenburg, to whom the new Chancellor bowed his head. Carl listened intently as 'Hindenburg a[nd] Hitler spoke together at the grave of Fr[ederick] t[he] Gr[eat]' before 'the first Reichstag session in the afternoon in the Kroll Opera', the building that was used as a replacement for the burned-out parliament.[23]

As much as he followed current events on the radio, to Carl, life wasn't about politics. 'The shop demanded all of our strength,' he wrote. This year, he had to deliver over 30,000 school books by lorry. His son would soon need textbooks too. Wilhelm was due to become a pupil at the nearby Herder Primary School. Carl proudly stuck a photograph of his boy into his diary that showed him with his *Zuckertüte*, a huge paper cone filled with sweets and stationery that German children receive as a present on their first day of school.[24] Life went on after 30 January 1933. Hitler's new regime didn't consider the Weirichs political or racial enemies.

For Kurt and Heddy Nehrling life got difficult. Not only were they both SPD members but Kurt was also in the pro-democratic paramilitary Reichsbanner. The Nazis feared fierce resistance from people like the Nehrlings, so they tried to purge them from public service. On 18 March, the Thuringian regime decreed that SPD members couldn't be civil servants. Only people who 'in their political views, their political work and their political aims are aligned with the politics of the nationalist Reich government of Adolf Hitler' could.[25] Kurt was suspended indefinitely.[26] He'd never work in his old job again.

The Nehrlings now faced a stark choice: stick to their convictions and risk persecution or opt for a quiet life. In the Nazis' racist world view, there was nothing biologically wrong with German communists, socialists and social democrats. They had simply adopted the wrong ideology. They were misguided Germans, but Germans nonetheless. While Jews would soon be stripped of their rights as citizens, the communist inmates of the Nohra concentration camp were allowed to vote in the elections on 5 March. A policeman and an official brought a ballot box up to the camp where all of the prisoners cast their vote for the KPD, skewing the election results for the Nohra district enormously. There were 172 communist votes, while it had only been ten at the last local election. The villagers were less concerned about having a concentration camp on their doorstep than about the misrepresentation of their community in the election results. '172 communists! Outrageous!' an official statement in the *Weimarische Zeitung* scoffed. 'Nohra's good old reputation is gone!' Relief spread when it was made public that it hadn't been the locals voting for the KPD: 'So the matter of the election is clarified sufficiently and Nohra shines once more in pure, old, patriotic light.'[27]

The camp inmates were released if they signed a declaration

committing 'not to further the communist movement in any way or take part in it in any form in the future'.[28] When Sauckel had inspected the makeshift prison he'd told the communists that 'it deeply hurt his government to incarcerate German workers'. He suspected that it had only been through the 'insane policies' of his predecessors that 'ever-increasing masses of people had allowed themselves to become confused'.[29] Political opponents of the Nazis had ways of reducing persecution: they could renounce their politics, retreat into the private sphere or emigrate. The Nazis would reward them with stable work, affordable holidays and potentially housing if they integrated into their system. The Nehrlings resolved to stand by their beliefs and fight.

They weren't alone. Some young left-wingers in particular were keen to resist Nazism. This was true for Cläre Herbst. A native Weimarer, she was a twenty-year-old shop assistant. She'd been active in the Socialist Workers' Youth (SAJ) since 1929, organizing events and activities for children. When the Nazis took over, Cläre and her boyfriend Heinz Adler attempted to hide incriminating books, membership cards and documents with her 'entirely unpolitical' grandmother. Soon, two police officers turned up at Cläre's workplace and told her that they'd found the books and confiscated them. A neighbour had tipped off the police.

The officers told Cläre to keep her head down in future, but she continued to attend secret meetings. At one gathering the police turned up and arrested everyone who hadn't fled out of the window. The detainees were taken to the Weimar police station but later released, not least because August Frölich, the former leader of Thuringia, was among the group and deemed too high profile to keep locked up.

Cläre's boyfriend Heinz also risked a lot in the spring of 1933.[30] He was told to procure weapons from a factory in Suhl in the Thuringian Forest. He managed to get hold of six pistols, keeping one for himself, which he later passed on to Cläre.[31] The couple found the guidance of older comrades reassuring as they tried to outsmart an increasingly ruthless security apparatus and its citizen spies. They soon connected with Kurt Nehrling and his friend Hans Eberling, a

Anti-Nazi resistance leaders Kurt Nehrling (left) and Hans Eberling (right).

wood-sculptor and fellow SAJ and SPD man. Kurt and Hans were in the process of establishing an underground resistance network. There weren't many comrades left who were willing to risk life and limb for their values, but those who remained formed a tight-knit group that resolved to carry on, whatever the cost.

Most of Weimar's Jews were doing their best to show that they were patriotic Germans. When the Thuringian Nazi government reintroduced the black-white-red flag of imperial Germany in January, the Jewish owners of the Hermann Tietz department store at the market did the same. They were proud to have a branch right in the heart of Weimar. The Kaufhaus Hermann Tietz had been there since 1887 – nearly half a century. It was thoroughly modern, complete with Weimar's first escalator. At the same time, the owners had taken great care to restore the exterior in a historic style that blended in.[32] Of course, the Tietz flew the imperial colours when everyone was supposed to. It was a respectable, law-abiding establishment. Rather than being appeased, the Nazis seethed in their party newspaper that 'Jews must not display symbols of honour.' On 13 March, SA troops were sent in to force the owners to take the flag down.

Such systematic bullying was just the beginning. The regime was testing how far it could go. As elsewhere, the Nazis encountered little resistance in Weimar when they attacked Jewish shop owners. So three days after the flag incident at the Tietz, they went further. On the afternoon of Thursday 16 March, they launched a boycott campaign against the few other shops that had Jewish owners. SA men walked through the town centre with signs that said 'Germans buy at German shops!' This would soon prove economically disastrous for Jewish businesses, but it was also deeply hurtful. The owners of the Heka department store by the theatre protested bitterly, putting a sign outside that said: 'We are Germans, too!' The SA simply removed it and carried on.

Their next victim was Ludwig Leopold, who ran a shoeshop at Rittergasse 15, just a stone's throw from Carl Weirich's house. The Leopolds were an ordinary German family. Incensed that he should be treated like this, Ludwig put a sign in the window: 'I only sell German wares, am a veteran and a war invalid.'[33] Like many German Jews, he believed the Nazis would run some kind of rules-based system that honoured loyalty and patriotism. It would prove a fatal misjudgement.

On 1 April, the regime carried out its first nationwide boycott against Jewish businesses. It proved that Hitler could rely not only on his underlings to carry out repressive measures, but also on the tacit support of much of the population. Harry Graf Kessler observed the situation from afar with great alarm. He had travelled to Paris just over three weeks earlier and had not dared return to Berlin, because of rumours that the SA were planning to target him as a vocal political opponent. Reading about the 'abhorrent Jew boycott in the Reich', he thought: 'this criminal insanity has destroyed everything . . . I don't know whether to feel more revulsion or pity for these extremely stupid and evil people.'[34]

The boycott appeal, printed in local newspapers, which were now under Nazi control, declared that 'in Weimar, too, the defence against the Jews began on Saturday morning at 10 o'clock'.[35] At the agreed time, SA troops left the restaurant Viktoriagarten, where they had gathered, and made their way into the town centre, where they stood in front of shops with signs that read: 'A Jew lives here, do not buy from him! If you buy from Jews, you will be photographed and publicly shamed.'[36]

While the owners of the Tietz decided to close their department store that day as a precaution, the Heka on the theatre square stayed open in defiance. A Stormtrooper stood by the entrance, camera in hand. One woman later recalled that she was remonstrating with the SA: 'They wouldn't let me in, this was supposedly a Jewish shop. I retorted: but the wares aren't Jewish; but I still wasn't allowed in.' A little girl watched her mother defy the SA. 'She'd always shopped at the Heka, and so she did that day,' she remembered later. But her mother had to brave the fact that 'she was photographed upon leaving the shop and her image publicly displayed, as if she was pilloried'.[37]

The boycott encompassed Jewish professionals too: doctors, lawyers, actors, everyone. Since there weren't any Jewish doctors or lawyers in Weimar, the Nazis resorted to fake news, calling on people to boycott a fictitious 'Dr Etzel'.[38] But they found real targets too, like Emmy Sonnemann's colleague, the prominent opera singer Emil Fischer. Active in the Jewish community and an SPD and Reichsbanner member to boot, he'd already stood up to the Nazis during their Weimar rally in 1926 when he'd reported their antisemitic slurs to the authorities.[39] Now the Nazis were the authorities. Emil's performance that night was cancelled. Soon, he received fewer roles, and eventually his contract was terminated. He felt helpless and depressed, telling an acquaintance: 'We feel so worthless as people, it's terrible.'[40]

A week after the boycott, a new law was passed that allowed only 'Aryans' to be civil servants, people who could prove that their parents and grandparents weren't 'non-Aryans, especially Jews'. Since so many German Jews were highly assimilated, the authorities began to use baptismal registers as one means of identifying them. In this way, three Weimarers lost their jobs who hadn't practised Judaism in years, if ever: Hans Bassermann, a professor at the music school, Cäcilie Ledermann, a teacher, and the musical director

Gustav Lewin, who'd converted to Protestantism over a decade earlier. Gustav was incensed, complaining to the authorities: 'My creed was always German and nationalist, I've felt German only . . . Being German in the spirit of Richard Wagner has been a fact of life for me.'[41] Cäcilie had Jewish parents but had converted to Protestantism. She was born in Weimar in 1900, attended the Sophienstift like so many other local girls and then became a teacher. As a law-abiding citizen, she'd accepted the new rule that civil servants, including teachers, had to disclose their background. She couldn't believe that she was being sacked for this, protesting that she hailed from a family that 'had lived in Thuringia for decades and always behaved positively towards the people and the state'. Too old to fight in the war, her father had bought war bonds for 60,000 marks and served on the home front. However, no amount of loyalty and patriotism could outweigh the visceral antisemitism of the new regime.[42]

Like Cäcilie, Rosa Schmidt descended from two Jewish parents. She wasn't a civil servant, but the boycotts were immensely destructive, and if they were to focus on the Hotel Hohenzollern, it could mean the end of the Schmidts' income. The Nazis called off the first boycott after a few days but more followed and the repression quickly took its toll, driving employees and customers away from Jewish enterprises. The Tietz department store was sold to the non-Jewish merchant Kröger within a year.

Rosa decided to keep a low profile. She had more than herself to worry about. Her three eldest children Alexandra, Arthur and Ernst were all grown up now, but little Horst was only eleven years old. Besides, like many other Jews, Rosa felt German and patriotic. If she just kept her head down, she decided, she would be all right. Since she hailed from Żółkiew, which was now in Poland, it was much harder for anyone to check her records. Her German passport revealed nothing about her Jewish ancestry, and she'd married into an old Weimar family. She and her war veteran husband had turned the Hotel Hohenzollern around from a seedy gambling den to a respectable establishment that had been good enough for Hitler himself to patronize repeatedly. Rosa had become a part of Weimar's social fabric. Nobody need ever know that she was Jewish.

Satisfied with the result of their first coordinated antisemitic boycott, local Nazis gathered in the market square in Weimar and proclaimed: 'You Jews in Germany, you Jews in the world. You believe you are our masters. National Socialism and its Führer have empowered us to become your executioners.'[43] The town awarded Adolf Hitler honorary citizenship on 1 April, the very same day.[44]

On 2 May, the Nazis destroyed the trade unions. In Weimar, this involved a brutal storm on the Volkshaus, the SPD stronghold, where SA and SS troops beat up the trade union leaders so badly that they were hospitalized. There followed raids on SPD and KPD members' homes and workplaces. Party assets were confiscated and bank accounts suspended. To symbolize the complete destruction of left-wing politics in Weimar, the Volkshaus was renamed the 'Deutsches Haus' or 'German House'.[45] Left-wing resistance was reduced to a few isolated groups who had yet to find methods of working underground.

Most Weimarers oscillated somewhere between outright support for Nazism and retreat into the private sphere. The economic situation was still dire, with 12,000 Weimarers requiring state welfare.[46] When the Nazis whipped up an atmosphere of antisemitism against moderately wealthy Jews, people either joined in and released their pent-up frustration or they looked the other way, busy with their own problems. Carl Weirich spent the spring working long hours in his shop, preparing his son for his first day at school, listening to radio programmes, observing Easter and going about his usual Sunday outings into the surrounding countryside. There is not a word about the waves of terror in his diary in 1933. With Jews and political opponents being minorities, the majority shut their eyes to their plight.

Emmy Sonnemann reflected later that 'everyone was focused on their own misery and on their own family . . . Germans were so full of confidence in happier years to come that they didn't notice the shadows that were slowly gathering.'[47] People like Carl Weirich or Rosa Schmidt may have had professional and private lives from which they could try to shut out reality, but for the girlfriend of Hermann Göring, this was impossible: Emmy was directly confronted with the ugly reality of Nazi repression. She tried to look away even as her own field of acting was hit hard. Years later, she still claimed that 'the Jewish Question wasn't carried to extremes in the beginning. It was only here and there that individual papers needed disgusting propaganda material.'[48]

That's not how it felt to colleagues at the Weimar theatre, who petitioned Emmy for help against measures that went well beyond propaganda. She remembered how a 'half-Jewish' actress and a 'fully Jewish' opera singer at the theatre asked her to protect them. Emmy tried to help from Berlin but failed. In other cases she was successful, intervening through Göring to shield Jewish friends, colleagues and strangers who wrote to her. Her efforts seemed sincere to many German Jews. Bella Fromm, a Jewish journalist who later emigrated to the US, wrote in her diary that 'Emmy has been wonderful in her loyalty to her non-Aryan friends.'[49] During the denazification process after the war, she was judged to have 'intervened in a number of cases on behalf of former (Jewish) colleagues, who turned to her in times of crisis. But anti-national-socialist motives can be ruled out.'[50] Emmy was swept along by the tides of Nazi euphoria that gripped so many in 1933 and made no effort to stay tethered to principles she may once have held. 'You had to look hard to find someone who didn't like the new direction,' she later said to justify her inaction.[51] 'I've been able to help all who wrote to me,' she recalled, never questioning what happened to those who didn't.[52]

Emmy also knew of the concentration camps her boyfriend had set up in his ministerial role. 'However, those weren't meant for Jews,' she reflected, 'but for communist enemies of the state.' This she agreed with 'for the sake of political peace'.[53] Like many Germans she chose to turn a blind eye to the grim reality of the camps and the fact that they operated outside the law. People who were held in them were never tried or convicted. Yet, this was accept-able to many Germans so long as it hit people they disagreed with. That such arbitrary state force could just as easily turn on them or their loved ones one day didn't occur to many citizens.

Harry Graf Kessler found out even from exile what Hermann Göring's camps meant in practice. At the end of April, he was having breakfast with the Berlin correspondent of the *Manchester Guardian* who'd just come from the German capital. The Englishman told him about the wife of a Berlin worker who'd opened the door to a group of Nazis holding a pistol to her chest. They demanded to arrest her husband and take him to a concentration camp without trial. The journalist told Harry that 'Nazis swarmed out to arrest workers and mistreat them in terrible ways.' It was always the same pattern: 'What they do is abduct the person from their flat, incarcer-ate him for eight to fourteen days, in which time they beat him again and again and threaten death. When the man comes back home, he is physically and mentally "a shell".'[54]

Emmy wished to neither see nor believe that her Hermann was responsible for such cruelty. The most effective strategy for her to live with the moral dilemmas in her life was escapism. In April 1933, she said goodbye to Weimar and moved on to the theatre in Berlin, where, furthered by Göring, who was responsible for culture in Prussia, her career soared. By his side, an irresistibly glamorous future lay ahead, and she wasn't going to sacrifice that. Baldur von Schirach's wife Henny later mused about Emmy: 'She would have been content if . . . the uniforms had been stage costumes, her palace the scenery, the noise of war the sound effects behind the scenes and her magnificent presents only props. She never wanted reality.'[55]

Elisabeth Förster-Nietzsche was also grappling with the reality that embracing Nazism meant tolerating antisemitic violence. Her response was to compartmentalize her life, giving each segment a different spin. Her longest-standing supporter Ernest Thiel had a German-Jewish mother. Writing to him on 12 May she complained about the 'sudden persecution of Jews'. In her view, the Nazis 'could have waited with this for a bit since excellent, highly talented people are suffering from it, good friends whom we feel for deeply'.[56] She reassured Thiel that she had 'hardly empathized' with the radical antisemitism of her late husband Bernhard Förster, who had set up an 'Aryan' settlement in Paraguay before Hitler was even born.

At the same time, she offered Thiel an explanation for the fervent antisemitism in Germany. After all, she wrote, 'our highest German court . . . has 138 positions for the highest judges of which 52 are occupied by Jews. In Berlin there are 3,800 lawyers of whom 3,000 are Jews and only 800 are German. In the famous, great Virchnow Hospital there are 80 doctors of whom 76 are Jews and only 4 are German.' Couldn't Thiel see how this would make people angry amid all that unemployment and misery? Still, she insisted, 'many among these Jewish civil servants are noble and good people, and now we are supposed to feel different about them compared to before. I can't do that.'[57]

Elisabeth told Henry van de Velde, the Belgian artist with whom she and Harry Graf Kessler had once endeavoured to build a New Weimar, the same thing: 'as far as art and science are concerned, I can't follow this antisemitic movement. People always think because I'm the widow of Dr Bernhard Förster, from the 70s of the last century, that I must be sympathetic towards this movement. But no, I never was, and my husband used to say in jest: "My wife has no talent for antisemitism."'[58] Like Emmy, Elisabeth received petitions from Jewish friends, and, she wrote, 'I help them as much as I can.' Ultimately, she hoped 'that this whole antisemitism thing will become milder and more reasonable over time'.[59]

Elisabeth presented a very different face to Hitler. On one of his visits to the Villa Silberblick that year, she ceremoniously gifted him Friedrich Nietzsche's cane-sword and explained that her brother and her husband could be seen as trailblazers to Nazism. She showed Hitler a petition Förster had initiated in the 1880s, which claimed that 'wherever Christian and Jew enter into social relations, we see the Jew as master and the native-born Christian population in a servile position'.[60]

The press reported that the Führer was astonished by the fervour German antisemites had displayed before he was even born.[61] Förster and the 265,000 signatories of his petition had demanded, among other things, that 'the Jews be excluded from all positions of authority', and 'that only Christian teachers be allowed in [primary] schools and that in all other schools Jewish teachers be placed only in special and exceptional cases'.[62] Otto von Bismarck, the Chancellor at the time, to whom this petition was presented, ignored it.

Now Hitler was Chancellor and had begun to enact the very measures Förster had proposed. Nietzsche's cane in hand, he walked out of Elisabeth's villa, without harbouring any doubt as to her loyalty. In exchange, she secured the Führer's support and with it the survival of the archive. He soon granted her a monthly stipend of 300 marks and public recognition of her life's work.[63] The archive's lead scholar and Nazi Party member Professor Emge solemnly declared at the end of the year that, 'as is well known, the Nietzsche Archive has a direct relationship with the Führer'.[64]

It wasn't just the Nietzsche Archive that tried to ensure it was central to Hitler's vision. Other Thuringian Nazis were keen to establish Weimar itself as the cultural capital of the Third Reich. Many locals had been central to the movement when it was still in its infancy. This made them part of a small group of 'old fighters' whom Hitler trusted. Baldur von Schirach was running the Hitler Youth. Wilhelm Frick, who wasn't a Weimarer but had cut his teeth as a Nazi politician in Thuringia, was now Minister of the Interior. Martin Bormann, who'd gone to school in Weimar and launched his Nazi career there under Fritz Sauckel, was appointed as Chief of Staff to Deputy Führer Rudolf Hess.

Gauleiter Sauckel assumed the new title of Reichsstatthalter in May 1933. This basically made him Hitler's governor in Thuringia with extensive powers. Though this role was later diminished as Hitler centralized his governance of the country, Sauckel confidently defended his position, demanding a 'strong Gau' structure while remaining fervently loyal to Hitler.[65] Hans Severus Ziegler became a powerful member of his government but also gained national influence over culture as president of the German Schiller Foundation, which was headquartered in Weimar. From 1936, Ziegler also became the director of the German National Theatre.

In contrast to most other German states, Thuringia had extensive continuity in personnel rather than having to exchange the political and cultural elite as was the case elsewhere, particularly in SPD strongholds. It had a head start in the Nazification of society too. By 1 January 1935, there would be nearly 100,000 registered Nazi Party members in Thuringia, which put it in the upper quartile when compared to the German population overall.[66] The Jewish accountant Rudolf Cohn, who was struggling to retain clients after the boycotts, complained that '90 per cent of Weimar business people were members of the party'.[67] While this figure is difficult to verify, it reflects the political atmosphere in town.

Broad support allowed the local regime to press ahead with the fulfilment of Hitler's ideology. On 15 July 1933, the State Office for Race Studies was established in Weimar at Marienstraße 13–15, just south of the old town. It was the first state-level institution in Germany to concern itself with racial and genetic engineering. Sauckel installed his friend and fellow Nazi Karl Astel as director and would soon add another position for him as professor of Eugenics and Hereditary Science at the University of Jena.[68] Astel took inspiration in concepts like the 'Master Race' and ideas on 'breeding' and marriage from the Nietzsche Archive, which readily handed him the required material in December 1934 to construe the case that Nietzsche would have approved of his work.[69]

Astel's team set up an extensive database that would eventually include records on one in three Thuringians. This charted things like racial ancestry and any diseases that were considered hereditary. This information was then used to implement forced sterilizations, which became legalized with the 'Law for the Prevention of Hereditarily Diseased Offspring' on 1 January 1934. Astel himself performed such operations on 1,593 men, women and children between 1934 and 1937 alone, believing this work to be necessary in order to cleanse the

German gene pool of the 'craziness of racial aliens and the racially perverted, Jews and degenerates'. He also ran a training centre from which he spread these ideas across Germany. By 1935, he'd run courses for over 10,000 Nazi officials, from politicians and doctors to leaders of the Nazi Women's League.[70]

Weimar dutifully carried out nationally coordinated events. In 1933, the Nazis hijacked Labour Day, a socialist tradition, celebrated on 1 May with demonstrations and marches. They declared it a public holiday and an 'Honour Day of National Labour'. Weimar organized a massive spectacle to mark the occasion. Carl Weirich was in awe of how it transformed the whole town. 'Houses were decorated with honeysuckle and flags and a huge march took place in Weimar up to the festive square (stadium behind the lido) with workers but also civil servants, teachers with children, priests, guilds and of course also the military with marching bands.' Since the day also marked the nineteenth anniversary of his takeover of the stationery shop and flat at Geleitstraße 10, Carl noted with wry amusement how this time 'all the inhabitants were forced to join in the celebrations'.[71]

When Nazi organizations, led by Baldur von Schirach's Hitler Youth and student groups, began to hold public book burnings between March and October, Weimar also joined in. On 21 June, in Niedergrunstedt, a small hamlet on the south-western outskirts of town, a book burning was combined with the annual summer solstice celebrations. Crowds gathered around a large bonfire. A leader called: 'Burn, un-German spirit!' and books like Erich Maria Remarque's *All Quiet on the Western Front* were cast into the flames.[72]

Hitler returned to Weimar on 1 November when the 'Weimar Day of the 100,000' took place, the largest Nazi spectacle the town had ever hosted. People were told to hang flags from their windows, and decorate the town with flowers. A massive tent with space for 50,000 people was erected on the modern sports grounds, and newspapers told readers to expect an event 'like towns of the size of Weimar have never seen'.[73]

Schools finished early, and public offices were closed so that people could welcome Hitler, who arrived by plane in Erfurt at 5 p.m. before driving into Weimar as part of an eleven-car motorcade. The town waited with mounting anticipation. The vast tent had been full for hours with another 30,000 people sitting on the ground around it. More people waited for live broadcasts in the German National Theatre and other 'historical sites of the development of the National Socialist Party', the press reported. Marching music blared from thirty loudspeakers.[74] But Hitler first spoke in the packed Weimarhalle and it was well past 9 p.m. when he finally entered the large event tent with Fritz Sauckel.

The atmosphere had reached fever pitch. According to the *Jenaische Zeitung*, people 'stand on their benches, scream and cheer. A huge wave is rolling towards the One. 50,000 hearts beat as one! Hitler!'[75] The Führer began to speak, was interrupted by applause and began again. He finally finished his speech with the words: 'You Thuringian man, you Thuringian woman, you Thuringians, stay loyal to me as I stay loyal to you!'[76]

After just fifteen minutes the spectacle was over. It was remarkably short, and formulaic. There was no special show for Weimar. Hitler chose to head to the Kaiser Café for some downtime rather than speaking for longer. This would prove to be typical for his relationship with Weimar. He did indeed love the town as he had once told Ziegler,[77] but this love was personal, not political. Hitler loved Weimar as a place to relax. It was beautiful, small and cosy with large parks and well-kept streets and houses. Its politics were broadly sympathetic to his, and that made it safe. Even his political opponents here had largely been law-abiding, preferring reports and demonstrations to physical assault. He never had to worry about being attacked and could move around freely, even telling his staff not to clear restaurants or cafés he wanted to sit in.

While Hitler understood the importance of the legacy of the likes of Goethe, Schiller and Nietzsche to his project, he wasn't personally invested in them in the way he was in Wagner, who made Bayreuth special for him. Being the size that it was, Weimar also couldn't compete with Nuremberg, which had taken over as a rallying ground after the first one in Weimar in 1926. An event of 100,000 people may have been huge for Weimar, but at Nuremberg, where director Leni Riefenstahl would film her propaganda masterpiece *Triumph of the Will* the following year, Hitler would speak to 700,000 spectators. Nor was Weimar Munich, the 'capital of the movement'. It wasn't Berlin, the capital of the Reich.[78] Weimar was nice and Hitler continued to visit, even in a private capacity, but it was no longer central to the Nazi cause.

The crowds of Weimarers themselves still felt special that November day. For the first time, vast swathes of the population had taken part in a Nazi event, not just activists and sympathizers. One paper commented: 'Weimar was looking back on a very big day, no, the biggest day in a row of political events . . . The shine of this day will continue to glow for a long time.'[79]

Carl Weirich wholeheartedly bought into this message by the end of 1933. Viewed from that cold December, when temperatures dropped to −15°C, things could only get better. The weather had exacerbated a painful boil on his body, which was soon diagnosed as 'malignant' by his doctor and had to be cut out. But even that couldn't spoil his festive optimism. He already saw how unemployment was dropping, which had an immediate effect on business in the shop. Carl wrote in his diary that he 'anticipated Christmas with hope for a better future'.[80]

1934

'One Führer, one people, one will,' Fritz Sauckel began, 'that is the watchword with which we shall launch the great, tremendous Battle of Labour.'[1] It was 21 March 1934 and Hitler's Reichsstatthalter in Thuringia was standing next to some churned-up earth in Oberweimar, a village on the south-eastern outskirts of Weimar. Behind the little swastika flags that served as a cordon around the construction site stood a group of people listening in solemn silence. Nazi officials, representatives of the town administration and students from local schools had gathered as bells rang out to mark the beginning of a Germany-wide 'Labour Offensive'.[2]

Launched by Hitler himself in a speech broadcast across the nation from a motorway construction site in Unterhaching near Munich, a public building initiative had begun that served the dual purpose of fostering the 'cooperation of everyone' and strengthening the belief in a 'German resurrection', as the Reich Chancellor laid out.[3] Germans were to feel that things were getting better and that this was because of their own labour, united under the banner of the swastika. In order to achieve this, visible changes had to happen quickly and everywhere at the same time so that the regime that coordinated such a national effort would become a 'font of the people's trust and optimism', as Hitler put it.[4] Whatever that looked like locally was in the hands of his lieutenants.

Sauckel wanted to impress Hitler with big plans for Thuringia. Emulating the Nazi leader in substance and style, he copied not just his mannerisms and speech but even grew a toothbrush moustache.[5] Prematurely bald and unable to shake off the Franconian accent of his upbringing, he never quite pulled it off. But this didn't taint his ambition to make Thuringia a *Mustergau* or 'model Gau' with a 'New Weimar' as its capital.[6]

The 'Labour Offensive' offered a chance to execute the Führer's will in Weimar. Speaking immediately after Hitler's broadcast from Unterhaching, Sauckel declared: 'We will follow him with joy in our hearts, we follow in his footsteps and begin our task with proud conviction.'[7] This task, he told those present, was to build 140 new houses so that Thuringian families might live in a 'lovely, cosy home with a garden, daylight and sunshine' rather than the 'depressing and inadequate houses' previous regimes had built for them.[8] In an effort to win over working-class families, many of whom were KPD or SPD voters, he had founded the Sauckel–Marschler Foundation to fund and organize a public-housing campaign.

After the Second World War, Sauckel would look back on these efforts with pride. In 1945, in prison while on trial as a major war criminal, he wrote that the purpose of his foundation had been to 'build houses for poor but hard-working families with many children. They were equipped with gardens and hutches for small livestock. Families needed no deposit but paid rent scaled according to their means . . . After twenty years, the little houses became the property of the families.' He added that the only precondition was that they had 'four children and a good reputation . . . Because a father of many children has other worries and duties, they were supposed to get an opportunity to acquire property. Isn't this a more beautiful form of socialism than the one that takes property?'[9]

Sauckel omitted that these houses were only for 'valuable, genetically viable' families, as he told the gathered crowds in Oberweimar while the foundation stone was laid for the first local 'Settlement of the People's Community'.[10] To apply for the scheme families had to prove their 'Aryan' descent with a certificate from the newly established State Office for Race Studies and their genetic worth through a document from the State Health Office that certified they had no hereditary conditions, or mental or physical disabilities, in the family.

By 1937, only 150 Sauckel–Marschler houses had been built and the scheme ground to a near halt, not least because it ran into financial difficulties. That's despite the fact that Weimar's population rose from 46,003 in early 1933 to 51,285 in 1936.[11] Public building schemes were financed mostly through borrowing. Weimar alone accumulated extra debt of over 450,000 marks in the financial year of 1933/34. The following year, it ballooned further, from 9.8 million to nearly 10.5 million marks.[12] More visible schemes took priority. As elsewhere across the Reich, a massive Autobahn or motorway project was under way in Thuringia, where work began in July 1934. The stretch between Weimar and Jena would open for traffic in August 1939.[13]

Sauckel's desire to make Weimar an impressive regional Nazi capital also took priority over housing. He had major plans to drag this small, old-fashioned town into the Third Reich with supersized building works. Since he saw his own role as a baron in Hitler's kingdom, he also began to plan for his very own castle on the hills to the south of the town centre, not far from the Nietzsche Archive. The Villa Sauckel in the Windmühlenstraße would be built in the style of a residential palace, complete with its own park and swimming pool. It received regular deliveries of caviar, oysters and champagne from the Hotel Elephant and selected market traders right up to 1945.[14] If there wasn't enough money left over to build more housing for families, so be it.

Sauckel was never particularly popular but the optics of his politics were effective. With feverish energy, he attended construction sites all across Thuringia. For the first time in years, it seemed, things were being built up and opened. This wouldn't be a 'fake blossom like 1924', Carl Weirich was sure. He was celebrating the twentieth anniversary of his shop this year. His enterprise had survived war, hyperinflation and the worst economic crisis in living memory. Business was still a little slow, but he had the distinct impression that he'd weathered the storm. The 'new Reich Chancellor demanded 4 years for reconstruction!' he wrote in his diary.[15] He was willing to give Hitler that time.

Carl wasn't particularly politically active. Unlike so many other business owners in Weimar, he wouldn't join the Nazi Party, but he became a Patron Member of the SS. This meant he wasn't a member of the SS and therefore didn't take part in any active duties but was associated with the organization and made financial contributions to it. As the monthly payments were scaled to reflect the income of members, Carl paid just 1 mark. For that, he received a membership number (1,031,415), a lapel pin and a monthly magazine.[16] It was a symbolic gesture, but he wanted to contribute to what he saw as a 'national rising in Germany' that seemed to come 'out of the people's own efforts'.[17]

The 'general security in the country that already became a little tangible' gave Carl the confidence to spend the spring of 1934 in a more carefree mood than he had done in years. He felt he no longer had to put on a brave face for Wilhelm and Marie. The family undertook many happy Sunday outings to the nearby Ettersberg hill. While the trees on it were beginning to recover from the mass deforestation after the war, Carl noted that winter storms had led to a lot of windthrow. But it was still a beautiful place to explore, whether by sledge in the winter or admiring the blooming woodland plants in the spring while stopping somewhere for a cup of coffee. For Carl, life was good in the spring of 1934.

Rosa and Arthur Schmidt were also optimistic about the future. On 3 June, their eldest daughter Alexandra gave birth to their first grandchild, a healthy baby girl called Marie-Luise. She was to grow up close to her grandparents, especially to grandmother Rosa, whom she would later fondly remember as a 'very, very nice and kind woman who worked very hard'.[18] There was certainly a lot to do in the family business, which was getting busier and more prosperous in the mid-1930s.[19] Since few people knew of Rosa's Jewish ancestry, the Hotel Hohenzollern hadn't been affected by the anti-semitic boycotts. On the contrary, their business now benefited from the steady stream of activity Sauckel's ambitions for Weimar was creating in the town.

In addition to sporting events that had already been arranged, like the German Swimming Championships in 1933 that were hosted at the new Schwanseebad lido, or the German Women's Athletic Championship the same year, the Nazis initiated a plethora of new conventions and conferences that drew people to the Thuringian capital. The Weimarhalle proved a particularly popular venue for events and exhibitions. It was used by cultural organizations like the Goethe Society and the Shakespeare Society but also for Nazi gatherings, due to its central location and size.[20]

All of this was excellent business news for the Schmidts, who now felt confident enough to expand their hotel. On 18 May, they applied to the town administration for permission to extend their licence to a beer garden and terrace.[21] Arthur signed the application on the Hohenzollern's own letterhead 'with German greetings', a phrase that Interior Minister Wilhelm Frick had prescribed for all official communication by law. It was easy to comply with such intrusions into language and habits since they appeared to have no negative effect. Non-compliance, on the other hand, would immediately have drawn attention to the Schmidts. Frick's decree affected everyone since it forced people to take part in Nazi rituals or be exposed as opponents. Passivity simply wasn't an option. So the Schmidts' youngest son Horst, despite being half Jewish, now began every lesson in school by raising his right arm in the Nazi salute and bellowing 'Heil Hitler!' in unison with his classmates. In light of the Schmidts' excellent reputation and their evident compliance with the new laws, Weimar town police raised 'no concerns against the granting of the aforementioned permission'. The Schmidts were free to grow their business.[22]

Weimarers who resisted the Nazis lived dangerous lives. The terror waves of 1933 had been out in the open, designed to show an approving majority that communists and socialists would be dealt with and to intimidate opponents. From 1934, there was a new strategy. On 1 January, the Thuringian Office of the Geheime Staatspolizeiamt or Gestapo was established and headquartered in Weimar.[23] As the secret police of the Nazi regime, the Gestapo identified, monitored and subdued political opponents. In the early years, it focused on what was left of the networks of former political parties and organizations like the trade unions, the SPD and especially the KPD, which had gone underground since it was banned in 1933.

Gestapo Weimar began operating with around a dozen members, mostly recruited from local police services where many loyal Nazis could be found since the regimes of Frick and Sauckel had placed them there from 1930 onwards. They operated out of the main police station in Sophienstraße 8–10, the long, broad avenue that led from the train station to the town centre. They soon expanded and, in 1936, moved into the Marstall, the former grand ducal mews. There, they installed two cells for solitary confinement and interrogation. Gestapo Weimar quickly outgrew those too, and carried on expanding the prison facilities in the Marstall until, from the late 1930s onwards, it operated twelve permanently overcrowded cells and a doubly sound-proofed interrogation room. This 'torture basement', where prisoners were viciously beaten, mistreated and murdered, gained infamy quickly.[24] The Nazis had brought terror to the heart of Weimar.

In order to get the desired convictions against political opponents, the regime established 'special courts'. One of them was in Weimar, where between 1933 and 1936 a total of 4,314 trials were held. Four out of every five cases were for anti-state agitation and sentences ranged from fines to death penalties.[25] Many ordinary people tried to use this system of terror to their advantage. In May 1934, the Thuringian Ministry of the Interior bemoaned the fact that it would have to spend significant resources on 'fighting denunciations'. Complaining that there had been a huge increase in citizen reports to the various branches of the police, it noted 'that these reports are almost entirely down to personal quarrels'. Especially in domestic or neighbourly contexts, 'enemies are often politically accused'. Even the Gestapo demanded that 'such careless reporting of unjustified cases' must stop, as it deemed it 'undignified for the German people and the National Socialist state'.[26]

Weimar's remaining social democrats and communists knew they faced danger from all sides: the regime, police, courts and the people around them. In December 1934, the Gestapo estimated that the surviving SPD groups in Thuringian towns, including in Weimar, oscillated between fifty and 150 members.[27] They resolved to identify and eliminate them.

This meant that the group led by Kurt Nehrling and his friend Hans Eberling had to be extremely careful. They usually met in people's houses or gardens or in the Nehrlings' textile shop at Zeppelinplatz. But even that was risky. Cläre Herbst had learned from experience that you couldn't trust anybody, especially not neighbours. So she and the others had to come up with ways of camouflaging their communications. One meeting at her house, for instance, was held in the garden as a 'Bratwurst Fest'. When they met comrades from other towns – which was far riskier, since they didn't know them as well and the Gestapo had begun to use 'turned' activists as undercover agents – they often did so under a pretext on public roads. They would pretend a bicycle tyre had gone flat and a friendly stranger was helping out. In reality, messages were hidden in the replacement tubes. Group cohesion required courage, regardless of such creativity. When one of Cläre's comrades was put on remand, she visited him in prison, pretending to be his cousin. This allowed her to arrange how and when to re-establish contact when he'd be released two years later, but it also served to reassure everyone that they wouldn't be abandoned if caught.[28]

Cläre's boyfriend Heinz was subjected to a lot of harassment by police from the moment the SPD was banned. He still lived with his parents, which didn't stop the agents from searching the house twice and confiscating all his books and magazines. He was ordered to report to the police headquarters daily, later twice-weekly. Within the Nehrling–Eberling group he was tasked with establishing contacts with other young socialists in Berlin, taking along brochures advertising hiking gear in case he was stopped and searched. After the Volkshaus had been raided and occupied by SA and SS troops, Heinz and his comrade Otto Schmuck took a horse-drawn cart that was normally used to collect kitchen waste to return to the building in the early hours of the morning to rescue the books from the SPD library. These were then hidden in the garden of another comrade, Walter Schaft, so that everyone could continue to read them.

It would have been easy for Kurt Nehrling to find good reasons to withdraw from such dangerous activism. As group leader he was particularly at risk. He could have told himself that he had two children, Ursula, who was now twelve, and Heinz, who was six. He could have withdrawn into 'inner emigration' as other activists and intellectuals did – keeping his opposition to Nazism inside while to all intents and purposes leading a conformist life. Being a non-Jewish war veteran, the Nazis would likely have let him run his shop, content that they had chastened him. Instead, Kurt worked hard to hold a group together that risked their lives for books and idealism.

Emmy Sonnemann spent much of the summer of 1934 on tour together with her colleague, the actor and director Gustaf Gründgens. The pair got on well and developed a symbiotic friendship that would elevate them both to the pinnacle of theatre in the early years of Nazi Germany. Everyone knew that Gründgens was gay, despite a short-lived marriage with Erika Mann, the daughter of the novelist Thomas Mann. Male homosexuality was not only illegal in Germany under Paragraph 175 of the German criminal code, but, since the Nazi takeover, outright dangerous, as the regime was arresting large numbers of gay men.

Gründgens was not only shielded from this but actively supported by Hermann Göring. At first, he renewed Gründgens's acting contract at the Prussian State Theatre. Then, one day in 1934, he said to Emmy: 'I think I will appoint Gustaf Gründgens as artistic director.'[29] This was to ensure that the man's glittering career shaped German theatre through much of the twentieth century. It was also a move that helped Emmy establish herself on the stage in Berlin. She got leading roles, often playing alongside Gründgens. Years later Emmy remembered that 'it was a gift to be able to work with him'.[30]

There were few clouds on Emmy's horizon in 1934. Even the fact that she continued to live with the spectre of Göring's dead wife Carin didn't seem to matter. He had her body moved from Sweden to Germany that summer and reburied in the grounds of his newly built house, which he'd named Carinhall in her honour. Emmy accepted this. What mattered to her was that she was somebody now. Playing another guest performance with Gründgens in Hamburg, she thought about how proud it would have made her late mother to see her like this. Her father, who had been so sceptical about her acting ambitions, attended the performance. Nearly eighty years old, 'he was very happy that fate still granted him this joy', Emmy thought.[31] But it didn't end there. In the autumn, Göring made her a Prussian State Actress, the highest title for stage actors in Nazi Germany. Emmy later remembered this period as 'the most joyful of my whole time in the theatre . . . I had achieved everything that I could have achieved as an actress in Germany.'[32]

In the early summer, Emmy Sonnemann's former place of work was busy preparing for a literary spectacle. Two years after the Goethe Year of 1932, it was Friedrich Schiller's turn to be celebrated. The playwright and poet had had a deep and productive friendship with Goethe, and together they were at the centre of the period celebrated as 'Weimar Classicism'. Their monument had been in front of the theatre since 1857, celebrated by dukes, democrats and dictators. On 10 November 1934, it would be 175 years since Schiller's birth, so it was expected that the annual youth festival organized by the Weimar-based German Schiller Association, or Deutscher Schillerbund, would be big.

To Hans Severus Ziegler, whose mentor Adolf Bartels had founded the Schillerbund in 1906, Schiller was the personification of German idealism, a 'spiritual Führer' for Nazi Germany. It was a concept that had the potential to elevate Weimar as a spiritual home of Nazism.[33] He had powerful backing for this idea from Berlin, where Hans Fabricius, a close ally of Wilhelm Frick, had in 1932 published a whole book dedicated to 'Schiller as Hitler's Battle Comrade' in which he claimed 'Schiller as a National Socialist'.[34] There was little resistance to such political appropriation from the cultural elites in Weimar.

Goethe scholar Max Hecker may have been a latecomer to the Nazi cause, but he used the *Goethe Yearbook* of 1933 to praise Hitler's 'rejuvenated Germany'.[35] His boss Hans Wahl was a founding member of the National Socialist Culture Community as the Militant League for German Culture was now called. Nobody objected when the youth festival was opened in June 1934 with a pledge that the Schillerbund now 'worked fully on behalf of the Führer Adolf Hitler'.[36]

According to the press, 'a large number of young, enthusiastic people, among them happily many Germans from outside of Germany', gathered for the opening ceremony. Entire school classes flocked to Weimar. 'Eight days of Weimar! One week of seeing, experiencing, enjoying – is this even responsible in today's serious, rather political times in which every day brings new work, new tasks and worries?' wondered one high school student from Zittau in Saxony. Yes, he concluded, because 'Weimar wasn't "enjoyment" for us in the usual sense but a great, inner experience, an acquaintance with entirely new values . . . So, we walked through Weimar under the impression of spending time in Germany's most significant place of culture, and we sensed how especially now in times of renewal the spirit of Weimar awoke in us, how it celebrated its resurrection as the precondition of a new German culture.'[37]

While the Schiller festivities were in full swing, the Weirich family hosted a party at Geleitstraße 10. It was Wilhelm's eighth birthday on 24 June. A dozen relatives and friends came to congratulate the boy and have coffee with his proud parents. Their son had been in school for over a year now. He'd learned to read and write, his clear, childlike hand now regularly appearing in the 'baby book' Carl was still keeping meticulously.[38]

In photos, Wilhelm often looked serious and contemplative, dressed in sailor suits or formal shirts tucked into traditional German leather shorts. Nazism was beginning to engulf his young life, its ideology and insignia ubiquitous at school and in private. He'd never experienced school life without the Hitler salute. One photo, taken in October, shows him at the wedding of his nanny Irma Götze in Niedergrunstedt, where the book burning had taken place the previous year. Irma's husband was in full SA uniform – by now a normal sight for a child growing up in Nazi Germany.

Carl had only just returned from a trip to Königsberg (today Kaliningrad) in East Prussia where the annual conference of the Federal Association of Bookbinders had taken place. Travelling by train, boat and bus, there had been an opportunity to see the giant Tannenberg Memorial along the way. It commemorated both the medieval battle by that name and the eponymous 1914 clash between Russia and Germany in which Paul von Hindenburg had made his name. When President Hindenburg died of lung cancer at the age of eighty-six, less than two months after Carl's trip, his coffin was placed at the Tannenberg Memorial in a huge ceremony, despite the late President's wishes to be buried on the family plot next to his wife.

Carl's memories of the trip were still fresh in his mind on 7 August as he and a few friends and neighbours gathered around the family radio to listen to a broadcast of the funeral. He also made a note of a plebiscite held on 19 August in which Hitler asked Germans for approval of a decision he had already made: to bury the office of the presidency with Hindenburg and transfer all its powers to himself. Carl recorded the result: '38 million yes'.[39] That was 90 per cent of the votes cast, a result that retrospectively approved a power grab and one obtained under widespread intimidation and fraud. Irrespective of these dubious methods, the plebiscite still gave an indication of the broad consent the Nazi government enjoyed in 1934.[40] Weimar's results reflected those of the Reich exactly.[41] Carl Weirich was among the many who took the plebiscite seriously and approved of 'Adolf Hitler's election as Führer of the German people'.[42]

When Hitler visited Elisabeth Förster-Nietzsche on the morning of 20 July, he brought flowers and greetings from Mussolini. A few weeks earlier, the two dictators had met for the first time, in Venice. Knowing that Mussolini was a fan of Nietzsche but sensing ongoing reticence from Hitler, Elisabeth had sent a telegram to Italy to make

Elisabeth Förster-Nietzsche welcoming Adolf Hitler at the Nietzsche Archive on 20 July 1934.

sure the dictators were thinking about her dead brother as they talked: 'The Manes of Friedrich Nietzsche are present at the conversation between Europe's two greatest statesmen.' Mussolini had responded, 'deeply moved' by her words.[43]

When Hitler called at the Villa Silberblick, he thanked Elisabeth for her telegram and talked animatedly about his impressions from Italy. He also explained that he had great plans for Bayreuth and Weimar.[44] Wagner and Nietzsche would be the spiritual pillars of the Third Reich. Karl Schlechta, a young Austrian scholar working at the Nietzsche Archive, was awed: 'The statesman in the house of the first state thinker: and yet not as a politician visiting a philosopher but as a generous, friendly and personal visitor of the "sister" who has been elevated to an almost surreal old age.'[45]

Karl and Elisabeth didn't always see eye-to-eye. The scholar had demanded to see her brother's original documents rather than Elisabeth's copies of them, and he had confronted her with incongruities and even outright forgeries, additions and changes he said he'd found. Elisabeth considered this an insolent accusation from the young man working under her roof. Karl even claimed that she threatened him with her walking stick, a heavy piece made from solid oak. 'I had the feeling that she wanted to beat me to death,' he shuddered many years later.[46] For all his differences with his boss, Karl was a Nazi Party member who saw tremendous symbolism in the personal meeting between her and Hitler. 'This is how, in ancient times, a great mother may have received her great son, a prophet, a hero, a great man, the priestess guarding a holy flame,' he wrote. 'Nobody who saw it will ever forget how the man whom all of Germany watches in hope, and whom all the world watches with the liveliest interest, said goodbye to the ethereal, waiflike old woman.'[47]

More-concrete plans on bringing Nietzsche and Nazism together were made during Hitler's next visit, on 2 October. This time, he brought two architects. One was Paul Schultze-Naumburg. Now in his mid-sixties, he was beginning to lose favour with younger Nazis who found his style old-fashioned, preferring the clean, orderly symmetry of a stripped-back form of neoclassicism. That was Hitler's style too, ideally oversized to monumental proportions to achieve impressive propaganda effects. But Schultze-Naumburg still had his uses. He was a true believer in the connection between art and race and had cleansed Weimar of the last traces of its Bauhaus past. A prolific writer, he'd also worked to destroy the cultural legacy of the movement. In the Nazi newspaper *Völkischer Beobachter* he described the Bauhaus as 'un-German', a 'cathedral of socialism' that looked so much like a 'synagogue that it's no wonder if their buildings all looked like they were from Asia Minor and Syria'.[48]

Hitler approved. After the Bauhaus had been driven from Weimar to Dessau, local Nazis had closed the school there in 1932. It briefly re-established itself in Berlin, where Hitler's regime forced it to close for good in 1933. Around a quarter of the Bauhaus artists fled abroad, which inadvertently helped their ideas become one of the most influential cultural movements of the twentieth century. But Hitler wasn't entirely averse to its modernism and made use of many of its non-Jewish artists and architects willing to collaborate. While at least twenty-four Bauhaus proponents were murdered by the regime, there were also 188 who became members of the Nazi Party.[49]

The Nazis' complex relationship with modern and traditional art and architecture was reflected in the meeting at Elisabeth's villa on 2 October 1934. She knew Schultze-Naumburg well, but she hadn't met the charismatic second architect Hitler had brought along. Albert Speer was not yet thirty, but it was clear that Hitler trusted him. Clean-shaven with prominent eyebrows framing keenly intelligent eyes, Speer exuded self-confidence and ambition. The young architect also knew Schultze-Naumburg was no competition. Hitler and Speer were on their way to Nuremberg, where Hitler wanted huge new structures erected for the Nazi rallies and he'd chosen Speer to design and build them.

When they'd arrived in Weimar for their brief stop, Hitler showed him plans for a new 'Party Forum' that was to be built in the Thuringian capital. They were Schultze-Naumburg's plans and they looked

Adolf Hitler gazing at a bust of the philosopher Friedrich Nietzsche at the Nietzsche Archive in Weimar in 1934.

it: conservative, traditional and in line with the pre-existing architecture. 'It looks like the oversized market square of a provincial town,' Hitler scoffed. 'There is nothing distinct, nothing to set it apart from former periods. If we are going to build a Party Forum, then everyone should see later that it was built in our time and in our style.' Speer noted that Hitler hadn't even invited the older man to defend his plans. He dismissed them out of hand and decided to hold a competition among other artists.[50]

Plans for the Nietzsche Archive were a different matter. Hitler put it to Elisabeth that it would be a good idea to build an extension to the Villa Silberblick or perhaps a separate building immediately adjacent. This could serve as a Nietzsche Memorial Hall, but more importantly it could be an educational space where young Germans could be brought to learn about 'Nietzsche's thoughts on the Herrenrasse [Master Race]'.[51] Speer watched with interest how the idea went down with Elisabeth. 'The odd and eccentric woman apparently didn't seem to get along with Hitler,' he thought. 'A strangely flat, confusingly meandering conversation ensued.'[52] In the end, however, everyone appeared to be happy. Hitler promised to finance the undertaking out of his own pocket, providing 50,000 marks and establishing a special fund for the purchase of books.[53] Schultze-Naumburg would design the Memorial Hall. Elisabeth was from the same generation as the architect and preferred his traditional style. Speer had bigger projects in Nuremberg. And Schultze-Naumburg had something to do. Hitler, Speer noticed, 'was visibly glad to be able to give the architect some small compensation' for losing out on the bigger job of designing the new Nazi buildings planned for Weimar.[54]

The gamble Rosa and Arthur Schmidt took in extending their business appeared to pay off. In November 1934, Sauckel's regime launched an intense campaign to promote tourism.[55] Under the slogan 'Every stranger who comes to Thuringia shall leave as a friend of our homeland', the Tourism Association, now headed by Minister President Willy Marschler, lobbied aggressively for people to visit Germany's 'green heart'. It seemed to work. By June 1935, the official statistics say that spa and holiday resorts had an increase of 163 per cent in bookings. Marschler encouraged restaurant owners to be as hospitable as possible, as 'a decent landlord with empathy will also have decent guests, who will always find their way back to him'.[56] The Schmidts were happy to oblige. They certainly had enough opportunity in November 1934 as several large events brought visitors to town.

One of these events began as a relatively small affair in the Erholung club at Karlsplatz, behind Carl Weirich's house. In the evening of 5 November it filled with guests for the first 'Week of the German Book', an event held in many German towns and cities simultaneously. A radio was turned on and the voice of Joseph Goebbels filled the room. The Propaganda Minister was delivering a fiery speech in Berlin's Sportpalast where he urged the nation to 'hold on fast to the German book, and you will preserve the precious treasure of our German spirit!'[57]

Shortly after, the Propaganda Minister decided to open all future German Book Weeks in Weimar, not Berlin, nor in the big German book fair cities of Frankfurt and Leipzig.[58] Explaining this choice the following year when he personally opened the next one in Weimar, he said that it had 'not been a coincidence . . . for there is probably no spiritual person in Germany who isn't tightly bound to this town's ideals and spiritual imagination. I remember the happy hour well when I came to this town for the first time, and ever since that day I have probably returned to Weimar once or several times every year with pleasure and out of my own motivation.'[59]

Hot on the heels of the first German Book Week followed a much bigger event. While the 1934 Schiller Youth Festival in the summer had been sizable, the poet's 175th birthday on 10 November was celebrated on an altogether different scale. There were festivities all over Germany, including in Schiller's birthplace of Marbach am Neckar, near Stuttgart, and in Jena, where Schiller had been professor of History and Philosophy. Jena used the opportunity to name its university after the famous poet. It is still called Friedrich Schiller University of Jena today.

Weimar, where Schiller had lived, worked and died, organized a 'Schiller Festival Week' from 7 to 11 November. The highlight was a state ceremony on 10 November. As in the Goethe Year of 1932, Grand Duchess Feodora laid a wreath at Schiller's tomb, which was next to Goethe's in the ducal burial chapel in Weimar's Historical Cemetery. The difference was that no SPD members nor anyone from any other party other than the NSDAP appeared. Instead, a representative of the Reich Propaganda Ministry laid a wreath with a quote from Goethe's epilogue to Schiller's poem 'Song of the Bell': 'Denn er war unser' – 'For he was ours'.[60]

In the evening, a state ceremony took place in the German National Theatre. At a few minutes to 8 o'clock, Hitler appeared, unusually for him in a formal tailcoat. The audience rose as one, their right arms shooting up in salute. Hitler warmly greeted the Grand Duchess Feodora and then took his seat in his box, where other Nazi politicians were already sitting. The Weimar State Orchestra played Beethoven's *Leonore* Overture No. 3 before Joseph Goebbels came on stage. 'If Schiller lived in these times,' the Propaganda Minister told the audience in Weimar and people listening on the radio all over Germany, 'he would doubtless have become the great poetic avant-garde of our revolution . . . He was one of us, blood of our blood and flesh of our flesh.'[61]

It was no coincidence that Hitler had remained in the background, merely lending the required weight by being there in person. He went through the motions, paying a brief visit to the Schillerhaus, where the poet had lived. But Schiller just wasn't his thing.[62] He liked Weimar well enough, however, to grant the town this moment in the national limelight, and there were key people like Goebbels, who held a doctorate in philology from the University of Heidelberg, and Baldur von Schirach, a Weimarer and Nazi poet, who stood ready to convince him that the cultivation of Weimar's literary heritage was worth his time. In November 1934, it looked as though Wilhelm Frick's aspiration from his time as minister in Thuringia was attainable: 'May Weimar always be at the centre of German culture and politics!'[63]

While Schillermania held Weimar in its grip, Ludwig Leopold had other worries. On 14 November, a trial began against him at the state court in Weimar. The shoeshop owner suspected he had been dragged to court for standing up against the Jewish boycott the previous year when he'd dared to point out that he was German and a war veteran to boot. The prosecution read out the charges: unfair business practices and indecent touching of female employees. Such cases appeared in courts all over the country. They fitted into the Nazi propaganda of Jews as depraved and corrupt, and they also served to prepare the population for antisemitic legislation. The following year the Nuremberg Laws would decree, among other restrictions, that Jews were no longer allowed to employ non-Jewish women under the age of forty-five, the implication being that this would prevent 'race-defiling behaviour'.[64]

Ludwig stood up for himself in court. He insisted that he hadn't done anything wrong and that he felt he was on trial for being Jewish. It was no use. The media coverage around the case had built up to a frenzy and Ludwig had been found guilty in the court of public opinion long before any legal judgment had been passed. The judge sentenced him to two and a half years in a house of correction plus five years' loss of civil rights. Ludwig appealed, taking the matter to the Reich court since no conclusive evidence had been brought against him in Weimar.

While his case was heard there, the Nazi propaganda machine cranked into full gear. The weekly tabloid *Der Stürmer*, a virulently antisemitic publication published by Julius Streicher, the Gauleiter of Middle Franconia, featured the case against Ludwig as a lead story on its cover: 'Jew L. Leopold – The Child Molester of Weimar'.[65] The unproven charges that he had inappropriately touched female employees had been escalated to allegations of paedophilia. Weimarers saw this too since the paper was displayed on a noticeboard on Karlsplatz.[66]

Ludwig's appeal was dismissed by the Reich court. The *Thüringische Staatszeitung*, as Hans Severus Ziegler's paper formerly known as *Der Nationalsozialist* was now called, sneered: 'In German courts there remain no more race comrades of his of whom the race defiler Leopold may have expected that they might look the other way. German courts are free of Jews, they don't judge according to Jewish doctrine any more, but here German law is practised.'[67] Ludwig was locked up at the correctional facility in Untermaßfeld in south-west Thuringia. He would never see his wife and daughter again.

Carl Weirich spent Christmas with his wife and son at home. It was a quiet one this year with just his niece Anny visiting. The weather was strange too. 'Almost autumnal, without snow,' Carl wrote in his diary.[68] But the Weirichs managed to make it as cosy as ever. Candles flooded the living room with warm light as the adults sat in front of the Christmas tree and watched Wilhelm unwrap his presents.[69] This year, he received a set of building blocks, a book of fairy tales and an alarm clock.[70]

1935

It was still early in the morning when the Weirichs set off on a winter walk. Come rain, come shine, they would take time out almost every weekend to spend a day together as a family. Sunday 20 January 1935 was no exception. This time, Carl, Marie and Wilhelm were on their way to one of their favourite places: the village of Ettersburg, which lay on the eponymous Ettersberg hill north-west of Weimar. It was a bit of a climb but it was worth it for the views, the beautiful scenery and the spectacular sight of the old hunting palace, Schloss Ettersburg. The Weirichs aimed to get up there by lunchtime so that they could have a meal at the Waidmannsheil, a traditional local inn.[1] Part of the attraction for visitors was that Ettersburg seemed timeless. Goethe and Schiller would have been greeted by much the same scene as the Weirichs were now. It was a place untouched by politics.

But by 1935 there was no escape from Nazism, not even on the Ettersberg. On their hike, the Weirichs passed large construction sites at the southern slopes of the hill. The first two barracks of an extensive military compound were being constructed there, re-establishing Weimar's status as a garrison town. Before the First World War, Weimar had been the home of the Grand Ducal regiment since 1702. The town had harboured a military presence of varying sizes for well over two centuries before the Treaty of Versailles temporarily put an end to that. In 1925, the first post-war troops had moved back into the local barracks. So what Hitler was planning to do in 1935 seemed to many Weimarers a return of normalcy rather than a prelude to war.

Preparing for the reintroduction of conscription in March 1935, Hitler saw the restoration of the German military, now called

Wehrmacht, as a national effort. This required many towns to house personnel and equipment. Weimar Mayor Walther Felix Mueller had immediately declared that 'all of Weimar . . . is proud to receive an extended garrison corresponding in its greatness to the past and the traditions of the town. For Weimar is not only the town of poets, but also a . . . garrison town.'[2]

Weimar had to provide land and build required infrastructure such as roads, water pipes, electricity supply and telephone lines. The airfield in Nohra was reactivated and extended. Where in 1933, the first Nazi concentration camp had incarcerated around 200 communists, 265 staff would run an air force training centre with 60 planes for 300 to 350 trainees from July 1935.[3] The build-up of the Luftwaffe, the Wehrmacht's aerial branch, was made official in 1935 in direct contravention of the Treaty of Versailles, which meant its facilities in Weimar could be extended without restraints. Barracks, runways and fuelling stations made Weimar-Nohra an important Luftwaffe hub in central Germany. In total at least 5,000 members of the Wehrmacht were stationed in Weimar by 1937 – around 10 per cent of the town's population.[4] Uniforms were ubiquitous, as were salutes and military jargon. Civilians too were affected by the spirit of combat readiness. They had to practise how to shut out all sources of light in case of aerial bombardment or what to do in case of general mobilization.[5] Air-raid shelters were installed and children were taught combat skills in the Hitler Youth.

Rearmament brought financial benefits for Weimar. Contracts stipulated that the Wehrmacht compounds would draw their supplies and services from the town, which brought steady business to the local economy.[6] Carl also saw this 'reconstruction' as a good thing. After all, it seemed an effective way to 'fight unemployment through the reintroduction of the Wehrmacht'.[7]

In February, Karl Astel hosted a prominent guest speaker. The director of the State Office for Race Studies in Weimar wanted his institution to lead Germany's eugenics programme. So he invited the Swiss-born geneticist Ernst Rüdin to speak. Rüdin's ideas had been instrumental in formulating the 'Law for the Prevention of Hereditarily Diseased Offspring' passed the previous year. Colleagues called him the 'Reichsführer for Sterilization'. In 1934, he'd argued that 'whoever is not physically or mentally fit must not pass on his defects to his children. The state must take care that only the fit produce children.'[8]

Astel agreed. His sterilization programme was well under way. At Weimar's municipal hospital on the northern slope of the Kirschberg, procedures had begun the previous year. In total, around 700 Weimar residents would be forcibly sterilized there by 1943. Court procedures to prove that the 'national body' had to be protected from an individual's 'harmful genetic material' could be called by the Gestapo or a medical official.[9] Reasons could be anything from physical disabilities to mental health issues or behaviour considered deviant such as repeated criminality, prostitution, alcoholism or homosexuality.

One victim was a thirty-two-year-old woman from Weimar. The town's public health officer and director of the State Health Office, Dr Waldemar Freienstein, sent her to the Psychiatric Clinic in Jena in August 1936 for a 'manic episode'. The woman had previously worked as an administrative assistant in the Ministry of the Interior and there was no prior record of unusual behaviour. Yet Freienstein suspected that she might have schizophrenia. On those grounds, he applied to the Hereditary Health Court (Erbgesundheitsgericht) in Weimar, where Astel worked as judge, for her to be sterilized.

The woman was neither notified nor asked for her input. When she found out from her brother what was about to happen to her, she was desperate to leave the clinic. Against her will, she was not only held there but subjected to insulin shock therapy, whereby patients were injected with large doses of insulin to induce repeated comas. The woman suffered from severe side effects such as vomiting, shivering and hot flushes. She resisted the injections, demanding to be let go. Staff increased the daily dosage until she fell into a temporary coma each time. When she was awake, she wrote increasingly desperate letters to her family pleading with them to take her home. Receiving no answer, she wrote to her employer and finally even to

Hitler for help. None of her letters ever left the building. Staff just placed them in her patient file. The woman was forcibly sterilized six months after her admission to the clinic. Only then was she released.[10]

Astel was keen to take things further. He'd joined the Nazi Party early, in July 1930, indicating a belief in its ideology that went much deeper than opportunism.[11] Obsessed with public health, he was prone to sudden outbursts when confronted with people or behaviours he considered a threat to it. Once, he spotted a young man smoking and slapped the cigarette out of his mouth.[12] The 'Sippenkartei' or 'Family Charts' he produced in Thuringia spoke of this personal obsession but they became a model for Nazi policy across the Reich. The files provided health information about an individual by tracing their ancestors back up to six generations and combined these details with police records in order to prove connections between behaviour and biology. With direct contacts in the SS, Astel found it easy to promote his ideas with the political elite. In 1937, he petitioned Heinrich Himmler, the Reichsführer-SS, with his idea that male criminals should be castrated. He also suggested to Himmler that he was able to predict deviant behaviours through his methods and advocated the pre-emptive 'killing of criminals even if they have not yet killed a person themselves'.[13]

His invitation for Rüdin to speak in Thuringia in February was one such move of merging science with politics to promote the 'elimination of the hereditarily ill and the unworthy from breeding', as Astel put it in his inaugural lecture at Jena University.[14] Rüdin chose to speak on 'Predictions of Hereditarily Diseased and Normal Children'. This was the strongest sign yet that Nazi eugenics would go further than forced sterilization. Soon children with mental and physical disabilities would be murdered. Over 650 Thuringians would eventually fall victim to Nazi 'euthanasia', one of the highest levels in the country.[15]

Emmy Sonnemann didn't think much about her old life in Weimar. Her thoughts were preoccupied with her future in Berlin. One morning in February, Hermann Göring was in his dressing room and appeared to be busy getting ready for the day. She was about to leave him to it and be on her way to theatre practice when he called through the door: 'I have to tell you something very important!' Emmy enquired whether it was good or bad news. 'Whether it's bad for you remains to be seen,' Göring replied unhelpfully. He passed her a folded piece of paper through the door and told her to open it on her way to the theatre. Emmy rushed outside and into the waiting car. On the back seat, she immediately unfolded the note. It said: 'Would you like to marry me at Easter? The Führer will be our best man.'[16]

The wedding took place on 10 April. It proved what Harry Graf Kessler had argued in 1919: autocratic regimes were better at pomp than democracies. Emmy loved every moment of the opulent festivities. 'Of course our wedding couldn't be seen as a purely private matter,' she wrote. 'It was decidedly an official one for Germany and especially for Berlin.'[17] Following a civil ceremony at the town hall, Hitler was the first to congratulate Emmy, telling her: 'If you ever have a personal concern, come to me.'[18] When the couple made their way to Berlin Cathedral for the religious ceremony, they travelled in an open-top car. Crowds cheered and Göring's new warplanes flew formations overhead. Then a feast was held at the Kaiserhof Hotel. 'A visitor . . . might well have thought that the monarchy had been restored,' Eric Phipps, the British ambassador to Germany, wrote in

Emmy and Hermann Göring on their wedding day, 10 April 1935, with their best man.

his dispatch to London. 'The streets were all decorated; all traffic was suspended . . . while two hundred military aircraft circled in the sky.'[19]

If Emmy had any regrets, it was only that she had to give up acting. She had given her last performance before the wedding. Now, she'd sighed to a friend, 'I must do what he wants.'[20] Hitler reminded her on her wedding day what her new role would be. He told her that he would never marry and that it would therefore fall to her to be First Lady of the Reich. 'I stared at him in shock,' Emmy recalled. Yet, her new life had long been all around her. She lived in the ever-expanding Carinhall, a sprawling mansion built in the style of a hunting lodge that featured a huge swimming pool, private cinema, library, banqueting hall and Göring's large art collection, to which he would soon add looted treasures from all over Europe. 'A new life began: the life of Emmy Göring,' she wrote. 'The world of Emmy Sonnemann appeared to be far away from me on another planet.'[21]

For Carl Weirich, the shine of Nazism was beginning to wear off a little. He could see that the work-creation measures were having an effect, but state control over the economy brought new problems. Carl had derived a substantial proportion of his income from being involved in the production and distribution of school books. 'For me personally,' he wrote, '[it was] a job without whose revenue I couldn't have bought my house.' Now the Nazi government threatened to award the book contracts elsewhere.[22] Without party membership, Carl didn't have a good case to argue to keep this lucrative strand of income.

When Labour Day came around in 1935, Carl felt less enthusiastic. Ostensibly, 1 May was an occasion to celebrate labour in all its forms and especially the skilled trades the Nazi regime said it was protecting from mass production and imports. This year, it was even someone from Carl's own field who was honoured in Weimar, the famous master bookbinder Otto Dorfner, who'd taught at the Bauhaus and crafted book covers for Harry Graf Kessler's Cranach Press. Dorfner had adapted to working under the new regime. He was commissioned to craft the elaborate certificates that declared people such as Hitler and Frick honorary citizens of Weimar. Carl appreciated Dorfner's skill and visited his workshop in Weimar with the board of the guild of bookbinders. But he wasn't in the mood for Labour Day. It didn't help that it was an unusually cold day for the time of year. There was even snowfall. The Weirichs joined the procession to the stadium where the main festivities were taking place, but they stole away at the first opportunity. Carl decided Nazi pomp wasn't worth 'contracting a mighty cold' for.[23]

If Carl's enthusiasm for the new regime was waning a little, his son was growing into the system as if it had always been there. For his ninth birthday someone gave Wilhelm a miniature replica of the 'Reich Chancellor's car'.[24] At school, too, there was no way around the ideology. Carl's focus was on Wilhelm's excellent grades as he planned to send his son to a specialized vocational school in a few years 'to become a master bookbinder, like his grandfather, so that in the shop at Geleitstr. 10 a master can continue the old ways'.[25] But Wilhelm learned a whole lot more at school than the skills he needed to be a tradesman. He learned about leading Nazi politicians, about their struggle for Germany and about their aims for the country in which he was to play a vital role. In lessons on religion, he learned that 'the highest form of fraternal love and the highest stage of the sacrifice mentality is death for the fatherland'.[26]

The activists around Kurt Nehrling and Hans Eberling were making increasingly large sacrifices to continue their resistance. Hans later remembered that, as 'the measures of the Hitler dictatorship became harsher and harsher, our circle of colleagues shrank further and further'.[27] The authorities appeared to be increasingly thin-skinned. Even humour was now criminalized. On 12 July, Gestapo Erfurt arrested the merchant Erich Kaiser because he'd made a joke about Hitler that, according to the police record, 'caused the greatest excitement among the population'. The accused was put in 'protective custody' for saying: 'Back in the day, we used to have a Kaiser sent from heaven above. Today, we have some arsehole from Berchtesgaden [Hitler's mountain retreat].'[28] Gestapo Weimar sent the factory worker Hermann Bischoff to the concentration camp of Bad Sulza, which had replaced the improvised early camps at Nohra and elsewhere in Thuringia. He told a co-worker that Gauleiter Fritz Sauckel had been arrested for embezzlement, which was deemed 'an attitude hostile to the state and alien to the people' as well as a 'threat to public security and order'.[29]

If jokes and grumbling were enough to get people incarcerated, the danger to political activists like Kurt Nehrling and his circle of social democrats was acute. That's why so many members dropped out. Kurt and Hans did their best to hold together what was left of their small band of young idealists with a mix of caution and solidarity. They helped people like Martin Seifert, an unemployed worker in his late twenties. Receiving just 7.50 marks a week in unemployment welfare, the temptation was there to join the Wehrmacht or a paramilitary organization in exchange for safety, shelter, food and a salary. But his comrades looked after Martin. August Frölich, former leader of Thuringia and SPD Reichstag deputy, invited him to his house for lunch twice a week. Willy Hüttenrauch, fellow member of the Nehrling–Eberling group (and future East German ambassador to Mongolia), allowed Martin to live at his parents' house, where he received shelter and food for 6 marks. Later, when Martin had his own flat, he repaid the favour, hosting illegal meetings camouflaged as art gatherings. Hans Eberling made oil paintings and sketches specifically for this purpose which they hung on Martin's walls. For all the solidarity, it was a perilous life. Martin would later be arrested and taken to the dreaded Gestapo basement in Weimar.[30]

Martin's girlfriend Ilse Odenthal knew the risks. The pair had met in Weimar a year earlier. Ilse worked as a maid while Martin was reliant on the charity of his friends and had no prospect of ever leading a stable or even a safe life. He explained to Ilse that he would fight fascism for as long as it took. Slowly, he introduced her to his friends and she too became part of the Nehrling–Eberling circle. She accepted that once they had their own flat it would become a resistance hub and that this would pose an enormous risk, not least because her paternal grandmother was Jewish.

In 1935, Martin came home with a Jewish man he introduced as Bruno Flörsheim. He asked Ilse to hide him while he prepared his emigration to South Africa. Ilse also helped another Jewish couple to hide and escape. Even when she was heavily pregnant and the Gestapo broke into her flat to search for evidence against her husband, Ilse was steely enough to remember to hide an anti-fascist pamphlet that Kurt Nehrling had written and given to Martin to copy on a typewriter.[31] Living life in permanent danger had become second nature to Kurt and his friends.

In August, signs appeared on the roads into Weimar: 'Jews aren't wanted here'. Jews were also banned from Weimar's Schwanseebad lido. SA troops dragged a wooden puppet hanging from a gallows through the town centre, chanting 'Germany, wake up! Jews, die a wretched death!'[32] Even though many Jews had already left town, the Nazis ramped up their efforts to make their antisemitism as visible as possible. Sauckel wanted Weimar to look like the Nazi *Musterstadt* or 'model town' he proclaimed it to be and pressed ahead with new measures. Many restaurants and hotels responded, displaying signs that Jews weren't invited, which ramped up the pressure on others to follow.

This put Arthur and Rosa Schmidt in a difficult position. If they didn't display antisemitic messaging, it might draw unwanted attention to Rosa. She was safe for now, but with Karl Astel's research into family backgrounds, how long could they hide hers? What if one of their children needed to prove their 'Aryan' ancestry for a wedding or a club membership? The SA columns marching through the town made it very clear that the line between Rosa Schmidt, the respected hotelier, and Rosa Schmidt, the Jewish threat to the 'People's Community', was paper thin. Signs on their big carts read: 'Jews are no compatriots'. The Gau newspaper reported that 'now it will be clear to the unwanted guests which way the wind is blowing'.[33]

On the morning of Wednesday 28 August, one of the most iconic sites of Weimar, the Goethe House, was buzzing with activity. On the Frauenplan square in front of it, swastika flags flapped in the summer breeze. Garlands, bunting and fir trees had been put up. Many Weimarers who weren't at work had come to catch a glimpse of the famous visitors who would be there. These included prominent politicians such as Reichsstatthalter Sauckel, Minister President Marschler as well as the ambassadors of the United States, Britain, Poland and the Free City of Danzig.[34] It was Johann Wolfgang von Goethe's 186th birthday and this year Weimar had a special cause to celebrate. A sizable extension to the poet's primary home had been built so that the Goethe National Museum could now separate the residential building from the exhibition space.

Hans Wahl, director of the museum since 1918, had tried to get an extension built for years, petitioning federal and Thuringian governments during the years of the Weimar Republic. But political and economic issues had repeatedly got in the way. When the Nazis seized power, Wahl saw another chance to realize his dream. He was also Gau advisor for scholarship and science. As vice president of the Goethe Society, he saw himself as an important link between culture and politics.[35] It was a position that he sought to use to draw funds and recognition to Weimar, offering the Nazis Goethe as a national figure in exchange.

Wahl told the Nazi authorities that furthering the Goethe legacy in Weimar was 'work of national importance'.[36] Eventually, he lobbied for Hitler himself to patronize the project. The Nazi leader's enthusiasm for the Goethe extension was at best lukewarm. The Thuringian authorities launched construction in 1934 anyway, without knowing whether Berlin would provide funding. They kept the ceremony of laying the cornerstone unusually low-key in case the project had to be aborted.[37]

But the Thuringian Nazis had an ace up their sleeves. They knew how fond their Führer was of Weimar. They'd have to catch him in person in a moment of enthusiasm for the town. So Fritz Wächtler, the Thuringian Education Minister, spent time with Hitler during the Schiller festivities in November 1934, showing him a model and drawings of the Goethe Museum expansion. Hitler didn't like

Wächtler, who was a notoriously thuggish drunk, but he liked what he showed him. Wächtler used the moment of Schillermania to explain that, sadly, the funding for the Goethe project was still not in place, and Hitler had agreed to provide the missing 160,000 marks from the national purse.[38]

When the finished extension opened to the public on 28 August, the local functionaries were full of praise for Hitler's supposed enthusiasm. A plaque in the foyer of the new building claimed: 'Extension built through the generous support of the Führer and Reich Chancellor ADOLF HITLER in the third year of his government inaugurated on Goethe's birthday 1935'.[39] Sauckel declared his hope that 'one day both names will shine in our town: Goethe and Hitler'.[40]

It had fallen to Hans Severus Ziegler to deliver the festive speech for the Goethe extension.[41] As a member of the Thuringian government, Reich culture senator and member of the leadership of the German National Theatre, he had carved out a significant role for himself in Nazi culture policy, but his mind was troubled throughout 1935. Writing to his friend, the writer Erich Ebermayer, he admitted that he felt 'hated and persecuted and so maliciously slandered'.[42] Ziegler had been cautious never to openly disclose his homosexuality. But rumours had spread, particularly in Weimar. Staff at the theatre gossiped about how Ziegler appointed male actors and staff who were rumoured to be gay. Even the Mayor of Frankfurt am Main, Friedrich Krebs, speculated that the Weimar theatre had 'almost no visitors to show for' because Ziegler 'had homosexual tendencies'.[43]

In the Third Reich, Ziegler's sexual orientation was no private matter. Male homosexuality was illegal and the Nazis put many gay men into concentration camps. At the beginning of the year, Ziegler was suspended from all public offices while a court inquiry investigated the rumours. Although the official report published in March stated that 'it is without a doubt that no deeds punishable according to the criminal code were committed by Dr Ziegler', this wasn't the end of the matter.[44]

Sauckel, who had long watched his colleague's powerful position in Thuringia and his close relationship with Hitler with envy, now tried to use the situation to get Ziegler moved to Dresden, where the post of a theatre directorship had become vacant. This time, Hitler intervened personally. He liked Ziegler and appreciated his loyalty. 'I want Ziegler to stay in Weimar,' Hitler insisted, 'he has far more important tasks here.'[45] This shielded Ziegler from the terrible fate other gay men endured under Nazi persecution. He was appointed general director of the theatre in Weimar in 1936. But neither that nor the constant threats Education Minister Wächtler issued in the press against anyone guilty of the 'dissemination of malicious rumours about State Councillor Dr Ziegler' made the man feel any safer.[46]

Hitler refused to see him personally about the matter, despite several pleas. By the summer, Ziegler was so downcast that he wrote to Ebermayer, who was also gay, that he felt he 'had no more energy for now and in the atmosphere of persecution and its consequences had few chances to help others . . . I am still suffering never-ending difficulties.'[47] These and other notes indicate that Ziegler might have had hopes that he could convince Hitler to ease the persecution of gay men so long as he could talk to him in private. In the meantime, he resolved to work even harder to prove his worth to the Nazi cause. Ziegler saw no paradox in the fact that that involved the deadly persecution of other minorities.

Joachim Appel's face went bright red. The whole class was staring at the teenager. When he had walked into the classroom, he had expected a normal lesson to begin. Then the German teacher entered the room. Normally, the class would stand up at this point for the Hitler salute, but today they sat in silence while the teacher showed no sign of starting the lesson. Instead, the man stood in front of the class and announced: 'I won't start teaching while that pig Jew is in the class.' All eyes turned on Joachim. One of the girls later recalled how beautiful he looked with his dark, slightly wavy hair, even as his face turned scarlet in indignation and anger. Joachim stayed utterly silent as he stuffed his belongings into his bag and stormed out of the room, the jeering and whooping of his class-mates ringing in his ears.[48]

Joachim had no idea what had happened. There had been no indication that he wouldn't be allowed to attend school any more. The Appels were a well-established Weimar family who had lived in a large house at Brühl 6 just north-east of the old town for three generations. They ran a leather shop from there and lived above it with a large garden to the back. 'Our family was so assimilated that we celebrated Christmas and Easter,' Joachim remembered later.[49] Even after 1933, the Jewish family had seemingly continued as normal or at least managed to shield their children from the growing antisemitism. Joachim and his older brother Günther played with other children in the neighbourhood, none of whom were Jewish. Even when the boycotts had started, the Appels still believed they could sit this out. His parents 'always believed that the Jew hatred would end soon', Joachim later recalled. 'That wasn't what one expected from the German people. The insanity and the inhumanity, those weren't German attributes.' It would prove a fatal misjudgement. Joachim, who decided to leave Weimar in 1938 and move to live with his uncle in Cincinnati in the United States, would be the sole member of his immediate family to survive the Holocaust.[50]

While it wasn't yet illegal for Jewish children to attend regular state schools in Weimar or anywhere else in Germany, many teachers and school heads acted on their own initiative. Lieselotte, the daughter of the imprisoned shoeshop owner Ludwig Leopold, was also the only Jewish child in her class. She was expelled in 1936, two years before the Nazis passed a law to ban Jews from attending non-Jewish schools. The Education Ministry bragged that, by July 1937, there were only seven Jewish and twenty-one half-Jewish pupils left in Weimar's state schools.[51] New legislation had emboldened people like Joachim's German teacher to press ahead with antisemitic measures. The Nuremberg Laws were enacted on 15 September 1935. Among other measures, they reduced the status of German Jews to subjects of the Reich rather than full citizens with political rights. They also banned future marriages and sexual relationships between Jews and people 'of German or related blood'.

A Jew was defined as someone with three or four Jewish grandparents while 'Mischlinge' or 'mixed-race' people were graded according to a complex, pseudo-scientific chart. This meant that Jews were now legally definable while simultaneously degraded in status. Pre-existing marriages like Rosa and Arthur Schmidts' weren't affected by this in principle. In practice, the family would have a problem the moment one of them needed to prove their 'Aryan ancestry' in order to get married or to apply for certain jobs or administrative processes. The Schmidt children would all be classed as 'Mischlinge of the first degree'. Alexandra was already married and Arthur lived abroad but if the two younger boys wanted to marry a non-Jewish German (as Alexandra had the year before the Nazis came to power), they would have to apply to the authorities for permission and that was rarely granted. In order to keep their Jewish ancestry a secret, all the Schmidts would have to be extremely careful, avoiding situations that required documentation of their 'Aryan' background. This applied to Ernst, for instance, who was now twenty-one and wanted to become a Luftwaffe pilot.

The immense power the Nuremberg Laws granted teachers, civil servants, shop owners and the non-Jewish population in general triggered a rapid escalation of antisemitic behaviour. People suddenly found they could preside over who used certain spaces, who got a contract, who sat next to them on the tram, who was treated with civility and who with scorn. This extended even to children. Joachim's classmates had treated him like any other friend before the Nazis passed antisemitic legislation but now hounded him out of their classroom, encouraged by the teacher. It was a hateful dynamic that spiralled to new heights month by month. Kurt Sachs, the Jewish owner of a textile shop at Jubiläumsplatz 2, diagonally opposite the Hotel Hohenzollern, was still awarded an honorary cross for front-line soldiers on 2 April 1935 – 'in the name of the Führer and Reich Chancellor'. Three years later, he was arrested and taken to Buchenwald concentration camp. He survived the Holocaust by emigrating to Colombia after his release.[52]

Life became more and more difficult for Weimar's Jews. Even everyday activities became risky. In November, after the annual autumn fair, the mayoral office received an angry letter claiming that 'displeasure was aroused by the fact that Jews move around at the fair as though there were no Third Reich'.[53]

On 11 November, Carl Weirich saw Hitler for the first time. He'd heard that 'the new Reich Chancellor was in Weimar briefly'. So he went out on to Karlsplatz behind his house where many other people had gathered to catch a glimpse of the Führer as he was driven past in an open-top car.[54] But Carl wasn't feeling the awed excitement that appeared to have gripped some of the Weimarers around him. He wasn't opposed to the regime. As far as he could tell, they were fixing the economy. Carl had turned fifty-two days earlier and enjoyed being able to celebrate without existential fears. Overall, things were heading in the right direction as far as he was concerned. But he was also fundamentally a non-political person who, while taking an interest in current affairs, wanted to be left alone by the state to live and work as he pleased. The political interference in the production and distribution of school book covers was just one of many signs that Nazism was an ideological project to the core that left nobody's life untouched, and Carl had mixed feelings about that.

He spent a pensive November withdrawing into the things that were important to him: family, religion and self-development. He attended religious services, concerts and an exhibition by the Weimar artist Irmgard von Bongé, who had studied at the Bauhaus. Carl was impressed by her skill and particularly moved by a painting depicting her own mother, who had been a much-valued customer of Carl's for many years.[55] The beauty of life itself was more important than politics. In November 1935, Carl decided not to be a Patron Member of the SS any longer.

When Carl Weirich saw Hitler on 11 November, the crowds were unusually quiet. There was a sombre, almost eerie atmosphere in Weimar despite thousands of people lining the streets. Hitler had arrived by special train from Munich together with Reich Youth Führer Baldur von Schirach and Nazi Press Chief Otto Dietrich. It was a brief but important visit for the regime. The spectators in Weimar sensed the gravity of the moment. As Hitler's entourage drove to the southern outskirts of Weimar, the townspeople stood in silence, their right arms raised in salute.[56] The Führer was on his way to the Villa Silberblick to pay his last respects to Elisabeth Förster-Nietzsche.

Friedrich Nietzsche's sister had died suddenly in her bed in the early hours of the morning of 8 November 1935. Ursula, the daughter of her cousin Max Oehler, mused that the woman who had been like a grandmother to her had wanted it that way. Elisabeth had slipped away 'without ringing a bell or calling for help', she wrote. 'Neither relatives nor friends had the opportunity to gather around her bed, nobody heard her speak her last words, no nurse cared for her.' It was as if she had 'given up her determined ghost'.[57]

Elisabeth died knowing her affairs were in order. Five years earlier, she'd acquired space for another grave in the church cemetery of the village of Röcken, where she and Friedrich had been born and raised. There she wanted to rest next to her brother. So she had her mother's remains and headstone moved to her father's grave on the right-hand edge of the small family plot. She would be buried in the middle between Friedrich and their parents. Elisabeth believed she had accomplished her life's aims. In her will, she'd stated with satisfaction: 'The way the Nietzsche Archive is set up today and works with such success is the last pleasure in my life.'[58] With the help of the 'most revered Führer Adolf Hitler', she had told her old friend Harry Graf Kessler in one last letter in September, the financial future of the archive was secured and an extension of the property was within reach.[59] 'You see, my revered friend, that the institution of the Nietzsche Archive is very large and expansive and now really stands in the centre of German intellectualism. If I was ten years younger, I'd be even more proud a[nd] joyful, but in my 90th year, I'm not the person you once knew.'[60]

The single-minded determination that had driven Elisabeth all those years had drained from her once she believed her brother's work safe in the hands of the Nazis and their sympathizers in the archive. She felt increasingly detached from things. It was time to go. She signed off the last letter to her friend 'with the warmest greetings and wishes, your old and frail Dr. h. c. Elisabeth Förster-Nietzsche'.[61]

Harry never responded. It may have taken a while for the letter to reach him. He had warnings from several sources that the Nazi regime was after him and with a heavy heart decided to remain in exile. He was also struggling with ongoing health issues, exacerbated by desperate attempts to save what was left of his estate in Germany. In July, he had looked on helplessly from exile in Paris as his furniture, books and personal effects from the house in Weimar were sold at auction. 'End of the central period of my life and of a home built with great love,' he wrote in his diary.[62] Almost exactly a year later, he lost the villa itself. 'My dear house in Weimar sold today,' he wrote wistfully. 'How many memories, how much of my life have I lost with it!'[63] When he died at the age of sixty-nine in a clinic in Lyon in the autumn of 1937, dejected and drained, Weimar was still on his mind. The last sentence he'd ever write in his diary compared the commune of Fournels in southern France with his old home: 'The town, old-fashioned, picturesque, reminds me in style and atmosphere of Weimar.'[64]

Two years earlier, it had been too dangerous for Harry to attend Elisabeth's funeral but he sent a brief telegram to her cousin Max Oehler, who was about to take over her leadership of the Nietzsche Archive. He sent his condolences, 'deeply shocked by the loss of my dear old friend'.[65] Hitler too seemed emotional as he sat in front of Elisabeth's coffin on 11 November. Richard Leutheußer, a former

DVP politician and chairman of the Nietzsche Archive, later wrote that he thought the Nazi leader really was affected by 'the death of a woman much respected by him'. Leutheußer had greeted Hitler when he arrived at the Villa Silberblick and reported that Elisabeth had, 'without suffering, never lost her rare mental strength right to the end and slipped away from her hardworking life very suddenly and without pain'. According to Leutheußer, Hitler's 'great grief was obvious'. As the Nazi leader left the archive after the hour-long ceremony, it seemed to Leutheußer as though 'He turned around once more at the gate with visible mourning and evident sadness and gazed at the now silent house once more with a deeply affected expression.'[66]

Whether Hitler grieved a woman he'd only met a few times is impossible to tell, but he was certainly appreciative of the intellectual legacy her work had gifted his cause. In the last few months of her life, Elisabeth cast aside whatever remaining reservations she may have harboured regarding the Nazis and their Führer. Their attention was flattering after the many years of financial insecurity and personal controversy. Now, 'the name Nietzsche is a magic word', she had told a friend at the end of July.[67]

Her last personal letters had been full of praise for individual members of the Nazi elite and not just for Hitler, whom she referred to as 'our worshipped Führer'.[68] Despite his crude mannerisms and lack of formal education, she was suddenly particularly taken with Reichsstatthalter Fritz Sauckel, who had spent more time at the Villa Silberblick of late to discuss the plans for the Nietzsche Memorial Hall with her. Elisabeth described him as 'one of the nicest and deepest men of our movement'.[69] Sauckel returned the compliment in his short speech at her memorial service, describing Elisabeth as a 'unique, noble and great German woman' and a 'fearless, determined and ambitious steward of a great German genius'. He added: 'Our German people may consider itself incredibly lucky to have been gifted such noble and glorious women alongside great statesmen, heroes, generals and mighty cultural creators.' Friedrich Nietzsche and his sister had become immortal, Sauckel said. Now it was time 'that National Socialist Germany protects the monumental intellectual legacy of the great philosopher for all times'.[70]

Many Nazi leaders embraced this. Chief ideologue Alfred Rosenberg retained an avid interest in Nietzsche right to the end of the Second World War when he told a delegation at the archive that in light of the lost war it was now time 'to love your destiny' in true Nietzschean spirit.[71] Eugenicists like Alfred Ploetz, who coined the term 'racial hygiene' and promoted 'mercy killings' of disabled children, claimed to follow Nietzschean ideas about eradicating weakness.[72] Nietzsche quotes appeared in many Nazi speeches and texts. Elisabeth's compilation of *The Will to Power* was more accessible than her brother's notes, creating a Nietzsche image that lent itself to the glorification of violence, might and superiority for people who couldn't or wouldn't bother with the originals, to which she had restricted access over many years. Nietzsche became an intellectual and spiritual resource for Nazis to draw ideas and words from selectively. The philosopher himself had been aware of the danger of his work being used for nefarious purposes. He'd once called his concepts 'dynamite'.[73]

But Nietzsche was also a controversial figure within Nazism. His adversarial relationship with Richard Wagner and Bayreuth – both adored by Hitler – counted against him. Nietzsche had argued that Jews could be assimilated into the German people over time, which ran contrary to the ever-intensifying ethnic antisemitism of Nazi Germany. Some Nazi intellectuals complained that Nietzsche's 'Master Race' wasn't a biological concept at all but based on class, education and intellectualism. Progress on the Nietzsche Memorial was sluggish since his place in Nazi ideology was never secure.

Hitler himself never returned to the Villa Silberblick. He didn't grant Elisabeth a state funeral nor attend her interment in Röcken. Nietzsche's sister had been important to the Führer but not all-important. He was wary of the cult-like obsession Nietzsche inspired in many people. Jealous of any rivals to the Führer cult, whether they were fellow politicians, Gods or dead philosophers, Hitler kept the Nietzsche legacy at arm's length.[74]

*

Max Hecker was deeply saddened by the death of Elisabeth Förster-Nietzsche. Like Hitler, he had been among the group of mourners at her memorial service at the Nietzsche Archive. The long-term scholar of the Goethe and Schiller Archive had visited Nietzsche's sister often in her villa and considered her a friend. Now he grieved not so much for the death of 'the enthusiastic founder of the archive', as he put it, as for the loss of 'a generous supporter who so often granted me her sympathy in word and deed, who in dark days became a magnanimous helper to me. This glowing image will never pale in my heart, the image of an understanding female soul who despite her great life's task never neglected the tender attention to the little things around her . . . She was kind, worthy of every kindness.'[75]

His daughter's thoughts were with a different Elisabeth. Jutta was now in her early thirties and still unsure about her future when her thoughts turned to a woman whose achievements were inspirational: Elisabeth Blochmann. She'd been a trainee teacher at Jutta's school during the war. Since then, she'd become an eminent scholar and education reformer. Unusually for a woman, she'd even been appointed as professor of Social and Theoretical Pedagogy at the Academy of Education at Halle an der Saale. Blochmann had developed a whole new concept for early education, elevating its status and the professions attached to it. She argued that early education should be available to all children and of the highest quality. Nursery teachers should therefore be fully qualified educators with their own professional code, decent pay and vocational dignity.

Jutta admired Blochmann because she was a woman with a fulfilling professional life, one that went beyond working out of necessity or only while single, as many women still did. Could Jutta do something similar? She thought she could, enrolling at the Friedrich Schiller University of Jena to study pedagogy. In November she received permission to begin the practical part of her teacher training under the condition that she joined either the Bund Deutscher Mädel (League of German Girls) or the NS-Frauenschaft

(National Socialist Women's League).[76] Jutta joined the latter, and passed the examination two years later with flying colours.

By that point, her role model Elisabeth Blochmann had been driven into exile. She was Jewish, which meant that she could no longer legally work at a German university. She was dismissed in 1933, and in 1934 she moved to England, where she eventually secured a position at the University of Oxford, teaching German Literature and Pedagogy. It would have been impossible, dangerous even, for Blochmann to attempt to pursue a professional career in Germany at the time Jutta did. Since 1933 only 'Aryans' could be teachers, professors and educators. Unlike Blochmann, Jutta had no problem proving that her descent was compliant with the law. So she did and looked forward to her own professional career.

On a cold, snowy day in December, Carl Weirich hiked up the Ettersberg hill. The frosty landscape looked magical. He stopped to look at blades of grass that were so glazed with frozen mist that they looked as though they were made from glass. Tapping them lightly with his foot, he delighted in the bright clink they made as they broke. Later, he wrote in his diary: 'Christmas 1935 was an especially joyful occasion for us and our lad, who showed how much he appreciated this by playing the piano beautifully and by being happy about the beautiful Christmas tree.' Life was good for the Weirichs.[77]

1936

Emmy Göring loved her life as First Lady of the Reich. It was true that Magda Goebbels had a much closer relationship with Hitler and was a permanent rival for that role, but Emmy had no political ambition and focused on the glamour and excitement of her new life. In that, Magda couldn't rival her. Unlike Goebbels, Göring was fabulously wealthy, and increased his fortune at every opportunity. As chief of the Luftwaffe, Emmy's husband presided over lucrative military contracts, which opened doors to embezzlement, bribery and corruption in his favour. Later in the year, Hitler would also appoint him as Plenipotentiary of the Four-Year Plan to boost economic growth and rearmament – a powerful position with yet more access to money. He was able to expand the Carinhall estate, acquire two huge yachts (*Carin I* and *Carin II*) and maintain several residences across the country.[1]

Emmy had been catapulted from small-town life as a provincial actress in Weimar to the national stage, and what she liked best about it was the constant drama. As surreal as life at Carinhall was between Göring's art collection, the grave of his first wife and the many famous visitors, Emmy took to it like a duck to water. One of her favourite things about the place was the presence of lion cubs. The Görings raised seven of them in succession, taking them from Berlin Zoo and exchanging them for a new one when they became too big and dangerous to be pets. 'It was admittedly a strange scene seeing a lion cub run around,' Emmy later remembered. 'Most of the time they would toddle by my side as well behaved as a dog.' One of them, called Mucki, was in the habit of getting up in the morning with Göring, who was an early riser. After her husband had his breakfast, he'd bring Mucki back into the bedroom, where the cub would jump on Emmy to wake her up.[2]

When they went out or received guests, both she and her husband loved to dress ostentatiously and play the magnanimous hosts for whom nothing was too expensive or too extravagant. They began 1936 by celebrating Göring's forty-third birthday on 12 January by throwing 'the most imposing and brilliant social event since the heyday of the Kaisers', the New York Times reported.[3] Over 2,000 guests flocked to the Prussian State Opera in Berlin to listen to the orchestra, drink champagne and take part in a tombola with prizes such as a diamond-encrusted swastika brooch.[4] 'General Goering, in the natty uniform of a general of aviators, occupied the chief box with his wife,' the New York Times wrote, while 'opposite them, in the brilliant pre-war uniform of the Black Hussars, was the former Crown Prince Friedrich Wilhelm', who shared a box with his siblings Eitel Friedrich and Oskar. Their brother August Wilhelm, nicknamed 'Auwi', had been an early Nazi supporter and appeared 'in the brown uniform of a Storm Trooper'. All-in-all, the New York Times concluded, the guests 'typified the imperial past, the Nazi present and the militarized future of Germany'.[5]

But Emmy hadn't entirely forgotten about her old life in Weimar. As the wife of a powerful Nazi politician she received plenty of pleas for help from individuals and institutions. She sometimes felt a little overwhelmed having 'become the "place" where people could deposit their concerns and their worries', as she put it.[6] Yet concerns from Weimar always found an open ear with her, especially when they came from the town's charitable care home for retired actors and performers, the Marie-Seebach-Stift.

The foundation had struggled through the difficult economic years of the Weimar Republic, as Emmy knew well. She and the other actors had each donated 50 pfennigs a month to it. With Emmy now in such a powerful position, director Wilhelm Hinrich Holtz saw an opportunity. He ensured Emmy would be elected to the board of governors, and Emmy in turn petitioned her husband for financial support. So for Christmas 1935 the foundation had been pleased to see that alongside the usual donations from people such as Reichsminister of the Interior Wilhelm Frick (20 marks) and ex-Kaiser Wilhelm II (100 marks), there was a 1,000-mark donation from Emmy Göring.[7]

This was excellent news, but both Emmy and Holtz were keen to ensure that the future of the Marie-Seebach-Stift was secured long-term. A chance to discuss this opened up when the Görings visited Weimar for the first time since getting married. Hermann was there to deliver a speech at the Weimarhalle on the eve of parliamentary elections on 29 March 1936 – the first one Jews and other ethnic minorities were banned from participating in. His wife accompanied him to her old home town.[8]

This time, Emmy did not stay in a modestly furnished flat as she had done for years, but at the prestigious Hotel Elephant, where Holtz greeted the power couple with a bunch of flowers from the garden of the Marie-Seebach-Stift. The next day, after they had voted, they walked up the hill to the actors' retirement home, where Göring officially announced that he would donate 5,000 marks to the foundation now and every year to come.[9] 'Well, dear Holtz,' he enquired in the informal conversation that ensued, 'how is everything, are things on track with your enterprise here?'[10]

Holtz explained that things were much better. He had installed a new kitchen. The rooms had each been fitted with electrical heating, and in general things were on the up. The ageing residents were also pleased about the new housing projects on the outskirts of Weimar. Many hoped soon to be surrounded by respectable young neighbours.[11] However, Holtz added, there were plenty more retired actors all across the country who would like to retire in Weimar, amid the glorious remnants of its literary past. Wouldn't it be 'incredibly beautiful to be able to help as *many* as possible?' Emmy remembered Holtz asking her husband.[12] Göring told Holtz to find a suitable property for an extension and start planning. In the meantime, he'd find the money somewhere. Emmy fell into her husband's arms. According to her, the director jumped up too, adding: 'If I could, I'd also hug you, Herr Minister President!'[13]

The extension was to be called the 'Emmy-Göring-Stift', a separate institution in its own building but near the Marie-Seebach-Stift and associated with it. It was everything Emmy dreamed of: a neo-baroque sanctuary that was evocative of Weimar Classicism. She could envision thespians retiring here 'free of the grinding concerns of everyday life, joyfully and peacefully'.[14] One year later, on a warm, sunny day in May 1937, the Görings returned for the opening ceremony. Himmler, Sauckel and Ziegler were among the high-profile guests.[15] Weimar had another strand to its self-image as the culture capital of the country and Emmy was 'as happy and grateful as one can only be very rarely in life'.[16] The Marie Seebach Foundation continues to use Emmy Göring's building to this day, though it no longer carries her name.

Two days after election Sunday and the Görings' visit to the Marie Seebach Foundation, Fritz Sauckel waited at Weimar train station for different guests. It was 10 o'clock in the morning of 31 March when dozens of uniformed men arrived. They marched in neat formation to be received by cheering crowds on the large square in front of the Hotel Hohenzollern. The men were very young, mostly between sixteen and twenty-three years old.[17] They were dressed entirely in black, their polished jackboots gleaming in the morning light. On their collars, the silver emblem of a skull and crossbones designated their unit.

This was the 8th Company of the SS Death's Head Unit 'Elbe' from Lichtenburg concentration camp in Prussia. The guard units responsible for running concentration camps had only officially been named 'Totenkopfverbände' or 'Death's Head Units' two days earlier. Now, the official SS newspaper *Das Schwarze Korps* (The Black Corps) reported, around 100 of them marched, accompanied by jubilant crowds, through Weimar. They passed 'Theatre Square, where Germany's two greatest poets tower on a stone plinth' and made their way to 'the new SS accommodation at Admiral-Scheer-Straße', where Sauckel handed a building over to them ceremonially.[18] In the evening, they were joined by an unexpected guest: SS Death's Head commander Theodor Eicke.

As commandant of Dachau, the large concentration camp just outside of Munich, Eicke had demanded his own SS unit. Training these guards at Dachau, he had developed a system deemed so brutally efficient that it was to be rolled out across Germany. And that was what he had come to discuss with Sauckel. When the two men met in Weimar, most of the early concentration camps of 1933 had been shut down. In Hitler's first year as Chancellor, there had been over seventy camps and dozens of other holding facilities, incarcerating around 45,000 people between them. A year later, five camps held around 3,000 prisoners.[19]

This drastic reduction was not a sign that the regime was becoming more moderate. On the contrary, the use of terror was becoming more systematic. Eicke had created the position of Inspector of Concentration Camps for himself and began, with Himmler's and Hitler's consent, to reorganize the remaining camps to mirror the Dachau system, complete with specially trained guards who didn't shy away from the application of violence to maintain control. The next step was to build new types of concentration camps from scratch. Thuringia still had a camp in Bad Sulza, but Eicke deemed this inefficient, 'because the administration and transport costs aren't in any proportion to the actual use and purpose of this institution', he told Sauckel.[20]

Eicke wanted new concentration camps: vast, efficient and with systematic violence replacing the haphazard brutality of the early years. He wanted purpose-built prisoner barracks and SS accommodation adjoining the camps. For that, he needed a blank canvas, not pre-existing structures. He told Sauckel that he'd agreed with Himmler to build a concentration camp in Thuringia for 3,000 prisoners and that all the men of SS Death's Head Unit 'Elbe' were to be moved there along with the existing prisoners from the Lichtenburg concentration camp. Since Eicke's system involved forced labour and eventually the Reich would cover the cost of running the camp, he told Sauckel that he saw 'only advantages for the Thuringian state with regards to the economy'.[21]

Sauckel agreed. This national project fitted into his plan to make Thuringia a 'Trutzgau' or 'Castle Gau', a Nazi stronghold against internal and external enemies. It was telling that Eicke and Sauckel held their meeting two days after an election in which supposedly 99 per cent of Germans had voted for Hitler and his party. This election may have been rigged but it proved nonetheless that organized opposition in Nazi Germany had been almost eradicated. Satisfaction with the regime was fairly high, not least due to the visible economic recovery and Hitler's flagrant breaches of the hated Treaty of Versailles.

At first glance it was an odd moment to introduce a new and vast concentration camp system. The explanation lies not in power politics but in Nazi ideology. While political opposition had effectively been squashed, the SS began to obsess over what it deemed to be 'Volksfeinde', biological enemies of the people, a group that included the disabled, criminals, ethnic minorities and, above all, Jews. While in February 1936, political prisoners still made up the vast majority of camp inmates, *Das Schwarze Korps* began to print pictures of people labelled 'habitual drunk', 'ruffian' and 'Jewish race defilers' as candidates for the new camps.[22] Himmler, Eicke and the SS began to see concentration camps as an instrument of 'racial hygiene'.[23]

Eicke told Sauckel that placing one of his new model camps in Thuringia was 'absolutely necessary because the state of Thuringia, as the heart of Germany, would during war be especially plagued by elements hostile to the state'.[24] He didn't need to tell Sauckel twice but Hitler might need some convincing if the funds for the project were to come out of Berlin. Eicke suggested that Sauckel speak to him directly, 'the Weimar Days (3rd to 5th July 36) are the best opportunity'.[25]

It was Mother's Day on 10 May, a relatively new addition to the German calendar. Before the First World War, the American Methodist Anna Jarvis had successfully campaigned to establish Mother's Day as an official public holiday in the US on the second Sunday in May. When the Nazis came to power, the veneration of motherhood fitted in well with their policies and they too made Mother's Day a public holiday. 'Another very nice tradition that National Socialism brought to Germany,' thought Carl Weirich.[26] He took Marie out for lunch at the Hotel Chemnitius, next door to their house. Then, they went hiking in the countryside with Wilhelm, having Bratwurst sausages and 'excellent cake' in the villages along the way. Soon dark clouds appeared out of nowhere and the Weirichs got drenched, but they took it in good spirits, with Carl joking that, since it was the fourth Sunday of Easter, this must be their 'baptism'. They took the train home, happy to enjoy a largely carefree year.[27]

Carl was also won over by another concept the Nazis had introduced: state-subsidized holidays laid on by an organization called Kraft durch Freude (KdF; Strength Through Joy). It had been set up in 1933 with the explicit aim of wooing the population, especially workers. Unlike communism, Nazism didn't seek to level society, but it aimed to integrate all Germans who were considered ethnically and biologically valuable into the 'People's Community', bridging class divides. The idea was that if all galleries, theatres, sports events and holidays were made affordable, then people would have similar experiences and, over time, society would harmonize. KdF was spectacularly popular. It became the world's largest travel agency. By 1939, 43 million holidays would be sold through it, most of them day trips, but 7 million were overnight holidays, including 690,000 cruises to Norway, Madeira and Italy.[28] Carl loved the idea of the cruises and booked tickets for himself and Marie.

On 23 July, the big day had come. Wilhelm was sent off to spend time with Carl's cousin. Then Carl and Marie boarded a special train from Weimar to Hamburg, a service included in the price of 50 marks per person for a five-day cruise around the Norwegian fjords. In Hamburg, they had a day to explore the city before strolling down to the St Pauli Piers in the evening to climb aboard the *Monte Sarmiento*, the passenger ship the KdF had chartered. Life on board was without frills. There were set times for getting up and lights out. The food was simple German fare, and the programme consisted of music, folk dancing, sports and presentations. Passengers were treated to a tour through Hamburg's impressive port before they set off towards the open sea.

Over the next few days, Carl and Marie saw breathtaking scenery. When they passed the tiny island of Heligoland, which Britain had ceded to Germany in 1890, the water began to glow in luminous shades of blue, an effect dubbed 'milky seas' by sailors. They passed through the Skagerrak strait where the late Weimar retiree Vice-Admiral Reinhard Scheer had fought the Battle of Jutland almost exactly twenty years earlier. Then they reached the Norwegian fjords. Carl, not normally given to flowery language, scribbled words like 'wildly romantic' and 'delightful' in his diary, overwhelmed by the sight of the majestic landscape. Then it was time to return through the North Sea to Hamburg and back to Weimar with fond memories and the newly confirmed impression that life was better now than it had been in years. If Carl had reservations about the Nazi regime, they were temporarily forgotten.

In May 1936, while Carl Weirich was looking forward to his cruise on the chartered *Monte Sarmiento*, work began on the first purpose-built KdF vessel. It would have space for nearly 1,500 passengers and contain a swimming pool as well as sea views from all cabins. Designed to be the organization's flagship, it was planned to be named *Adolf Hitler*. But the Führer changed his mind when in February Wilhelm Gustloff, the leader of the Swiss branch of the Nazi Party, was assassinated by a Jewish student in Davos. Like other 'fallen Nazis' he was declared a martyr or 'Blutzeuge' ('Blood Witness'). Hitler decided to name the KdF ship *Wilhelm Gustloff*.

Never one to miss an opportunity to emulate his Führer, Fritz Sauckel founded a 'Wilhelm Gustloff Foundation' in Weimar on 27 May. The money for this came from the 'Aryanization' of the Jewish-owned Simson company in the Thuringian Forest, a manufacturer of vehicles and weapons. In the 1920s, Simson had been given a monopoly by the Allies to produce handguns, rifles and light machine guns for the German Army, so that supply could be controlled and limited. Simson also survived the crisis years by producing luxury cars, other vehicles and prams. When the Nazis took power, Sauckel didn't wait long to claim that the Jewish owners, Arthur and Julius Simson, had embezzled state funds.[29]

This was a complaint that found an open ear with many aggrieved small business owners and workers in the area who had experienced personal catastrophes while envying the Simsons for their continued success. A trial found the company not guilty, but Sauckel seized it anyway in 1935. The Simsons fled into exile the following year. Now the Reichsstatthalter had the funds for his Wilhelm Gustloff Foundation. Using the stolen money, Sauckel acquired the small wagon factory in Weimar. He had big plans for it, beginning by converting it into a weapons and munitions factory. This would be extended year on year, eventually also including new high-tech factories to produce things like anti-aircraft guns, machine tools and wind turbines. It would soon be by far the largest employer in Weimar and from 1937 it would carry the founder's name: Fritz-Sauckel-Werk.[30]

Sauckel thought that Weimar could only be a Nazi 'model town' if it had a sizable population of workers. He planned to attract more and then train them in Nazi ideology at the factory, house them in purpose-built accommodation nearby and ensure that they lived in accordance with Nazi principles, as he explained in a speech in October 1936: 'In the factories of the Wilhelm Gustloff Foundation a permanent office for National Socialist ideological schooling of all employees of the factories . . . will be installed.' Social policies would particularly benefit the 'child-rich and most genetically worthy families in our factories', Sauckel added, so that 'strong, healthy and happy offspring' would be supported. There would also be all-encompassing medical care to 'permanently monitor the health of the children of our workers'. This system of control was to be accompanied by excellent sports facilities, including a gym and a swimming pool, modern working conditions and free technical training for apprentices. 'It is of course obvious,' Sauckel concluded, 'that the workers of the Wilhelm Gustloff Foundation can and must only be loyal, reliable followers of the Führer.'[31] This was the Nazis' offering to workers: submit to comprehensive state control and you will be rewarded with better living and working conditions than you have ever known under previous regimes. It was a compelling offer to some, especially younger workers, who had known little but economic instability.

Others, like Kurt Nehrling's group of young SPD activists, doubled down in their resistance. Heinz Adler remembered later that this was a time when 'our illegal Group Eberling/Nehrling became tighter and tighter. We paid membership fees and met around once a month in the flats of comrades Seifert, Nehrling, Köth, Iggesen and . . . at our place in Oberweimar in the factory apartment of the Coal Plant Gispersleben.' The group was not only audacious enough to meet in their workers' flats, but they also came up with ever new and inventive ways of disguising their communications. Heinz, whose job it was to establish and maintain links to other groups, took to hiding small pamphlets and other texts in the frame of his bicycle.[32]

Kurt was also able to maintain contacts with SPD groups in Berlin, Erfurt and Vienna. Although the Gestapo came close to his circle, sometimes even close enough to arrest members, they kept going. Outwardly, Kurt and his wife Heddy were simply running a fabric shop at Zeppelinplatz. Daughter Ursula, who was now fourteen, and son Heinz, who was eight, were healthy German children attending local schools. This allowed them to stay under the radar. The Nehrlings were a working family that proved total control was impossible, even for the Nazi regime. But they were intensely aware that the price for their principled objection was economic deprivation, social isolation and acute and permanent danger.

Many other workers took the Nazis up on their offer, consenting at least outwardly to Nazi ideology in exchange for security. Now that there was work in the arms industry in Weimar, more people moved to the town. In early 1933, there were 46,003 inhabitants. In 1936, this rose to 51,285 and by 1939 it would go up to nearly 60,000.[33] This helped local businesses like Carl Weirich's stationery shop by providing a larger customer base.

That people like Carl had disposable income again to travel

and eat out was in turn good news for Rosa and Carl Schmidt at the Hotel Hohenzollern. By 1937, the number of annual visitors to Weimar would rise to nearly 80,000. This was partially because Sauckel and the Thuringian Nazis did everything to sell Weimar as the most German of German towns.[34] This meant the town increased its popularity for conferences, congresses and school trips. But there was also plenty of private tourism again, which Sauckel and his men promoted heavily. In October, the Nazi Gau newspaper reported that a new hiking trail had been established that visitors could use to view a new dam on the River Saale. 'With this, one of the most naturally beautiful areas of Thuringia is completely accessible to ramblers,' the paper promised.[35] The Schmidts didn't really mind if visitors came for Thuringia's natural beauty, Weimar's history or Nazi projects. For the first time since they'd taken over the Hotel Hohenzollern after the war, they were making a steady and comfortable income.[36]

On 3 July, it was Marie Weirich's fiftieth birthday, and it was as if Weimar were celebrating with her. Inside Geleitstraße 10, a party had gathered for coffee and cake. Wilhelm played songs for his mother on the piano. Outside, there was also plenty of music. The streets were decked with flowers and swastikas. When the commotion outside made it clear that important visitors were about to arrive, Marie's guests crowded around the window, craning their necks to see better. A large, open-top car emerged, slowly making its way past jubilant crowds. There he was. Adolf Hitler, standing in his car and greeting the gathered Weimarers. 'Something to talk about over birthday coffee,' mused Carl.[37]

The spectacle the Weirichs observed that day had taken a year to organize. In the summer of 1935, Fritz Sauckel had proudly announced that Hitler had put him in charge of 'launching the preparations for the ten-year anniversary of the first party rally in the year of 1926 in Weimar'.[38] The town in turn had responded by making a staggering sum of 50,000 marks available. Mayor Walther Felix Mueller wrote in a letter to the Gau Organization Office: 'I of

Adolf Hitler looking on to Weimar Market Square from a window of the Hotel
Elephant, 3 July 1936.

course consider it a duty of honour of the Weimar town community that it too will do everything to make these days an unforgettable event.'[39] The town pulled out all the stops, erecting 500 flagpoles and renovating all the squares and streets earmarked for marching routes and events.[40] A radio station was set up to ensure that 'every single participant who comes to Weimar has the opportunity to take part in the event by listening to the broadcasts on all the main squares in the town', a newspaper reported.[41] Restaurants and hotels worked with the Gau Organization Office to organize catering and accommodation. Weimar residents also offered up over 4,000 private rooms in their homes. Schools, gyms and other large buildings were transformed into sleeping halls. On the outskirts of Weimar, 'tent towns' were set up for tens of thousands of men from the Nazis' paramilitary formations. Even the balcony of the town hall was reserved as a sleeping space for Hitler Youth groups from Sweden, Austria and the Baltic. Traffic coordination alone required 10,000 people over the course of the three-day festivities.[42] Special postage stamps were introduced and temporary electricity and water supply installed for the tent towns.

The final bill showed how many small businesses had contributed. There were entries for flowers from the town gardener. The removals company headed by Elisabeth Förster-Nietzsche's friend Lisbeth Staupendahl provided vehicles for transport. Local craftsmen made the flagpoles. Drivers offered lifts throughout town.[43] It was a mammoth effort that left no Weimarer untouched. Around 300,000 people were expected. The Gau newspaper gloated that the festivities would be on such an enormous scale that 'Weimar and the world will never have seen anything like it!'[44] The Nazified local press chimed in, announcing that Weimar was ready for the greatest 'mass event ever to have taken place in Thuringia and central Germany . . . And so the quiet and dignified former [grand ducal] residence and town of the arts has become a stronghold of National Socialist life.'[45]

The anniversary festivities certainly didn't disappoint on that front. In total, 110 special trains from all over Germany brought visitors to town. Among them were about half of the participants of the much smaller gathering of 1926 that many Weimarers had resented for the ugly violence that had accompanied it. Hitler picked up on this theme during his speech at the first big event: 'Then, in the year 1926, we launched an assault on this town, an assault on this state and with it an assault on Germany. Today, barely ten years later, we are already completing victory. The belief that filled a few hundred thousand back then, has today become the belief of the entire German people!'[46]

The masses that thronged to Weimar contained many ordinary, law-abiding people who would have abhorred the brutish thuggery ten years earlier. The Weirichs also had visitors. The Zemlin family of Carl's first wife stayed over, as did Marie's brother Karl from Nuremberg. What the family had witnessed on Marie's birthday on 3 July was just the beginning of the three-day event. Hitler and other Nazi leaders had just arrived at the station by special train in the afternoon. One local paper reported that 'thousands of happy people crowded, especially on the market square, to welcome the Führer'.[47] Goebbels, who accompanied Hitler as he had done ten years earlier, was delighted, jotting in his diary: 'Weimar: big reception. Town in flags. 10-year-anniversary. What a journey 1926–1936! A beautiful feeling of triumph.'[48]

The next days were filled with events labelled 'historical' in the official programme, such as a repeat of the 1926 conference at the German National Theatre, propaganda marches, military parades and public speeches. When Hitler watched a performance of Richard Wagner's *Tannhäuser* at the German National Theatre, hundreds of people gathered outside to see him re-emerge. When that took too long, the crowds began to chant: 'Dear Führer, please come out, before our breath runs out!'[49] The Weirichs too were impressed by the spectacle. They watched a march on Karlsplatz on 4 July and went back out in the evening to admire the festive lighting that had been put up all around town.[50]

Hitler reminded everyone again and again how important the events of 1926 had been for his rise. It was in Weimar, he declared, where the 'format of the National Socialist Party rallies' had been developed. This had begun to rectify the 'shame the town of Weimar, the town of the German spirit, German science and German art, had been subjected to in the year 1919 by the convention of the so-called National Assembly . . . But we have raised Weimar once again to its German importance.'[51]

These developments were personified by Baldur von Schirach. At the party conference of 1926, he had been a teenager in awe of his Führer while the Hitler Youth received its name in his home town. Now, he stood on Weimar's market square, addressing boys and girls in his role as Reich Youth Leader. Above him, Hitler appeared at a window of the Hotel Elephant to wave to his young followers, who cheered, clapped and beat their drums. 'My Führer,' Schirach finished, 'the German youth is yours.'[52]

The finale of the celebrations was a gathering of a quarter of a million people at the Weimar stadium. Goebbels told the crowds that, after Munich and Nuremberg, Weimar was one of the few places 'especially familiar and dear' to the Nazis.[53] For his part, Hitler promised another huge gathering in Weimar for the twentieth anniversary of the first rally in 1946.[54] By then, Hitler would be dead and much of Weimar reduced to rubble.

Amid all the excitement of the anniversary, Sauckel had not forgotten what Concentration Camps Inspector Theodor Eicke had told him: the 'Weimar Days' would be an opportunity to speak to Hitler in person about a new concentration camp in Thuringia. Building works on a comparable structure had already begun in Sachsenhausen, north of Berlin. Weimar would provide the middle point between this new camp and Eicke's prototype in Dachau, Munich.[55] They just needed the definitive go-ahead from the Führer.

It's unclear whether Sauckel just hadn't found the right moment to speak to Hitler or whether the Führer didn't want to make a decision there and then, but by October, when Eicke next contacted Sauckel, the Reichsstatthalter still didn't have an answer. Without Hitler's consent, the funding of a massive Thuringian camp remained uncertain. Eicke had told Sauckel that it would cost around 1.2 million marks and that the state of Thuringia should provide the money upfront and then try to retrieve it from the Reich, but that was risky, given the chaotic decision-making processes in Nazi Germany, where competing agencies had overlapping responsibilities and Hitler himself could be very difficult to get hold of for a final call. Eicke now pressed Sauckel. He was increasing the plans to 6,000 prisoners and told him that 'several Prussian towns have asked for the camp to be moved and allocated to them and made the funds for it available'. He really needed to know soon 'if Thuringia was still interested in the building of a new conc. camp'.[56]

There was one building project that Hitler was happy to launch during the party rally anniversary. Sauckel's plan was for Weimar to become not just bigger but also visibly Nazified. Like the other Gau capitals such as Bayreuth, Hamburg, Cologne and Dresden, Weimar was to receive a Gau Forum. This was where the Gau administration would have its headquarters in massive buildings that projected power, symmetry and order. These party complexes were all supposed to contain the same elements: a vast marching square, a 'people's hall' for several thousand spectators and a bell tower. Several such projects were planned but Weimar's Gau Forum would be the only one to be built.

Sauckel wanted even more. In the 'foreseeable future', he wrote in 1936, Weimar's population should double in size, growing to 100,000 inhabitants. The town had to both expand and change, blending layers of the 'old' Classical Weimar with a 'new' National Socialist one.[57] 'The old, traditional core of the town, the old buildings which are witnesses of a great past, they should . . . be maintained. Next to them a new Weimar is materializing,' Sauckel explained.[58] In his ambition to make Weimar integral to Nazism, Nazism would also become integral to Weimar.

The centrepiece of this 'new Weimar' was the 'Platz Adolf Hitlers' or 'Adolf Hitler Square', on which the Gau Forum would be placed. For that, the park in front of the State Museum, between the old town and the train station, had to go. This was a crucial space that every visitor passed on their way from the station to the old town. Hitler was initially reluctant about sacrificing the park with its elaborate fountain depicting Vimaria, a personification of Weimar. He changed his mind when he was told that this was the only suitable area for the ambitious project.[59]

A competition for architectural designs was called on which – uniquely among the plans for these kinds of party forums – Hitler reserved the right to make the final decision. He chose a model proposed by Hermann Giesler, his second most favoured architect after Albert Speer. The final design was to provide the blueprint not just for Weimar's Adolf Hitler Square but for all such projects across the Gau capitals.[60] A few days after he'd made his final decision, Hitler had travelled to Weimar for the ten-year-anniversary. One of the highlights on the programme was a ground-breaking ceremony. On the afternoon of 4 July, the space in front of the museum was teeming with people. The Vimaria Fountain had already been removed, and a large model showed the plans for the expansive Adolf Hitler Square. Mayor Mueller had warned that the 'barracks-like' complex might jar with the quaint old town. But his concerns had been brushed aside.[61] The project would happen whether Weimarers liked it or not. At 5 p.m., Hitler, Sauckel, Frick and Giesler stepped on to the podium in front of the model. Suddenly dark storm clouds gathered and the heavens opened. Struggling to make himself heard through the torrential rain despite the loudspeakers, Frick said something about Weimar and Thuringia being 'Nazi strongholds' and the new buildings carrying the 'true spirit of Weimar' into the nation. Then, Sauckel ceremoniously turned the first sod.[62] Goebbels noted: 'Ground-breaking for the party building. A terribly rainy affair. The speeches sound thoroughly hollow.'[63]

At Christmas 1936, Carl Weirich looked back on what had been a wonderful year for him, the best since before the outbreak of the First World War over two decades earlier. What he and many other Germans saw was recovery, reinvigoration even. Everything seemed to move forward at blinding speed. People had money in their pockets again. Carl's turnover had risen so much in 1936 that 'after 22 years we hope to look to the future with fewer worries'. He was beginning to believe that the Nazis' economic success was steady. So, he decided to invest, installing a central heating system and a bespoke glass cabinet in his shop.[64] It felt good to be able to make plans. Carl spent 'New Year's Eve 1936 with good hopes for 1937'.[65] He had no idea how soon catastrophe would strike.

PART V

Darkness

Unleashing the Furies of war

1937

The day was too beautiful for politics. Blue skies and spring sunshine drew the Weirich family out into the countryside on 1 May 1937. On this 'Honour Day of National Socialist Labour', newspapers claimed, 'the thoughts of every German are with the Führer'.[1] But when Hitler appeared at the Olympic Stadium in Berlin to address 120,000 Hitler Youth members,[2] Carl, Marie and Wilhelm were out hiking. Their family radio remained silent on its stand at Geleit-straße 10. They also missed a political spectacle in Weimar. As they'd left the town in the morning, tens of thousands had travelled the other way to observe a ceremony led by Hitler's Deputy Führer Rudolf Hess that would transform the town forever.

On the giant construction site of the Adolf Hitler Square, boys and girls from the Hitler Youth stood in formation alongside SA and SS units and political representatives. Together, they listened to Hitler's speech, broadcast from Berlin. When the loudspeakers fell silent, Hess announced that Weimar was about to build 'the first Hall of the People's Community'.[3] Six masons lowered its foundation stone into the ground. Then Hess performed three ceremonial hammer blows. As the heavy tool hit the stone, he accompanied each strike with a rallying call: 'All for the People's Community! All for National Socialism! All for Germany!'[4]

The scale of the project was enormous. By the time it was aborted at the end of the war, nearly 25 million marks had been poured into it. Hitler partly funded it himself and followed its progress. In the autumn of 1944, when the war was as good as lost, architect Hermann Giesler met him at the 'Wolf's Lair' military headquarters, 850 kilometres away in present-day Poland, where the two men discussed a subterranean car park underneath the square in Weimar.[5]

May Day 1937 in Weimar. A vast model of the People's Hall had been erected for the foundation stone ceremony.

The works involved drastic changes to the townscape. A large viaduct was removed. The street that ran across it had already been renamed Adolf-Hitler-Straße in 1933. Now it was completely altered, not least because Weimar lost the tram line that ran on it, connecting the town with the train station. Trams were abolished altogether and replaced by buses. In all, 139 properties were demolished and with them 462 flats for 1,650 people. Giesler reckoned he needed to resettle 530 families. Restaurants, hotels, pharmacies, around fifty shops and one car repair garage were also affected.[6]

Weimar's rebranding as a Nazi Gau capital involved a huge amount of upheaval and destruction. Yet, the regime did not see this as a break with history. On the contrary. The Gau newspaper commented that 'Weimar's big legacy as the town of Goethe and Schiller, as a centre point of cultural life in German Classicism, will be continued with this in a way previous generations could not have imagined in their dreams.'[7] The Nazi regime in Thuringia was determined that Weimar should punch above its weight, comparing its building project to similar developments in Munich, Nuremberg, Hamburg and Berlin. Hitler was happy to indulge them.

Carl resented what was happening to Weimar. His shop and house lay in the old town, perilously close to the areas to be remodelled. He didn't like that the 'glorious parks had to vanish', replaced by 'party buildings that don't fit into the townscape'. He thought the 'huge congress hall' was particularly monstrous. So he sought solace in 'God's beautiful nature' while the town he called home was churned up.[8]

Goethe scholar Max Hecker stayed in Weimar on 1 May. His presence was essential since he was to receive the Goethe Medal for Art and Science from Reichsstatthalter Fritz Sauckel on behalf of Hitler. This was a huge moment for Max. The Goethe Medal had previously been given to Nobel Prize winners like Thomas Mann and Max Planck. Now it was Max Hecker's turn to be recognized for 'his great services to Goethe scholarship'. Following the award ceremony in Sauckel's office, Max was invited to the Hotel Elephant to talk to Rudolf Hess about his research.[9] The Gau newspaper praised Max as a world-renowned scholar and 'interpreter of the great works of German Classicism who is always ready to elevate the Weimar experience' for visitors.[10]

On the day Max had tea with Hess, his daughter Jutta joined the Nazi Party.[11] She would later say that she found this necessary to protect herself and her work from Nazi interference. Now a woman in her early thirties with round glasses and blonde, wavy hair cut in a bob, Jutta felt she had found her calling: teaching. She wasn't going to risk that. After graduating, there had been a moment when she feared she might not find a job. Then, an old family friend rang. 'Margarethe Mittell here!' a firm voice announced from the telephone receiver. Jutta admired Margarethe, a formidable woman in her early seventies who owned one of the most prestigious private girls' schools in Hamburg.[12]

Margarethe was remarkable in all sorts of ways. She lived with her partner Meta Redlich, a woman thirteen years her junior. The women ran the school together according to their own values, following the playful principles of the Swiss education reformer Johann Heinrich Pestalozzi in the lower years before applying rigorous academic criteria in the upper classes. There was also a deep religiosity underpinning school life with daily morning prayers and regular Christian

Jutta Hecker as a young teacher, 1942.

services punctuating the girls' education. Margarethe and Meta both adored Goethe. They undertook regular study trips to Weimar, where Margarethe had formed a deep friendship with the Heckers. Now she'd heard that Jutta, the daughter of one of the most respected Goethe scholars in the country and a woman holding a doctorate and a teaching degree in her own right, was without a job. She immediately invited her to join her in Hamburg to teach at her school.

It was a lucky break. As a private school, Margarethe's institution was still comparatively free in the way it educated girls. Jutta saw it as a place to raise them according to 'eternal values of humanity'.[13] The headmistress was stubbornly refusing to join the Nazi Party, despite increasing pressure to do so. For those who could afford it, her school continued to provide at least some intellectual refuge. By 1938, there were still twelve Jewish girls enrolled. But Margarethe would soon find out that mere lip service to the regime wasn't enough. When Jutta left the school again in the spring of 1939 to return to Weimar, Margarethe wrote her a reference for future jobs that attested how well she had encouraged the girls to become 'conscious, striving members of the new Germany' and she had signed the letter 'Heil Hitler!' as required by law. Nonetheless, her school was forced to shut down a few months later.[14]

★

On 14 June 1937, Baldur von Schirach was back in his home town of Weimar. But this was no family visit. He was here in his capacity as Reich Youth Leader, lending gravity to the annual Schiller youth festival, which had just been renamed Weimar Festival of the German Youth. Schirach led the opening ceremony at the German National Theatre himself, telling his young audience to 'wander through the streets of Weimar, be elevated in the evenings by noble plays, [and] to leave here with grateful and awed minds'. After a brief lecture on Goethe as a patriot, he concluded: 'The German Reich called you here so that in this place, Germany's greatness, vastness and depth becomes apparent to you.' It was important, Schirach implored, that they embrace 'the concept of Goethe and Weimar . . . so that you'll always know what it's all about when you must fight for Germany'.[15]

The town leadership used the opportunity to make Schirach the youngest honorary citizen of Weimar. The elaborate leather-bound certificate, made by master bookbinder Otto Dorfner, honoured Schirach as a 'son of the town of Weimar' who had 'opened up the world of Goethe to the young nation and revealed the greatness of the German genius to it'.[16]

Mid-morning on 15 July, the deep rumble of lorry engines reverberated around the beech forests of the Ettersberg hill. Eight kilometres south-east, down in Weimar, church bells struck eleven as the convoy turned into a lane flanked by two striped guardhouses. Then it reached its destination, a busy, if somewhat untidy construction site. Raw tree stumps protruded from the ground where beeches had hastily been hacked down. Wooden pallets, wheelbarrows, ladders, piping and tools lay strewn across the clearing. Long, single-storey, wooden barracks were in various states of completion. A group of men was working on them as the lorries pulled up. It was a hot day in high summer, and many of the workers had taken their shirts off. Others wore full uniform, the silver skulls on their caps gleaming in the sun.[17]

When the convoy came to a halt, two SS men jumped out of the back, barking orders of 'Raus! Raus!' – 'Out! Out!' – at the other

149 passengers. Dishevelled and tired-looking men disembarked and were told to line up in rows of three. They all wore bits of discarded uniform: boots or heavy shoes with coats or jackets. On their chests, white patches of cloth displayed their prisoner numbers. Until that morning, they had been inmates at Sachsenhausen concentration camp, ninety-seven of them as 'Professional Criminals', fifty-two as 'Political' prisoners.

Among the men was Fritz Gerlitz from Kassel. He later described how disoriented he felt as they arrived on the hill outside of Weimar: 'We left Sachsenhausen in the morning only with the clothes we were wearing, a blanket, a bag of bread and a canteen.' He and the others had been chosen for the transfer because they were trades-men and builders with specific skills. That much was obvious. But they hadn't been told the purpose or destination of their journey. Standing to attention with the others in the stifling heat, clutching his last few personal belongings in a small bag, Fritz was surprised to see a photographer arrive. Weimar Criminal Police had sent a man up to document the building site. He'd been taking pictures for nearly a week, accompanying the SS as they felled trees, erected fencing, set up a rudimentary field kitchen and began to build the first barracks. Now he captured the tired faces of Fritz and the other prisoners as they were marched to a barracks that looked as though it had only just been finished enough for people to move in. The outer shell of the building had been fully assembled, but the rest was only 'in parts completed in terms of its internal layout'. Once they had put their belongings inside, the prisoners 'were divided into work commandos'.[18] Fritz didn't know it yet, but they had been brought here to construct KZ Buchenwald. What was a rudi-mentary building site when they arrived in July 1937 would in time become the largest concentration camp on German soil.[19]

The whole set-up seemed haphazard to Fritz. There was an aggressive urgency to the way in which he and the other prisoners were worked hard, often twelve hours a day, to construct further barracks and other facilities for the camp. There was no running water or electricity nor enough food, medicine, work clothes or machinery.[20] The communist Bruno Apitz from Leipzig, who was brought to Buchenwald in November, remembered that he and the others 'waded through ankle-deep mud laden with planks, boards and stones like animals. We transported the huge trunks of ancient beeches. 20 to 30 men for each trunk.'[21] Fritz recalled how the unhygienic conditions quickly deteriorated further and led to the outbreak of disease. The constant hunger and thirst were particularly cruel. As he laboured through the hot summer months, he took to drinking water from puddles whenever he could.[22]

What appeared improvised to Fritz had indeed been a rushed and chaotic process. For a long time, Sauckel had stuck to his idea of extending the Bad Sulza concentration camp rather than building a new one from scratch as Eicke demanded. In the late spring of 1937, one of Sauckel's underlings, Hellmuth Gommlich, who was responsible for police matters in the Thuringian Interior Ministry, feared that if they didn't act fast Thuringia would lose its place in Eicke's new camp system altogether. He asked geologists in Jena to find a suitable site 'of a size of about 75 hectares (bad soil or even forest), which is near usable clay or earth'. As part of Hermann Göring's Four-Year Plan, the inmates were to produce bricks. Within two days, the Jena experts had got back to Gommlich, suggesting a location on the northern slopes of the Ettersberg. Eicke inspected the location on 18 May for its suitability for what he now envisioned as a camp for 8,000 prisoners and 1,300 SS staff and told Sauckel that he was happy to establish his new camp on the outskirts of Weimar.[23]

Fritz Gerlitz arrived on the site ten weeks later. At that point, the negotiations over the procurement of the land hadn't even been completed yet. The leader of the Ettersberg Forestry Office complained after the war that 'construction happened without any notice . . . The Forestry Office was simply confronted with a fait accompli.' The man claimed he was made an SS Hauptsturmführer against his will but that he accepted this because it helped him negotiate with the SS. In the end, the Forestry Office received 240,000 marks for the land.[24] Businesses and private individuals who owned parts of the plot received 46,000 marks in total for land used by the camp itself and nearly

80,000 marks for property to build the accompanying SS settlement on.[25] The whole process was only completed by March 1938, at which point the camp already contained 2,500 inmates.[26]

On 28 July the camp on the Ettersberg still looked chaotic. Bits of building material were lying around. Splintered wood from the felled trees littered the ground. What had changed was that the images taken by Weimar police now showed inmates working while their SS captors watched them, hands on hips and dressed in full uniform. As the concentration camp was beginning to emerge through the labour of its first prisoners, it also received its official name: 'Concentration Camp Buchenwald/Post Weimar'. It was an awkward compromise. When Franz Gerlitz and his fellow prisoners had arrived less than two weeks earlier, their destination had been 'K.L. Ettersberg' (Concentration Camp Ettersberg). This name had provoked the only objection to the establishment of the camp from any institution in Weimar.[27]

Paradoxically, it was the local chapter of the National Socialist Culture Community that complained. It counted many members of the town's cultural elite among its supporters. They didn't have a problem with the concentration camp system as such, nor even with one so close to Weimar. What they objected to was linking a place of brutality so overtly to the Weimar Classicism they cherished. Goethe had enjoyed spending time on the Ettersberg. It was a place where he felt 'great and free', the poet told his friend Johann Peter Eckermann when the two men enjoyed a picnic of roast partridge, bread and wine in 1827, almost exactly in the same spot where Fritz Gerlitz and his fellow prisoners drank dirty water from puddles just over a century later. Legend had it that Goethe had carved his initials into an ancient oak on the Ettersberg. Preserved by the Nazis' environmental protection laws, this was the only tree that was spared the deforestation for the camp, standing tall between the camp kitchen and laundry. Prisoners would fell this 'Goethe Oak' in 1944 after it was hit by a bomb.[28]

Eicke, usually so single-minded in the pursuit of his camp system, respected the concerns of the self-appointed guardians of German culture. On 24 July, he wrote to his boss, Reichsführer-SS Heinrich Himmler, to inform him that the 'ordered naming of "K.L. Ettersberg" cannot be implemented, because the NS Culture Community in Weimar objects to it, as the Ettersberg is connected to the life of the poet Goethe'.[29] Himmler relented, opting for the neutral 'Buchenwald' or 'Beech Forest'.

From the beginning, starvation, disease and violence were deliberate features of Buchenwald. They lurked behind a facade of order upheld by a strict hierarchy among staff and prisoners and complex bureaucracy.[30] Himmler praised the 'unheard-of cleanliness in accommodation and bodily hygiene, impeccable food [and] strict but fair treatment'.[31] The Buchenwald administration even occasionally invited visitors, such as in August 1939, when sixty-eight German-Americans toured the camp as part of a 'study visit to get to know the Greater German Reich better'. Press coverage stressed that 'there, they could convince themselves with their own eyes how ridiculous the lies of the Jewish world press' about the terrible conditions in the camp had been.[32]

Behind Buchenwald's veneer of civility lay lawless barbarism. Eicke's Dachau system deliberately insulated the camps from regular legislation. What happened to inmates behind the high, electrified fences was for SS personnel to decide. Prisoners were there not because they'd been convicted of a crime and sentenced by a court but because the SS said so. In fact, people were often apprehended at the gates of regular prisons when their sentence had ended and taken to concentration camps without any further legal process.

The Dachau model had rules for camp discipline that encouraged wanton brutality at all levels.[33] A prisoner hierarchy developed, with 'criminals' topping the chain, and fellow inmates could often be even crueller than the SS guards. This was seen as a form of self-administration that reduced the need for paid personnel. The omnipresence and unpredictability of violence, the idea that any prisoner could be beaten, humiliated, tortured or even killed at any moment without cause or consequence, had a powerful psychological impact. The collective terror and apathy played its part in breaking resistance, individuality and willpower among prisoners.

Underneath the surface of an efficient system, malice and corruption festered.[34] Buchenwald became particularly notorious for its unscrupulous commandant Karl Otto Koch, a forty-year-old, mid-ranking SS commander. Inmate and camp barber Franz Eichhorn found him 'a very creepy person, brutal and unpredictable; bordering on perverse', as he remembered after the war.[35] He had long developed a reputation for his lack of self-control and his greed, having previously fallen foul of the law for embezzlement and forgery. His doings at Buchenwald, where he and his family lived in a large villa, involved the same behaviour as well as sexual offences and murder. Things would get so out of hand that he would be investigated in 1941, but the charges were dropped and he was moved to Majdanek extermination camp in German-occupied Poland. Koch was charged again with corruption and murder in 1944 and sentenced to death. He ended up at Buchenwald, where an SS firing squad executed him in April 1945.[36]

If Koch was infamous, his reputation was still overshadowed by that of his wife Ilse, whose sadistic behaviour became so notorious that she was known as the 'Beast of Buchenwald'. After the war, she was accused of acts of excessive cruelty such as riding through the camp on horseback while hitting prisoners with a whip. It's hard to distinguish the wild rumours about her from fact. One accusation was that she had prisoners killed to make lampshades from their skin. Two prisoners testified that they had seen such a lampshade made and presented to Ilse Koch. The item still exists and was tested in 2024, with experts confirming it to be made of human skin.[37]

There is no shortage of evidence of the savage regime at Buchenwald. At the quarry where inmates were forced to work, many were pushed over the steep edges by SS staff to die or be seriously injured. For punishment, prisoners were sometimes hung from trees for hours as SS men whipped or tortured them. Some of the victims died from this, others suffered permanent damage from dislocated joints or torn ligaments. There were arrest cells collectively called the 'bunker' by prisoners, for solitary confinement with no light, furniture or heating.[38] SS Sergeant Martin Sommer, a young man in his early twenties, who served at Buchenwald right from the beginning, had free rein to do what he wanted. This allowed him to torture and murder inmates with unparalleled cruelty. He often personally strangled people to death or injected air or milk into their veins.[39]

If Buchenwald was a model camp, as Eicke and Himmler claimed, it was only in that it set previously unimaginable standards of lawlessness and cruelty. Over the first two years, up until the outbreak of the Second World War, Buchenwald had the highest mortality rate of all German concentration camps. In 1937 alone, when the camp was not yet used to detain Jews but was supposedly set up as a corrective facility for criminals and political opponents, fifty-three people died. By the end of the war, its death toll would rise to an estimated 56,000, including 1,600 children and teenagers.

People died at Buchenwald of a wide range of causes, from the terrible living conditions and malnourishment to work accidents, epidemics, violence, torture, execution and hypothermia. The very first victim was Hermann Kempek, a twenty-three-year-old worker from Hamburg, who had been sent to Buchenwald as a 'Professional Criminal'. He ended his own life by hanging on 13 August, less than a month after the first prisoners arrived.[40]

Four days after his suicide, Hermann Kempek's body arrived in Weimar. On 17 August, the crematorium at the town cemetery received a crudely cut wooden box containing his remains alongside two more boxes with the bodies of fellow Buchenwald inmates. The three dead men had been transported down from the Ettersberg and through the town to the crematorium on the southern outskirts of Weimar. Cemetery manager Rudolf Winkler or one of his colleagues wrote their names into the 'Body Log Book' (*Leicheneingangsbuch*) where they immediately stood out on the page. These weren't the bodies of ordinary people who had died a natural death in Weimar. They were special bodies from Buchenwald. Winkler had instructions to record them in a different manner. So he made a note of the two civilian bodies that had arrived on the same day in pencil and switched to red for the Buchenwald victims. In the column labelled 'Address', he put 'K.L.' for *Konzentrationslager* or 'Concentration Camp'.

The Buchenwald bodies were to receive less than a pauper's funeral. Ordinary Weimarers who'd received state welfare were usually cremated at the expense of the town, for which the cemetery administration charged 97.50 marks. Of that, 75 marks were for the coffin, 2.50 marks for a funeral gown and 20 marks for the cremation itself. Bodies sent down from the Ettersberg would have to be burned for 20 marks each, naked and without a coffin. According to one witness, the SS sometimes simply wrote the reference number of the dead on their bare skin to save costs.[41]

The SS may have managed to create practically lawless spaces in its new concentration camps but it had no lawful means of disposing of human bodies. According to a cremation law passed in 1934, only municipalities with public cemeteries were allowed to run crematoria. The SS was explicitly not a public institution. The only solution for the Buchenwald administration was to ask the nearby town of Weimar for use of its facilities at the main cemetery. Its request arrived at the office of Mayor Walther Felix Mueller on 29 July. Mueller never replied. His simmering disagreements with Sauckel had finally boiled over. He had been suspended on 14 June. So it fell to his deputy Karl Thomas, a fanatical Nazi, to agree that Weimar would 'undertake the cremation of the bodies in question'.[42]

The cremation law also decreed that for each body there had to be a death certificate, a document issued by police declaring that death hadn't been caused by criminal activity, documentation that the deceased or their next-of-kin agreed to the cremation and a document by the chief medical officer certifying that they had seen the body and were satisfied that the person had died of natural causes. Manufacturing this paper trail in order to legalize Buchenwald's body count required compliance from many people. Few of the bodies looked as though they had died from a natural death. The very first one bore bruises of strangulation on his neck from hanging.

Future ones would be malnourished, display marks of physical abuse or medical experimentation or be so famished by disease that their bodies became difficult to burn. Martin Klettner, an engineer who was repeatedly sent in to fix the cremation oven, explained in his technical report that the problems were caused by the 'extremely malnourished and desiccated bodies from Buchenwald'.[43]

In Weimar, all the people in the reporting chain did their bit to enable the processing of the bodies, even if this meant breaking the law. Cemetery manager Winkler and his stoker Max Jacobi admitted that they sometimes added 'significant amounts of wood' during the cremations – something that was illegal and considered unethical – because the emaciated bodies didn't burn as intended.[44]

Registrar Heinrich Fleischhauer issued ordinary death certificates. Mayor Otto Koch (not to be confused with the camp commandant), who replaced Mueller in October 1937, had a direct telephone line installed between his office and the camp. Chief medical officer Waldemar Freienstein didn't view each body, as required by law, and helped argue the case for the installation of a new furnace for 'hygienic reasons'. There were people in the municipal administration deciding whether to spend money on new cremation facilities as they discussed how quickly the body count racked up. Hans Wahl, the director of the Goethe Museum, was one of the councillors present when this was debated in a non-public session in December 1938.[45] Nobody raised any concerns beyond efficiency and funding.

On 30 September, Fritz Sauckel was celebrating ten years as Gauleiter of the Nazi Party in Thuringia. Local newspapers featured a two-page supplement outlining a life's journey that had allowed him to become 'the decisive force that moves everything in Thuringia'.[46] Sauckel felt he had Nazified his realm with zeal. Just before the anniversary, the Reichsstatthalter had landed another coup. He was going to give Hitler his own apartment in Weimar, in his favourite place, the Hotel Elephant. The 400-year-old building was to be demolished and a new one built. Sauckel had been able to secure the services of architect Hermann Giesler, the man who also worked on the Adolf

Hitler Square. Giesler promised to make the new Elephant 'Europe's most modern hotel', which would be 'trailblazing in its facilities and architecture'. Hitler loved the idea and helped finance the project from Nazi Party funds. In exchange, he expected to get an exclusive apartment with garden views, in a quiet part of the hotel that would never be used by other guests.[47] There would be a balcony out on to the market square, complete with flagpoles and the eagle emblem of the Reich.[48]

Sauckel knew the reinvention of the Elephant had the potential to be hugely unpopular with the Weimar population. Carl Weirich wasn't the only one grumbling about Nazi buildings that didn't fit. So the regime made it known that the old Elephant suffered from 'extraordinary dereliction' as testified by 'detailed surveys by the foremost experts'.[49] In the end it didn't matter what Weimarers thought. Sauckel stuck a splinter of the new era into Weimar's old heart.

Emmy Göring was delighted. Weimar was making her and her husband honorary citizens. She was being celebrated by the town she'd called home for so many years. Hinrich Holtz, the director of the Marie-Seebach retirement home for actors, had initiated this. Their massive support for his institution, he insisted, proved the Görings' 'love for Weimar', and receiving honorary citizenship would strengthen the 'friendly bond between the town of Weimar and Colonel General Göring'.[50] Emmy's document thanked her as a 'former fellow resident and highly valued actress of the great female roles of Goethe and Schiller at the German National Theatre' and for creating a 'new old people's home for German stage actors'.[51]

As her public role at the top of Nazi society was beginning to crystallize, Emmy's future was taking a new turn. On 28 September, the Italian dictator Benito Mussolini was running around her Carinhall home, delirious with childlike glee as he played with Mucki the lion cub. Laughing as he play-wrestled her pet, Mussolini told Emmy that he was going to deliver a speech in German at the Olympic Stadium that evening. He invited her to join him in his car to travel there.

She politely declined. Her doctor had cautioned against unnecessary travel.[52] At the age of forty-four, Emmy had fallen pregnant.

Mussolini reacted with an outburst of joy, hugging both expectant parents. By contrast, Göring's response had been so muted that Emmy was 'disappointed by Hermann for the first time in our marriage'. 'Aren't you happy at all?' she demanded incredulously. 'No,' he responded, 'I can't be happy, I'm so terribly frightened I could lose you. If only the child was here now.'[53] After an anxious nine-month wait, a baby girl was born on 2 June 1938, whom the couple named Edda. Given her warm relationship with the Italian dictator, Emmy was keen to point out that they had not named her after Mussolini's daughter by the same name but after one of her friends.[54] The Mayor of Weimar was among the many well-wishers, sending a congratulatory telegram from 'the Gau and State Capital' to 'its highly revered Honorary Citizens'.[55]

On 1 November, Goebbels and Sauckel stood outside the Villa Silberblick and looked at a construction site. Sauckel was keen to show the Propaganda Minister how fast the building of the Nietzsche Memorial Hall was progressing. Building works had started in mid-July to coincide with work on the Adolf Hitler Square and the establishment of the new housing estates that would make Weimar a 'Stadt der SS' or 'SS Town'. While on the Ettersberg, villas were being constructed for the Buchenwald leadership and barracks for the troops of SS Death's Head Unit Thuringia, in the town centre new party-political buildings emerged. Sauckel was trying to convince Goebbels that on the hills to the south this axis of Nazification should be completed with a monument to Nietzsche.

Initially, nothing had stood in the way of enfolding Nietzsche into the Nazified 'New Weimar'. Hitler personally got involved with the design of the building, increasing its floor plan, which was now supposed to have an antechamber and a corridor leading up to a large hall with room for up to 600 people. Hitler envisioned a monumental bust of Nietzsche to greet visitors and for there to be a large wing with workrooms and office spaces for the archive and its scholars.

The villa itself could then become a memorial and museum.[56] This was good news in principle for the Nietzsche Archive, but the total estimated costs for the project were now 500,000 marks.[57] Sauckel had tried to raise some of the funds. His Wilhelm Gustloff Foundation stepped in, as had the town of Weimar and the state of Thuringia.[58] But it wasn't enough. Nonetheless, building had begun on a tight schedule, as Sauckel aimed to have it finished for Hitler's fiftieth birthday on 20 April 1939.

Sauckel had taken Goebbels up to the construction site in the hope that his Propaganda Ministry would patronize the project. But Goebbels wasn't fired up. In the spring of 1938, his ministry pulled funding of the archive's flagship project, the Critical Nietzsche Edition, on account of its being 'a prime example of the scientification of great works and personalities'. In other words, it was deemed too academic, inaccessible and elitist.[59]

Meanwhile, Nazi ideologues continued to debate whether Nietzsche really worked as a pioneer of Nazi ideology. Some protested that the philosopher hadn't been racist enough in his concept of what constituted the 'German people'. He had repeatedly claimed to have Polish roots.[60] There was no evidence for this. But the Nazis found it difficult to embrace an intellectual ancestor who appeared to have been proud to have Polish blood when they regarded Poles as a 'subhuman' race. Goebbels was also aware that Hitler hadn't returned to the Nietzsche Archive since Elisabeth's death. With Hitler's interest waning, there was no personal advantage for Goebbels in supporting the building of the Memorial Hall.

So the project progressed in fits and starts. Hitler himself gave another 100,000 marks in the autumn of 1938 but there wasn't wholehearted commitment in the way he afforded Richard Wagner's legacy in Bayreuth. Rather, this donation may have been made in gratitude to Sauckel for the new suite at the Hotel Elephant.[61] Hitler's big birthday in 1939 came and went without the Nietzsche Memorial Hall being completed. Eventually, even Sauckel lost interest, causing the head of the archive, Max Oehler, to enquire in June 1939 'whether the building should provisionally stay in its current [unfinished] state'.[62]

In the autumn of 1939, structural work was halted altogether. Mussolini, a greater Nietzsche fan than Hitler, donated an antique sculpture of Dionysus, which was delivered in early 1944 to take pride of place in the Memorial Hall. But this only highlighted the sorry state of the project. The sculpture was too large and wouldn't fit through the door. For a while, it stood forlorn in the garden of the Villa Silberblick before eventually finding a home in the Pergamon Museum in Berlin. To this day, the Memorial Hall has not been completed nor has it ever been used for its intended purpose. While the Nietzsche Archive has survived, Elisabeth Förster-Nietzsche's legacy remains tainted by the way she enabled the Nazis' selective use of her brother's philosophy.

Carl Weirich finished 1937 in an upbeat mood. While he didn't like the way Weimar was changing, in his shop things couldn't have turned out better. Even the increasing militarization of society had commercial upsides. There were blackout exercises during which private households covered doors and windows. For this purpose, dark paper was recommended. 'The minds of Weimarers were haunted by blackouts,' Carl recorded in his diary, 'piles of the paper were sold in the shop!' Overall, business was excellent and Carl and Marie were 'glad that we had enough energy' for the run-up to Christmas.

Wilhelm was a little annoyed because the snow appeared to have run out by mid-December. But Christmas was Christmas. When the boy found his parents still working in the shop downstairs late on Christmas Eve, he ran down the spiral staircase and nagged: 'When is it finally going to be Christmas?' It was 8 p.m. when Carl and Marie at last called it a day. The family went upstairs together, lit the candles on the tree and turned on the radio to listen to the church bells toll in Eisenach, where much of Carl's family sat together. The Weirichs sang 'dear old Christmas songs together, and all tiredness was forgotten', Carl thought, as 'the bells ringing from the church in town hopefully proclaimed a blessed New Year of 1938'.[63]

1938

In mid-February, snow returned to Weimar. It had been an unusually mild winter and Wilhelm Weirich was impatient to get his sledge out. On Sunday 20 February, his father took the family up to the village of Ettersburg, where his son enjoyed himself all day, sledging down the northern slopes of the Ettersberg hill.

Around 2 kilometres downhill, at Buchenwald, prisoners were working on a wrought iron gate for the concentration camp. The austere entrance complex with its main guard tower and a block of detention cells had been under construction over the winter. It had taken longer to decide on the design and messaging of the gate itself. As the only way for prisoners to get in and out of the camp, it was highly symbolic and its commission was delayed until the final decision came back from Berlin. Sachsenhausen and Dachau, like later camps such as Auschwitz, displayed the phrase 'Arbeit macht frei' or 'Work makes you free' on their gates in a mocking nod to their supposed function as correction facilities rather than as punishment, detention, exploitation and killing centres.

Buchenwald was the only camp for which a different message was chosen: 'Jedem das Seine', a German translation of the Latin 'Suum cuique' – 'To each his own' or 'To each what he deserves'. Prisoners were to know that their incarceration, the abuse they suffered and the terrible conditions they were made to live in were their just deserts as far as the SS was concerned. Since this message was for the prisoners rather than the outside world, Commandant Karl Otto Koch made another decision that distinguished his camp from the others. Its slogan faced inward so that inmates could see it from the roll call square every day. The iron lettering was to be bright red while the rest of the gate was painted white. It was meant to stand out, and the camp leadership ensured it would stay that way. While they only coated the side facing outward once, when the gate was first installed, the side facing inward got a fresh, crimson coating eight times between 1938 and 1945.[1]

Since the gate was deemed to be crucial, the SS wanted to commission an expert to design it. As it happened, there was one among the prisoners. Franz Ehrlich had been incarcerated at Buchenwald since the previous September, when the camp had only just been established. Not quite thirty years old, he'd been fit enough to be worked hard in the quarry, but the other political prisoners soon recognized him. They confirmed that he was a highly trained architect. When the SS realized this, they immediately placed him into a carpentry unit and then into a commando tasked with camp construction. Franz was happy to oblige since mentally engaging, non-physical labour indoors was infinitely preferable to the life-threatening conditions in the quarry.

Franz had been one of Walter Gropius's most promising students at the Bauhaus. The star architect had personally ensured that he'd be admitted to the school in 1927. At that point, it had already moved to Dessau, but Franz's first fascination with the movement's modern design principles had been sparked by the early Bauhaus in Weimar. He'd been a fifteen-year-old apprentice fitter in Leipzig when the Bauhaus held its controversial exhibition in the Thuringian capital. Franz had been desperate to see this avant-garde movement, but hyperinflation made it difficult to pay for train tickets to Weimar. Undeterred, he had made his way there on foot, walking nearly 100 kilometres each way.

Franz's enthusiasm never waned. When studying at the Bauhaus in Dessau, he took in everything teachers such as Paul Klee, Wassily Kandinsky and Joost Schmidt had to offer, and he absorbed the left-wing politics associated with the movement, joining first socialist, then communist youth groups. By the time the Gestapo arrested him in 1934, Franz was a skilled typographer involved in the printing of illegal newspapers. He was held in custody for ten months before being sentenced to three years in prison. Once he'd done his time, the Gestapo immediately took him to Buchenwald.[2]

When Franz arrived at the concentration camp, the whole complex was still in its infancy. The primitive barracks for prisoners were being built quickly, but there were many areas that required more architectural skill and an eye for design. Buchenwald was supposed to become a model camp with luxurious villas for the leadership and comfortable housing for SS personnel. Plans for the SS facilities foresaw a parade ground, a casino, bathhouses and even a zoo with monkeys and bears for the 'distraction and entertainment' of the men and their families.[3] SS construction manager Robert Riedl was beginning to worry how he was supposed to fulfil the demands of Commandant Koch. So he was glad to hear that an inmate had arrived with great talent for building and design. From a working-class background and with practical training under his belt, Franz was as good with a hammer as he was with a pencil. He soon impressed the camp leadership when he and the carpentry commando designed and built temporary accommodation for the commandant. Franz later bragged that the interior design he and his fellow prisoners had realized under the conditions had been 'a sensation . . . among the entire SS'.[4] He moved on to furniture, designing a cradle for Karl and Ilse Koch, who were expecting their first child, Artwin.

By the time the Weirichs went sledging a little further up the Ettersberg, Franz had been ordered to design the typography of the entrance gate. To him, there was only one way to do this. He once said that he hadn't joined the Bauhaus in order to 'become an architect, a designer or an artist but a Bauhauser'. The movement's design principles were what he knew and cared about. So he designed the lettering for the Buchenwald gate in a Bauhaus font, very visibly inspired by the influence of some of his teachers, particularly Joost Schmidt, who had designed the poster for the 1923 exhibition in Weimar. Franz remembered later that rather than being appalled by the influence of an art movement the Nazis had denounced and destroyed, 'The gate was deemed so satisfactory by the SS that we were allowed to design and make the gate for Sachsenhausen as well.'[5]

The gate of Buchenwald concentration camp with its inscription designed by the imprisoned Bauhaus graduate Franz Ehrlich. Image taken shortly after the liberation, April 1945.

His compliance ensured his own survival and that of comrades working with him on buildings and furniture. Franz and the SS had come to an arrangement that suited both sides. When he was released in the autumn of 1939, shortly after the war had begun, he was declared 'unworthy to serve', which allowed him to work in his old field of architecture and design. He chose to stay at Buchenwald, no longer as a prisoner but as a civilian employee, drawing a decent salary, moving into his own flat and getting married. In 1941, he decided to apply for a role in the SS Construction Planning headquarters in Berlin and was successful. Eventually, his SS employment ended because he was drafted after all in 1943. He survived the war and continued to be successful in East Germany.[6]

While work was going on at Buchenwald, Gestapo Weimar was running out of space in its headquarters at the Marstall mews. It had been promised a brand-new home as part of the Gau Forum complex at the Adolf Hitler Square, but that was taking too long. It needed more office and interrogation space now. As an interim solution, they built a large wooden barracks in the courtyard of the Marstall with staff offices and a doubly sound-proofed interrogation room.[7] One officer working at Gestapo Weimar at the time later described that the wooded barracks was where 'mistreatments were mainly carried out. It was generally known that this is where the so-called Initiation Collation (25 cane strokes) was administered. I myself was never involved but I know it reliably. Permission for the administration of 25 cane strokes was supposed to have been applied for on a case-by-case basis from Reich Security Main Office Berlin. But this rule was mostly not adhered to and the beatings happened anyway. It was generally known that the prisoners in the barracks were beaten mercilessly.'[8]

Gestapo Weimar was running out of space because it continued to crack down on the political opponents no matter how small circles of resistance had become. Kurt Nehrling and his comrades knew that they lived in permanent danger of being arrested and tortured. The Gestapo headquarters were right in the centre of Weimar and everyone knew what was going on since released prisoners would talk about their mistreatment. Rather than hide the violence, the Gestapo relished the terror it spread and its deterrence potential.

Kurt's friend and co-leader of the resistance group, Hans Eberling, worried that this might erode group cohesion. There was always a risk of people dropping out or beginning to mistrust one another, given how heavily the Gestapo relied on denouncements and informants. Hans felt that 'only the power of the idea could hold them together'. A little taller and more solidly built than his tuberculosis-suffering friend Kurt, the thirty-two-year-old Hans was fit and healthy. He travelled around in Thuringia and the Rhineland where he had contacts, maintaining links between groups, lecturing younger members and trying his best to shore up morale. 'But the measures of Hitler's dictatorship became harsher and harsher,' he wrote, 'our circle of members became smaller and smaller.' He took pride in the fact that, 'even if we couldn't hold everyone, we still managed to raise them to become decent blokes, so that not a single traitor has emerged from our ranks'.[9]

Hans was also realistic enough to understand that the dwindling Weimar group wouldn't last without outside support. Yet their contacts were picked off by the Gestapo one by one. When a friendly group in the town of Gera had been discovered, its members had received long sentences. Hans had only been spared because they'd refused to give up his name. The underground group Communist Party Opposition in Weimar was also discovered and every single one of its members arrested and badly maltreated. In the town of Nord-hausen, there were rumours that members were wavering. Gestapo crackdowns were relentless in 1938 and 'tore us apart', Hans wrote.

Kurt and Hans saw no other choice. It was risky but they needed to establish contact with the larger group of social democrats. In Berlin, they could contact courageous and capable people like Hermann Brill, who had interrogated Hitler and Frick in 1932 about their botched attempts to get Hitler German citizenship. So Kurt and Hans travelled back and forth between Weimar and Berlin, taking every precaution. But the Gestapo tightened its noose around the Weimar group. It didn't take long for them to identify Hans. They arrested him in October 1938 together with the former leader of Thuringia and SPD Reichstag MP August Frölich. 'Our work was on hold during that time,' Hans remembered. 'Our efforts to connect to a leading movement had failed.'[10] Kurt and Heddy were left isolated and vulnerable.

Many Thuringians had mixed feelings about the evident applica-tion of state violence. It was no secret that Gestapo and police regularly arrested, mistreated and even murdered people, and that those who were taken to Buchenwald were held there without trial. On 2 March, the president of the higher regional court in Jena had impressed on the Reich Justice Minister that the mood in the general population had reached a tipping point. 'People understand that notorious communist and Bolshevik leaders are locked away safely,' he conceded in a report to Berlin, 'but not that people who aren't generally regarded as criminals at all are still vanishing in con-centration camps without trial.' He finished with a piece of advice that would never be heeded: 'More restraint should be displayed in administrative acts that may easily be regarded as arbitrary.'[11]

The arbitrary nature of the terror was beginning to frighten people. Many of Weimar's middle-class residents and pensioners hadn't been averse to the idea of locking up leftists when the Hitler regime first took power in times of economic crisis and social angst. Now the various enforcers of Nazism seemed to be emboldened to a point where their attention could get anyone arrested. In May, two older civil servants and the surgeon Maximilian Schreiner experienced just how quickly one could fall foul of the regime. They had intervened in a brawl in a Weimar tavern between a member of the public and three high-ranking Nazis. What happened didn't seem right to them and they demanded the Nazis pay the man for the damage they had done. All three men were arrested for their efforts to stand up for a fellow citizen. They were carted off to Buchenwald for a few weeks to learn not to challenge authority even when that authority acted with impunity. The men were shocked. They'd been on good terms with the regime previously, going hunting and drinking with local Nazi officials.[12] Now they found out that nobody was safe in a state that didn't abide by the rule of law.

Beyond the terrifying arrests, Weimarers felt the presence of the concentration camp in many ways. From 1 April, Buchenwald was an incorporated constituency of Weimar. The town councillors had agreed to this since they were hoping to benefit from this economically by using forced labour from the camp in Weimar factories, businesses and construction sites. They were also told that the merger had been Sauckel's personal wish because he wanted town and camp connected.[13] Buchenwald got a Weimar telephone number and post office. Until the camp built its own infirmary in the summer, Weimar's hospitals were responsible for the treatment of Buchenwald inmates and SS staff. Forced sterilizations of inmates were also carried out by Weimar doctors (on 221 prisoners in 1938 alone[14]). Weimar's firefighters were responsible for the camp. Buchenwald's water and electricity supply was drawn from the town.[15]

Weimarers knew that the camp existed and what it was for. Prosecutor General Werner Wurmstich, who had acted as a Gestapo informant since 1937, recorded their reactions in a report with remarkable frankness.[16] He wrote that 'it's interesting that the Weimar population isn't happy at all about the building of the camp and that the business owners aren't in the mood to have dealings with it. People are pleased when occasionally a prisoner manages to escape.'[17]

Buchenwald may not have been popular, but most Weimarers got used to it all the same. Contrary to Wurmstich's report, some business owners were 'in the mood' to do business with Buchenwald either directly or indirectly. Weimar butchers supplied meat to the camp kitchen. Bookbinders made the cardboard boxes in which the urns with the ashes of victims were sent to their families if they requested this and had paid the 3-mark administration fee.[18] The local construction company Grosch supplied transporters for the building works on the camp and processed the timber that was cut down on the Ettersberg. Hotels and restaurants benefited from the increased custom from SS personnel and their visitors.

Compared to Dachau, the town near Eicke's original model camp by the same name, which struggled economically and built intense economic connections to the camp, Weimar was somewhat warier of its new neighbour. As Wurmstich's report indicated, business interest remained lukewarm at first. There was more business to be had in the town itself given the enormous construction works there and the steady growth of the population and tourism. This changed significantly during the war when forced labour was widely deployed in construction, in the Gustloff works and across private businesses and households.[19]

The initial lack of enthusiasm for business with Buchenwald may partially have derived from the notion that something terrible was going on up on the Ettersberg. While the general population had no way of knowing details of the cruelties that went on under the Koch regime, it didn't escape Weimarers that Buchenwald's death toll was accelerating. Before the camp was built, the town cemetery conducted around 450 cremations a year. In 1938, this tripled to 1,351 bodies. The following year it would be 2,900 or six times the normal rate.[20] This enormous increase didn't just concern cemetery staff; ordinary people noticed it too. It was hard not to, given the logistics involved. While the camp lacked its own crematorium, dead prisoners were first taken to a storage shed near the camp zoo. From the summer of 1938, when more and more Jews were taken to Buchenwald, this task fell entirely to the Jewish prisoners themselves. They wrapped the bodies in blankets and carried them to the camp gate, where they reported to the SS officer on duty how many had died and who they were. The bodies were placed in wooden crates, covered in sawdust and the lid was closed with a simple hook. Vehicles then took the boxes down to the town cemetery in regular transports that Weimarers couldn't help but notice.[21]

Several eyewitness reports claim that the wooden crates sometimes fell off the back of the loaded vehicles. Since the lids were only held down with hooks, some of the boxes were said to have opened, with the naked, emaciated bodies of Buchenwald victims tumbling on to Weimar's streets. One young woman said this happened in the Schützengasse; a couple claimed it occurred on Karlsplatz. Both were central, highly frequented places in Weimar where many people would have witnessed this. Rumours of such incidents even spread back up to Buchenwald itself, where prisoners like Eugen Kogon heard the story.[22] True or not, the presence of such rumours itself shows that knowledge of the death toll of the camp was widespread.

It was also impossible for Weimarers not to notice the thick plumes of smoke emanating from the crematorium in the cemetery. It was just a stone's throw from the Nietzsche Archive and Harry Graf Kessler's old villa at Cranachstraße. If in either building the windows were open at the wrong time, black, foul-smelling fumes wafted in. There were frequent complaints about this to the town authorities, as the fifty-five-year-old architect and construction official Wolfgang Holz bemoaned in a letter to Topf & Söhne (Topf and Sons), the company based in Erfurt that provided the crematorium ovens.[23] SS personnel were also buried in the regular cemetery. When the first two died in 1938, there had been discussions whether to use camp prisoners to tend to their graves, but the idea was dismissed because the Buchenwald leadership thought 'it would be an unfortunate image if inmates were to maintain the graves under surveillance'. They decided to pay the cemetery administration 10 marks a year to do the job.[24]

While the Buchenwald SS wasn't keen for Weimarers to see the ugly reality of the camp first hand, it made no attempt to hide its existence. Concentration camps were an overt feature of the Nazi system, signalling control and discipline as well as spreading terror and fear, as an incident at the first annual 'Weimar Poets' Convention' in 1938 proved. Run by Goebbels' Propaganda Ministry and held at the Hotel Elephant, it attracted the most prominent authors in the Reich. They came together in Weimar to discuss literature and to network. In 1938, one delegate turned up physically broken and with his head shorn down to a short stubble. Everyone knew why he looked that way.

Ernst Wiechert was Germany's most-read author and critical of the Nazi regime, a potent combination, especially as the authorities continually failed to intimidate him. He defended the pastor Martin Niemöller, a vocal and powerful opponent of the regime and leading figure of the Confessing Church movement that rejected Nazi interference in faith matters. Wiechert had also openly refused to take part in the rigged, retrospective referendum that asked voters to approve the Anschluss, Germany's annexation of Austria in March. He was arrested on 8 May and taken to Buchenwald on 4 July.

Goebbels hated the writer with a vengeance, fuming in his diary: 'this piece of dirt wants to rise up against the state. 3 months concentration camp. Then I will deal with him personally.'[25] Widespread protests abroad and in Germany itself forced the Nazis to release Wiechert after two months, but it didn't stop Goebbels summoning him. The Propaganda Minister wrote: 'Have the writer Wiechert brought to me from the K.Z. and deliver a right royal Philippic [dressing down] . . . I'm in top form and butcher him intellectually. One last warning! I have no doubt about that . . . Any renewed misdemeanour will be followed only by physical annihilation. Now we both know that.'[26] To make sure other authors knew it too, Goebbels forced Wiechert to take part in the first poetry summit in Weimar. Here was Germany's most successful author, visibly maltreated by the regime and paraded in this pitiful state in front of his most distinguished colleagues.

The lines between high culture and barbarism blurred further when Hans Severus Ziegler put on the romantic operetta *The Land of Smiles* at Weimar's theatre while the librettist of the piece was incarcerated just a few kilometres away at Buchenwald.[27] The Austrian Fritz Löhner-Beda had been arrested shortly after the Anschluss in March. While Ziegler performed Löhner-Beda's operettas in town, the man who had been one of Vienna's most popular lyricists co-wrote with fellow prisoner and Jewish-Austrian Hermann Leopoldi the 'Buchenwaldlied' or 'Buchenwald Song' on the Ettersberg at the end of 1938. Commissioned by SS officer Arthur Rödl, it was sung at roll calls and when marching to and from work. It is now known as the 'Buchenwald anthem' and sung at commemoration ceremonies. Löhner-Beda never knew how long this legacy would last. He was beaten to death at Auschwitz III Monowitz in 1942 for being too ill to work.

> *O Buchenwald, I cannot forget you,*
> *because you are my fate.*
> *Only he who leaves you can appreciate*
> *how wonderful freedom is!*
> *O Buchenwald, we don't cry and complain;*
> *and whatever our destiny may be,*
> *we nevertheless shall say 'yes' to life:*
> *for once the day comes, we shall be free!*[28]

Carl Weirich had very personal reasons to become disenchanted with Nazism in 1938. In many ways, he still wanted to be impressed by the Hitler regime. He approved of the annexation of Austria and the creation of the 'Greater Germany' this 'achieved for us Germans'.[29] Carl was also impressed with the Autobahn network that was being built at great speed, using one of his Sunday outings on his newly

The German National Theatre in Weimar, decorated in swastika flags, 1938.

acquired three-gear bicycle to admire the 'monumental' stretch between Jena and Weimar.[30] But the regime dealt him a personal 'blow' so heavy that it overshadowed everything else.

On 24 May, a group of men appeared at Geleitstraße 10. They explained that they were from the building association and that Fritz Sauckel's plan for a 'New Weimar' would soon require the demolition of Carl's house.[31] The route from the station down to the old town was to be made more uniform. Karlsplatz behind Carl's house would be remodelled and the adjacent buildings removed or altered to blend in with the disciplined symmetry of the Gau Forum. The Hotel Chemnitius next door to Carl's shop and home was to be demolished alongside the rest of Geleitstraße to make room for a colonnade. The project had a budget of 1.2 million marks and was to begin in the summer of 1939.[32]

Carl was numb with shock. How could they do this to him? Surely there were laws to protect people from such whims? 'We let the news sink in with a deep sigh,' Carl wrote, feeling dejected and helpless, 'we only bought the house 11 years ago and now we must sell it for maybe half the price?'[33] A few days after this depressing meeting, Carl decided to take legal counsel from the renowned local lawyer Georg Mardersteig.[34] He wasn't the only one to cling on to the mistaken belief that Nazi Germany was built on a rules-based order and that state power could be held to account.

By August, Carl Weirich was so beset by anxiety that 'the uncertainty over the fate of the house drove me out on my bike by myself'.[35] He went on a long cycling tour. He needed to get out of Weimar to think.

Meanwhile, another family lost everything. The Berlowitzs ran a textile department store at Schillerstraße 17–19, on the corner of Theatre Square. The Nazis forced them to sell up, not for town-planning purposes but because they wanted to drive the family out of Weimar. As Jews, the Berlowitzs stood no chance to fight back legally. The regime had already changed legislation to speed up the 'Aryanization' of businesses and property.

The Berlowitzs had initially hoped they could weather the anti-semitic storm the Nazis had unleashed. The head of the family, Israel Berlowitz, was seventy years old. Together with his wife Lucie and their business partner Rudolf Sachs he'd opened a shop for women's wear just before the turn of the century. In 1911, they'd invested in a large, three-storey newbuild. They'd installed a lift and turned the business into a modern department store, which they ran without Sachs from 1924. Even in the 1930s, the small shopping centre continued to thrive. The Berlowitzs had tried hard to keep a low profile. During the early boycotts in 1933, they had closed their store. They had done no more public advertising since Hitler became Chancellor and simply continued running their very popular business in the heart of Weimar.[36]

In 1937, the turnover of the Sachs & Berlowitz Department Store had been close to 1 million marks and it employed seventy-three people, among whom the Berlowitz couple were the only Jews.[37] It was the last large Jewish-owned business in Sauckel's Gau capital, Weimar. Since the annexation of Austria, there had been increasing pressure from the regime to push the remaining Jews out of public and economic life so that the 'Greater Germany' Hitler sought to create might be rid of all traces of Jewish life. In the spring of 1938, a formal 'Aryanization Commission' was set up in the 'Wilhelm Gustloff House' at Johann-Albrecht-Straße 1. This hit Weimar's few remaining Jewish-owned shops hard. In March, their addresses – now only seven in total – were published to locally stationed SS staff by order of the commandant of Buchenwald with a view to intimidating the owners, some of whom were women.[38] This included Elfriede Leopold, who continued to run her husband Ludwig's shoeshop since he'd been arrested and imprisoned in 1935.

Now Elfriede was told she had to sell her shop to an 'Aryan' owner. Desperate because she had no other means to feed herself, her daughter and her elderly mother, Elfriede pleaded with the authorities. A Gau official noted in his report that in a meeting she 'completely lost her composure . . . Frau Leopold frequently breaks out in tears during the discussions because she allegedly doesn't know how she is supposed to spend the rest of her life if she doesn't have any form of income at all . . . If she sells her shop, she will be left without means. A forced sale would be unbearable to her and she would have to turn on the gas tap.' This threat to take her own life had no effect on the Gau leadership. The official just coldly noted: 'I gave Frau Leopold an ultimatum of 14 days.'[39] Elfriede lost her shop. Her daughter Lieselotte emigrated to New York and Elfriede moved to Leipzig. In May 1942, she was deported from there on a train that also contained nineteen Jews from Weimar. Three months after that, she was murdered at Majdanek extermination camp.[40]

Israel Berlowitz's business was the most lucrative target for 'Aryanization'. By July, the Thuringian Ministry of the Interior and Sauckel's office wrote to Weimar Mayor Otto Koch that 'the Aryanization of the Jewish department store Sachs and Berlowitz in Weimar is under way'.[41] A conglomerate headed by businessman Hugo Oxen from Bochum bought it for 715,000 marks, of which 10 per cent immediately went into the coffers of the 'Aryanization' department. The Berlowitzs decided that the situation was getting too dangerous. They'd just sell the business and emigrate but keep hold of the land it sat on so that they could return one day when this madness had passed.

This compromise wasn't good enough for the regime. The SA continued to bully and intimidate the family, marching in front of the department store to pressure them to sell everything. In the end they resorted to violence. They dragged the seventy-year-old Israel up to Buchenwald and would only let him go if he agreed to sell up and emigrate. Broken, frightened and with no options left, he signed. The vast bulk of the sale price never reached the family. It was transferred to a state-controlled holding account and only 6,000 marks were paid out to Israel and Lucie. They took that and emigrated to the British Mandate of Palestine, settling in Tel Aviv.

Their adult daughter Edith managed to join them eventually but the family would never see Edith's older sister Lena again. She sold her Weimar house in February 1939 and fled to a relative in Libau (now Liepāja in Latvia) with no way of predicting that it would be captured by German troops in 1941. Her mother wrote in 1946 that she never heard from her again, nor from her grandchildren, twin boys called Hans and Peter. But she'd heard rumours that they 'had suffered the same fate as almost all Jews in that area'. Other reports later confirmed what had happened to Lena and her children. The arriving German troops had rounded up all Jews on the market square. Lena was separated from Hans and Peter, who were ordered to wait in a different area. Terrified, the two boys ran across the square towards their mother. They were both shot before they could reach her. Shortly after, Lena was murdered too.[42]

In Weimar, the Berlowitz name had long been wiped out by then, replaced by that of Hugo Oxen, the new non-Jewish owner of their business, who enticed customers in with a heart-shaped advert that promised a 'Department Store for All in the Heart of the Gau Capital'.[43]

Adolf Hitler returned to Weimar on 5 November. Nothing that day suggested that this would be his last official visit. When the Führer arrived by special train at 11 a.m., the town welcomed him with the usual fanfare. If Rosa Schmidt had looked out of one of the windows of the Hotel Hohenzollern, she would have seen a significant proportion of the Nazi top brass emerge from the station. Among others, Hitler was accompanied by Heinrich Himmler, Martin Bormann and Albert Speer. In the square, formations of the Wehrmacht, the SS and the Hitler Youth stood to attention.[44] All the church bells in the town rang out and the deep thud of salutary shots rumbled through the air. A military band began to play but, according to the press, 'it was immediately drowned out by an incomparable storm of jubilation'.[45] It was a spectacle no less impressive than on previous visits.

An appreciative Hitler slowly walked along the formations before boarding an open-top car. This took him down the broad Sophien-straße boulevard to the enormous construction site of the Adolf Hitler Square. Sauckel had ensured that a temporary street was built across the area that was now flanked by construction workers who stood to rigid attention. Further down, Weimarers were leaning out of their windows, waving to the Führer, while tens of thousands of people lined the decorated streets. Many had arrived by special trains from all over Thuringia to witness this tenth Thuringian Gau Day.[46]

To Sauckel's delight, Hitler had agreed to attend personally. His last visit now lay two years in the past. While the Führer enjoyed spending time in Weimar privately, something he'd do one last time in the summer of 1940, he was busy expanding the Reich and preparing for war. He'd just annexed the Sudetenland territory from Czechoslovakia; there just wasn't time for coffee, theatre and walks in Weimar. Yet Sauckel had managed to entice Hitler back because he had more to offer than the Gau Day. The new Hotel Elephant was ready, complete with an exclusive 80-square-metre Führer suite. Hitler was excited about this. He had an emotional attachment to a hotel in which, as the Gau newspaper put it, 'many a decision of historical importance for the movement and therefore for Germany' had been made ever since he had switched from the Hohenzollern to the Elephant in 1926.[47]

The relaunch of the hotel was observed well beyond Weimar. The *Berliner Tageblatt* reported after the opening: 'That Adolf Hitler in these times demanded to be kept abreast of all phases of planning, that he was the first guest to move into the transformed rooms, shows the importance of this architectural feat. It is not only a part of the party buildings which the Thuringian capital is erecting, but at the same time it is the most modern hospitality enterprise in Europe.'[48] Hitler had not only decided on the style, materials and details of the building but also made conceptual decisions on pricing and image. According to the architect Hermann Giesler, he'd said: 'Sauckel, make sure that the costs for overnight stays remain low. Guests who have to save up must not be excluded from the Hotel Elephant . . . Hire good staff who get paid decently . . . Everything has to be so good that word gets round.'[49]

Now that the opening day had arrived, Hitler couldn't wait to see the place. As his car made its slow way through the masses of people that had thronged on to the market square, Hitler stood gripping the top of the windshield with both hands as he looked up at the facade of the brand-new Elephant. When he got down from the car, he was immediately greeted by Giesler and some of Sauckel's ten children, who gave him flowers.[50]

As Hitler was shown around the hotel, the people outside shouted themselves into a frenzy. The new building had a balcony above the door and the crowds wanted Hitler to come out and speak to them. They began to chant: 'Dearest Führer, pretty please – Direct your feet to the balcony.'[51] He obliged, briefly appearing to frenetic applause. He'd barely gone back inside when the crowds started chanting again, coming up with increasingly creative messages from 'Dearest Führer, please come out, from your noble Elephant house!' to 'Dearest Führer, can't you hear, we're running out of breath down here!' and 'Dearest Führer, be so bold, come out soon or our dinner will get cold!' When Hitler took too long admiring his apartment, the crowds began to address the Gauleiter instead: 'Dearest Sauckel, be a star, bring back our Führer!'[52] As far as Hitler and Sauckel were concerned, the opening was a complete success.

The next day, over 100,000 people cheered the Nazi leader at the grand finale of the Gau Day, a rally on the sports track in Weimar. Hitler spoke about the achievements of annexing Austria and the Sudetenland but, ranting against Winston 'Churchill and his comrades', he warned that 'from this we must draw the realization and the determination never to leave this victorious path again'.[53] It was an ominous sign to Weimar, Germany and the world that Hitler wasn't done redrawing the map of Europe.

Propaganda claimed that 'the masses, who listened to the Führer's words, [were] deeply moved' and that their 'love, gratitude and loyalty' reflected that of 'the entire German people'.[54] In reality, the picture of the public mood was changing. Internal reports collated by police, Gestapo and officials all over Germany were beginning to speak of a certain 'rally fatigue'. They suggested that there were simply too many mass events, that their content and the attendant rituals were repetitive and that people were often coerced to attend.[55] There was also widespread fear of another war. The last one was only a generation ago and had caused such loss, trauma and humiliation that many Germans felt deeply uneasy about Hitler's actions and rhetoric, despite the territorial gains made without war thus far. Reports to the authorities warned of 'war psychosis'. One added that 'should the worst case happen, the population will do its duty, but a glowing enthusiasm like in 1914 . . . has so far not materialized'.[56] This certainly applied to Carl Weirich. Towards the end of 1938, it wasn't just the matter of the 'ludicrous construction works of the building association that our house is supposed to be sacrificed for' that made Carl anxious but also the fact that an 'increasing persecution of Jews began that blasphemed against God Himself'.[57]

On 9 November, three days after Hitler's departure from Weimar, Carl Weirich celebrated his fifty-third birthday. While he enjoyed a family meal with Marie, Wilhelm and relatives from Nuremberg, Hitler had dinner at the Old Town Hall in Munich to celebrate a different occasion. 'The ninth of the eleventh' had become one of the most important days in the Nazi calendar. It marked the anniversary of the botched Munich Putsch in 1923. Hitler was attending this when the news reached him that the German diplomat Ernst vom Rath had died in Paris.

Vom Rath had been shot two days earlier by Herschel Grynszpan, a seventeen-year-old German-born Polish Jew whose family had been expelled from Germany in October as part of the 'Polenaktion', a coordinated purge that forcibly deported 17,000 Polish Jews living in Nazi Germany. Upon hearing the news that vom Rath had succumbed to his wounds, Hitler discussed the matter with Goebbels at dinner, telling him: 'This time, the Jews must be exposed to the wrath of the people.' Then he got up and left. Goebbels took Hitler's comment for what it was: an order to launch a state-sponsored pogrom. The Propaganda Minister noted in his diary: 'I immediately give instructions to this effect to police and party . . . Now the people will act.'[58]

A wave of brutality swept over Germany that night – and soon over Austria, too, with even greater intensity. Euphemistically referred to as 'Kristallnacht' or 'Crystal Night', the pogrom involved arson, looting, vandalism, violence, arrests and murder against Jews and their synagogues, shops and homes. It was launched and coordinated by arms of the Nazi regime, particularly the SA, while police were told to stand by, only intervening to stop theft or damage to nearby 'Aryan' properties.

While a number of ordinary German civilians joined the lawless outbursts, many others were deeply shocked by the events. The Social Democratic Party of Germany in exile (Sopade), which operated out of Prague and published 'Germany Reports' through a network of informants, concluded that 'the excesses are strongly condemned by the great majority of the German people'.[59] Other reports suggest that many abhorred the violence, the destruction of property in times of economic crisis and the general lawlessness that the party had deliberately created, but not the principle that Jews should be punished. Many Germans managed to simultaneously feel pity for their Jewish neighbours but approve of their expulsion from the economy.[60] On the night of his birthday, Carl knew nothing of the antisemitic violence that wrought destruction and death in Germany. He spent the evening with friends and family, noting later that he'd been 'ignorant of the political consequences the day would bring through the persecution of Jews in Germany'.[61]

It's possible that Carl didn't hear anything that night because 'Kristallnacht' was comparatively quiet in Weimar. The town's Jewish community had never been large enough to sustain a synagogue, and most of the Jewish-owned shops and businesses had already been 'Aryanized'. While in Erfurt, the Great Synagogue was looted, vandalized and set on fire, there were few targets left to burn and smash in Weimar. On the evening of 9 November, the local Gestapo office received the same message that went out across the country: 'With very short notice, actions against Jews, particularly against their synagogues, will take place all over Germany. They are not to be disrupted . . . Prepare the arrest of around 20–30,000 Jews in the Reich. Select especially wealthy Jews.'[62]

In Weimar, SA and SS men targeted the one remaining Jewish-owned shop, that of Hedwig Hetemann. In her early seventies, Hedwig was an institution in Weimar. She ran a toy shop in Teichgasse 6 in the old town stocked with teddy bears, carved wooden animals, wind-up toys and marbles. But what many locals remembered most fondly was that she repaired broken toys in her 'Doll Clinic'. One resident recalled later that, when she was a little girl, 'the toy shop of Doll Mother Hetemann was a small paradise for us children. How I loved going there as a child!' Another remembered that Hedwig helped adults too, for instance when she agreed to sell a pram on credit to a young mother who was unemployed and impoverished in the middle of the Great Depression. Other shops had not wanted to take the risk that the woman might not be able to pay back at the agreed rates. Hedwig showed compassion, despite not being particularly wealthy herself. She still ran her shop at her advanced age because her husband had died in 1925 and she needed the income.[63]

Neither her reputation nor her long-standing place in Weimar's social fabric protected Hedwig from the violence of Kristallnacht. Men appeared at her shop and smashed in the window. They scattered her dolls all over the street and demolished everything inside. Hedwig came running out and pleaded with them to stop. She cried and begged for them to leave her her livelihood. But the men only mocked and assaulted the elderly woman until she retreated into the house, sobbing and frightened. Nobody came to help. One young woman who saw the incident later explained that she 'didn't know the meaning of this destruction at the time and was thoroughly shaken up' herself. Another resident said she was confused when she saw that there were SA men everywhere on the streets. 'The next day when I heard about the destruction of the Hetemann shop, I understood.' One young woman heard her colleague, who was in the SA, brag about his crimes at work: 'Yesterday, we sorted out the place of the old Hetemann, that Jewess,' the man gloated. 'You should have seen it!'[64]

After her ordeal, Hedwig retreated from public life. She closed the shop and was so afraid and isolated that she barely left her flat. Since nobody had helped her during or after the attack she lost faith in her fellow Weimarers. It was hard to tell who had sympathy for her but didn't speak up for fear of being seen as being too friendly with Jews and who would attack her, given that they could clearly do so with impunity. Simple things like going to the dentist felt like running the gauntlet, especially when a law later compelled all Jews in Germany to wear a yellow star from September 1941. Hedwig's dentist remembered how the old lady 'came to me with a tooth-ache. Since she feared to be accosted because of the yellow star, she covered the star with her handbag. I treated her as always. It was shocking.'[65] In September 1942, aged seventy-six, Hedwig was deported together with many of the remaining Jews from Weimar. She died at Theresienstadt Ghetto in 1943.

Carl Weirich and other Weimarers may have been oblivious to the fate of Hedwig Hetemann initially, but they found out very soon what was going on. Not only did the story of the vicious attack on her make the rounds in town, but Goebbels also delivered a national explanation for the violence across Germany. Local papers in Thuringia spread his message: 'The justified and understandable outrage of the German people about the cowardly, Jewish assassination of a German diplomat in Paris found a comprehensive vent last night. In numerous cities and towns of the Reich, acts of revenge were under-taken against Jewish buildings and shops.'⁶⁶

It wasn't just this message, designed to portray the state-coordinated attacks as a spontaneous outbreak of justified anger, that gave Weimarers an idea as to what was going on. The reality of what Nazi antisemitism looked like in practice came home to them. Over the next few days, close to 30,000 Jewish men were arrested across the country and taken to Nazi Germany's three large concen-tration camps: Dachau, Sachsenhausen and Buchenwald.

From her windows at the Hotel Hohenzollern, Rosa Schmidt could see train after train arrive between 10 and 14 November. Hundreds of men spilled out of each one. Some looked dazed and confused, others angry or desperate. SS and police beat them through the tunnel underneath the platforms and out on to the large square in front of her hotel, where ugly scenes unfolded every day. Ernst Cramer was one of 964 men on a transport from Breslau arriving at Weimar station on 11 November. He remembered later how his group was 'apparently entirely unnecessarily herded like cattle and beaten against the wall'. Then a shrill whistle gave the signal, and their captors shouted, 'Los, los!' – 'Go, go!' – while beating the men on to overcrowded lorries. Ernst recalled how 'An elderly man, who had stumbled and fallen, was first assaulted by those sadistic pigs with kicks, then they grabbed him by his arms and legs and shoved him into the lorry, which was already full.'⁶⁷

It was a frightening thing to observe for many Weimarers. Pris-oners sat in front of the station, huddled in blankets and holding on to a few belongings in small bags as they waited for the next trans-port to Buchenwald. One bystander remembered that she was 'deeply moved' by what she saw: 'Every generation was there, old and young, children too; they were broken and apathetic, looking down all the time, as if they were ashamed of their expulsion.' A young Weimar couple sat in the Kulmbach tavern in nearby Röhrstraße when a friend walked by and whispered: 'At the station, a Jew transport is due to arrive at 11 o'clock, come along if you want to see something.' They did, watching the arrivals being beaten, shouted at and loaded on to lorries until 3 o'clock in the afternoon, fascinated by the horrific spectacle. Recalling the scene later, they said: 'We just didn't understand it, we were frightened. How could they treat people like that?'[68] Klaus Engelhardt, the ten-year-old son of a Wehrmacht officer, had also heard the rumours. Like many Weimar children, he too rushed to the station to gape at the 'well-dressed, bearded men being beaten on to lorries with sticks', as he recalled later. Too young to know a Germany without Nazi ideology, he approved of what he saw, seeing the mistreatment of Jews as 'something normal'.[69]

Rosa wasn't so different from the people who were beaten and carted off to a concentration camp a few metres away from her front door. According to the Nazis' race laws, her four Jewish grandparents made her a 'Volljude' – a 'full Jew'. It didn't matter that she didn't regard herself as a religious Jew. Hedwig Hetemann was a baptized Protestant. In the Nazis' racist world view, only blood made one a member of the 'People's Community'. Many Jews hoped that a mixed marriage with a non-Jew, like that of the Schmidts, would protect them from Nazi persecution, but among the people now dragged off to Buchenwald were Weimarers like Julius Wiener, who had until recently run a curtain shop at Adolf-Hitler-Straße 14 and whose wife wasn't Jewish.

The fact that Arthur Schmidt was a decorated war veteran wasn't an iron-cast shield against the persecution of his family. Julius Katz, a new Buchenwald arrival from Sontra in Hesse, remembered how a fellow prisoner had screamed at his captors: 'I fought for Germany. I lay at the front for over four years. I'm a German Jew. We've been persecuted for 2,000 years, and you claim to be a cultured people!' He was punished immediately, receiving twenty-five cane strokes on his bare buttocks. Julius recalled the man's screams when he described the incident, 'you could really hear how the SS man took aim, cut the air with his cane so that it whistled . . . I just thought of Weimar, Buchenwald, Goethe. It made no sense.'[70]

The Schmidts had been spared maltreatment so far because there was no paper trail that pointed to Rosa's background. They had simply ignored the new rule, introduced on 17 August, that forced

Jewish men arrested in the days after the pogrom night of 9 November 1938, standing for roll call at Buchenwald.

male and female Jews to add 'Israel' or 'Sara' respectively as additional first names if their names weren't overtly Jewish already. When in October the passports of German Jews became invalid until they were altered to contain the additional name and a large, red letter 'J', Rosa ignored that too. She applied for a new passport around that time and was issued one on 15 October, ten days after the rule had come in. It simply named her as 'Rosa Schmidt' – no added 'Sara', no red 'J'. The difference was beginning to be a matter of life or death.

If her secret had come out then, Rosa would not have ended up among the mistreated prisoners in front of her hotel in November 1938. For one thing, the Nazis concentrated on arresting Jewish men after Kristallnacht. For another, the Schmidts' relationship would have been classed as a 'privileged mixed marriage' since it was between a Jewish woman and a 'German-blooded' man in which the children were raised without the Jewish faith. Such families were for now exempted from the sharp end of Nazi persecution since the regime was worried about resistance from non-Jewish relatives and friends. But the rules introduced up to 1938, including the need to register as Jewish, 'Aryanize' property and change of name still applied. There was also never official legislation protecting 'privileged' families, only an internal directive from Hermann Göring in December 1938. Given the escalation of antisemitic rhetoric and action already, there was no guarantee that the regime would stick to its own rules.

There were twelve Jews from Weimar among those torn from their regular lives and incarcerated. Weimarer Ernst Bendix perished at Buchenwald. Chemist Hans Adolf Salomon and salesman Albert Ortweiler died in Weimar shortly after their release in December from the consequences of their imprisonment on the Ettersberg.[71] This time, the prisoners were all men, but women were not exempt from Nazi violence as the callousness with which Hedwig Hetemann had been treated readily demonstrated. One look out of the Hohenzollern in mid-November, where nearly 10,000 innocent people arrived in four days to be taken to a concentration camp, showed the kind of future Adolf Hitler, once a warmly received guest at Rosa's hotel, had in mind for people like her.

Christmas 1938 was bitterly cold. As temperatures dropped to $-18°$, Carl Weirich didn't have to worry about his pipes bursting again, since Nazi Germany's economic recovery had enabled him to install a modern heating system. But what good was that now? The house and its pipes were to be demolished the following year to make room for Nazi dreams of a 'New Weimar'. Carl's unease about the extreme violence Weimar had witnessed in November also tainted his outlook for 1939. That was supposed to be a happy year. May would mark the twenty-fifth anniversary of his takeover of the shop and his new life in Weimar. These achievements, the blood, sweat and tears of a quarter of a century's worth of labour, were to be wiped out at the whim of a regime capable of wanton brutality. Carl didn't feel much like celebrating.

Between Christmas and New Year, staff at Weimar cemetery worked overtime. Throughout December, bodies from Buchenwald had arrived daily. On 27 December alone, employees burned the bodies of twenty-five concentration camp victims and four regular civilians. In the previous two months the bodies brought down from the Ettersberg had made up well over 80 per cent of all cremations. In total, 802 Buchenwald prisoners had died in 1938; around half of them were Jewish.[72] The two furnaces at the Weimar crematorium were ill-suited to cope with such numbers. They had never been designed to burn bodies on an industrial scale.

The town-planning department had got in touch with the Erfurt-based company Topf & Söhne, which specialized in chimneys, incinerators and crematoria. This company would later also develop and supply the ovens and ventilation systems for the crematoria and gas chambers at Auschwitz and other concentration and extermination camps. For Weimar, it was a local company and a trusted business partner, situated around 20 kilometres away. It had already installed one of the old ovens at the town crematorium in 1926.

When the company's engineer turned up in the middle of December to see what the problem was, it turned out that 'due to the increasing use of the oven in the last few months' one of the cremation chambers, which had only been installed four years earlier, had to be replaced. Topf & Söhne, the cemetery management and the Weimar planning department came to the conclusion that there was simply no point trying to keep the old ovens going. As the company explained, the models it had installed were perfectly adequate for the 'cremation of bodies that burned well or normally, but failed with frequent cases of cremations of bodies that burned badly (tuberculosis, cancer)'. Buchenwald would eventually get its own Topf & Söhne crematorium, but, for now, Weimar town council adapted to the new realities with remarkable ease. In a non-public session on 21 December, it decided to order a new crematorium oven for Weimar town cemetery. Everyone knew the bodies would keep coming.[73]

Conditions in Theodor Eicke's model camp had deteriorated quickly. Before the November pogroms, there had already been over 10,000 prisoners at Buchenwald. This number had doubled when 9,845 Jewish men arrived after Kristallnacht. One huge problem was that there simply wasn't enough water to maintain basic standards of hygiene, and a typhoid epidemic broke out.[74]

Doubling the camp's size in a matter of days also led to chaos, not least because the SS had only been notified of the planned arrests late in the evening of 9 November. There just wasn't room in the already overcrowded barracks. So the prisoners were made to construct an emergency camp on site. Hastily built, the new blocks had no floors, windows, heating or toilets. The inmates were made to use just two open latrines while living in units of 2,000 men per block. Crammed in cheek by jowl, they were denied sleep, food, water and medical treatment as they caught diseases and frostbite.[75] Like the elderly Weimar department store owner Israel Berlowitz, who was among the detainees, many of the men were constantly and deliberately maltreated by the SS until they gave up their property and agreed to leave Germany. The pogrom camp was dissolved in February 1939 – too late for over 250 men who died in its cold and dark barracks in the middle of a country they called home.

1939

An iron-grey sky hung over Weimar as Carl Weirich set out on his Sunday outing on 12 February. The bitterly cold weeks of December and January had given way to an unusually mild spell. The previous week had been sunny, raising hopes of longer days and shorter nights ahead. But today was gloomy. Thick, dark clouds brooded above, threatening rain.

Carl was walking alone, in search of a peace of mind that was hard to come by these days. He wasn't feeling well. The prospect of losing his home and livelihood was sapping his strength. He could see it in Wilhelm too. Now twelve years old and helping his father in the shop whenever he could, the boy sensed something was troubling his father to the point of exhaustion. Carl had always been a thin man but now he looked gaunt. His hair had turned white and thin. His cheekbones were beginning to protrude and bags had appeared under his troubled eyes. Wilhelm doubled down in helping him, carrying, packaging and delivering books for the shop. But father and son were both rapidly approaching their limits.

As Carl walked up the slopes of the Ettersberg in the drizzle, determined to leave his sorrows behind in Weimar for the day, he found he was simply going through the motions, having lunch at the Waidmannsheil tavern and coffee on the way back down at the Rödchen forest on the southern slopes. As he navigated unfamiliar routes, around fences and blocked footpaths, he found there was little relaxation to be had 'on our Ettersberg, which was badly affected by the concentration camp'.[1]

Two days after Carl's hiking trip, Weimar's chief medical officer Waldemar Freienstein made his way up the Ettersberg. The town authorities were alarmed by the fact that thirteen civilians from the village of Ottmannshausen, around 4 kilometres north of Buchenwald, had somehow contracted typhoid. Some had to be treated in the town hospital. By the time that Carl undertook his walk, three of the victims had died, all young people, including a ten-year-old child. The entire area had been quarantined. The village school had been closed. People were banned from using the local stream, and the sufferers and their immediate families had been isolated.

There was significant concern since the sister of one of the typhoid sufferers worked for a butcher in Weimar, who in turn delivered produce to Buchenwald. The whole thing was beginning to spiral out of control and the town authorities were furious that they had not been told about the hygiene issues at the nearby concentration camp. They had only found out what was going on when they began to investigate the matter themselves, working out that raw sewage had appeared in the stream at Ottmannshausen, which could only have come from Buchenwalds further uphill. When they called the responsible medical official there, they were told that there had indeed been cases of typhoid in the camp but that no details would be passed on, due to the 'classified nature of conditions in the K.L.'.[2]

The authorities took immediate action, restricting public access to the entire area beyond specific, designated routes. They sent in experts from the Institute for Hygiene at the University of Jena as well as Dr Freienstein, who was shocked by what he saw at Buchenwald. Conditions in the camp were beyond atrocious, and the leadership appeared to have made no effort to remedy the situation, isolate the risks of epidemics spreading beyond the camp or even report the matter. In his scathing report, Freienstein complained that SS staff at Buchenwald had refused to cooperate with Weimar on public-health matters.[3] Freienstein, normally more concerned with the prevention of human life when authorizing and carrying out forced sterilizations, was worried that this negligence 'had so far unfortunately claimed three human victims, all of a youthful age'.[4] Karl Astel, leader of the State Health Department and president of the Thuringian Race Office, who was responsible for thousands of sterilizations and the identification of supposed racial enemies of the 'People's Community', also insisted that in future 'notification is given immediately after cases of typhoid are noted'. This, he argued, was necessary due to 'the close proximity and complex interaction between the town of Weimar and K.L. Buchenwald'.[5]

Both medical officials were right to suspect that the SS had been well aware of the scale of the problem. SS hygiene officer Dr Joachim Mrugowsky, who had been asked to inspect Buchenwald shortly after the arrival of the 10,000 pogrom detainees, noted in his report on 10 December that the camp provided 'ideal conditions for the spread of an epidemic. There was the greatest scarcity of water so that each SS man only had ½ litre of water a day, each prisoner had only ¼ litre . . . It's a miracle that, given the overly primitive conditions, the epidemic hasn't become even greater in scale.'[6]

Freienstein's promise to be quiet about the conditions in the camp following his threat to take the matter to Himmler led to the camp authorities liaising with Weimar to solve the problem – not for the sake of the prisoners but in order to prevent the spread of disease beyond Buchenwald. Town and camp now worked closely together to build better facilities, including a new sewage treatment plant, which Weimar's Planning Office agreed to build. Inmates were vaccinated against typhoid, water was chlorinated, open sewers shut. Buchenwald was placed under a strict quarantine between February and April 1939. The camp authorities monitored the situation and sent regular reports down to the Health Department in Weimar. The makeshift pogrom camp was shut down on 15 February, the day after Freienstein's visit.[7]

By the time Hitler launched the Second World War in September 1939, around 1,000 inmates had died at Buchenwald since it had first been built in 1937. Between those deaths and prisoner releases, the population of the camp was reduced to 5,400. But the typhoid epidemic would not be the last to befall Buchenwald, nor was it the only cause of death. Deteriorating conditions coupled with the cruelty of staff and outright executions would kill around 56,000 people or roughly one in five inmates between 1937 and 1945. The scale of the brutality was known to plenty of town officials who had seen it with their own eyes or were directly involved.[8]

In Weimar, references to the camp slipped into everyday parlance. People would threaten or joke: 'Just watch out or they'll take you to Buchenwald.' The caretaker at the Hotel Fürstenhof one day made a joke about the Wehrmacht in front of two young women who worked there. One of them responded: 'If you carry on like that, you'll end up in Buchenwald', to which the caretaker retorted: 'but you'd bring up some soup for me.' One of the women reported the conversation to the Gestapo, but even their interrogation couldn't clarify just how much the caretaker actually knew about the camp. So he was released. It's likely that he had a good idea what the camp was for. Most people knew that many prisoners never returned. 'What's the highest hill in Germany?' Weimarers asked each other. 'It's the Ettersberg! It's so tall that once you're up there, you'll never get back down.'[9]

A month after his visit to the Ettersberg, Carl Weirich felt seriously ill. The whites of his eyes and his skin had turned a sickly yellow colour. Family physician Dr Schmidt diagnosed jaundice and prescribed an effective treatment so that Carl was back on his feet a week later. But then Wilhelm got sick, and his case was a lot worse. Carl was beginning to think that 1939 was shaping up to be a terrible year. The twenty-fifth anniversary of his takeover of the 'little shop' at Geleitstraße 10 came and went on 1 May, affording him no 'special kind of joy in these times of crisis'.[10]

While Wilhelm Weirich was recovering from jaundice at home, a short walk away, Gestapo Weimar was looking to expand its premises at the Marstall building. In January, it had applied to the Thuringian Finance Ministry to install further prisoner cells in the basement, ideally three solitary units and one communal one. After all, it had argued, 'Weimar is now a hub for the through traffic of prisoner transports.'[11] Although Himmler's office had denied permission, citing building regulations, Gestapo Weimar pressed ahead, installing temporary new cells in the former coach house of the Marstall 'since the question of prisoner accommodation must be solved urgently'.[12] Buchenwald inmates built those twelve cells, soon followed by more converted space in the main building. Four cells were specifically designed for torture, as a report explained: 'They are just 0.70m wide and 1.40m long with a height of about 2m. They don't have windows, only a small opening in the door. Two large heating pipes create a constant sauna temperature of nearly 50 degrees C. In the cell the light is always on. There is neither food nor water . . . No prisoner has survived this treatment for more than 9 days.'[13]

Kurt Nehrling knew from incarcerated comrades like his friend Hans Eberling what it meant to be arrested by the Gestapo. His resistance group discussed if it wouldn't be better for the few remaining members to join the Nazi Party for cover. Hans later said that he vehemently argued against this because he still believed that the Nazi system would fall one day and when it did how could they say with integrity that they were any different from fellow Germans who had marched along with the Nazi regime? Hans and Kurt resolved to fight for their principles or die trying.[14]

Nazi leaders knew they couldn't rely on terror alone to control the population. Propaganda and culture were to play key roles in shaping the hearts and minds of the 'People's Community' whose members were to feel invested in their project of laying the foundation for a 'Thousand-Year Reich'. Part of this effort was an exhibition called *Degenerate Art* (*Entartete Kunst*), which began in Munich and then toured Germany and Austria. Not to be outdone, Weimar Nazis pushed for their town to be included on the exhibition tour. *Degenerate Art* had been to Berlin, Leipzig, Düsseldorf, Salzburg, Hamburg and Stettin before it opened at the State Museum in Weimar on 23 March 1939.[15]

Hans Severus Ziegler, whose initiative had brought the exhibition to town, was extremely pleased. Speaking at the opening, he expressed his hope that it would 'expose the mistakes of the past as clearly as possible'. Thuringia, he argued, had been 'a brave early outpost' of Nazi culture policy. Now, it would continue in this vein, 'exposing the damage of the past to young people'.[16] Then he released the guests to roam around the twenty rooms of the exhibition.

In an effort to give the impression of moral depravity, the authorities banned anyone under the age of eighteen from visiting. Tickets were sold through the Strength Through Joy scheme at a reduced price of 35 pfennigs as opposed to the regular fee of 50 pfennigs. According to the press, 6,000 people visited the State Museum in the first week alone. It's impossible to know who attended and why. Some may indeed have hoped to 'gain harrowing impressions of Jewish cultural Bolshevism as depicted in over 700 visual documents', as the Nazified press claimed. But it's unlikely that 'everyone left the exhibition with a feeling of gratitude towards the Führer, who had had these products of madness removed from the museums'.[17] Some Weimarers may have regarded it as their last chance to see works of art that had vanished from view. The regime had seized around 21,000 pieces. It sold some and destroyed others. Weimar's state collections alone had lost 450 items. Among the artists displayed at the *Entartete Kunst* exhibition in Weimar were people who had lived and worked in the town during the Bauhaus years such as the painters Wassily Kandinsky and Paul Klee.[18]

Regarding himself as one of the Reich's foremost musical experts, Ziegler was particularly pleased by his own contribution to the exhibition called *Degenerate Music*, which filled two rooms on the upper floor with information and listening booths. He'd tested it during the Reich Music Days in Düsseldorf in May 1938. After Weimar, it would also go on to be shown in Munich and Vienna. Ziegler wanted his exhibition understood as a 'depiction of the triumph of subhumanity, arrogant Jewish impudence and complete spiritual stupidity'.[19] While not disagreeing with him in principle, his enemies took the opportunity to discredit him. The rumours regarding his homosexuality had never gone away and neither had old rivalries. Isolated and thinly shielded by Hitler's tacit goodwill, Ziegler's exhibition was widely – if not publicly – criticized by those who regarded them-selves as the Reich's music experts. Among them was the composer and conductor Peter Raabe, president of the Reich Music Chamber. He complained directly to Goebbels about Ziegler's trespassing into his field, calling him a 'layman' and an 'amateur'. *Degenerate Music* received minimal coverage and was soon shelved.[20]

In Weimar, *Degenerate Art* had a successful run, not least because many residents sought refuge where they could from permanent overexposure to politics. It was possible to ignore the vicious propa-ganda that came with the works of art on display and visit the museum as a gallery. People could sit in one of Ziegler's booths, put on a pair of headphones and tap their toes to a bit of jazz music. Nazi propaganda may have intruded into every aspect of life but people's thoughts remained free.

Many Germans began to look for ways to at least temporarily escape the mounting fear of war. The regime trod an awkward line between trying to assuage concerns and shoring up a spirit of war readiness. On 10 November 1938, the day after he had given the order to unleash terror on Jewish communities, Hitler had delivered a secret speech to German journalists, by now state-approved enforcers of Nazi propaganda. He'd explained that 'circumstances' had 'forced me to talk almost exclusively about peace for decades'. Now it was time to 'slowly transition the German people psychologically and make it clear to them that there are things which, if they can't be done by peaceful means, must be brought about by means of violence'.[21]

Hitler had followed this up with a public speech on 30 January 1939, the sixth anniversary of his ascension to the chancellorship, in which he discussed his foreign policy. Preparing the country for the prospect of armed conflict as well as further brutality against Jews, he thundered:

The German people feels no hatred towards England, America, or France; it just wants peace and quiet. Those nations, however, are being continuously stirred up against Germany and the German people by

Jewish or non-Jewish agitators . . . Should international financial Jewry
in and outside of Europe succeed in plunging the nations once again
into a world war, the result will not be the Bolshevization of the world
and thus the victory of Jewry, but the annihilation of the Jewish race
in Europe.[22]

Hitler was preparing the nation for a large-scale, genocidal war in
Europe, and this had a direct psychological effect on a population
that hadn't forgotten the devastation of the last total war. Reports
from Nazi sources and the social democratic resistance agreed that
many Germans were ready to believe that tension was whipped up
by the Western powers and Poland, but this didn't allay their unease.
The population still 'trust the Führer completely', one report reassured Nazi leaders, but it added that 'it wouldn't be right to speak
of enthusiasm for war'.[23]

Weimarers didn't openly resist the advent of war but many went out
of their way to bury their fears. With the Ettersberg an increasingly
frustrating and depressing destination for hiking excursions, the
Weirichs joined the local chapter of the Rennsteig Club. The Rennsteig is a famous long-distance ridge trail high up in the Thuringian
Forest – beautiful and far away from Weimar. Carl had to take an
early-morning train to get there and would often only return late in
the evenings, but it was worth it for the spectacular scenery and the
company. The Rennsteig ramblers were a 'funny tribe', Carl noted,
'in which many members had nicknames and went on cheerful foot
hikes'.[24]

There were distractions in Weimar too. Carl and Marie went to
the cinema to watch the newly released motion picture *The Immortal
Heart*, which was filmed in Marie's home town of Nuremberg but
set in the early modern period. When the nightingales returned
from migration, Carl went on a night walk to hear their beautiful birdsong. But the highlight of June was a family outing to
the southern Thuringian town of Meiningen. They took a special
train on 2 July to join 40,000 other people to watch the airship

Graf Zeppelin II land. The Weirichs didn't know that they were witnessing the last of its kind. The airship would be mothballed in August and scrapped by Hermann Göring a few months later. Göring was uneasy to even fly in them for propaganda purposes since the *Hindenburg* airship had caught fire in 1937, causing thirty-six fatalities. When pressed to board a Zeppelin after that, he had responded: 'Nah, you won't get me into one of those, those things burn.' When Hitler invaded Poland in September, Göring decided to scrap the airship scheme altogether: 'In war, they are useless,' he had ranted, 'one match is enough and the whole thing goes up in flames.'[25]

On 24 August, a week before German troops invaded Poland, Fritz Sauckel opened an exhibition called 'The Old and the New Weimar'. With Albert Speer's support, he had managed to get Weimar on the regime's official list of towns and cities to be remodelled according to Hitler's wishes.[26] 'Weimar will forever be grateful to Adolf Hitler for making this small German Grand Ducal residence the Gau Capital,' Sauckel said at the Weimarhalle. From being linked to the Reich Autobahn to erecting new buildings like the Hotel Elephant, the Nietzsche Memorial Hall, the extension of the Goethe Museum or the new military barracks, the Gauleiter argued, 'through Adolf Hitler's movement, Weimar was effectively woken to new life like Sleeping Beauty'. The best things were yet to come, Sauckel promised. The Adolf Hitler Square with its huge People's Hall would be the crowning glory, a place where the 'geniuses of the nation can speak to the people'. There would be an enormous new machine-tool factory for the Gustloff works in which 'German workers of the mind and the hand' would find 'clean and great' working conditions. There would be more housing in which 'happy families, dear German mothers live and cheerful, plentiful children grow up'.[27]

The Reichsstatthalter in Thuringia planned to present the Führer with a completely transformed Gau capital for the twentieth anniversary of the Nazi Party rally of 1926.[28] That would be in August 1946. Weimar would indeed be completely transformed by then, but not as Sauckel had intended. He would have only a few months to live. His Führer would be dead. Weimar would lie in ashes and ruins.

Emmy Göring knew something was very wrong. She sat at the breakfast table at Carinhall with her husband and didn't dare say a word to break the stony silence between them. He had drawn the curtains, and now sat brooding on his chair with his head hung low. 'We all thought about the war,' she remembered later, 'but nobody voiced any thoughts. We were waiting for a word of redemption from Hermann. But he remained silent.'[29]

It was 31 August, the day before the German invasion of Poland, and Göring knew what was coming. He had accompanied Hitler on his path right up to this point, from participating in the Munich Putsch in 1923 to founding the Gestapo and cracking down on political opponents after Hitler took power. He'd helped organize the destruction of Jewish life in Germany and built a Luftwaffe for his Führer, personally profiting from both through bribery and embezzlement. Emmy felt no remorse, just 'the fear of a woman who hates war'.[30]

When Göring returned home later that day his face was ashen. 'We are at war!' he told Emmy. 'It will be terrible – As terrible as nobody can imagine.'[31]

Carl Weirich was out hiking when he learned that Germany was at war. He, Marie and Wilhelm had met up with friends in the countryside just south of Weimar. While they were walking downhill to the station to catch a train back to Weimar, they heard the 'sad news'.

Carl's heart sank. Another world war. The last one had stolen his family. Memories of rationing, hardship, hunger and death came flooding back. The fear of aerial bombardment added new terror. This war would come home to Germany. For the first time in his life, there was neither solace nor 'joy in hiking', Carl wrote. His fears were visceral, gnawing away at his very soul. He worried for his livelihood, his wife and most of all little Wilhelm. What would become of them? 'The year of 1939 came to a quiet end,' Carl wrote, as 'Hitler's Germany unleashed the Furies of war.'[32]

Epilogue: War

Poets and hangmen

When death and destruction finally came to Weimar, it sounded surprisingly innocuous to Carl Weirich. At lunchtime on 9 February 1945, he and the other occupants of Geleitstraße 10 sat huddled in the basement when a deep, rumbling sound shook the ceiling. It sounded as if a train had rolled through the house. Before Carl could even contemplate leaving the shelter, a loud boom marked the first explosion. Then another one. And another one. They waited for thirteen minutes while American warplanes dropped 1,925 explosive bombs. Weimar would remember this as Black Friday, the single most deadly and destructive day in the town's history.

When Carl emerged, he found himself in a dystopian hellscape. 'Rubble and roof tiles and dust everywhere!' he wrote in his diary. As he looked around, dazed by the sheer scale of destruction, Frau Wendelmuth, who lived a few houses down, came running towards him, wringing her hands in obvious distress. 'Why, please help,' she cried. 'My dead mother-in-law is in the house of the clockmaker Bayer, who is also dead.'[1] Harrowing scenes took place all over Weimar, where 462 people had perished. In the nursery in Richard-Strauß-Straße, all the staff and most of the ninety children had been killed. Once the dust had settled, teenager Margot Köhler, who worked there part-time, witnessed a horrific scene: 'Everywhere sat or lay children and grown-ups, their lungs having burst. Soulless, they stared at us.' Among the dead infants were two girls, Monika and Christa. Their mother Friedel had now lost her entire family, as her husband Herbert never returned from the front.[2]

Over the next few weeks, more bombs rained down on

Weimar, killing 1,254 residents in all. Six hundred Buchenwald inmates died while engaged in forced labour in Fritz Sauckel's Gustloff works. The camp itself had also been targeted in earlier strikes, with hundreds dead and injured. In total, 325 houses were destroyed, and many more were damaged. Among them were some of Weimar's most cherished cultural sites, including the church of St Peter and Paul and the Goethe and Schiller museums. The German National Theatre, which had been transformed into an armaments factory, was hit by an explosive and burned down. The iconic Goethe and Schiller memorial in front survived amid a landscape of ash and rubble, having been encased for protection. The tombs of Weimar's two famous poets were also saved, having been moved to Jena.[3]

Carl's house was badly damaged. There was a bitter irony in this. He hadn't lost it to the Nazi building schemes after all. Those plans had suddenly been abandoned in 1939. Instead, the war came for it. The Weirich family now slept together in what was left of their home, on the bare floor in the one small room at the back that was still intact. The roof had been blown wide open. The shop windows had been smashed and only rudimentarily covered with cardboard to protect the stock from the elements, a feeble attempt to maintain order in the midst of chaos.

The dying regime lashed out viciously. Gestapo Weimar

Bomb-ravaged Weimar, 1945.

murdered all its surviving prisoners. The SS tried to evacuate Buchenwald and murdered many inmates before abandoning the site
amid a prisoner rebellion on 11 April, shortly before the arrival of
American troops.

Despite the utter breakdown of humanity in Weimar, Carl and
his neighbours attempted to maintain a semblance of purpose.
They helped each other procure materials for house repairs as
well as food and supplies. What was left of Carl's front door was
nailed shut. 'It looked terrible in the shop,' Carl wrote misera-
bly.[4] But he still had his wife and his son – that was more than
many other families had. Carl was nearly sixty now, which had
saved him from military service. He had been drafted into the
'Volkssturm' militia the previous year and was often called out
for work details, but, crucially, he wasn't sent to the front lines.
Wilhelm had been drafted into the Wehrmacht in 1944, when he
turned eighteen. He returned home for leave at the end of March
1945, wounded three times but alive and deemed fit enough to go
again in April. Carl accompanied his son back to the barracks,
dreading the prospect of having to let him go once more. But
Wilhelm never had to fight again. On 12 April, American troops
arrived in Weimar.

The liberation of Weimar came too late for many of its residents.
Thousands had died in battle, in bombing raids or due to the increasingly desperate supply situation. The chances of survival of anyone
deemed a political or racial enemy of the Nazi 'People's Community' were particularly slim in wartime. Kurt Nehrling managed to
evade both capture and the front lines of Hitler's war for some time
after 1939. He was forty years old at the time and still within the draft
age range. It was only because of the tuberculosis he'd contracted
in the First World War that he was deemed unfit and seconded as a
bookkeeper at the Weimar police station. With many of his friends
in prison, in hiding or living withdrawn from political activity, Kurt
could have chosen to give up the fight against Nazism to save himself
and his family. But he didn't.

Keen to effect change in whatever small way he could, he talked to his colleagues at the police station. Perhaps he could sow seeds of doubt in their minds. A court later judged that 'from the very start of the war, he didn't share the enthusiasm of his comrades'. Kurt explained to his colleagues that the Soviet Union, the US and Britain had a numerical advantage. The Wehrmacht simply couldn't destroy houses and people at the rate at which the enemy was able to replenish them. When he visited relatives in western Germany during a holiday in 1942, he returned with stories of bombed cities like Cologne and Mainz and told his colleagues that the public mood there had reached 'boiling point'. They mustn't believe the propaganda in the newspapers, he insisted. The war was going badly, and the German public would soon rise in protest. When challenged, he replied defiantly that, unlike many of his fellow social democrats, he was proud not to have denied his convictions.[5]

When a colleague growled that 'people like Nehrling should be hanged', Kurt knew he was in trouble. He hastily applied to be moved to a different office, but it was too late. The next day, one of his closest co-workers wrote an itemized denunciation of all the things he had said and gave it to the Gestapo. Kurt was suspended from his job on 1 December 1942. He expected to be sentenced to one, perhaps two years in prison. Worst-case scenario, he might end up in a concentration camp, which may well have been akin to a death sentence given his weak lungs. But these things had happened to plenty of his comrades, and most had come out the other end. Kurt, Heddy and their children were bracing themselves for these scenarios. They had done so for years in an attempt to normalize the horror that might one day tear their family apart.

What they hadn't been able to anticipate was the timing of Kurt's arrest. He was taken into custody on 16 February 1943, just after the defeat of the Wehrmacht at the Battle of Stalingrad. This costly military loss shattered the myth of German invincibility. It broke morale and raised the spectre of rebellion. Kurt had been denounced at the worst possible moment. The Nazis would make an example of him. The SS judge who tried him admitted freely that he should have taken into account that 'the accused has no prior convictions, and there is also no other evidence to prove that he has acted in a treasonous way'. But that didn't matter now. 'The fateful struggle of the German people demands of the entire people that they summon all their strength.' Since Kurt had 'diminished the achievements and attitudes of his own people', he had 'forsaken his life'.[6] Kurt Nehrling was sentenced to death. On the morning of 22 December 1943, he was told that he was to be executed that afternoon at the Dachau concentration camp. He wrote one last letter to his wife.

My Dear Heddy,

Merry Christmas! I was picked up from Stadelheim prison this morning a[nd] I was just told that my death sentence will be executed at 2 o'clock this afternoon.

You know I'm not a traitor, and I have not had one moment yet when I felt that I have been guilty of anything . . .

I ask you not to despair and not to lose courage even when I'm no longer with you. I'm not worried about Ursula; she is 21 years old a[nd] will marry soon after all. I'm only worried about Heinz's future. I doubt that you can make it happen to get Heinz his place at university as intended. If you can't make it possible for Heinz to go to university, then make sure he learns a decent trade. Maybe he could become a dental technician or a dentist . . .

As for the shop, you have a completely free hand. If you think it necessary, feel free to give up the shop, but it seems best to me if you don't give it up.

Please give my regards to everyone I know. In this hour, I think of every one of them. A[nd] if one of them would like something to remember me by, let them take one book from my bookcase.

It brought me joy that you a[nd] Ursula visited me one last time eight days ago today, a[nd] it brings me solace that you have all been well so far.

*In my thoughts, I kiss you one more time. Please send my love to
my parents a[nd] tell them I didn't deserve this.*

*I will die thinking of you a[nd] in the knowledge to have had the
best intentions.*

Your Kurt[7]

Rosa Schmidt had managed to hide her Jewish background for years,
but this was proving increasingly difficult. The regime cracked down
on people it considered racial enemies harder the longer the war
dragged on. What had started with antisemitic boycotts in 1933 led to
extermination camps such as Auschwitz, where the first mass transport of Jews arrived in early 1942. That same year, Rosa's daughter
Alexandra had needed to apply for an 'Aryan certificate' from Karl
Astel's Thuringian State Office for Race Questions. On 18 June 1942,
she received a full report. She was classified as 'Jewish mixed-race
with two racial full Jews as grandparents'.[8]

The document brought misery and death to the Schmidts.
Alexandra's non-Jewish husband Artur, who refused to divorce
her, was summoned to a forced labour camp in 1944 that left him
physically and mentally broken for the rest of his life. Alexandra, who had small children to look after, was also forced to work
together with other 'mixed-race' people at Weimar cemetery. Her
brother Horst managed to escape from his forced labour camp and
went into hiding in Berlin. Ernst, who had been born on the eve of
the First World War, was suspended from his job as a Wehrmacht
pilot. He married his non-Jewish fiancée in secret and went underground until the end of the war. Even the eldest Schmidt child,
Arthur, who had emigrated to America before the Nazis came to
power, fell into the regime's hands. Fighting as a soldier in the US
Army, he was captured in December 1944 and incarcerated at Stalag
IX-B prisoner-of-war camp, not so far from his old home town of
Weimar.[9]

The worst fate hit Rosa and Arthur Schmidt. Nazi antisemitism
took no heed of the fact that Weimar's Jewish community had been

small and highly assimilated. At the beginning of 1945, there were only three Jewish residents left. Given the constant threat of deportation, the Schmidt couple did everything possible to maintain a low profile. Arthur handed the Hotel Hohenzollern over to the Wehrmacht for soldiers' accommodation in April 1943, keeping only the Beer Tunnel as a means of income.[10] In October, he submitted a list of household members that neither mentioned Rosa's Jewish background nor added the mandatory name 'Sara' to her name. But the Gestapo, keen to track down every single remaining Jew, soon found the paper trail leading to Rosa. In June 1944, Waldemar Eißfeld, director of the 'Department for Jews', summoned Arthur to the Gestapo headquarters in the infamous Marstall building. He was given a fine of 150 marks for not reporting that his wife was Jewish.[11]

That wasn't the end of the matter. Soon, Rosa herself was ordered to the Gestapo offices for questioning by Eißfeld, who was notorious for his cruel interrogations. She was sent home again. Then, in September, the Gestapo appeared at her door. Rosa was taken to the train station in the clothes she was wearing, with no time to pack or tell anyone where she was going. A woman spotted her waiting in front of the station. Understanding that this could mean only one thing, she ran to find Arthur to warn him that his wife was being deported imminently. Arthur hurried to the station to save Rosa or at least say goodbye, but when he got there the train had already departed.[12]

Two months later, a Gestapo officer informed Arthur that Rosa had died at Auschwitz on 28 November 1944. Arthur was heartbroken. How had it come to this? He suspected that his wife hadn't died 'of gastroenteritis with weak heart' as claimed.[13] But he had no way of knowing that nearly a million Jews had been murdered at Auschwitz, nor that the camp operated large gas chambers and crematoria to conduct genocide on an industrial scale. He didn't know that Jews were robbed of their last personal belongings upon arrival, nor that even their bodies were plundered for labour, hair and gold teeth. How could he begin to imagine that, even in death, they had neither dignity nor individuality?

Desperate, he clung to the notion that, even in concentration camps, they surely adhered to some German values like order, discipline and honesty. He wrote a letter directly to the commandant of Auschwitz weeks before the camp was evacuated by the SS and then liberated by the Red Army.

Re: The deceased female prisoner in protective custody Ruchel Schmidt, Nr. 88794 – Block 13 A[14]

Herr Camp Commandant,

On the 4th of this month, I was told by a member of the Gestapo that my wife died from gastroenteritis with accompanying cardiac arrest.

I now request that you send me an official death certificate so that I can start the necessary procedures regarding the probate. As far as the personal effects of my wife are concerned, which she took to Auschwitz with her (especially wedding ring, coat etc.), I would appreciate it if I could gain possession of those soon, and I request politely to receive notification regarding what has been done so far.

And then I have another question. Would it be possible for me to receive the urn with the ashes of my late wife? This is of the greatest importance to me.[15]

Arthur received no coat and no wedding ring, only a formal death certificate. He would never learn that the ashes of his wife lay strewn or buried with those of hundreds of thousands of other victims on the grounds of Auschwitz, that her wedding ring and coat had been stolen from her, that there was nothing left of Rosa.

Arthur was a broken man. With his last strength, he arranged for mourning cards to be printed in Rosa's name and for a small symbolic funeral at Weimar cemetery. He died on 30 January 1945, three days after the liberation of Auschwitz. His daughter Alexandra placed a brief obituary in the local paper for her 'much-loved, caring father' who, 'after just a few weeks, followed his beloved wife into eternity'.[16]

Death did not relinquish its grip on Weimar. Even many of those who had most fervently supported Hitler weren't shielded from the storm they had helped unleash. Weimarers were furious when Gauleiter Fritz Sauckel was seen fleeing the town in April 1945 in an attempt to escape justice for the crimes he had committed. But he was soon arrested by American troops and was among the twenty-four major war criminals accused in the Nuremberg trials. From 1942, he had been General Plenipotentiary for Labour Deployment, organizing the ruthless mobilization of forced labour. Found guilty of war crimes and crimes against humanity, he was executed by hanging in October 1946.

Hermann Göring would have suffered the same fate, having been found guilty on all four counts: conspiracy to commit crimes against peace; crimes against peace; war crimes; and crimes against humanity. He was also sentenced to death by hanging, but took his own life by poisoning himself with cyanide the night before his scheduled execution. Emmy Göring was arrested and classified as an active Nazi, for which she received a one-year prison sentence, and 30 per cent of her property was confiscated. She was never able to reconcile herself with the idea that her husband had done terrible things for Nazism and his own and her benefit. In prison, she got into trouble for repeatedly displaying a picture of him. Later, she would write an autobiography entitled My Life with Goering. Her daughter Edda was only eight years old when her father died. His long shadow would hang over her life forever. Like her mother, she found it impossible to remember him as a corrupt Nazi and war criminal.

Carl Weirich was forced to face the terrible reality of Nazi crimes first hand. Following his harrowing first visit to Buchenwald concentration camp together with the acting mayor and 1,000 fellow Weimarers on 16 April, he was ordered to help clear up the camp as part of a work detail. American commanders had demanded that civilians be brought up from Weimar to Buchenwald every day. On 28 April, it was Carl's turn. He was tasked with clearing out the camp's sewage plant. Clinton C. Gardner, who had been put in charge of Buchenwald, wrote home to his parents in the United States: 'My first job was the cleaning of the camp, removal of all rubbish, burial of all bodies. To accomplish this I requested and got 500 citizens of Weimar every day for several weeks. Not only did this give the people a nice tour of the camp but afforded them opportunity to bale out latrines. In one big latrine they had to bale out considerable muck before they could remove a body that had been dumped there.'[17]

Remaining former political prisoners taunted the townspeople as they worked. One jeered: 'Weimar, town of poets and hangmen'. As Carl laboured among the filth and human remains left behind by the SS, an organization he had once supported, he was gripped by 'revulsion and shame over our German fall!'[18] In the evening, he walked the 8 kilometres home from the camp deeply dejected. It wasn't just the moral decay of his country that weighed on his mind. He was returning to a place that had once regarded itself as the epitome of German civility and high culture. Now, what he could see from the slopes of the Ettersberg was a broken town. Burned-out houses stood like skeletons among their collapsed neighbours. There was 'no light, no water, no gas'.[19]

Carl had to hurry home by 7 p.m., as the Americans had imposed a strict night-time curfew. Nonetheless, former Buchenwald inmates roamed the streets, many still wearing their striped uniforms. Some were bent on revenge on the German population. Others were after food, alcohol, weapons or clothing. In the Geleitstraße, Carl's neighbour, the old weapon-maker Seelig, had been beaten to death because he'd had a few rifles in his shop for repairs. This frightened Carl to the core. If an old man could be murdered in his house for something as trivial as this, what did this mean for Wilhelm, who had been in full uniform and barracked when the Americans arrived? 'What will become of our son?' he anxiously asked his diary.[20]

Wilhelm had been arrested and taken to the Weimar stadium. He was now a prisoner of war. Under the watchful gaze of their American captors, he and the other captives slept on the ground, out in the open. The Weirichs took a blanket and some food for their teenage son, but they weren't allowed to pass anything inside. Then, they lost sight of him. With the complete breakdown of infrastructure, there was no way to communicate with anybody. When Carl walked down from the Ettersberg, Wilhelm had been gone for nearly three weeks, and he had no idea whether he was dead or alive. Two days later, Hitler killed himself in his bunker in Berlin. On 8 May, Germany officially surrendered, marking the end of the war in Europe. Carl didn't feel like celebrating.

There was much joy, however, when Wilhelm suddenly appeared on 28 May. He looked dreadful, gaunt and filthy, like an old man rather than the teenager he was. But he was alive. He'd crawled through the barbed wire of the Rheinwiesenlager camp, built by the US Army to hold German prisoners of war. Conditions there had been atrocious. Wilhelm was in a camp intended for 45,000 people, which ultimately held more than twice that number, including 1,000 women. People died in their droves, sleeping on the ground while starving and lacking toilet and washing facilities. The camp quickly became known as the 'Field of Mourning' or, as Carl called it, the 'Hunger Camp'.[21]

Wilhelm may well have died there if he hadn't managed to escape. When his nineteenth birthday arrived on 24 June, he and his parents celebrated it as though he had been born anew. 'Our Wilhelm is H o m e,' Carl wrote.[22] They put bunting up in an elevated alcove of their bombed-out house, whose broken walls now afforded splendid views into the courtyard. Wilhelm's makeshift birthday venue was christened 'The Field View', and friends gathered for a get-together to celebrate the return of the birthday boy. Carl burst with joy when his son announced that he would like to train as a bookbinder with the famous Otto Dorfner, who had once taught at the Bauhaus but was most recently included on Goebbels' list of 'God-gifted' artists. Dorfner was a star bookbinder, renowned well beyond Weimar, and now Wilhelm was going to study under him to follow in his father's footsteps one day.

Everything changed when Thuringia was handed over to the Red Army. The Allies had long agreed for the state to become part of the Soviet Zone of Occupation. Now, three Russian officers were billeted in the Weirichs' house, and Carl's work details were soon supervised by Red Army troops rather than American ones.

The Soviets were keen to denazify thoroughly, and they also feared resistance, especially from young men and teenage boys. Waves of arrests followed. Anyone who had been a Nazi Party member or part of any other Nazi organization, was seen in uniform or was suspected of having supported the regime in any way could be apprehended at any moment. Terror spread through Weimar once again. Carl knew a teacher who took his own life together with those of his entire family, a wife and four children. Carl himself kept his brief stint as a Patron Member of the SS a secret. Wilhelm tried to keep a low profile. But it didn't take long before the Soviet occupiers found out that he had been a soldier.

On 9 August 1946, Carl left his house in the morning to cycle into the countryside in the hope of procuring food. When he returned, Marie told him that a man had appeared at their door during the day to ask about Wilhelm. She had told him where their son worked, and he'd left. Carl's heart sank. At 10 p.m., his worst fears were confirmed. Wilhelm had been arrested. Two uniformed Russians appeared at the Weirich home and searched the whole house for incriminating evidence. They also took coats, blankets and bed sheets. Carl had to sign a document. What was happening to Wilhelm? Where was he? Could they bring him some food? The Russians told them nothing. Desperate and helpless, Carl wrote in his diary: 'As parents, we can't understand how they can lock up young people just like that without giving a reason.'[23] He sought solace in his faith. 'God never sends us more than we can bear,' he told himself. It became increasingly difficult to believe.

There was no miraculous return this time. Wilhelm had been taken to the Marstall. Like so many others who had been held there without trial over the previous thirteen years, he disappeared. He was transported to the former Nazi concentration camp of Sachsenhausen, where the Soviet occupying forces had set up a special camp for those deemed enemies of the people. Wilhelm was twenty years old when he died there in the spring of 1947. For the second time in his life, Carl lost his only child in the aftermath of war.

Conclusion

Berlin is not Weimar

In January 1971, Carl Weirich felt a sudden pang of sorrow. Anniversaries often had this effect on him. Exactly a century earlier, the German state had been founded. He was born in 1885 when the German Empire was just fourteen years old. Otto von Bismarck was still Chancellor then before he was dismissed by Kaiser Wilhelm II. Carl still lived in the same house, now in socialist East Germany, into which he had moved when Wilhelm II was Emperor. An old man now, he recalled 'happy childhood memories', growing up in the infant nation state.[1] History seemed to promise progress then. Germany was a newly unified country with a growing economy. A great future seemed to lie ahead. Carl travelled Germany and Europe with a light heart and a head full of plans. He would master the trade of bookbinding and set up his own business, maybe marry his girlfriend Friedel.

Carl's mood darkened as his thoughts turned to all the things that had happened since then. 'Oh, how one decade after the next tore us from the dream of a unified Europe!' he lamented.[2] There had been the First World War and the terrible humanitarian catastrophe that came with it. Then, 'for the second time in our lives, war befell Germany, drawing in our neighbours just as it did us. The megalomania of the Hitler Party with their Buchenwald concentration camp and finally with their attack on Russia embroiled us all and made us victims of the terrible destruction that such a war was bound to wreak.'[3]

Carl was now eighty-five and had nobody to pass anything on to. Each war had robbed him of a child. So he had managed his stationery shop himself until he gave it up in 1965 after more than fifty years. He'd taken it over when Germany was a monarchy, had steered it through the instability of the post-war republic, then through Nazism, war and East German socialism. It was with a heavy heart that he dissolved it and watched a florist move in, but he was looking forward to retirement as a fit and healthy eighty-year-old who still had a lot of walking and travelling to do. As a pensioner, he found it easier to get permission to leave East Germany, and he was eager to see Paris once more. But then his wife Marie had died suddenly in 1965, leaving him alone and heartbroken. Carl still undertook his 'Western Journey' in 1966, and, as ever, he found much solace in walking and nature. Yet anniversaries of all kinds tended to catch him off guard. They had a habit of tearing open half-healed wounds, suggesting continuity where there were deep fractures. His only son's birthdays were particularly painful each year. 'Our Wilhelm was born 50 years ago † 1947,' he noted in his diary on 24 June 1976.[4]

Where had it all gone wrong? Like most people, Carl viewed history as something that happens to people, big waves of events and developments that individuals can't control or break. The best a person can do is navigate the tides in an effort not to drown. Could he have done anything to change his family's fate? Carl accepted that Germans had collectively brought about terrible things. He visited Buchenwald a number of times after it had first been used by the Soviet occupiers as an internment camp, much like the one his son Wilhelm had died in, and then been transformed into a National Memorial of East Germany. He grumbled about the fact that the Soviets took much higher reparations out of East Germany than the Western Allies did from West Germany, but, overall, he accepted German guilt and responsibility.

What never occurred to him, however, even after seeing the horrors at Buchenwald in 1945, was the question of his personal responsibility for the Nazi dictatorship, its concentration camps, the war or the Holocaust. Carl had, after all, cheered Hitler's ascent to the chancellorship along with millions of his compatriots. He had briefly been a Patron Member of the SS. He had taken advantage of Nazi programmes to go on holidays and had embraced new Nazi rituals and traditions like Mother's Day. He had watched Wilhelm draw swastikas in his school books and wear the uniform of the Hitler Youth. He had watched him be drafted into the Nazi Wehrmacht and kissed him goodbye as he went to fight in a genocidal war. Carl had accepted these things as set in stone at the time, and he continued to do so to the very end of his life.

Could he have saved his son's life somehow? That was the only question Carl pondered from time to time, the private sphere being the only area where he felt he had any agency. 'We should have dared look the danger in the eye more ruthlessly back then,' Carl mused with hindsight, the danger he spoke of being entirely that to his own family. 'Perhaps,' he continued, 'we should have left Weimar [before the war] for southern Germany.' Nuremberg, where his wife Marie was from, had ended up in the American Zone of Occupation. Carl thought perhaps Wilhelm might not have been arrested and incarcerated until he died of the terrible conditions in the Soviet special camp in Sachsenhausen. 'Perhaps we may have saved the life of our only child,' he wondered sadly. But no. How could he have known? 'Man proposes, God disposes,' he mused.[5] Carl believed he never stood a chance to change the path of history, not even his own, never mind that of his country. He took this conviction to his grave when he died in 1978 at the age of ninety-two.

The American occupiers had hoped to teach Carl a different lesson when they confronted him with Buchenwald in 1945. They believed all German civilians bore some responsibility for what had taken place there, implying that Carl, too, could and should have done something to prevent Nazi atrocities. Much of history education is based on the same premise. After all, what would be the point in teaching young people about the rise of Nazism in Germany if we didn't believe that this knowledge would enable them to make better choices than Germans had in the 1920s and 1930s? In history education, we hope to have found an effective means to prevent a repeat of such terrible crimes and human suffering.

In German 'memory culture' (*Erinnerungskultur*), especially, Weimar remains an important and evocative name. The thinking behind founding the republic after the First World War in Weimar was that Weimar was not Berlin. The shift in location was intended to mark a break from the Prussia-Germany of 1871, whose militarism was seen as a cause of war. Germany has now reversed this pledge. The current-day, reunified Germany is often defiantly referred to as the 'Berlin Republic' to mark it out as different from the 'Weimar Republic'.

Today, much of Germany is concerned about the rise of new right- and left-wing parties, parliamentary fragmentation and widespread disaffection with mainstream politics. As political, economic and social instability looms, the spectre of 'Weimar' is haunting Germany once more. 'Berlin isn't Weimar' is a defiant slogan used with increasing frequency by journalists and politicians. It's the post-reunification edition of 'Bonn isn't Weimar', a phrase that was used in West Germany after the war when a new republic had been founded in a new capital. Weimar was once supposed to denote high culture and positive German traditions. Now, it seems, it carries frightening notions of the sudden death of democracy and civility. The Weimar Republic is the most stark and terrifying example of a collapsed democracy in Western history. The name of the town where it was founded is intrinsically linked to this history.

Weimar today strives to do justice to its complex legacy. Most tourists still come for the same reasons they have always done. They come for Goethe, Schiller and the many other famous names associated with the town. However, book a town tour and you will also be told about Hitler's suite in the Hotel Elephant, which is now called the Lyonel-Feininger-Suite, after the first faculty appointment at the Bauhaus school in 1919. Weimar's theatre has been rebuilt and is still called the German National Theatre. A replica of the Bauhaus-designed plaque commemorating the founding of the Weimar Republic, which the SA had removed in 1933, has been reinstated on its walls. Opposite the theatre is a museum and education centre about the Weimar Republic. Buchenwald remains a memorial and museum. Today, a footpath leads from Ettersburg Castle to the former concentration camp, reminding visitors of the close proximity of high culture and barbarity.

Weimar itself continues to bear the scars of all the contradictions of the interwar period, no matter how much they appear to have blended in with a modern townscape. Hitler's Gau Forum is today mostly used as office space by the Thuringian State Administration. The 'Hall of the People's Community' is a shopping centre. An exhibition on forced labour is housed in a small wing by the bell tower of the complex. The Villa Sauckel, which the Gauleiter had built for himself, is a training centre for Germany's Federal Employment Agency. Sauckel's plans were never fully implemented, but Nazism has left its permanent mark. The street layout was forever altered. Only a few remaining bits of track and cable fixtures on house walls remind visitors that Weimar had a tram system before it was abolished in 1937. The large viaduct on the way into town, which had to make way for the Adolf Hitler Square, is gone forever, as is the iconic Vimaria Fountain.

Many of the people featured in this book have also left physical traces in Weimar. Step out of the train station today, and to your left you can still see the tall white building that once housed the Hotel Hohenzollern. It is no longer a hotel. Only a small 'Stolperstein' brass plate, set into the pavement in front, tells you that Rosa Schmidt once lived there and that she was murdered at Auschwitz. Resistance fighter Kurt Nehrling has a street named after him where he once lived with Heddy and their children. Elisabeth Förster-Nietzsche's Villa Silberblick still sits on its hill south-west of the old town, containing an exhibition about both her and her brother. The half-finished, Nazi-built extension was empty during my last visit, but a foundation has now bought it and wants to put it to use. Goethe scholar Jutta Hecker died where she was born, in Weimar. Her gravestone sits beside that of her father on the family plot in Weimar cemetery.

As for Carl, he left his traces too, albeit in a less visible way. His meticulously kept diary and the loving baby book he continued

417

throughout the short life of his son Wilhelm are invaluable records for any historian studying the period. By sheer coincidence, they were being acquired by the Weimar Town Archive just as I was beginning my research for this book in Weimar. Carl's memory is also still alive in Weimar. As I pieced together his life story in the archive, I frequently found myself just around the corner from there, in front of his former home in Geleitstraße 10. It contains a different shop today, but the layout of the house and the street remains the same. One day in 2024, as I stood in the cobbled street looking into the shop to see if the iron staircase was still at the back, leading to the apartments above, two elderly women approached me and asked me what I was looking for. I explained that I was studying the life of the former owner of the shop, and their eyes lit up. 'Herr Weirich?' one of them said. 'He was the kindest man. I used to buy my school books and pens from him. He was very old.' I spoke with the two a bit more about Carl, the street and life in Weimar, and found myself oddly touched by this human bridge to my subject of study.

Such encounters were a powerful reminder that what we are studying as historians is the behaviour of fellow humans in the past, real people who acted the way they did for specific reasons and in the circumstances they found themselves in. They are shaped by historical events and in turn shape them with their responses. If we are to learn anything from history, we must allow that fact to sink in. The Nazis couldn't take away people's free will, regardless of their exceptionally effective means of propaganda and repression. Carl chose to quit his patron membership of the SS after just a few months and eventually stopped attending major events. But he didn't leave the country or join a resistance group. He reported for duty in the Nazis' 'Volkssturm' militia when ordered to, just as he did for the Americans shortly after when they forced him to help clear up Buchenwald. Like many people of his generation in Weimar, he lived through monarchy, democracy, Nazism and socialism, in each case trying to look after his family, his business and himself as best he could. Asking why he chose to act the way he did in each instance is not the same as justifying his choices. It's a way of understanding why ordinary Germans like him found it possible to go hiking and sledging a stone's throw from a concentration camp and sleep soundly in their beds at night. It is always easier to condemn than it is to explain, but in the latter lies the key to understanding history and ultimately to drawing meaningful conclusions from it.

Weimar, with all its inherent contradictions, with all the hopes and fears of a nation stamped on to its houses and streets, acted as a crucible of German history between the two world wars. It was here that both good and evil ideas were forged, tried and tested. The people of Weimar were observers, participants, perpetrators, bystanders and victims of events that shaped Germany, Europe and the world. Studying their behaviour both as individuals and as members of society can get us closer to understanding how Nazism took hold and how it was able to spread its pernicious influence far beyond its fanatical core. It is in these dynamics that we may find lessons to safeguard democracy and freedom in our own time.

Bibliography

All quotes from sources originally in the German language were translated by the author.

PRIMARY SOURCES

Carl Weirich's Diary. Stadtarchiv Weimar. 53 50/68 Bd1.

Death Mills. Orientation Film no. 19. Accessed at United States Holocaust Memorial Museum, courtesy of National Archives & Records Administration. In: https://collections.ushmm.org/search/catalog/irn1000182 (last accessed 27 June 2025)

Speech by German President Roman Herzog on 19 February 1999. In: https://www.bundespraesident.de/SharedDocs/Reden/DE/Roman-Herzog/Reden/1999/02/19990219_Weimar_Kulturhauptstadt.html (last accessed 30 June 2025)

Recollections of Hanns Wagner. In: Wagner, Martin. *Vier Generationen Buchdrucker Wagner in Weimar, 1879 bis 2009. Von Familienunternehmen zur Gutenberg GmbH*. Privately published, 2010, pp. 46–122.

Letter from Ludwig Sckell to his father Otto. Sent from Nouvion le Comte to Weimar on 30 June 1916. ThHStA Weimar, Familiennachlass Sckell, Nr. 225. In: Bechmann, Denis and Mestrup, Heinz (Eds). *Quellen zur Geschichte Thüringens. 'Wann wird das Morden ein Ende nehmen?' Feldpostbriefe und Tagebucheinträge zum Ersten Weltkrieg*. Landeszentrale für politische Bildung Thüringen, Erfurt, 2008, pp. 127–9.

Ration cards held by Stadtmuseum Weimar. In: Rößner, Alf (Ed.). *Demokratie aus Weimar. Die Nationalversammlung 1919. Ausstellung des Stadtmuseums Weimar zur Nationalversammlung*. Begleitheft, 2015, p. 25.

Down with the War! Announcement, 3 August 1914, Stadtmuseum Weimar.

Sophienstift, Oberlyzeum, zu Weimar. Festschrift zur Feier des 75 jahrigen Bestehens der Anstalt am 5.–7.Mai 1929. 1854–1929. Stadtarchiv Weimar. 89-1590.

Police Report, 4 September 1919. Stadtarchiv Weimar. II-10B-532.

Letter from Ludwig Sckell to his father Otto. Sent from Linselles to Weimar
on 21 June 1917. ThHStA Weimar, Familiennachlass Sckell, Nr. 225.
In: Bechmann, Denis and Mestrup, Heinz (Eds). *Quellen zur Geschichte
Thüringens. 'Wann wird das Morden ein Ende nehmen?' Feldpostbriefe und
Tagebucheinträge zum Ersten Weltkrieg.* Landeszentrale für politische
Bildung Thüringen, Erfurt, 2008, pp. 129–30.

Letter from Ludwig Sckell to his parents. Sent from Neuvilly to Weimar
on 6 June 1917. ThHStA Weimar, Familiennachlass Sckell, Nr. 225. In:
Bechmann, Denis and Mestrup, Heinz (Eds). *Quellen zur Geschichte
Thüringens. 'Wann wird das Morden ein Ende nehmen?' Feldpostbriefe und
Tagebucheinträge zum Ersten Weltkrieg.* Landeszentrale für politische Bildung
Thüringen, Erfurt, 2008, p. 270.

First Proclamation of the Weimar Soldiers' Council, 8/9 November
1918. In: John, Jürgen (Ed.). *Quellen zur Geschichte Thüringens. 1918–1945.*
Landeszentrale für politische Bildung Thüringen, Erfurt, 1996,
pp. 55–6.

Die Nationalversammlung in *Wort und Bild.* Sonderheft der *Berliner
Illustrierten Zeitung.* Thüringisches Hauptstaatsarchiv Weimar.
Stahlarmbrust-Schützengesellschaft Weimar. Archivalien-Signatur: 576.
Bestandssignatur: 6-96-1701, 1919.

Goethe zu der Armbrustgesellschaft. In: Thüringisches Hauptstaatsarchiv
Weimar, Stahlarmbrust-Schützengesellschaft Weimar. Archivalien-
Signatur: 356-46, 1925.

Letter of 1 May 1917. In: Thüringisches Hauptstaatsarchiv Weimar,
Stahlarmbrust-Schützengesellschaft Weimar 581-16, 1917.

Chronicle of the Crossbow Society. In: Thüringisches Hauptstaatsarchiv
Weimar, Stahlarmbrust-Schützengesellschaft Weimar 197-343, 1919.

Friedrich Ebert's opening speech of the National Assembly, 6 February 1919.
In: http://www.reichstagsprotokolle.de/Blatt2_wv_bsb00000010_00008.
html (last accessed 10 March 2024)

Harry Graf Kessler. *Die Tagebücher 1880–1937.* Literatur- und
Wissenschaftsverlag, Göttingen, 2020.

Ilse-Sibylle Stapff's recollections 1. In: Weimar. Die Geburtsstunde der
Demokratie und ihre Gegner, Focus Online, 19 January 2016. In:
https://www.focus.de/wissen/videos/1919-gruendung-der-ersten-republik-
weimar-die-geburtsstunde-der-demokratie-und-ihre-gegner_id_5220698.
html (last accessed 14 April 2024)

Ilse-Sibylle Stapff's recollections 2. In: Schulportal Thüringen. Zeitzeugen
erzählen: Die Weimarer Republik (1919–1933), 2011. In: https://www.
schulportal-thueringen.de/tip/resources/medien/14289?dateiname=

Zeitzeugen_WeimarerRepublik_Textauszuege.pdf (last accessed 14 April 2024)

Georges Clemenceau's speech and Ulrich Graf Brockdorff-Rantzau's response on 7 May 1919, Paris. In Weimarer Republik e.V., 'Clemenceau an Deutschland: "Die Stunde der Abrechnung ist da" '. In: https://www.weimarer-republik.net/jubilaeum/revolution-und-gruendung-der-republik-tag-fuer-tag/mai-1919/clemenceau-an-deutschland-die-stunde-der-abrechnung-ist-da/ (last accessed 19 April 2024)

Hohenzollern file. Stadtarchiv Weimar. Abtlg: II. Locat: 10B. Nr: 532.

Adreß-Buch der Landeshauptstadt Weimar. 1920–1922. Weimar, Putze & Hölzer. Stadtarchiv Weimar / Thulb. ZDB-ID 2687467-2.

Elisabeth Förster-Nietzsche's letter to Edvard Munch, 17 September 1921. In: Edvard Munchs Tekster. Digitalt Arkiv. MM K 2974, Munchmuseet. In: https://emunch.no/HYBRIDNo-MM_K2974.xhtml (last accessed 30 July 2024)

Programme of the 'Great German Culture Avowal' of the 'National Socialist Freedom Party' in Weimar, 17.8.1924. In: John, Jürgen (Ed.). *Quellen zur Geschichte Thüringens. 1918–1945.* Landeszentrale für politische Bildung Thüringen, Erfurt, 1996, pp. 120–21.

Great inquiry of the SPD faction in the Thuringian parliament about the behaviour of the Thuringian government regarding the Republican and Nazi-völkisch organizations, 22 August 1924. In: John, Jürgen (Ed.). *Quellen zur Geschichte Thüringens. 1918–1945.* Landeszentrale für politische Bildung Thüringen, Erfurt, 1996, pp. 123–5.

Harry Graf Kessler's Diary, 17 August 1924. In: John, Jürgen (Ed.). *Quellen zur Geschichte Thüringens. 1918–1945.* Landeszentrale für politische Bildung Thüringen, Erfurt, 1996, pp. 122–3.

Joseph Goebbels's Diary 1924–1945. In: Reuth, Ralf Georg (Ed.). *Tagebücher 1924–1945. Band 1. Einführung. 1924–1929.* Piper, Munich and Zurich, 2003.

Letter from Elisabeth Förster-Nietzsche to Harry Graf Kessler, 30 January 1925. In: Föhl, Thomas (Ed.). *Elisabeth Förster-Nietzsche und Harry Graf Kessler. Band 2: Der Briefwechsel 1895–1935.* Weimarer Verlagsgesellschaft, Weimar, 2013, pp. 1031–3.

Letter from Elisabeth Förster-Nietzsche to Harry Graf Kessler, 16 April 1925. In: Föhl, Thomas (Ed.). *Elisabeth Förster-Nietzsche und Harry Graf Kessler. Band 2: Der Briefwechsel 1895–1935.* Weimarer Verlagsgesellschaft, Weimar, 2013, pp. 1056–7.

Letter from Harry Graf Kessler to Elisabeth Förster-Nietzsche, 11 March 1926. In: Föhl, Thomas (Ed.). *Elisabeth Förster-Nietzsche und Harry Graf Kessler. Band 2: Der Briefwechsel 1895–1935.* Weimarer Verlagsgesellschaft, Weimar, 2013, pp. 1057–8.

Order of summary punishment, 10 June 1926. In: Hohenzollern file, Stadtarchiv Weimar. Abtlg: II. Locat: 10B. Nr: 532/75.

Unser Kinderbuch. Baby book recording Wilhelm Weirich's life. Stadtarchiv Weimar.

Letter from Elisabeth Förster-Nietzsche to Harry Graf Kessler, 26 August 1926. In: Föhl, Thomas (Ed.). *Elisabeth Förster-Nietzsche und Harry Graf Kessler. Band 2: Der Briefwechsel 1895–1935*. Weimarer Verlagsgesellschaft, Weimar, 2013, pp. 1067–70.

Otto Daube: Weimar – Bayreuth. In: Neumann, Thomas (Ed.). *Quellen zur Geschichte Thüringens. Kultur in Thüringen 1919–1949*. Landeszentrale für politische Bildung Thüringen, Erfurt, 1998, pp. 114–17.

Note by the chief secretary of the town council of Weimar to the Assessment Commission of the Hospitality Association, 15 February 1927. In: Hohenzollern file, Stadtarchiv Weimar. Abtlg: II. Locat: 10B. Nr: 532/79.

Arthur Schmidt's letter to the town manager, 15 February 1927. In: Hohenzollern file, Stadtarchiv Weimar. Abtlg: II. Locat: 10B. Nr: 532/76.

Police assessment of Arthur Schmidt's request to extend his alcohol licence, 18 February 1927. In: Hohenzollern file, Stadtarchiv Weimar. Abtlg: II. Locat: 10B. Nr: 532/80.

Police assessment of Arthur Schmidt's request to extend his alcohol licence, 15 March 1927. In: Hohenzollern file, Stadtarchiv Weimar. Abtlg: II. Locat: 10B. Nr: 532/82.

Kurt Nehrling's application for a building grant, 1926–1927. In: Gewährung von Baudarlehen zum Wohnungsbau. Stadtarchiv Weimar. Abtlg: 7. Locat: 77. Nr. 91.

Letter from Elisabeth Förster-Nietzsche to Harry Graf Kessler, 9 September 1927. In: Föhl, Thomas (Ed.). *Elisabeth Förster-Nietzsche und Harry Graf Kessler. Band 2: Der Briefwechsel 1895–1935*. Weimarer Verlagsgesellschaft, Weimar, 2013, pp. 1092–4.

Letter from Harry Graf Kessler to Elisabeth Förster-Nietzsche, 12 October 1927. In: Föhl, Thomas (Ed.). *Elisabeth Förster-Nietzsche und Harry Graf Kessler. Band 2: Der Briefwechsel 1895–1935*. Weimarer Verlagsgesellschaft, Weimar, 2013, pp. 1098–9.

Letter from Elisabeth Förster-Nietzsche to Harry Graf Kessler, 12 April 1928. In: Föhl, Thomas (Ed.). *Elisabeth Förster-Nietzsche und Harry Graf Kessler. Band 2: Der Briefwechsel 1895–1935*. Weimarer Verlagsgesellschaft, Weimar, 2013, pp. 1119–20.

Nietzsche, Friedrich. *Fragmente von Frühjahr 1884 bis Herbst 1885*, Band 5, 26, [173]. In: Gutenberg Edition 16. 2. vermehrte und verbesserte Auflage.

https://www.projekt-gutenberg.org/nietzsch/fragmen5/chap002.html (last accessed 11 December 2024)

Letter from Harry Graf Kessler to Elisabeth Förster-Nietzsche, 13 April 1928. In: Föhl, Thomas (Ed.). *Elisabeth Förster-Nietzsche und Harry Graf Kessler. Band 2: Der Briefwechsel 1895–1935.* Weimarer Verlagsgesellschaft, Weimar, 2013, pp. 1121–3.

Appeal for the Kampfbund für deutsche Kultur, Munich, January 1929. In: Neumann, Thomas (Ed.). *Quellen zur Geschichte Thüringens. Kultur in Thüringen 1919–1949.* Landeszentrale für politische Bildung Thüringen, Erfurt, 1998, pp. 130–33.

Court File Hotel Hohenzollern. In: Akten des Thür. Amtsgerichts Weimar. Landesarchiv Thüringen, Hauptstaatsarchiv Weimar, Nr. 250.

Letter from Elisabeth Förster-Nietzsche to Harry Graf Kessler, 17 June 1929. In: Föhl, Thomas (Ed.). *Elisabeth Förster-Nietzsche und Harry Graf Kessler. Band 2: Der Briefwechsel 1895–1935.* Weimarer Verlagsgesellschaft, Weimar, 2013, p. 1138.

Letter from Harry Graf Kessler to Elisabeth Förster-Nietzsche, 15 June 1929. In: Föhl, Thomas (Ed.). *Elisabeth Förster-Nietzsche und Harry Graf Kessler. Band 2: Der Briefwechsel 1895–1935.* Weimarer Verlagsgesellschaft, Weimar, 2013, p. 1137.

Letter from Harry Graf Kessler to Elisabeth Förster-Nietzsche, 21 June 1929. In: Föhl, Thomas (Ed.). *Elisabeth Förster-Nietzsche und Harry Graf Kessler. Band 2: Der Briefwechsel 1895–1935.* Weimarer Verlagsgesellschaft, Weimar, 2013, pp. 1141–2.

Letter from Elisabeth Förster-Nietzsche to Harry Graf Kessler, 7 October 1929. In: Föhl, Thomas (Ed.). *Elisabeth Förster-Nietzsche und Harry Graf Kessler. Band 2: Der Briefwechsel 1895–1935.* Weimarer Verlagsgesellschaft, Weimar, 2013, p. 1145.

Letter from Elisabeth Förster-Nietzsche to Harry Graf Kessler, 14 March 1930. In: Föhl, Thomas (Ed.). *Elisabeth Förster-Nietzsche und Harry Graf Kessler. Band 2: Der Briefwechsel 1895–1935.* Weimarer Verlagsgesellschaft, Weimar, 2013, p. 1154.

Decree IV CII/771, Nr. 53 'Against the Negro Culture for German Folkdom' [April 1930]. In: Neumann, Thomas (Ed.). *Quellen zur Geschichte Thüringens. Kultur in Thüringen 1919–1949.* Landeszentrale für politische Bildung Thüringen, Erfurt, 1998, pp. 144–6.

Reinhard Buchwald: 'On Weimar Art and Scholarship' [1930]. In: Neumann, Thomas (Ed.). *Quellen zur Geschichte Thüringens. Kultur in Thüringen 1919–1949.* Landeszentrale für politische Bildung Thüringen, Erfurt, 1998, pp. 140–41.

Letter from Elisabeth Förster-Nietzsche to Harry Graf Kessler, 17 June 1930. In: Föhl, Thomas (Ed.). *Elisabeth Förster-Nietzsche und Harry Graf Kessler. Band 2: Der Briefwechsel 1895–1935.* Weimarer Verlagsgesellschaft, Weimar, 2013, pp. 1164–5.

Letter from Harry Graf Kessler to Elisabeth Förster-Nietzsche, 19 November 1930. In: Föhl, Thomas (Ed.). *Elisabeth Förster-Nietzsche und Harry Graf Kessler. Band 2: Der Briefwechsel 1895–1935.* Weimarer Verlagsgesellschaft, Weimar, 2013, p. 1170.

Letter from Harry Graf Kessler to Elisabeth Förster-Nietzsche, 27 December 1930. In: Föhl, Thomas (Ed.). *Elisabeth Förster-Nietzsche und Harry Graf Kessler. Band 2: Der Briefwechsel 1895–1935.* Weimarer Verlagsgesellschaft, Weimar, 2013, p. 1173.

Letter from Lisbeth Staupendahl to Elisabeth Förster-Nietzsche, 8 July 1930. In: GSA 72/BW 5263.

Harry Graf Kessler: 'Frick über Deutschland'. In: Neumann, Thomas (Ed.). *Quellen zur Geschichte Thüringens. Kultur in Thüringen 1919–1949.* Landeszentrale für politische Bildung Thüringen, Erfurt, 1998, pp. 149–50.

Statistisches Jahrbuch für das Deutsche Reich. In: Statistische Bibliothek, Statistische Ämter des Bundes und der Länder, 2019. In: https://www.statistischebibliothek.de/mir/receive/DESerie_mods_00007448 (last accessed 15 March 2025)

Letter from Elisabeth Förster-Nietzsche to Harry Graf Kessler, 30 July 1931. In: Föhl, Thomas (Ed.). *Elisabeth Förster-Nietzsche und Harry Graf Kessler. Band 2: Der Briefwechsel 1895–1935.* Weimarer Verlagsgesellschaft, Weimar, 2013, pp. 1187–8.

Speech by Werner Deetjen, 10 July 1931. In: Neumann, Thomas (Ed.). *Quellen zur Geschichte Thüringens. Kultur in Thüringen 1919–1949.* Landeszentrale für politische Bildung Thüringen, Erfurt, 1998, pp. 150–51.

Announcement of *Campo di Maggio* at the German National Theatre, 30 January 1932. In: Landesarchiv Thüringen, Hauptstaatsarchiv Weimar, Generalintendanz des Deutschen Nationaltheaters und der Staatskapelle Weimar, 1902 / 158. In: https://staatsarchive.thulb.uni-jena.de/receive/ThHStAW_archivesource_00012036 (last accessed 22 March 2025)

Völkischer Beobachter (Münchener Ausgabe), Nr. 201, 24/25 August 1930. In: Naake, Erhard. *Nietzsche und Weimar. Werk und Wirkung im 20. Jahrhundert.* Böhlau Verlag, Cologne, Weimar, Vienna, 2000, p. 210.

Paul von Hindenburg's 'Appeal! German People's Donation for Goethe's Place of Birth', 22 March 1931. In: Stadtarchiv Weimar. Goethefeier 1932. 12 4-43-6.

Letter from Harry Graf Kessler to Elisabeth Förster-Nietzsche, 2 November 1932. In: Föhl, Thomas (Ed.). *Elisabeth Förster-Nietzsche und Harry Graf Kessler. Band 2: Der Briefwechsel 1895–1935.* Weimarer Verlagsgesellschaft, Weimar, 2013, p. 1208.

Ban on the membership of civil servants and public sector workers of the Social Democratic Party, 18 March 1933. In: John, Jürgen (Ed.). *Quellen zur Geschichte Thüringens. 1918–1945.* Landeszentrale für politische Bildung Thüringen, Erfurt, 1996, pp. 157–8.

The Union of Thuringian Towns grants Adolf Hitler and Dr Wilhelm Frick Honorary Citizenship. In: Stadtarchiv Weimar. 107-04/9.

Antisemites' Petition (1880–1881). In: German Historical Institute, German History in Documents and Images (GHDI), https://ghdi.ghi-dc.org/sub_document.cfm?document_id=1801 (last accessed 4 April 2025)

Fritz Sauckel's Nuremberg Notes. In: Lehnstaedt, Stephan and Lehnstaedt, Kurt. 'Fritz Sauckels Nürnberger Aufzeichnungen. Erinnerungen aus seiner Haft während des Kriegsverbrecherprozesses'. In: *Vierteljahrshefte für Zeitgeschichte.* Institut für Zeitgeschichte München-Berlin. Jahrgang 57, Heft 1, 2009, pp. 130–50.

Carl Weirich's Stasi File. In: Landesarchiv Thüringen, Hauptstaatsarchiv Weimar, NS-Archiv des Ministeriums für Staatssicherheit, Objekt 9 ZA 533.

Overburdened Gestapo – Decree of the 'struggle against denunciations' in Thuringia, 26 May 1934. In: Gräfe, Marlis, Post, Bernhard and Schneider, Andreas (Eds). *Quellen zur Geschichte Thüringens. Die Geheime Staatspolizei im NS-Gau Thüringen 1933–1945.* Landeszentrale für politische Bildung Thüringen, Erfurt, 2009, p. 88.

Reports from participants of the current Schillerbund Festival [1934]. In: Neumann, Thomas (Ed.). *Quellen zur Geschichte Thüringens. Kultur in Thüringen 1919–1949.* Landeszentrale für politische Bildung Thüringen, Erfurt, 1998, pp. 179–84.

Extract from Karl Astel's Inaugural Lecture at the University of Jena. In: John, Jürgen. *Quellen zur Geschichte Thüringens. 1918–1945.* Landeszentrale für politische Bildung Thüringen, Erfurt, 1996, pp. 179–80.

Essay samples and lesson plans for comprehensive schools, 1934–1936. In: John, Jürgen (Ed.). *Quellen zur Geschichte Thüringens. 1918–1945.* Landeszentrale für politische Bildung Thüringen, Erfurt, 1996, pp. 172–5.

The political joke in the secret situation report of the Gestapo for the municipal area of Erfurt, 12 July 1935. In: Gräfe, Marlis, Post, Bernhard and Schneider, Andreas (Eds). *Quellen zur Geschichte Thüringens. Die Geheime Staatspolizei im NS-Gau Thüringen 1933–1945.* Landeszentrale für politische Bildung Thüringen, Erfurt, 2009, p. 144.

Warrant for Protective Custody by Gestapo Weimar for Utterances against the Reichsstatthalter Fritz Sauckel. In: Gräfe, Marlis, Post, Bernhard and Schneider, Andreas (Eds). *Quellen zur Geschichte Thüringens. Die Geheime Staatspolizei im NS-Gau Thüringen 1933–1945.* Landeszentrale für politische Bildung Thüringen, Erfurt, 2009, pp. 161–2.

Julius Petersen's speech for the festivities of the 50th anniversary of the Goethe Society on 27 August 1935. In: Neumann, Thomas (Ed.). *Quellen zur Geschichte Thüringens. Kultur in Thüringen 1919–1949.* Landeszentrale für politische Bildung Thüringen, Erfurt, 1998, pp. 191–5.

Petition of the Gau Business Association Thuringia to the Mayor of Weimar, 16 November 1935. In: Gibas, Monika (Ed.). *Quellen zur Geschichte Thüringens. 'Arisierung in Thüringen': Entrechtung, Enteignung und Vernichtung der jüdischen Bürger Thüringens 1933–1945.* Landeszentrale für politische Bildung Thüringen, Erfurt, 2006, pp. 150–51.

Letter from Elisabeth Förster-Nietzsche to Harry Graf Kessler, 10 September 1935. In: Föhl, Thomas (Ed.). *Elisabeth Förster-Nietzsche und Harry Graf Kessler. Band 2: Der Briefwechsel 1895–1935.* Weimarer Verlagsgesellschaft, Weimar, 2013, pp. 1212–18.

Telegram from Harry Graf Kessler to Max Oehler, 9 November 1935. In: Föhl, Thomas (Ed.). *Elisabeth Förster-Nietzsche und Harry Graf Kessler. Band 2: Der Briefwechsel 1895–1935.* Weimarer Verlagsgesellschaft, Weimar, 2013, p. 1223.

Extract from the memoirs of Richard Leutheußer. In: Naake, Erhard. *Nietzsche und Weimar. Werk und Wirkung im 20. Jahrhundert.* Böhlau Verlag, Cologne, Weimar, Vienna, 2000, pp. 214–16.

Letter from Theodor Eicke to Fritz Sauckel, 3 June 1936. In: John, Jürgen (Ed.). *Quellen zur Geschichte Thüringens. 1918–1945.* Landeszentrale für politische Bildung Thüringen, Erfurt, 1996, pp. 243–5.

Extract from the speech of the NSDAP Gauleiter Sauckel about the Wilhelm Gustloff Foundation, 27 October 1936. In: John, Jürgen (Ed.). *Quellen zur Geschichte Thüringens. 1918–1945.* Landeszentrale für politische Bildung Thüringen, Erfurt, 1996, pp. 182–5.

'Massive, natural water reserves in Thuringia' – Report of the NSDAP Gau newspaper, 23 October 1936. In: John, Jürgen (Ed.). *Quellen zur Geschichte Thüringens. 1918–1945.* Landeszentrale für politische Bildung Thüringen, Erfurt, 1996, pp. 168–9.

Letter from Weimar Mayor Walther Felix Mueller to the Gau Organization Office of the Nazi Party, 15 November 1935. Stadtarchiv Weimar. 100-06/9, 3.

Newspaper report, 29 April 1936. Stadtarchiv Weimar. 100-06/9, 4.

Gau newspaper report, 23 May 1936. Stadtarchiv Weimar. 100-06/9, 6.

Summary of costs for the 10-year anniversary of the first Reich Party Rally 1936. Stadtarchiv Weimar. 100-06/9, 27.

Gau newspaper report, 23 June 1936. Stadtarchiv Weimar. 100-06/9, 19.

Adolf Hitler's speech at the State Reception at Weimar Palace at 5 p.m. on 3 July 1936. In: Domarus, Max (Ed.). *The Complete Hitler. A Digital Desktop Reference to His Speeches and Proclamations 1932–1945.* Bolchazy-Carducci Publishers, Inc., 2007, pp. 627–8.

'German Festive Day under glowing May sun.' In Gau newspaper, 3 May 1937. In: Neumann, Thomas (Ed.). *Quellen zur Geschichte Thüringens. Kultur in Thüringen 1919–1949.* Landeszentrale für politische Bildung Thüringen, Erfurt, 1998, pp. 198–201.

'Professor Hecker as a Scholar'. In: Gau newspaper, 3 May 1937. In: Neumann, Thomas (Ed.). *Quellen zur Geschichte Thüringens. Kultur in Thüringen 1919–1949.* Landeszentrale für politische Bildung Thüringen, Erfurt, 1998, pp. 202–4.

Baldur von Schirach's Goethe Speech, 14 June 1937. In: Neumann, Thomas (Ed.). *Quellen zur Geschichte Thüringens. Kultur in Thüringen 1919–1949.* Landeszentrale für politische Bildung Thüringen, Erfurt, 1998, pp. 204–8.

Award of honorary citizenship to Baldur von Schirach. In: Stadtarchiv Weimar. 107-04/11.

Pictures taken by Criminal Police Weimar on 15 July 1937, Fotoarchiv Buchenwald, Archiv der Gedenkstätte Buchenwald. In: https://fotoarchiv.buchenwald.de/results?strategy=categories&provenance=2&place=176&dates=343 (last accessed 9 May 2025)

Letter from Theodor Eicke to Heinrich Himmler, 24 July 1937. In: John, Jürgen (Ed.). *Quellen zur Geschichte Thüringens. 1918–1945.* Landeszentrale für politische Bildung Thüringen, Erfurt, 1996, p. 245.

Newspaper 'Deutschland', 20 September 1937. In: Stadtarchiv Weimar. 100-06/14, 1.

Report of a likely budget deficit, 25 September 1937. Stadtarchiv Weimar. 100-06/14, 3.

Gau newspaper, 28 September 1937. Stadtarchiv Weimar. 100-06/14, 5.

Hinrich Holtz's petition to grant Emmy and Hermann Göring honorary citizenship, 27 April 1937. Stadtarchiv Weimar. 107-04/10.

Draft letter of Honorary Citizenship for Emmy Göring, 29 May 1937. Stadtarchiv Weimar. 107-04/10.

Telegram from Otto Koch to Hermann and Emmy Göring, 3 June 1938. Stadtarchiv Weimar. 107-04/10.

Extract from the Interrogation of Gestapo Officer Junge by the Criminal Office Weimar, 19 May 1945. In: Gräfe, Marlis, Post, Bernhard and

Schneider, Andreas (Eds). *Quellen zur Geschichte Thüringens. Die Geheime Staatspolizei im NS-Gau Thüringen 1933–1945*. Landeszentrale für politische Bildung Thüringen, Erfurt, 2009, pp. 173–4.

Report by the President of the Higher Regional Court in Jena to the Reich Minister for Justice about the Attitudes of the Population to Protective Custody, 2 March 1938. In: Gräfe, Marlis, Post, Bernhard and Schneider, Andreas (Eds). *Quellen zur Geschichte Thüringens. Die Geheime Staatspolizei im NS-Gau Thüringen 1933–1945*. Landeszentrale für politische Bildung Thüringen, Erfurt, 2009, p. 165.

Aryanization Questionnaire for the Buyers of the Department Store Sachs & Berlowitz. In: Gibas, Monika (Ed.). *Quellen zur Geschichte Thüringens. 'Arisierung in Thüringen': Entrechtung, Enteignung und Vernichtung der jüdischen Bürger Thüringens 1933–1945*. Landeszentrale für politische Bildung Thüringen, Erfurt, 2006, pp. 330–33.

Letter from the Reichsstatthalter in Thuringia to the Mayor of Weimar about the sale of a Jewish company. In: Gibas, Monika (Ed.). *Quellen zur Geschichte Thüringens. 'Arisierung in Thüringen': Entrechtung, Enteignung und Vernichtung der jüdischen Bürger Thüringens 1933–1945*. Landeszentrale für politische Bildung Thüringen, Erfurt, 2006, pp. 324–25.

Telegram from the Gestapo Office to all State Police Offices, 9 November 1938. In: Gräfe, Marlis, Post, Bernhard and Schneider, Andreas (Eds). *Quellen zur Geschichte Thüringens. Die Geheime Staatspolizei im NS-Gau Thüringen 1933–1945*. Landeszentrale für politische Bildung Thüringen, Erfurt, 2009, pp. 338–9.

Application from the Gestapo to the Thuringian Finance Ministry about the Installation of Further Prison Cells in the Basement of the State Police Office Weimar, 18 January 1939. In: Gräfe, Marlis, Post, Bernhard and Schneider, Andreas (Eds). *Quellen zur Geschichte Thüringens. Die Geheime Staatspolizei im NS-Gau Thüringen 1933–1945*. Landeszentrale für politische Bildung Thüringen, Erfurt, 2009, p. 176.

Plan for the Rental of a Coach House from the Grand Ducal Estate Management for Conversion into a Temporary Prison, 25 March 1939. In: Gräfe, Marlis, Post, Bernhard and Schneider, Andreas (Eds). *Quellen zur Geschichte Thüringens. Die Geheime Staatspolizei im NS-Gau Thüringen 1933–1945*. Landeszentrale für politische Bildung Thüringen, Erfurt, 2009, p. 177.

'Four cells of special construction'. In: Gräfe, Marlis, Post, Bernhard and Schneider, Andreas (Eds). *Quellen zur Geschichte Thüringens. Die Geheime Staatspolizei im NS-Gau Thüringen 1933–1945*. Landeszentrale für politische Bildung Thüringen, Erfurt, 2009, p. 178.

Excerpts from Hitler's Speech before the first 'Greater German Reichstag', 30 January 1939. In: *Rede des Führers und Reichskanzlers Adolf Hitler vor dem Reichstag am 30. Januar 1939*, M. Müller & Sohn, Berlin, pp. 5–63. Translated by Thomas Dunlap in: https://ghdi.ghi-dc.org/pdf/eng/English35.pdf (last accessed 22 May 2025)

Fritz Sauckel on 'The Old and the New Weimar', 24 August 1939. In: John, Jürgen (Ed.). *Quellen zur Geschichte Thüringens. 1918–1945*. Landeszentrale für politische Bildung Thüringen, Erfurt, 1996, pp. 203–4.

Field Judgment against Kurt Nehrling, 23 September 1943. In: Stein, Harry and Wohlfeld, Udo. *Sozialdemokraten gegen Hitler. Die Widerstandsgruppe Nehrling-Eberling in Weimar*. Eigenverlag Geschichtswerkstatt Weimar/Apolda e.V., Weimar, 2003, pp. 12–19.

Kurt Nehrling's farewell letter, 22 December 1943. In: Stein, Harry and Wohlfeld, Udo. *Sozialdemokraten gegen Hitler. Die Widerstandsgruppe Nehrling-Eberling in Weimar*. Eigenverlag Geschichtswerkstatt Weimar/Apolda e.V., Weimar, 2003, pp. 24–7.

Alexandra Greulich's report from the Thuringian State Office for Race Questions, 18 June 1942. In: Landesarchiv Thüringen, Hauptstaatsarchiv Weimar, Bezirkstag und Rat des Bezirkes Erfurt, VdN Nr. 884, 11.

Letter from Arthur Schmidt to Business Police, 6 May 1943. In: Hohenzollern file, Stadtarchiv Weimar. Abtlg: II. Locat: 10B. Nr: 532/94.

Rosa Schmidt's Death Certificate, 14 December 1944. In: Landesarchiv Thüringen, Hauptstaatsarchiv Weimar, Bezirkstag und Rat des Bezirkes Erfurt, VdN Nr. 885, 14.

Arthur Schmidt's Obituary, 2 February 1945. In: Hohenzollern file, Stadtarchiv Weimar. Abtlg: II. Locat: 10B. Nr: 532/95.

Letter from Clinton C. Gardner to his parents, 16 July 1945. Held by United States Holocaust Memorial Museum. Quoted from https://www.buchenwald.de/en/geschichte/themen/dossiers/buchenwald1945/im-befreiten-lager-arbeiten (last accessed 3 June 2025)

NEWSPAPERS

Allgemeine Thüringische Landeszeitung
Der Nationalsozialist
Evangelisches Gemeindeblatt für Weimar
Jenaer Volksblatt
Thüringer Tageszeitung für deutsche Art und Arbeit in Stadt und Land (previously *Weimarische Zeitung*)
The New York Times

Völkischer Beobachter
Weimarische Volkszeitung
Weimarische Landeszeitung
Weimarische Zeitung

ARTICLES

Ackermann, Ute. '"Es ist ein Jammer, daß man nun wieder kämpfen muss, anstatt zu arbeiten." Die Vertreibung des Bauhauses aus Weimar 1925'. In: Blümm, Anke, Otto, Elizabeth and Rössler, Patrick (Eds). *Bauhaus und Nationalsozialismus*. Katalog zur Ausstellung im Museum Neues Weimar, Bauhaus-Museum Weimar und Schiller-Museum. Klassik Stiftung Weimar, Hirmer, 2024, pp. 28–31.

Adler, Bruno. 'Damals in Weimar . . .' In: Droste, Magdalena and Friedewald, Boris (Eds). *Unser Bauhaus. Bauhäusler und Freunde erinnern sich*. Prestel, Munich, London, New York, 2019, pp. 11–15.

Barth, Tobias. 'Vor 100 Jahren: Die "Schicksalswahl" in Thüringen 1924'. In: MDR Thüringen, 10 February 2024. In: https://www.mdr.de/ nachrichten/thueringen/schicksalswahl-nsdap-hitler-weimarer-republik-demokratie-100.html (last accessed 31 August 2024)

Blümm, Anke and Rössler, Patrick. 'Bauhaus und Nationalsozialismus. Eine statistische Annäherung'. In: Blümm, Anke, Otto, Elizabeth and Rössler, Patrick (Eds). *Bauhaus und Nationalsozialismus*. Katalog zur Ausstellung im Museum Neues Weimar, Bauhaus-Museum Weimar und Schiller-Museum. Klassik Stiftung Weimar, Hirmer, 2024, pp. 72–7.

Dickmann, Fritz. 'Die Regierungsbildung in Thüringen als Modell der Machtergreifung. Ein Brief Hitlers aus dem Jahre 1930'. In: *Vierteljahrshefte für Zeitgeschichte*. Institut für Zeitgeschichte München-Berlin. Jahrgang 14, Heft 4, 1966, pp. 454–64.

Dietrich, Andrea and Dell, Claudia. 'Geschichte, Geschichten & Geschichtenerzähler'. In: Dell, Claudia (Ed.). *Das Hotel Elephant in Weimar. Haus der Geschichte, Geschichten und Geschichtenerzähler*. Hotel Elephant Weimar und Wartburg Verlag GmbH, Weimar, 2022, pp. 11–56.

Driesch-Foucar, Lydia. 'Erinnerungen an die Anfänge der Dorburger Töpferwerkstatt des Staatlichen Bauhauses Weimar 1920–1923'. In: Droste, Magdalena and Friedewald, Boris (Eds). *Unser Bauhaus. Bauhäusler und Freunde erinnern sich*. Prestel, Munich, London, New York, 2019, pp. 89–99.

Fischer, Jens-Uwe. 'Franz Ehrlich. Zwischen Widerstand und Kollaboration'. In: Blümm, Anke, Otto, Elizabeth and Rössler, Patrick (Eds). *Bauhaus und Nationalsozialismus*. Katalog zur Ausstellung im Museum Neues Weimar,

Bauhaus-Museum Weimar und Schiller-Museum. Klassik Stiftung Weimar, Hirmer, 2024, pp. 78–83.

Gerstenberg, Günther. 'Sozialistische Arbeiterjugend (SAJ), 1922–1933'. In: Historisches Lexikon Bayerns, 2006. https://www.historisches-lexikon-bayerns.de/Lexikon/Sozialistische_Arbeiterjugend_(SAJ),_1922-1933 (last accessed 18 July 2024)

Graeff, Werner. 'Das Bauhaus, die Stijl-Gruppe und der Konstruktivistenkongress von 1922'. In: Droste, Magdalena and Friedewald, Boris (Eds). *Unser Bauhaus. Bauhäusler und Freunde erinnern sich*. Prestel, Munich, London, New York, 2019, pp. 121–3.

Hundehege, Stefanie. 'Writing the Nazi Movement. The Poetry of Baldur von Schirach'. Doctor of Philosophy (PhD) dissertation, University of Kent. (KAR id:62985). In: https://kar.kent.ac.uk/62985/1/235Hundehege_Writing%20the%20Nazi%20Movement.pdf (last accessed 8 August 2024)

Hyperinflation in Deutschland 1923. In: Deutscher Bundestag, Parlament, Geschichte, 100 Jahre Weimar. In: https://www.bundestag.de/parlament/geschichte/100-jahre-weimar/hyperinflation-970722 (last accessed 31 July 2024)

Iken, Katja and Frank, Alexandra. 'Konfrontation mit der Hölle'. In: Spiegel Online. 23 February 2018. https://www.spiegel.de/geschichte/kz-buchenwald-zwangsbesichtigung-am-16-april-1945-a-1193659.html (last accessed 27 June 2025)

Jüllig, Carola. 'Die NS-Gemeinschaft "Kraft durch Freude" (KdF)'. In: Deutsches Historisches Museum, Berlin, 2021. https://www.dhm.de/lemo/kapitel/ns-regime/ns-organisationen/kdf (last accessed 29 April 2025)

Kelm, Zsófia. 'Ausbildung in Weimar nach dem Bauhaus 1926–1933. Von der Bauhochschule zu den Vereinigten Kunstlehranstalten Weimar'. In: Blümm, Anke, Otto, Elizabeth and Rössler, Patrick (Eds). *Bauhaus und Nationalsozialismus*. Katalog zur Ausstellung im Museum Neues Weimar, Bauhaus-Museum Weimar und Schiller-Museum. Klassik Stiftung Weimar, Hirmer, 2024, pp. 32–5.

Lernort Weimar. 'Das Paradies war in der Teichgasse 6'. In: https://lernort-weimar.de/stolpersteine/hedwig-hetemann-und-johanna-straubing/das-paradies-war-in-der-teichgasse-6/ (last accessed 18 May 2025)

Lernort Weimar. 'Ein gefährliches Geheimnis: Rosa Schmidt'. In: https://lernort-weimar.de/stolpersteine/rosa_schmidt/ein-gefaehrliches-geheimnis/ (last accessed 15 March 2024)

Lernort Weimar. 'Marstall'. In: https://lernort-weimar.de/stolpersteine/marstall/ (last accessed 15 May 2025)

Lernort Weimar. ' ". . . und laß, falls noch einer ein Andenken an mich haben will, sich jeden ein Buch aus meinem Bücherschrank aussuchen . . ." Kurt Nehrling'. In: https://lernort-weimar.de/stolpersteine/kurt_nehrling/und-lass-falls-noch-einer-ein-andenken-an-mich-haben-will-sich-jeden-ein-buch-aus-meinem-buecherschrank-aussuchen/ (last accessed 21 March 2025)

Lernort Weimar. 'Weimarhalle'. In: https://lernort-weimar.de/stolpersteine/weimarhalle/#:~:text=Die%20im%20M%C3%A4rz%201932%20er%C3%B6ffnete,aus%20%E2%80%9EHitlerismus%20und%20Goethe%E2%80%9C (last accessed 24 March 2025)

Lernort Weimar. 'Zwischen Anwerbung und Auslöschung. Spuren jüdischen Lebens in Weimar'. In: https://lernort-weimar.de/juedisches-leben/ausloeschung/#:~:text=Das%20Gesch%C3%A4ft%20Hermann%20Tietz%20befindet,Marktstra%C3%9Fe%202%20eine%20Filiale%20einrichten (last accessed 3 April 2025)

Lissner, Erich. 'Rund ums Bauhaus 1923'. In: Droste, Magdalena and Friedewald, Boris (Eds). *Unser Bauhaus. Bauhäusler und Freunde erinnern sich.* Prestel, Munich, London, New York, 2019, pp. 215–17.

Loos, Karina. 'Die Inszenierung der Stadt. Planen und Bauen im Nationalsozialismus in Weimar'. Doktoringenieur (Dr.-Ing.) dissertation, Bauhaus University Weimar, 1999. In: https://www.db-thueringen.de/receive/dbt_mods_00035546 (last accessed 22 April 2025)

Lorenz, Robert. 'Reichsjugendtag der Arbeiterjugend 1920 in Weimar – Dem Morgenrot entgegen'. In: Walter, Franz and Butzlaff, Felix (Eds). *Mythen, Ikonen, Märtyrer. Sozialdemokratische Geschichten.* Vorwärts Verlag, 2013, pp. 96–104 and https://www.rlorenz.de/texte/reichsjugendtag-der-arbeiterjugend-1920-in-weimar/#_ftn6 (last accessed 18 July 2024)

Ludwig, Annette. 'Zur Einführung. Bauhaus und Nationalsozialismus – Brüche, Widersprüche, Kontinuitäten'. In: Blümm, Anke, Otto, Elizabeth and Rössler, Patrick (Eds). *Bauhaus und Nationalsozialismus.* Katalog zur Ausstellung im Museum Neues Weimar, Bauhaus-Museum Weimar und Schiller-Museum. Klassik Stiftung Weimar, Hirmer, 2024, pp. 8–11.

MDR Thüringen. 'Gutachten: Lampenschirm doch aus Menschenhaut gefertigt, 21 March 2024'. In: https://www.mdr.de/nachrichten/thueringen/mitte-thueringen/weimar/kz-gedenkstaette-buchenwald-lampenschirm-aus-menschenheit-gutachten-benecke-100.html (last accessed 10 May 2025)

Müller, Manfred. 'Nationalsozialistische Einflüsse auf die Vorbereitung und den Ablauf der Reichsgedächtnisfeier für Goethe 1932 in Weimar'. In: *Zeitschrift für Germanistik,* 2004, Neue Folge, Vol. 14, No. 3, 2004, pp. 608–13. In: https://www.jstor.org/stable/23980547 (last accessed 24 March 2025)

Naake, Erhard. 'Die Beziehungen zwischen Elisabeth Förster-Nietzsche und dem Thüringischen Innen- und Volksbildungsminister Wilhelm Frick'. In: Ehrlich, Lothar and Jürgen, John (Eds). *Weimar 1930. Politik und Kultur im Vorfeld der NS-Diktatur*. Böhlau Verlag, Cologne, Weimar, Vienna, 1998, pp. 275–92.

Ochaba, Sabine. 'Mehr als nur Schrott. Die Abwrackung des LZ 127 und des LZ 130 im Frühjahr 1940 in Frankfurt – Teil 1'. In Zeppelin Museum, Blog. https://www.zeppelin-museum.de/entdecken/abwrackung-des-lz-127-und-des-lz-130-teil-1 (last accessed 22 May 2025)

Oehler, Richard. 'Unsere Zeit im Spiegel von Nietzsches Kulturphilosphie'. In: Oehler, Max (Ed.). *Den Manen Friedrich Nietzsches. Weimarer Weihgeschenke zum 75. Geburtstag der Frau Elisabeth Förster-Nietzsche*. Musarion Verlag, Munich, 1921, pp. 127–41.

Orwell, George. 'What is Fascism?' In: *Tribune*, 24 March 1944. https://orwell.ru/library/articles/As_I_Please/english/efasc.html (last accessed 29 June 2025)

Overesch, Manfred. 'Die Einbürgerung Hitlers 1930'. In: *Vierteljahrshefte für Zeitgeschichte*, Nr. 40, Issue 4, 1992, pp. 543–66. In: https://www.ifz-muenchen.de/heftarchiv/1992_4_3_overesch.pdf (last accessed 23 March 2025)

Pollmann, Joachim. 'Hans Severus Ziegler'. In: Grotjahn, Rebecca (Ed.). *Kollaborateure – Involvierte – Profiteure. Musik in der NS-Zeit*. Universität Paderborn, Hochschule für Musik Detmold, 2020. In: https://kollaborateure-involvierte-profiteure.uni-paderborn.de/index.php/Hans_Severus_Ziegler.html (last accessed 22 May 2025)

Post, Bernhard. ' "Na so schlimm wird es ja wohl nicht gleich werden." Die Mobilmachung im Großherzogtum Sachsen-Weimar-Eisenach.' In: Holler, Wolfgang et al. (Eds). *Krieg der Geister. Weimar als Symbolort deutscher Kultur vor und nach 1914*. Sandstein. Klassik Stiftung Weimar, 2014, pp. 44–7.

Rauch, Elena. 'Marlene in Weimar'. In: *Ostthüringer Zeitung*, 15 June 2019. In: https://www.pressreader.com/germany/ostthuringer-zeitung-schleiz/20190615/282548724786160 (last accessed 22 July 2024)

Reuth, Ralf Georg. 'Glaube und Judenhaß als Konstanten im Leben des Joseph Goebbels'. In: Reuth, Ralf Georg (Ed.). *Tagebücher 1924–1945. Band 1. Einführung. 1924–1929*. Piper, Munich and Zurich, 2003, pp. 20–46.

Riederer, Jens. 'Das städtische Krematorium im Dienste der Lager-SS von 1937 bis 1940'. In: Verein Grüne Wahlverwandtschaften (Ed.). '. . . *dem*

Gottesacker ein freundliches gartenähnliches Ansehen'. Zum 200jährigen Bestehen des Weimarer Hauptfriedhofs. Weimar, 2018, pp. 59–90.

'Rittergut und Brauerei. Industrie-Geschichte in Ehringsdorf'. In: Geschichte Sichtbar Machen. Denkmale in Oberweimar & Ehringsdorf, 2022. https://www.geschichte-sichtbar-machen.de/denkmale/rittergut-und-brauerei (last accessed 1 July 2024)

Schley, Jens. 'Weimar und Buchenwald'. In: Knigge, Volkhard and Baumann, Imanuel (Eds). *'. . . mitten im deutschen Volke'. Buchenwald, Weimar und die nationalsozialistische Volksgemeinschaft.* Wallstein Verlag, Göttingen, 2018, pp. 33–57.

Schwarz, Manuel. 'Die letzten Regierungsjahre von Großherzog Wilhelm Ernst'. In: Klassik Stiftung Weimar. Blog Archiv. 2018. https://blog-archiv.klassik-stiftung.de/die-letzten-regierungsjahre-von-grossherzog-wilhelm-ernst/ (last accessed 6 August 2023)

Stadtwerke Weimar. 'Die Chronik des Schwanseebades'. In: https://sw-weimar.de/fileadmin/user_upload/SWG/Sportstaetten/Bad/Schwanseebad_Tafeln_PDF.pdf (last accessed 7 January 2024)

Stein, Harry. 'Eine Stadt für die SS. Die Errichtung des Konzentrationslagers Buchenwald'. In: Knigge, Volkhard and Baumann, Imanuel (Eds). *'. . . mitten im deutschen Volke'. Buchenwald, Weimar und die nationalsozialistische Volksgemeinschaft.* Wallstein Verlag, Göttingen, 2018, pp. 12–32.

Stein, Sabine. 'Franz Ehrlich. Ein Bauhäusler im Widerstand und Konzentrationslager'. In: Thüringer Museumshefte 2/2008. https://lag-buchenwald.vvn-bda.de/2009/09/29/franz-ehrlich-ein-bauhausler-im-widerstand-und-konzentrationslager/ (last accessed 13 May 2025)

Stenzel, Burkhard. '"Buch und Schwert". Die "Woche des deutschen Buches" in Weimar (1934–1942). Anmerkungen zur NS-Literaturpolitik'. In: Härtl, Ursula, Stenzel, Burkhard and Ulbricht, Justus H. (Eds). *Hier, hier ist Deutschland . . . : Von nationalen Kulturkonzepten zur nationalsozialistischen Kulturpolitik.* Wallstein Verlag, Göttingen, 1997, pp. 83–122.

Stenzel, Burkhard. '"Pg. Goethe"? Vom politischen und philologischen Umgang mit einem Weimarer Klassiker'. In: Ehrlich, Lothar, John, Jürgen and Ulbricht, Justus H. (Eds). *Das Dritte Weimar. Klassik und Kultur im Nationalsozialismus.* Böhlau Verlag, Cologne, Weimar, Vienna, 1999, pp. 219–43.

Studiengruppe 'Naturwissenschaftsnahes Philosophieren und Hintergrundpolitik-Kritik seit 1900. Ludendorff-Bewegung'. In: Blogarchiv Studiengruppe Naturalismus, 30 January 2018. https://studiengruppe.

blogspot.com/2018/01/erich-ludendorff-im-jahr-1924_30.html (last accessed 15 September 2024)

Stutz, Rüdiger. 'Weimar als "Stadt der Arbeit". Fritz Sauckel und die Gustloff-Werke'. In: Knigge, Volkhard and Baumann, Imanuel (Eds). '. . . mitten im deutschen Volke'. Buchenwald, Weimar und die nationalsozialistische Volksgemeinschaft. Wallstein Verlag, Göttingen, 2018, pp. 89–101.

Thüringer Landtag. 'Thüringer Verfassungsgeschichte. Landtag, Geschichte, Landesverfassung'. In: https://www.thueringer-landtag.de/landtag/geschichte/landesverfassung/ (last accessed 1 August 2024)

Thüsing, Matthias. 'Bauhaus Weimar. "Haus für Marsmenschen" von "verzweifelter Ähnlichkeit mit einer Bedürfnisanstalt"'. In Die Welt, 1 September 2023. In: https://www.welt.de/geschichte/article246919662/Bauhaus-Verzweifelte-Aehnlichkeit-mit-einer-Beduerfnisanstalt.html (last accessed 13 August 2024)

Ulbricht, Justus H. 'Von der "Heimat" zum "Trutzgau" Kulturgeschichtliche Aspekte der "Zeitenwende" 1933'. In: Ehrlich, Lothar, John, Jürgen and Ulbricht, Justus H. (Eds). Das Dritte Weimar. Klassik und Kultur im Nationalsozialismus. Böhlau Verlag, Cologne, Weimar, Vienna, 1999, pp. 163–217.

Ullrich, Volker. 'Generalprobe in Thüringen. Wie die NSDAP 1930 die Zerstörung der Demokratie übte'. In: Blätter für deutsche und internationale Politik, September 2024, pp. 63–72. In: https://www.blaetter.de/ausgabe/2024/september/generalprobe-in-thueringen (last accessed 9 February 2025)

von Bradish, Joseph A. 'Elisabeth Förster-Nietzsche, Gestorben 8. November 1935'. In: Monatshefte für Deutschen Unterricht, Vol. 27, No. 8, 1935, pp. 321–5. In: JSTOR, http://www.jstor.org/stable/30169117 (last accessed 10 March 2025)

Wahl, Volker. 'Sie war "von Kopf bis Fuß" auf Weimar eingestellt. Marlene Dietrich als private Musikschülerin in der Goethestadt 1920/21'. In: Beiträge zur Weimarer Geschichte. Jahresschrift des Vereins der Freunde und Förderer des Stadtmuseums Weimar im Bertuchhaus e.V. Weimar, 2021, pp. 9–36.

Weber, Petra. ' "Siegerjustiz" oder Volksgerichte? Thüringen unter amerikanischer Besatzungsherrschaft'. In: Justiz und Diktatur: Justizverwaltung und politische Strafjustiz in Thüringen 1945–1961. Veröffentlichungen zur SBZ-/DDR-Forschung im Institut für Zeitgeschichte. R. Oldenbourg Verlag, Munich, 2000, pp. 17–24.

Weimar Werk. 'Album "50 Jahre Volkshaus" in Weimar'. In: VEB Weimar-Werk, Weimar, 1958. https://weimar-werk.de/album-50-jahre-volkshaus-in-weimar-1958/ (last accessed 17 December 2023)

Weindling, Paul. '"Mustergau" Thüringen. Rassenhygiene zwischen Ideologie und Machtpolitik'. In: Frei, Norbert (Ed.). *Medizin und Gesundheitspolitik in der NS-Zeit*. R. Oldenbourg Verlag, Munich, 1991, pp. 81–97.

Wendermann, Gerda. '100 Jahre Dada in Weimar!' In: Klassik Stiftung Weimar. Blog. 25. September 2022. https://blog.klassik-stiftung.de/100-jahre-dada-in-weimar/ (last accessed 11 August 2024)

Wohlfeld, Udo. 'Das Konzentrationslager Nohra in Thüringen'. In: Benz, Wolfgang and Distel, Barbara (Eds). *Terror ohne System. Die ersten Konzentrationslager im Nationalsozialismus 1933–35*. Metropol Verlag, Berlin, 2001, pp. 105–22.

Zinn, Alexander. 'Hans Severus Ziegler. Staatsrat und Generalintendant'. In: Rosa Winkel. Die Verfolgung Homosexueller im Nationalsozialismus, 2017. http://www.rosa-winkel.de/bio-ziegler.htm (last accessed 24 April 2025)

Zuschlag, Christoph. 'Kampf gegen die Avantgarde. Die Ausstellung "Entartete Kunst" in Weimar 1939'. In: Blümm, Anke, Otto, Elizabeth and Rössler, Patrick (Eds). *Bauhaus und Nationalsozialismus*. Katalog zur Ausstellung im Museum Neues Weimar, Bauhaus-Museum Weimar und Schiller-Museum. Klassik Stiftung Weimar, Hirmer, 2024, pp. 60–61.

WEBSITES

Das Gauforum in Weimar – Ein Erbe des Dritten Reiches. https://www.gauforum.de/ (last accessed 4 May 2025)

Gedenkstätte Buchenwald. 'Chronologie des KZ Buchenwald'. https://www.buchenwald.de/geschichte/chronologie/konzentrationslager (last accessed 18 May 2025)

Gedenkstätte Buchenwald. 'Weimar im Nationalsozialismus. Chronik'. https://www.weimar-im-ns.de/chronik (last accessed 9 May 2025)

Klassik Stiftung Weimar. 'Park an der Ilm'. https://www.klassik-stiftung.de/park-an-der-ilm/#:~:text=%E2%80%9EWeimar%20ist%20eigentlich%20ein%20Park,%E2%80%9C&text=Der%2048%20Hektar%20gro%C3%9Fe%20Park,verwirklichten%20hier%20ihre%20gartenk%C3%BCnstlerischen%20Ideen (last accessed 29 June 2025)

Stocker, Frank. https://www.inflation1923.de/ (last accessed 12 August 2024)

ORAL TESTIMONY

Seyfarth, Marie-Luise. In: Visual History Archive of Holocaust oral testimonies from the USC Shoah Foundation Institute. Interview Code: 14861.

BIBLIOGRAPHY

BOOKS

Baudert, August. *Sachsen-Weimars Ende. Historische Tatsachen aus sturmbewegter Zeit.* Panse, Weimar, 1923.

Boblenz, Frank and Post, Bernhard. *Die Machtübernahme in Thüringen 1932/33.* Landeszentrale für politische Bildung Thüringen, Erfurt, 2013.

Churchill, Winston. *The Unknown War: The Eastern Front.* Thornton Butterworth Ltd., New York, 1931.

Decker, Kerstin. *Die Schwester. Das Leben der Elisabeth Förster-Nietzsche.* Berlin Verlag, Munich and Berlin, 2016.

Diethe, Carol. *Nietzsche's Sister and the Will to Power: A Biography of Elisabeth Förster-Nietzsche.* International Nietzsche Studies. Kindle Edition. University of Illinois Press, Urbana and Chicago, 2023.

Dietrich, Marlene. *Marlene.* Kindle Edition. The University Press of Kentucky, Lexington, 2022.

Domarus, Max (Ed.). *The Complete Hitler. A Digital Desktop Reference to His Speeches and Proclamations 1932–1945.* Bolchazy-Carducci Publishers, Inc., 2007.

Dressel, Guido. *Quellen zur Geschichte Thüringens. Wahlen und Abstimmungsergebnisse 1920–1995.* Landeszentrale für politische Bildung Thüringen, Erfurt, 1995.

Droste, Magdalena and Friedewald, Boris (Ed.). *Unser Bauhaus. Bauhäusler und Freunde erinnern sich.* Prestel, Munich, London, New York, 2019.

Epkenhans, Michael (Ed.). *Mein lieber Schatz! Briefe von Admiral Reinhard Scheer an seine Ehefrau. August bis November 1918.* Verlag Dr. Dieter Winkler, Bochum, 2006.

Evans, Richard J. *Hitler's People: The Faces of the Third Reich.* Allen Lane, London, 2024.

Faludi, Christian. *1919 in Weimar. Die Stadt und die Republik.* Weimarer Verlagsgesellschaft, Weimar, 2019.

Faludi, Christian. *1920 in Weimar. Das Ringen um Normalität.* Weimarer Verlagsgesellschaft, Weimar, 2021.

Föhl, Thomas (Ed.). *Elisabeth Förster-Nietzsche und Harry Graf Kessler. Band 2: Der Briefwechsel 189–1935.* Weimarer Verlagsgesellschaft, Weimar, 2013.

Gibas, Monika (Ed.). *Quellen zur Geschichte Thüringens. 'Arisierung in Thüringen': Entrechtung, Enteignung und Vernichtung der jüdischen Bürger Thüringens 1933–1945.* Landeszentrale für politische Bildung Thüringen, Erfurt, 2006.

Göring, Emmy. *An der Seite meines Mannes. Begebenheiten und Bekenntnisse.* Nation Europa Verlag, Coburg, 1996.

Gräfe, Marlis, Post, Bernhard and Schneider, Andreas (Eds). *Quellen zur*

Geschichte Thüringens. Die Geheime Staatspolizei im NS-Gau Thüringen 1933–1945. Landeszentrale für politische Bildung Thüringen, Erfurt, 2009.

Gropius, Walter. *Ausgewählte Schriften. Band 3*. Probst, Hartmut and Schädlich, Christian (Eds). VEB Verlag für Bauwesen, Berlin, 1988.

Günther, Gitta and Hoffmann, Gerhard. *Konzentrationslager Buchenwald 1937 bis 1945. Kleines Lexikon*. Rhinoverlag, Ilmenau, 2016.

Günther, Gitta and Wallraf, Lothar (Eds). *Geschichte der Stadt Weimar*. Hermann Böhlaus Nachfolger, Weimar, 1975.

Günther, Gitter, Huschke, Wolfram and Steiner, Walter. *Weimar. Lexikon zur Stadtgeschichte*. Hermann Böhlaus Nachfolger, Weimar, 1993.

Hamann, Brigitte. *Hitlers Wien: Lehrjahre eines Diktators*. Piper, Munich and Zurich, 1996.

Hecker, Jutta. *Wunder des Worts. Leben im Banne Goethes*. Verlag Weimardruck GmbH, Weimar, 1993.

Hesselbarth, Mario. '*Gegen das Hissen der roten Flagge auf dem Rathaus erheben wir keinen Einspruch'. Novemberrevolution 1918 in Thüringen*. Rosa-Luxemburg-Stiftung Thüringen, Jena, 2018.

John, Jürgen (Ed.). *Quellen zur Geschichte Thüringens. 1918–1945*. Landeszentrale für politische Bildung Thüringen, Erfurt, 1996.

Jones, Mark. *1923: The Forgotten Crisis in the Year of Hitler's Coup*. Basic Books, London, 2023.

Kater, Michael. *Weimar: From Enlightenment to the Present*. Yale University Press, New Haven and London, 2014.

Kershaw, Ian. *Hitler 1889–1936: Hubris*. W. W. Norton, New York, 1999.

Kirsten, Holm. '*Weimar im Banne des Führers': Die Besuche Adolf Hitlers, 1925–1940*. Böhlau Verlag, Cologne, 2001.

Knigge, Volkhard and Baumann, Imanuel (Eds). '*. . . mitten im deutschen Volke'. Buchenwald, Weimar und die nationalsozialistische Volksgemeinschaft*. Wallstein Verlag, Göttingen, 2018.

Kowalczuk, Ilko-Sascha. *Walter Ulbricht. Der deutsche Kommunist 1893–1945*. C.H.Beck, Munich, 2023.

Löffelsender, Michael. *Das Konzentrationslager Buchenwald 1937 bis 1945*. Wallstein Verlag, Göttingen, 2025.

Longerich, Peter. *Unwillige Volksgenossen. Wie die Deutschen zum NS-Regime standen. Eine Stimmungsgeschichte*. Siedler Verlag, Munich, 2025.

Ludendorff, Erich. *Vom Feldherrn zum Weltrevolutionär und Wegbereiter Deutscher Volksschöpfung. Meine Lebenserinnerungen von 1919 bis 1925*. Ludendorffs Verlag, Munich, 1940.

Lüttgenau, Rikola-Gunnar (Ed.). *Weimar im Nationalsozialismus. Ein Stadtplan*. AVISO Verlagsgesellschaft, Weimar, 2011.

McDonough, Frank. *The Weimar Years: Rise and Fall 1918–1933*. Head of Zeus, London, 2023.

Mauersberger, Volker, *Hitler in Weimar. Der Fall einer deutschen Kulturstadt*, Berlin: Rowohlt Berlin 1999.

Merseburger, Peter. *Mythos Weimar. Zwischen Geist und Macht*. Pantheon Verlag, Munich, 1998.

Müller, Erika and Stein, Harry. *Jüdische Familien in Weimar. Ihre Verfolgung und Vernichtung*. Weimar Schriften. Stadtmuseum Weimar, Weimar, 1998.

Müller, Ulrike. *Bauhaus-Frauen. Meisterinnen in Kunst, Handwerk und Design*. Insel Verlag, Berlin, 2014.

Naake, Erhard. *Nietzsche und Weimar. Werk und Wirkung im 20. Jahrhundert*. Böhlau Verlag, Cologne, Weimar, Vienna, 2000.

Neumann, Thomas (Ed.). *Kultur in Thüringen 1919–1949. Quellen zur Geschichte Thüringens*. Landeszentrale für politische Bildung Thüringen, Erfurt, Weimar, 1998.

Nielsen, Jens and Freienstein, Kirsten. *Schweigepflicht. Dr. Waldemar Freienstein. Ein Thüringer Arzt im Nationalsozialismus*. Kirschlager, Arnstadt, 2021.

Raßloff, Steffen. *Fritz Sauckel. Hitlers 'Muster-Gauleiter' und 'Sklavenhalter'*. Landeszentrale für politische Bildung Thüringen, Erfurt, 2008.

Rathkolb, Oliver. *Schirach. Eine Generation zwischen Goethe und Hitler*. Piper, Munich, 2022.

Rehbein, Maja and Bosse, Dankmar. *Jutta Hecker. Ein Leben für die Weimarer Klassik*. Quartus-Verlag, Bucha bei Jena, 2022.

Riva, Maria. *Marlene Dietrich*. Kindle Edition. Pegasus Books, New York, 2021.

Rößner, Alf (Ed.). *Demokratie aus Weimar. Die Nationalversammlung 1919*. Stadtmuseum Weimar, 2015.

Sauckel, Fritz (Ed.). *Der Führer in Weimar 1925–1938. Allen Volksgenossen Thüringens ein Dokument der großen Zeit Adolf Hitlers. Dem Führer ein Zeichen des Dankes für unseres Volkes Glück, das er uns gab*. publisher, Weimar, 1938.

Sauckel, Fritz. *Fritz Sauckels Kampfreden. Dokumente aus der Zeit der Wende und des Aufbaus*, selected and edited by Fritz Fink. Fritz Fink Verlag, Weimar, 1934.

Schaefer, Dirk. *Im Namen Nietzsches, Elisabeth Förster-Nietzsche und Lou Andres-Salomé*. Fischer Taschenbuch Verlag, Frankfurt am Main, 2001.

Schau, Reinhard. *Die Stiftung der Marie Seebach. Ein Altenheim für Bühnenkünstler. Seit 1895 in Weimar*. Böhlau Verlag, Cologne, Weimar, Vienna 2015.

Schley, Jens. *Nachbar Buchenwald. Die Stadt Weimar und ihr Konzentrationslager 1937–1945*. Böhlau Verlag, Cologne, Weimar, Vienna, 1999.

Sieg, Ulrich. *Die Macht des Willens. Elisabeth Förster-Nietzsche und ihre Welt*. Carl Hanser Verlag, Munich, 2019.

Sigmund, Anna Maria. *Die Frauen der Nazis*. Ueberreuter Verlag, Vienna, 1998.

Speer, Albert. *Erinnerungen*. Ullstein Verlag, Berlin, 1969.

Stein, Harry and Wohlfeld, Udo. *Sozialdemokraten gegen Hitler. Die Widerstandsgruppe Nehrling-Eberling in Weimar*. Geschichtswerkstatt Weimar/Apolda e.V., Weimar, 2003.

Tucker, William H. *The Science and Politics of Racial Research*. University of Illinois Press, Urbana and Chicago, 1994.

v. Lang, Jochen. *Der Hitlerjunge. Baldur von Schirach. Der Mann, der Deutschlands Jugend erzog*. Rasch und Röhring Verlag, Hamburg, 1991.

Wagener, Otto. *Hitler aus nächster Nähe: Aufzeichnungen eines Vertrauten 1929–1932*. Ullstein, Frankfurt am Main, Berlin, Vienna, 1978.

Wagner, Martin. *Vier Generationen Buchdrucker Wagner in Weimar, 1879 bis 2009. Von Familienunternehmen zur Gutenberg GmbH*. Privately published, 2010.

Wilson, W. Daniel. *Der Faustische Pakt. Goethe und die Goethe-Gesellschaft im Dritten Reich*. DTV Verlagsgesellschaft, Munich, 2018.

Winkler, Heinrich August. *Weimar 1918–1933. Die Geschichte der ersten deutschen Demokratie*. Beck, Munich, 1993.

Wohlfeld, Udo. *Und unweigerlich führt der Weg nach Buchenwald. Der Geist von Weimar hinter Gittern*. Eigenverlag Verein Prager-Haus-Apolda e.V, Langenhagen, 1999.

Wyllie, James. *Nazi Wives: The Women at the Top of Hitler's Germany*. The History Press, Cheltenham, 2019.

Ziegler, Hans Severus. *Entartete Musik. Eine Abrechnung von Staatsrat Dr. H. S. Ziegler*. Völkischer Verlag, Düsseldorf, 1938.

Notes

INTRODUCTION: GERMANY IN A NUTSHELL

1. Quoted in Schley, *Nachbar Buchenwald*, p. 1.   **2.** Quoted in Iken and Frank.
3. *Death Mills*. Orientation Film no. 19.   **4.** Carl Weirich's Diary, 16 April 1945
and 1 May 1945.   **5.** Klassik Stiftung Weimar. 'Park an der Ilm'.   **6.** Speech by
German President Roman Herzog on 19 February 1999.

PRELUDE: WAR

1. Carl Weirich's Diary, first page of continuous writing, undated.   **2.** Ibid., 1
May 1914.   **3.** Ibid.   **4.** Ibid.   **5.** Recollections of Hanns Wagner, p. 48.   **6.**
Lokales. In: *Jenaer Volksblatt*. Vol. 25, No. 174, Tuesday 28 July 1914, p. 3.   **7.**
Down with the War! Announcement, 3 August 1914.   **8.** *Weimarische Volkszeit-
ung*, Jahrgang 9, Beilage zu No. 173.   **9.** *Weimarische Zeitung*, Jahrgang 160, No.
184, p. 1.   **10.** *Lokales*. In: *Jenaer Volksblatt*. Vol. 25, No. 185, Sunday 9 August
1914, p. 2.   **11.** Ibid.   **12.** *Weimarische Volkszeitung*, Jahrgang 9, No. 184, S.3.
13. Quoted in Schwarz.   **14.** Recollections of Hanns Wagner, p. 61.   **15.** Carl
Weirich's Diary, 31 July 1914.   **16.** Recollections of Hanns Wagner, p. 67.   **17.**
Carl Weirich's Diary, 29 November 1914.   **18.** Ibid., 9 November 1914.   **19.** Ibid.
20. Rehbein and Bosse, p. 24.   **21.** Sophienstift, Oberlyzeum, zu Weimar, p.
41.   **22.** Recollections of Hanns Wagner, p. 68.   **23.** Carl Weirich's Diary, 22
February 1915.   **24.** Ibid., 22 August 1916.   **25.** Letter from Ludwig Sckell to
his father Otto. Sent from Nouvion le Comte to Weimar on 30 June 1916.   **26.**
Ration cards held by Stadtmuseum Weimar.   **27.** Average monthly income
was around 100 marks.   **28.** *Bread and Potatoes*. In: *Jenaer Volksblatt*. Vol. 26, No.
42, Friday 19 February 1915, p. 7.   **29.** Letter from Ludwig Sckell to his father
Otto. Sent from Nouvion le Comte to Weimar on 30 June 1916.   **30.** Ibid.   **31.**
Ibid.   **32.** Recollections of Hanns Wagner, p. 72.   **33.** Ibid., p. 69.   **34.** Ibid., p.
78.   **35.** Ibid., p. 79.   **36.** Rehbein and Bosse, p. 29.   **37.** Carl Weirich's Diary,
23 June 1917.   **38.** Ibid.   **39.** Letter from Ludwig Sckell to his father Otto. Sent
from Linselles to Weimar on 21 June 1917.   **40.** Letter from Ludwig Sckell to

his parents. Sent from Neuvilly to Weimar on 6 June 1917.   **41.** Carl Weirich's Diary, June 1918.   **42.** Quoted in Post, p. 47.   **43.** Sophienstift, Oberlyzeum, zu Weimar, p. 38.   **44.** Weimar Werk.   **45.** Baudert, p. 10.   **46.** Ibid., p. 1.   **47.** Günther and Wallraf , p. 516.   **48.** Baudert, p. 2.   **49.** Ibid., p. 11.   **50.** Ibid., p. 12.   **51.** Ibid.   **52.** Ibid., p. 14.   **53.** Carl Weirich's Diary, 9 November 1918. **54.** First Proclamation of the Weimar Soldiers' Council, 8/9 November 1918. **55.** Baudert, p. 19.   **56.** Ibid., p. 21.   **57.** Recollections of Hanns Wagner, p. 121.

1919

1. Diary of Catharina Louise Lehmann. Quoted in Faludi, *1919*, p. 31.   **2.** Kater, p. 132.   **3.** Recollections of Hanns Wagner, p. 122.   **4.** Diary of Catharina Louise Lehmann. Quoted in Faludi, *1919*, p. 32.   **5.** Ibid.   **6.** Faludi, *1919*, p. 18.   **7.** Sophienstift, Oberlyzeum, zu Weimar, p. 10.   **8.** Rehbein and Bosse, p. 31.   **9.** Winkler, p. 70.   **10.** Diary of Carl Weiß. Quoted in Faludi, *1919*, p. 38.   **11.** Baudert, p. 42.   **12.** See also Rößner, p. 47f.   **13.** *Weimarische Landeszeitung*, 12 January 1919.   **14.** Ibid.   **15.** Ibid.   **16.** Diary of Catharina Louise Lehmann. Quoted in Faludi, *1919*, p. 42.   **17.** Advert in *Weimarische Zeitung*. **18.** Gertrud Bäumer's Heimatchronik. Quoted in Faludi, *1919*, p. 36.   **19.** Diary of Carl Weiß. Quoted in Faludi, *1919*, p. 38.   **20.** Ibid.   **21.** Ibid.   **22.** Diary of Catharina Louise Lehmann. Quoted in Faludi, *1919*, p. 42.   **23.** Ibid.   **24.** Ibid. **25.** Kowalczuk, p. 159, and *Volkszeitung*, 21 January 1919. Quoted in Faludi, *1919*, p. 49.   **26.** *Weimarische Landeszeitung*, 6 February 1919.   **27.** Gertrud Bäumer's Heimatchronik. Quoted in Faludi, *1919*, p. 48.   **28.** Diary of Catharina Louise Lehmann. Quoted in Faludi, *1919*, p. 46.   **29.** Gertrud Bäumer's Heimatchronik. Quoted in Faludi, *1919*, p. 48.   **30.** Emma Witte's 'Appeal to German women'. Quoted in Faludi, *1919*, p. 40.   **31.** Gertrud Bäumer's Heimatchronik. Quoted in Faludi, *1919*, p. 48.   **32.** *Weimarische Landeszeitung*, 19 January 1919.   **33.** Figures own calculations based on *Volkszeitung*, 21 January 1919. Quoted in Faludi, *1919*, p. 49.   **34.** Ibid., pp. 49–50.   **35.** Goethe zu der Armbrustgesellschaft. In: Thüringisches Hauptstaatsarchiv Weimar, Stahlarmbrust-Schützengesellschaft Weimar 356-46.   **36.** Chronicle of the Crossbow Society. In: Thüringisches Hauptstaatsarchiv Weimar, Stahlarmbrust-Schützengesellschaft Weimar 197-343.   **37.** Baudert, p. 45.   **38.** Ibid.   **39.** Ibid.   **40.** Rößner, p. 88.   **41.** Sophienstift, Oberlyzeum, zu Weimar, p. 11.   **42.** *New York Times*, 7 February 1919.   **43.** Friedrich Ebert's opening speech of the National Assembly, 6 February 1919. **44.** See seating plan in Die Nationalversammlung in *Wort und Bild*, p. 22.   **45.** Friedrich Ebert's opening speech of the National Assembly, 6 February 1919. **46.** Ibid.   **47.** Carl Weirich's Diary, 6 February 1919.   **48.** Ibid.   **49.** Harry Graf Kessler's Diary, 24 February 1919.   **50.** Ibid., 23 February 1919.   **51.** Ibid.   **52.**

Vossische Zeitung, 6 February 1919, in Rößner, p. 72.   **53.** *Weimarische Landeszeitung*, 8 February 1919. Quoted in Faludi, *1919*, p. 76.   **54.** Ilse-Sibylle Stapff's recollections 1.   **55.** Quoted in Faludi, *1919*, p. 76.   **56.** Ibid., p. 78.   **57.** Harry Graf Kessler's Diary, 27 February 1919.   **58.** Quoted in Rößner, p. 63.   **59.** Quoted in Faludi, *1919*, p. 196.   **60.** Carl Weirich's Diary, 1919/1920.   **61.** Adreß-Buch der Landeshauptstadt Weimar. 1920–1922, pp. 135–6.   **62.** Ibid., p. 189.   **63.** Ibid., p. 136.   **64.** Georges Clemenceau's speech and Ulrich Graf Brockdorff-Rantzau's response on 7 May 1919, Paris.   **65.** Ibid.   **66.** Quoted in Faludi, *1919*, p. 83.   **67.** Both ibid., pp. 88f.   **68.** Harry Graf Kessler's Diary, 12 June 1919.   **69.** Quoted in Decker, p. 545.   **70.** Quoted in Rößner, p. 63.   **71.** Harry Graf Kessler's Diary, 8 August 1919.   **72.** Faludi, *1919*, p. 87.   **73.** Harry Graf Kessler's Diary, 25 July 1919.   **74.** Ibid., 22 June 1919.   **75.** *Thüringer Tageszeitung*, 28 June 1919, p. 1.   **76.** Quoted in Faludi, *1919*, p. 97.   **77.** Quoted in ibid., p. 98.   **78.** Harry Graf Kessler's Diary, 21 August 1919.   **79.** Ebert's speech, on 21 August 1919. Quoted in Faludi, *1919*, p. 104.   **80.** Ebert's letter to Weimar, on 23 August 1919. Quoted in Faludi, *1919*, p. 106.   **81.** Foundation Programme of the Weimar Bauhaus, April 1919. Quoted in John, p. 71.   **82.** Ibid. Quoted in Ulrike Müller, p. 14.   **83.** Walter Gropius to Adolf Behne on 22 May 1919. Quoted in Faludi, *1919*, p. 252.   **84.** Walter Gropius to Max Osborn on 16 December 1919. Quoted in ibid., p. 253.   **85.** Complaint of Weimar Citizens to the State Ministry of Saxe-Weimar-Eisenach, 19 December 1919. Quoted in Faludi, *1919*, pp. 260–63.   **86.** Kater, p. 141.   **87.** Sophienstift, Oberlyzeum, zu Weimar, pp. 12f.   **88.** Carl Weirich's Diary, September 1919.   **89.** Quoted in Faludi, *1919*, p. 236.   **90.** Quoted in ibid., p. 237.   **91.** Police Report, 4 September 1919.   **92.** Carl Weirich's Diary, October 1919.   **93.** Ibid., Christmas 1919.

1920

1. Baudert, p. 57.   **2.** Carl Weirich's Diary, Christmas 1919.   **3.** Figures from Frank Stocker. In: www.inflation1923.de / Berliner Volkszeitung / Berliner Tageblatt / Statistisches Reichsamt   **4.** *Weimarer Landeszeitung*, 21 May 1920. Quoted in Faludi, *1920*, p. 295.   **5.** Ibid., p. 28.   **6.** Cf. Ibid., p. 29.   **7.** Ibid., p. 31.   **8.** Quoted in ibid., p. 32.   **9.** Carl Weirich's Diary, August 1920.   **10.** Baudert, p. 57.   **11.** Ibid.   **12.** Ibid., p. 59.   **13.** Ibid.   **14.** Rehbein and Bosse, p. 32.   **15.** Quoted in Faludi, *1920*, p. 88.   **16.** Baudert, p. 73.   **17.** Rittergut und Brauerei. Industrie-Geschichte in Ehringsdorf.   **18.** Hohenzollern file, No. 62.   **19.** Ibid., No. 63.   **20.** Figures from Faludi, *1920*, p. 296.   **21.** Günther and Wallraf, p. 543.   **22.** Quoted in Faludi, *1920*, p. 298.   **23.** Ibid., p. 142.   **24.** *Thüringer Tageszeitung*, 21 June 1920, p. 1.   **25.** Baudert, p. 75.   **26.** Description based on Lorenz.   **27.** Figure from Gerstenberg.   **28.** Lorenz.   **29.** Ibid.   **30.** Stein and Wohlfeld,

p. 6. **31.** Ibid. **32.** Carl Weirich's Diary, 1920/1921. **33.** Based on *Weimarische Landeszeitung*, 10 October 1920. Quoted in Faludi, *1920*, p. 290. **34.** *Thüringer Tageszeitung*, 11 October 1920. Quoted in Faludi, *1920*, p. 291. **35.** From a letter Scheer wrote in 1921. Quoted in Epkenhans, p. 53. **36.** From Scheer's memoir. Quoted in ibid. **37.** Cf. Kater, p. 165. **38.** *Thüringer Tageszeitung*, 11 October 1920. Quoted in Faludi, *1920*, p. 290. **39.** Dietrich, Location No. 516. **40.** Ibid. **41.** Ibid. **42.** Marlene Dietrich's Diary, 10 October 1920. Quoted in Wahl, p. 12. **43.** Dietrich, Location No. 516. **44.** Marlene Dietrich's Diary, 10 October 1920. Quoted in Wahl, p. 15. **45.** Dietrich, Location No. 539. **46.** Marlene Dietrich's Diary, 13 February 1921. Quoted in Wahl, p. 17. **47.** Carl Weirich's Diary, December 1920. **48.** Ibid. **49.** Ibid.

1921

1. *Evangelisches Gemeindeblatt für Weimar*, Nr. 4, 13 February 1921, p. 1. **2.** Ibid. **3.** Wahl, p. 24. **4.** Marlene Dietrich's Diary, 2 July 1923. Quoted in Wahl, p. 17. **5.** Riva, pp. 54, 57. **6.** Ibid. **7.** Marlene Dietrich's Diary, 2 July 1923. Quoted in Wahl, p. 19. **8.** Carl Weirich's Diary, 6 January 1921. **9.** Ibid., Oranienburg 1909. **10.** Stein and Wohlfeld, pp. 6–7. **11.** Diethe, p. 159. **12.** Oehler, p. 131. **13.** Sieg, p. 286. **14.** Kater, p. 110. **15.** Elisabeth Förster-Nietzsche's letter to Edvard Munch, 17 September 1921. **16.** Quoted in Sieg, p. 286. **17.** Decker, p. 561. **18.** Kater, p. 169. **19.** Sieg, p. 290. **20.** Elisabeth Förster-Nietzsche's letter to Edvard Munch, 17 September 1921. **21.** McDonough, p. 157. **22.** Ibid., p. 158. **23.** Hyperinflation in Deutschland 1923. **24.** https://www.inflation1923.de/ **25.** Elisabeth Förster-Nietzsche's letter to Edvard Munch, 17 September 1921. **26.** Quoted in Baudert, p. 77. **27.** Ibid., p. 79. **28.** Thüringer Landtag. 'Thüringer Verfassungsgeschichte'. **29.** Quoted in Baudert, p. 77. **30.** Ibid. **31.** Ibid., p. 78. **32.** Ibid. **33.** Dietrich, Location No. 564. **34.** Quoted in Wahl, p. 22. **35.** Quoted in ibid., p. 23. **36.** Ibid., p. 25. **37.** Ibid. **38.** Dietrich, Location No. 564. **39.** Quoted in Wahl, p. 33. **40.** Quoted in ibid., p. 17. **41.** Carl Weirich's Diary, Christmas 1921.

1922

1. Carl Weirich's Diary, January 1922. **2.** Ibid. **3.** Ibid., February 1922. **4.** Günther and Wallraf, p. 548. **5.** Rehbein and Bosse, p. 32. **6.** Ibid., p. 37. **7.** Quoted in ibid., p. 52. **8.** Carl Weirich's Diary, 17 June 1922. **9.** Ibid., 18 June 1922. **10.** Baudert, pp. 82–3. **11.** Adler, p. 13. **12.** Gropius, pp. 97–100. **13.** Kater, p. 142. **14.** Driesch-Foucar, p. 93. **15.** Graeff, p. 122. **16.** Wendermann. **17.** Ibid. **18.** Quoted in ibid. **19.** Quoted in ibid. **20.** Quoted in ibid. **21.**

Plans of Hotel Hohenzollern in Hohenzollern file. Stadtarchiv Weimar. Abtlg: II. Locat: 10B. Nr: 532. **22.** *Jenaer Volksblatt*, No. 80, 6 October 1922, Sports Pages (Sportblatt).

1923

1. Carl Weirich's Diary, May 1923. **2.** Stocker. **3.** Carl Weirich's Diary, 18 February 1923. **4.** McDonough, p. 205. **5.** Ibid., pp. 205–6. **6.** Jones, pp. 178–9. **7.** Carl Weirich's Diary, September 1923. **8.** Jones, p. 180. **9.** Rehbein and Bosse, p. 33. **10.** Jones, p. 182. **11.** Ibid., p. 183. **12.** *Jenaer Volksblatt*, Nr. 117, Wednesday 23 May 1923, p. 6. **13.** Ibid. **14.** Ibid. **15.** Stocker. **16.** Lissner, p. 215. **17.** Ibid., p. 216. **18.** Ibid. **19.** Ibid. **20.** *Jenaer Volksblatt*, Wednesday 8 August 1923. **21.** Quoted in Merseburger, pp. 304–5. **22.** Ibid., p. 304. **23.** Quotes in this paragraph in Thüsing. **24.** Quoted in Hundehege, p. 45. **25.** Merseburger, p. 305. **26.** Kater, p. 146. **27.** Carl Weirich's Diary, 9 November 1923. **28.** Günther and Wallraf, pp. 540–41.

1924

1. Quoted in Decker, p. 568. **2.** Quoted in Sieg, p. 290. **3.** Harry Graf Kessler's Diary, 20 April 1925. **4.** Carl Weirich's Diary, beginning of 1924. **5.** Ibid., 23 February 1924. **6.** Mauersberger, pp. 170–71. **7.** Ibid., p. 172. **8.** Quoted in Barth. **9.** Quoted in Mauersberger, p. 163. **10.** Quoted in ibid., p. 164. **11.** Müller and Stein, pp. 51–5. **12.** Ibid., p. 162. **13.** Ibid., p. 184. **14.** Rehbein and Bosse, p. 33. **15.** Ibid., p. 34. **16.** Evans, p. 204. **17.** Ibid., p. 205. **18.** Ibid., p. 291. **19.** Quoted in ibid., p. 293. **20.** Quoted in Lernort Weimar. 'Ein gefährliches Geheimnis'. **21.** Oral testimony of Marie-Luise Seyfarth. **22.** Quotes in this paragraph from Mauersberger, p. 119. **23.** Quoted in Ackermann, p. 28. **24.** Ibid., p. 30. **25.** Quoted in Mauersberger, p. 152. **26.** Quoted in ibid., p. 153. **27.** Quoted in ibid., p. 152. **28.** Quoted in Ackermann, p. 30. **29.** Quoted in ibid. **30.** Ibid. **31.** Quoted in Mauersberger, p. 153. **32.** *Jenaer Volksblatt*, 24 July 1924. **33.** Ludendorff, p. 333. **34.** Quoted in Rathkolb, p. 46. **35.** Quoted in ibid. **36.** Quoted in Mauersberger, p. 118. **37.** Quoted in ibid. **38.** Programme of the 'Great German Culture Avowal' of the 'National Socialist Freedom Party' in Weimar, 17.8.1924. **39.** Quoted in Mauersberger, p. 117. **40.** Quoted in ibid., p. 121. **41.** *Weimarische Zeitung*, 17 August 1924. Quoted in Neumann, p. 111. **42.** Ludendorff, p. 349. **43.** Quoted in Studiengruppe. 'Naturwissenschaftsnahes Philosophieren und Hintergrundpolitik-Kritik seit 1900'. **44.** Programme of the 'Great German Culture Avowal' of the 'National Socialist Freedom Party' in Weimar, 17.8.1924.

45. Great inquiry of the SPD faction in the Thuringian parliament about the behaviour of the Thuringian government regarding the Republican and Nazi-völkisch organizations, 22 August 1924. **46.** Harry Graf Kessler's Diary, 17 August 1924. **47.** Quoted in Mauersberger, p. 123. **48.** Quoted in ibid., p. 122. **49.** Harry Graf Kessler's Diary, 17 August 1924. **50.** Ibid. **51.** Carl Weirich's Diary, 11–18 August 1924. **52.** Quoted in Studiengruppe 'Naturwissenschafts-nahes Philosophieren und Hintergrundpolitik-Kritik seit 1900'. **53.** Joseph Goebbels' Diary, 15 August 1924. **54.** Ibid. **55.** Mauersberger, S. 154. **56.** Quoted in Mauersberger, p. 155. **57.** Carl Weirich's Diary, 24 December 1924.

1925

1. Hundehege, p. 25. **2.** Kirsten, p. 21. **3.** Kater, p. 200. **4.** Raßloff, pp. 38–40. **5.** Kater, p. 199. **6.** Kirsten, p. 21. **7.** Quoted in Rathkolb, p. 48. **8.** Hundehege, p. 25. **9.** Kirsten, p. 22. **10.** Quoted in ibid. **11.** Quoted in Rathkolb, p. 48. **12.** Hundehege, p. 25. **13.** Kirsten, pp. 22–3. **14.** Kater, p. 202. **15.** Quoted in Rathkolb, p. 49. **16.** Quoted in ibid., p. 50. **17.** Quoted in ibid. **18.** Kirsten, p. 23. **19.** Raßloff, p. 46. **20.** Kelm, p. 33. **21.** Ibid. **22.** Ibid., p. 34. **23.** Quoted in ibid., p. 33. **24.** Harry Graf Kessler's Diary, 20 April 1925. **25.** Ibid. **26.** Letter from Elisabeth Förster-Nietzsche to Harry Graf Kessler, 30 January 1925. **27.** Quoted in Sieg, p. 303. **28.** Harry Graf Kessler's Diary, 15 May 1925. **29.** Ibid. **30.** Ibid. **31.** Extract from a letter by Harry Graf Kessler to Henry van de Velde, 29 June 1925. Quoted in Föhl, p. 1036. **32.** Carl Weirich's Diary, June 1925. **33.** Ibid., beginning of 1925. **34.** Reuth, p. 34. **35.** Kirsten, p. 24. **36.** Joseph Goebbels' Diary, 10 November 1925. **37.** Quoted in Rathkolb, p. 53. **38.** Quoted in Kirsten, p. 24. **39.** Günther and Wallraf, p. 556. **40.** Quoted in Mauersberger, p. 212. **41.** Quoted in ibid., p. 214. **42.** Kirsten, p. 25. **43.** Rathkolb, pp. 51–2. **44.** Quoted in Hundehege, p. 54. **45.** Quoted in ibid. **46.** Quoted in Rathkolb, p. 51. **47.** Quoted in ibid., p. 52. **48.** Quoted in Kirsten, p. 25. **49.** Kater, p. 203. **50.** Quoted in Mauersberger, p. 217. **51.** Quoted in Sieg, p. 300. **52.** *New York Times*, 9 November 1924, p. 7. **53.** Quoted in Decker, p. 577. **54.** Carl Weirich's Diary, Christmas 1925.

1926

1. Letter from Harry Graf Kessler to Elisabeth Förster-Nietzsche, 11 March 1926. **2.** Harry Graf Kessler's Diary, 18 March 1926. **3.** Ibid., 11 February 1926. **4.** Quoted in Sieg, p. 300. **5.** Günther and Wallraf, p. 558. **6.** Order of summary punishment, 10 June 1926. In: Hohenzollern file, item 75. **7.** Carl Weirich's Diary, 10 May 1926. **8.** Quotes and information from *Jenaer*

Volksblatt, 11 May 1926, p. 1.   **9.** Details from Unser Kinderbuch, pp. 6–13.   **10.** Carl Weirich's Diary, 3 July 1926.   **11.** Joseph Goebbels' Diary, 6 July 1924.   **12.** Lernort Weimar. 'Ein gefährliches Geheimnis: Rosa Schmidt'.   **13.** Joseph Goebbels' Diary, 6 July 1924.   **14.** Dietrich and Dell, p. 17.   **15.** Quoted in ibid.   **16.** Quoted in Mauersberger, p. 216.   **17.** Joseph Goebbels' Diary, 6 July 1926.   **18.** v. Lang, p. 26.   **19.** Kirsten, p. 27.   **20.** *Jenaer Volksblatt*, 5 July 1926, p. 2.   **21.** Quoted in Kirsten, p. 28.   **22.** *Allgemeine Thüringische Landeszeitung Deutschland*, Weimar, 2 July 1926, No. 181, p. 10.   **23.** Joseph Goebbels' Diary, 6 July 1926.   **24.** Quoted in Rathkolb, p. 56.   **25.** *Allgemeine Thüringische Landeszeitung Deutschland*, Weimar, 2 July 1926, No. 181, p. 10.   **26.** Quoted in Mauersberger, p. 224.   **27.** Quoted in Rathkolb, p. 54.   **28.** Kirsten, p. 30.   **29.** Ibid.   **30.** *Jenaer Volksblatt*, 5 July 1926, p. 2.   **31.** Kirsten, p. 31.   **32.** *Allgemeine Thüringische Landeszeitung Deutschland*, Weimar, 5 July 1926, No. 184, p. 8, and Mauersberger, p. 227.   **33.** Quoted in Mauersberger, p. 227.   **34.** *Allgemeine Thüringische Landeszeitung Deutschland*, Weimar, 5 July 1926, No. 184, p. 8.   **35.** Kirsten, p. 32.   **36.** Ibid., pp. 31–2.   **37.** *Jenaer Volksblatt*, 5 July 1926, p. 2.   **38.** *Allgemeine Thüringische Landeszeitung Deutschland*, Weimar, 5 July 1926, No. 184, p. 8.   **39.** *Jenaer Volksblatt*, 16 April 1931, p. 6.   **40.** Ibid., 5 July 1926, p. 2.   **41.** Quoted in Mauersberger, p. 230.   **42.** Mauersberger, p. 230.   **43.** All quoted in Mauersberger, pp. 225–6, 233.   **44.** Joseph Goebbels' Diary, 6 July 1926.   **45.** Sieg, p. 305.   **46.** Letter from Elisabeth Förster-Nietzsche to Harry Graf Kessler, 26 August 1926.   **47.** Quoted in Föhl, pp. 1065–6.   **48.** Quoted in Decker, p. 577.   **49.** Letter from Elisabeth Förster-Nietzsche to Harry Graf Kessler, 26 August 1926.   **50.** Otto Daube: Weimar – Bayreuth, p. 117.   **51.** Letter from Elisabeth Förster-Nietzsche to Harry Graf Kessler, 26 August 1926.   **52.** Harry Graf Kessler's Diary, 22 October 1926.   **53.** Föhl, p. 1075.   **54.** Letters from Elisabeth Förster-Nietzsche to Harry Graf Kessler, 26 August and 1 December 1926.   **55.** Ibid., 1 December 1926.   **56.** Kirsten, pp. 25–6.   **57.** Carl Weirich's Diary, 10 November 1926.   **58.** Ibid., 30 December 1926.

1927

1. Kirsten, p. 26.   **2.** Günther and Wallraf, p. 561.   **3.** Note by the chief secretary of the town council of Weimar to the Assessment Commission of the Hospitality Association, 15 February 1927.   **4.** Arthur Schmidt's letter to the town manager, 15 February 1927.   **5.** Police assessment of Arthur Schmidt's request to extend his alcohol licence, 18 February 1927.   **6.** Ibid., 15 March 1927.   **7.** Stein and Wohlfeld, p. 7.   **8.** All information from Kurt Nehrling's application for a building grant, 1926–1927.   **9.** Details from Unser Kinderbuch, p. 26.   **10.** Unser Kinderbuch, p. 28.   **11.** Carl Weirich's Diary, beginning of

1927.   **12.** Joseph Goebbels' Diary, 8 May 1926, p. 247.   **13.** His exact combination of subjects is somewhat disputed. See Hundehege, p. 54.   **14.** Quoted in Hundehege, p. 55.   **15.** v. Lang, pp. 34–5.   **16.** Quoted in Rathkolb, p. 75.   **17.** v. Lang, p. 36.   **18.** Raßloff, p. 46.   **19.** Quote in ibid.   **20.** Kater, p. 200.   **21.** Raßloff, p. 46.   **22.** Carl Weirich's Diary, 12 October 1927.   **23.** Letter from Elisabeth Förster-Nietzsche to Harry Graf Kessler, 9 September 1927.   **24.** Ibid., 8 October 1927.   **25.** Harry Graf Kessler's Diary, 5 October 1927.   **26.** Ibid.   **27.** Letter from Harry Graf Kessler to Elisabeth Förster-Nietzsche, 12 October 1927.   **28.** Harry Graf Kessler's Diary, 13 October 1927.   **29.** Ibid., 15 October 1927.   **30.** Quote and information from Kirsten, p. 39.   **31.** Ibid.   **32.** Carl Weirich's Diary, October–December 1927/prelude to 1928.

1928

1. Kater, p. 170.   **2.** Letter from Elisabeth Förster-Nietzsche to Harry Graf Kessler, 12 April 1928.   **3.** Ibid.   **4.** Nietzsche, *Fragmente von Frühjahr 1884 bis Herbst 1885*, Band 5, 26, [173].   **5.** Letter from Elisabeth Förster-Nietzsche to Harry Graf Kessler, 12 April 1928.   **6.** Letter from Harry Graf Kessler to Elisabeth Förster-Nietzsche, 13 April 1928.   **7.** Kater, p. 175.   **8.** Ibid.   **9.** Ulbricht, p. 173.   **10.** Appeal for the Kampfbund für deutsche Kultur, pp. 131–2.   **11.** Wilson, pp. 10–11.   **12.** Rathkolb, p. 77.   **13.** Ibid., p. 76.   **14.** *Jenaer Volksblatt*, 21 May 1928, p. 1, and Dressel, pp. 42–7, 70–75.   **15.** *Jenaer Volksblatt*, 21 May 1928, p. 2.   **16.** Ibid., p. 1.   **17.** Ibid., 22 May 1928, p. 6.   **18.** Stadtwerke Weimar.   **19.** Günther and Wallraf, p. 562.   **20.** *Jenaer Volksblatt*, 21 September 1928, p. 11.   **21.** 'Annual value' = 'Ertragswert'.   **22.** Court File Hotel Hohenzollern No. 250.   **23.** Quoted in Epkenhans, p. 56.   **24.** Ibid., p. 54.   **25.** Quoted in ibid., p. 55.   **26.** Quoted in ibid., p. 56.   **27.** Quoted in ibid., p. 57.   **28.** *Jenaer Volksblatt*, 1 December 1928, p. 12.

1929

1. Carl Weirich's Diary, 3 February 1929.   **2.** Letter from Elisabeth Förster-Nietzsche to Harry Graf Kessler, 17 June 1929.   **3.** Letter from Harry Graf Kessler to Elisabeth Förster-Nietzsche, 15 June 1929.   **4.** Letter from Elisabeth Förster-Nietzsche to Harry Graf Kessler, 17 June 1929.   **5.** Summary of Kessler's conversation with Elisabeth Förster-Nietzsche in: Letter from Harry Graf Kessler to Elisabeth Förster-Nietzsche, 21 June 1929.   **6.** Ibid.   **7.** Letter from Elisabeth Förster-Nietzsche to Harry Graf Kessler, 7 October 1929.   **8.** Ibid.   **9.** Sieg, p. 310.   **10.** Letter from Elisabeth Förster-Nietzsche to Harry Graf Kessler, 17 June 1929.   **11.** Carl Weirich's Diary, 23

July 1929. **12.** Hecker, p. 8. **13.** Rehbein and Bosse, p. 37. **14.** Hecker, p. 8. **15.** Rehbein and Bosse, p. 37. **16.** Hecker, pp. 71–2. **17.** Rehbein and Bosse, p. 38. **18.** Hundehege, p. 65. **19.** Quoted in ibid. **20.** Quoted in ibid. **21.** *Jenaer Volksblatt*, 12 September 1929, p. 7. **22.** Carl Weirich's Diary, 12 September 1929. **23.** Harry Graf Kessler's Diary, 3 October 1929. **24.** *Jenaer Volksblatt*, 25 October 1929, p. 1. **25.** Ibid., 1 November 1929, p. 5. **26.** Stein and Wohlfeld, pp. 7–8. **27.** Anecdote and quote from Mauersberger, pp. 242–3. **28.** *Jenaer Volksblatt*, 7 December 1929, p. 1. **29.** Figures from Dressel, pp. 86–9. **30.** Ibid., p. 86. **31.** *Jenaer Volksblatt*, 9 December 1929, p. 1. **32.** Quoted in Mauersberger, p. 248. **33.** Quoted in ibid., p. 244. **34.** Quoted in ibid., p. 240. **35.** Quoted in Kater, p. 206. **36.** Carl Weirich's Diary, 2 June 1929. **37.** Ibid.

1930

1. Wagener, p. 313. **2.** Ibid., p. 312. **3.** Quoted in Kirsten, p. 34. **4.** Joseph Goebbels' Diary, 11 January 1930. **5.** Ibid. **6.** Ibid. **7.** Ullrich. **8.** Quotes and information from ibid., pp. 63ff. **9.** Dickmann, p. 455. **10.** Quoted in ibid., p. 460. **11.** Quoted in ibid., p. 461. **12.** Quoted in ibid. **13.** Quoted in ibid. **14.** Quoted in ibid., pp. 462–3. **15.** Quoted in ibid., p. 464. **16.** Quoted in ibid. **17.** Letter from Elisabeth Förster-Nietzsche to Harry Graf Kessler, 14 March 1930. **18.** Sieg, p. 312. **19.** Quoted in ibid. **20.** Quoted in Decker, p. 587. **21.** Ibid. **22.** Letter from Elisabeth Förster-Nietzsche to Harry Graf Kessler, 14 March 1930. **23.** Günther and Wallraf, p. 563. **24.** Ibid. **25.** Ibid., p. 564. **26.** Lernort Weimar. 'Ein gefährliches Geheimnis: Rosa Schmidt'. **27.** Carl Weirich's Diary, 1930. **28.** Günther and Wallraf, p. 564. **29.** Carl Weirich's Diary, February 1930. **30.** Ibid., 1930. **31.** Stein and Wohlfeld, pp. 7–8. **32.** Günther and Wallraf, pp. 565–6. **33.** Quoted in Ullrich. **34.** *Jenaer Volksblatt*, 14 March 1930, p. 5. **35.** Quoted in Mauersberger, p. 263. **36.** Ullrich. **37.** Günther and Wallraf, p. 569. **38.** Mauersberger, p. 264. **39.** Ullrich. **40.** Quoted in Mauersberger, p. 266. **41.** Quoted in Ullrich. **42.** Quoted in Müller and Stein, p. 39. **43.** Quotes and information from Rehbein and Bosse, p. 40. **44.** Quoted in Ullrich. **45.** Wilson, p. 21. **46.** Mauersberger, p. 267. **47.** Joseph Goebbels' Diary, 6 December 1930. **48.** Quoted in Mauersberger, pp. 269–70. **49.** Quoted in ibid., p. 271. **50.** Decree IV CII/771, Nr. 53 'Against the Negro Culture for German Folkdom' [April 1930], p. 144. **51.** Ibid., p. 146. **52.** Quoted in Ullrich. **53.** Elisabeth Förster-Nietzsche's letter to the Duchess of Schwarzburg on 19 February 1930. Quoted in Naake, 'Die Beziehungen', p. 279. **54.** Reinhard Buchwald: 'On Weimar Art and Scholarship'. **55.** Quoted in Ullrich. **56.** Joseph Goebbels' Diary, 18

June 1930.   **57.** Naake, 'Die Beziehungen', p. 279.   **58.** Letter from Elisabeth Förster-Nietzsche to Lisbeth Staupendahl, 28 March 1930. Quoted in Naake, 'Die Beziehungen', p. 279.   **59.** Letter from Elisabeth Förster-Nietzsche to Friedrich Stier, 17 June 1930. Quoted in Naake, 'Die Beziehungen', p. 282.   **60.** Letter from Elisabeth Förster-Nietzsche to Wilhelm Frick, 23 May 1930. Quoted in Naake, 'Die Beziehungen', p. 280.   **61.** Unser Kinderbuch, p. 34 and photographs.   **62.** Carl Weirich's Diary, 24 July 1930.   **63.** Harry Graf Kessler's Diary, 25 August 1930.   **64.** Quoted in von Bradish, p. 323.   **65.** Sieg, p. 310.   **66.** Naake, 'Die Beziehungen', p. 282.   **67.** Harry Graf Kessler's Diary, 15 September 1930.   **68.** *Jenaer Volksblatt*, 15 September 1930, p. 1.   **69.** Ibid.   **70.** Joseph Goebbels' Diary, 15 September 1930.   **71.** Ibid.   **72.** Harry Graf Kessler's Diary, 15 September 1930.   **73.** Ibid.   **74.** Dressel, pp. 92–7.   **75.** Naake, 'Die Beziehungen', p. 282.   **76.** Ibid., p. 283.   **77.** Letter from Harry Graf Kessler to Elisabeth Förster-Nietzsche, 27 December 1930.   **78.** Naake, *Nietzsche und Weimar*, p. 101.   **79.** Naake, 'Die Beziehungen', p. 284.   **80.** Ibid., p. 283.   **81.** Letter from Lisbeth Staupendahl to Elisabeth Förster-Nietzsche, 8 July 1930.   **82.** Quotes and information from Naake, 'Die Beziehungen', p. 285.   **83.** Quotes from ibid., p. 286.   **84.** Harry Graf Kessler: 'Frick über Deutschland'.

1931

1. Quoted in Mauersberger, p. 253.   **2.** *Jenaer Volksblatt*, 16 April 1931, p. 6.   **3.** Statistisches Jahrbuch für das Deutsche Reich.   **4.** Boblenz and Post, p. 19.   **5.** Günther and Wallraf, pp. 564–5.   **6.** Carl Weirich's Diary, 1931.   **7.** Quoted in McDonough, p. 451.   **8.** Ibid.   **9.** Carl Weirich's Diary, 1931.   **10.** McDonough, p. 458.   **11.** Carl Weirich's Diary, 1931.   **12.** Quoted in Kirsten, p. 41.   **13.** *Jenaer Volksblatt*, 9 February 1931.   **14.** Ibid., and Kirsten, p. 40.   **15.** *Jenaer Volksblatt*, 9 February 1931.   **16.** Ibid.   **17.** Quoted in Kirsten, p. 41.   **18.** Raßloff, p. 57.   **19.** Quoted in Kirsten, p. 37, and Boblenz and Post, p. 18.   **20.** *Thüringer Allgemeine Zeitung*, 2 April 1931. Quoted in Kirsten, p. 37.   **21.** *Jenaer Volksblatt*, 2 April 1931.   **22.** Quoted in Boblenz and Post, p. 20.   **23.** Ibid.   **24.** Quoted in Ullrich.   **25.** Raßloff, p. 59.   **26.** Quoted in ibid.   **27.** Harry Graf Kessler's Diary, 12 November 1931.   **28.** Quoted in Föhl, p. 1186.   **29.** Letter from Elisabeth Förster-Nietzsche to Harry Graf Kessler, 30 July 1931.   **30.** Speech by Werner Deetjen, 10 July 1931.   **31.** Quoted in Naake, 'Die Beziehungen', pp. 287–8.   **32.** Letter from Elisabeth Förster-Nietzsche to Harry Graf Kessler, 30 July 1931.   **33.** Decker, p. 588.   **34.** Rathkolb, p. 99.   **35.** Quoted in ibid., p. 93.   **36.** Ibid.   **37.** See v. Lang, who interviewed Baldur von Schirach after the war, p. 59.

38. Information and quote from Rathkolb, pp. 97–8.   **39.** Ibid., pp. 98–9.
40. Quoted in v. Lang, pp. 64–5.   **41.** Lernort Weimar. 'Kurt Nehrling'.
42. Unser Kinderbuch, pp. 42–3.   **43.** Letter from Harry Graf Kessler to
Elisabeth Förster-Nietzsche, 23 December 1931.   **44.** Harry Graf Kessler's
Diary, 9 December 1931.   **45.** Ibid., 31 December 1931.

1932

1. She told Harry Graf Kessler about her impressions when she met him in
August. Harry Graf Kessler's Diary, 7 August 1932.   **2.** Details of the performance from Announcement of *Campo di Maggio* at the German National Theatre,
30 January 1932.   **3.** *New York Times*, 7 February 1932, p. 3.   **4.** *Völkischer
Beobachter* (Münchener Ausgabe), Nr. 201, 24/25 August 1930.   **5.** Föhl, pp.
1188–9.   **6.** Harry Graf Kessler's Diary, 7 August 1932.   **7.** Ibid., 16 April 1932.
8. Quoted in Decker, pp. 593–4.   **9.** Harry Graf Kessler's Diary, 7 August 1932.
10. Ibid.   **11.** Quoted in Hamann, p. 565.   **12.** Quoted in ibid., p. 574.   **13.**
Quoted in Overesch, p. 545.   **14.** Quoted in ibid.   **15.** Joseph Goebbels' Diary, 4
February 1932.   **16.** Quoted in Kirsten, p. 46.   **17.** Ibid.   **18.** Joseph Goebbels'
Diary, 15 March 1932.   **19.** *Jenaer Volksblatt*, 16 March 1932, p. 6.   **20.** Joseph
Goebbels' Diary, 15 March 1932.   **21.** Quoted in Boblenz and Post, p. 22.   **22.**
Kirsten, p. 46.   **23.** Results of the 1932 German presidential election in Dressel,
pp. 104–7.   **24.** Quoted in Kirsten, p. 47.   **25.** Quoted in Lernort Weimar. 'Wei-
marhalle'.   **26.** Carl Weirich's Diary, 1932.   **27.** Lernort Weimar. 'Ein gefähr-
liches Geheimnis: Rosa Schmidt'.   **28.** Carl Weirich's Diary, March 1932.   **29.**
Paul von Hindenburg's 'Appeal!'   **30.** Quoted in Manfred Müller, p. 608.   **31.**
Quoted in ibid., pp. 608–9.   **32.** Boblenz and Post, p. 23.   **33.** Quoted in Merseburger, p. 335.   **34.** Quote and information from Rehbein and Bosse, p. 42.   **35.**
Quoted in ibid., p. 43.   **36.** Quoted in Wyllie, p. 75.   **37.** Göring, p. 27.   **38.**
Ibid., p. 24.   **39.** Ibid., p. 26.   **40.** Ibid., p. 28.   **41.** Ibid., p. 29.   **42.** Ibid., p. 21.
43. Ibid., pp. 30–31.   **44.** Rathkolb, p. 97.   **45.** Results from Dressel, pp. 114–15.
46. v. Lang, p. 80.   **47.** Quoted in Rathkolb, p. 103.   **48.** Results from Dressel,
pp. 108–11.   **49.** Quoted in Raßloff, p. 60.   **50.** Quoted in Mauersberger, p.
282.   **51.** *Jenaer Volksblatt*, 19 October 1932, p. 10.   **52.** Naake, *Nietzsche und
Weimar*, p. 104.   **53.** Harry Graf Kessler's Diary, 24 October 1932.   **54.** Ibid.
55. Ibid.   **56.** Letter from Harry Graf Kessler to Elisabeth Förster-Nietzsche,
2 November 1932.   **57.** Quoted in Raßloff, p. 60.   **58.** Quoted in Müller and
Stein, p. 62.   **59.** Ibid., pp. 66–7.   **60.** Quoted in Raßloff, p. 61.   **61.** *Jenaer
Volksblatt*, 24 October 1932, p. 3.   **62.** Kirsten, p. 48.   **63.** Joseph Goebbels'
Diary, 1 December 1932.   **64.** Ibid.   **65.** Carl Weirich's Diary, Christmas 1932.
66. Ibid., 1933.

1933

1. Göring, p. 42. **2.** Ibid., pp. 31–2. **3.** Ibid., p. 38. **4.** Ibid. **5.** Ibid., p. 39. **6.** Ibid. **7.** Harry Graf Kessler's Diary, 30 January 1933. **8.** Carl Weirich's Diary, 30 January 1933. **9.** Unser Kinderbuch, Insert. **10.** Carl Weirich's Diary, winter and spring of 1933. **11.** Ibid., 30 January 1933. **12.** Kater, p. 223. **13.** Naake, *Nietzsche und Weimar*, p. 112. **14.** Boblenz and Post, p. 34. **15.** Harry Graf Kessler's Diary, 28 February 1933. **16.** Boblenz and Post, p. 36. **17.** Wohlfeld, 'Das Konzentrationslager Nohra', p. 109. **18.** Ibid., p. 114. **19.** Müller and Stein, p. 65. **20.** *Weimarische Zeitung*, 31 January 1933, p. 1. **21.** Election results of 5 March 1933 in Dressel, pp. 134–9. **22.** Announcements in *Jenaer Volksblatt*, 22 April 1933 and 13 August 1933. **23.** Carl Weirich's Diary, 21 March 1933. **24.** Unser Kinderbuch, Inlay. **25.** Ban on the membership of civil servants and public sector workers of the Social Democratic Party, 18 March 1933. **26.** Ibid. **27.** Quote and information from Wohlfeld, 'Das Konzentrationslager Nohra', p. 118. **28.** Quoted in ibid., p. 119. **29.** *Jenaer Volksblatt*, 7 March 1933, p. 5. **30.** Cläre Adler's biography in Stein and Wohlfeld, pp. 34–5. **31.** Heinz Adler's biography in ibid., pp. 36–7. **32.** Lernort Weimar. 'Zwischen Anwerbung und Auslöschung'. **33.** Müller and Stein, p. 70. **34.** Harry Graf Kessler's Diary, 1 April 1933. **35.** Quoted in Müller and Stein, p. 72. **36.** Quoted in ibid., p. 71. **37.** Quoted in ibid., p. 73. **38.** Ibid. **39.** Lernort Weimar. 'Zwischen Anwerbung und Auslöschung'. **40.** Müller and Stein, p. 96. **41.** Ibid., p. 77. **42.** Ibid., pp. 79–81. **43.** Ibid., p. 73. **44.** Ibid., p. 71. **45.** Günther and Wallraf, p. 599. **46.** Müller and Stein, p. 63. **47.** Göring, p. 80. **48.** Ibid., p. 66. **49.** Quoted in Wyllie, p. 95. **50.** Quoted in Sigmund, p. 64. **51.** Göring, p. 51. **52.** Ibid., p. 65. **53.** Ibid. **54.** Harry Graf Kessler's Diary, 25 April 1933. **55.** Quoted in Wyllie, p. 104. **56.** Quoted in Sieg, p. 321. **57.** Quoted in Decker, p. 596. **58.** Quoted in ibid., pp. 596–7. **59.** Quoted in ibid., p. 597. **60.** Antisemites' Petition (1880–1881). **61.** Sieg, pp. 325–6. **62.** Antisemites' Petition (1880–1881). **63.** Kater, p. 224. **64.** Naake, *Nietzsche und Weimar*, p. 111. **65.** Raßloff, p. 66. **66.** Mauersberger, pp. 282–3. **67.** Quote and figures from Kater, p. 212. **68.** Ibid., p. 218. **69.** Naake, *Nietzsche und Weimar*, p. 116. **70.** Figures and quotes from Kater, p. 219. **71.** Carl Weirich's Diary, 1 May 1933. **72.** *Weimarische Zeitung*, 22 June 1933. **73.** Quoted in Kirsten, p. 52. **74.** Quotes and information from ibid. **75.** Quoted in ibid., p. 53. **76.** Ibid. **77.** Raßloff, p. 68. **78.** On the status of Weimar in Nazi Germany see also Kater, pp. 220–29. **79.** Quoted in Kirsten, p. 54. **80.** Carl Weirich's Diary, December 1933.

1934

1. Sauckel, *Kampfreden*, p. 173. 2. *Jenaer Volksblatt*, 22 March 1934, p. 8. 3. Quoted in *Jenaer Volksblatt*, 23 March 1934, p. 6. 4. Quoted in ibid. 5. Raßloff, p. 67. 6. Seemann, p. 295. 7. Sauckel, *Kampfreden*, p. 173. 8. Ibid., p. 175. 9. Fritz Sauckel's Nuremberg Notes, p. 141. 10. Sauckel, *Kampfreden*, p. 175. 11. Kater, p. 214. 12. Günther and Wallraf, p. 608. 13. Kater, p. 214. 14. Raßloff, p. 70. 15. Carl Weirich's Diary, 1934. 16. Carl Weirich's Stasi File. 17. Carl Weirich's Diary, 1933. 18. Oral testimony of Marie-Luise Seyfarth. 19. Lernort Weimar. 'Ein gefährliches Geheimnis: Rosa Schmidt'. 20. Günther and Wallraf, p. 609. 21. Hohenzollern File, No. 88. 22. Ibid., No. 90. 23. Gräfe, Post and Schneider, p. 38. 24. Ibid., pp. 50–51. 25. Günther and Wallraf, p. 601. 26. Overburdened Gestapo – Decree of the 'struggle against denunciations' in Thuringia, 26 May 1934. 27. Stein and Wohlfeld, p. 34. 28. Cläre Adler's recollections in Stein and Wohlfeld, p. 35. 29. Göring, p. 59. 30. Ibid., p. 81. 31. Ibid., p. 89. 32. Ibid. 33. Quoted in Merseburger, p. 343. 34. Quoted in ibid., p. 344. 35. Quoted in Rehbein and Bosse, p. 44. 36. Quoted in *Jenaer Volksblatt*, 12 June 1934, p. 1. 37. Reports from participants of the current Schillerbund Festival [1934], p. 180. 38. Unser Kinderbuch, p. 44. 39. Carl Weirich's Diary, 19 August 1934. 40. For a deeper analysis see Kershaw, p. 526. 41. Results in Dressel, p. 150. 42. Carl Weirich's Diary, 19 August 1934. 43. Quoted in Naake, *Nietzsche und Weimar*, p. 112. 44. *Jenaer Volksblatt*, 21 July 1934. 45. Quoted in Naake, *Nietzsche und Weimar*, p. 113. 46. Quoted in Schaefer, p. 244. 47. Quoted in Naake, *Nietzsche und Weimar*, p. 113. 48. *Völkischer Beobachter*, 14 October 1932, second inlay. 49. Ludwig, p. 8, and Blümm and Rössler, p. 77. 50. Speer, p. 77. 51. Quoted in Naake, *Nietzsche und Weimar*, p. 112. 52. Speer, p. 78. 53. Naake, *Nietzsche und Weimar*, p. 112. 54. Speer, p. 78. 55. Kater, p. 214. 56. *Jenaer Volksblatt*, 18 June 1935, p. 8. 57. Quoted in Stenzel, ' "Buch und Schwert" ', p. 84. 58. Ibid. 59. Quoted in ibid., p. 93. 60. Kirsten, p. 55. 61. Quoted in ibid., p. 56. 62. ibid., p. 57. 63. Quoted in Stenzel, ' "Buch und Schwert" ', p. 94. 64. Müller and Stein, p. 115. 65. *Der Stürmer*, January 1935, Nr. 2, p. 1 in Müller and Stein, p. 116. 66. Müller and Stein, p. 117. 67. *Thüringische Staatszeitung*, 12 February 1935, quoted in Müller and Stein, p. 117. 68. Carl Weirich's Diary, Christmas 1934. 69. Photograph 'Christmas 1934' in Unser Kinderbuch. 70. Unser Kinderbuch, Christmas 1934.

1935

1. Carl Weirich's Diary, 20 January 1935.   **2.** Quoted in Loos, p. 206.   **3.** Ibid., p. 209.   **4.** Ibid., p. 210.   **5.** Günther and Wallraf, p. 600.   **6.** Loos, p. 209.   **7.** Carl Weirich's Diary, beginning of 1935.   **8.** Quoted in Tucker, p. 121.   **9.** Lüttgenau, No. 22. Krankenhaus am Kirschberg.   **10.** Nielsen and Freienstein, pp. 104–6.   **11.** Weindling, p. 86.   **12.** Ibid., p. 91.   **13.** Quoted in ibid., p. 90.   **14.** Extract from Karl Astel's Inaugural Lecture at the University of Jena.   **15.** Kater, p. 219.   **16.** Göring, p. 113.   **17.** Ibid., p. 114.   **18.** Ibid., p. 116.   **19.** Quoted in Wyllie, p. 101.   **20.** Göring, p. 115.   **21.** Ibid., p. 119.   **22.** Carl Weirich's Diary, beginning of 1935.   **23.** Ibid., 1 May 1935.   **24.** Unser Kinderbuch, Inlay, note for 24 June 1935.   **25.** Ibid., p. 46.   **26.** Essay samples and lesson plans for comprehensive schools, 1934–1936.   **27.** Hans Eberling's report to the KPD Thuringia, 17 October 1945 in Stein and Wohlfeld, pp. 38–9.   **28.** The political joke in the secret situation report of the Gestapo for the municipal area of Erfurt, 12 July 1935.   **29.** Warrant for Protective Custody by Gestapo Weimar for Utterances against the Reichsstatthalter Fritz Sauckel.   **30.** Martin Seifert's biography in Stein and Wohlfeld, pp. 42–3.   **31.** Ibid. and Ilse Seifert's biography in Stein and Wohlfeld, pp. 43–4.   **32.** Quoted in Wagner, p. 129.   **33.** Quoted in Müller and Stein, pp. 89–90.   **34.** *Jenaer Volksblatt*, 29 August 1935, p. 8.   **35.** Wilson, p. 166.   **36.** Quoted in Loos, p. 171.   **37.** Ibid., pp. 174–5.   **38.** Ibid., pp. 175–6.   **39.** Quoted in ibid., p. 176.   **40.** Quoted in Kirsten, p. 78.   **41.** Quoted in *Jenaer Volksblatt*, 29 August 1935, p. 8.   **42.** Quoted in Zinn.   **43.** Quoted in ibid.   **44.** Quoted in ibid.   **45.** Quoted in Kirsten, p. 112.   **46.** Quoted in Zinn.   **47.** Quoted in ibid.   **48.** Based on John Appel's account and that of one of his Weimar classmates. Both in Müller and Stein, pp. 106–7.   **49.** Quoted in Müller and Stein, p. 157.   **50.** Ibid., p. 160.   **51.** Ibid., p 107.   **52.** Ibid., p. 111.   **53.** Petition of the Gau Business Association Thuringia to the Mayor of Weimar, 16 November 1935.   **54.** Carl Weirich's Diary, 11 November 1935.   **55.** Ibid., 20 November 1935.   **56.** *Jenaer Volksblatt*, 12 November 1935, p. 5.   **57.** Quoted in Decker, p. 604.   **58.** Quoted in Sieg, p. 338.   **59.** Letter from Elisabeth Förster-Nietzsche to Harry Graf Kessler, 10 September 1935.   **60.** Ibid.   **61.** Ibid.   **62.** Harry Graf Kessler's Diary, 20 July 1935.   **63.** Ibid., 6 July 1936.   **64.** Ibid., 30 September 1937.   **65.** Telegram from Harry Graf Kessler to Max Oehler, 9 November 1935.   **66.** Extract from the memoirs of Richard Leutheußer.   **67.** Quoted in Sieg, p. 338.   **68.** Quoted in ibid., p. 339.   **69.** Quoted in ibid.   **70.** Sauckel's speech on 11 November 1935 printed in *Jenaer Volksblatt*, 12 November 1935, p. 5.   **71.** Quoted in Kater, p. 226.   **72.** Ibid., p. 227.   **73.** Naake, *Nietzsche und Weimar*,

p. 118.   **74.** Kater, pp. 228–9.   **75.** Letter from Max Hecker to Max Oehler, 24 November 1935. Quoted in Decker, p. 605.   **76.** Rehbein and Bosse, pp. 46–7.   **77.** Carl Weirich's Diary, December 1935.

1936

1. Wyllie, pp. 102–7.   **2.** Göring, p. 130.   **3.** *New York Times*, 13 January 1936, p. 6.   **4.** Wyllie, p. 103.   **5.** *New York Times*, 13 January 1936, p. 6.   **6.** Göring, p. 119.   **7.** Schau, p. 135.   **8.** Ibid.   **9.** Ibid.   **10.** Ibid., p. 136, and Göring, p. 198.   **11.** Schau, p. 134.   **12.** Göring, p. 198.   **13.** Ibid., p. 199.   **14.** Loos, p. 385.   **15.** Ibid., pp. 381–2.   **16.** Göring, p. 199.   **17.** Harry Stein, 'Eine Stadt für die SS', pp. 16, 19.   **18.** Quoted in ibid., pp. 16–17.   **19.** Ibid., p. 17.   **20.** Letter from Theodor Eicke to Fritz Sauckel, 3 June 1936.   **21.** Ibid.   **22.** Quoted in Harry Stein, 'Eine Stadt für die SS', p. 21.   **23.** Ibid., p. 22.   **24.** Letter from Theodor Eicke to Fritz Sauckel, 3 June 1936.   **25.** Ibid.   **26.** Carl Weirich's Diary, 10 May 1936.   **27.** Ibid.   **28.** All statistics from Jüllig.   **29.** Extract from the speech of the NSDAP Gauleiter Sauckel about the Wilhelm Gustloff Foundation, 27 October 1936.   **30.** Schley, *Nachbar Buchenwald*, pp. 19–20.   **31.** Extract from the speech of the NSDAP Gauleiter Sauckel about the Wilhelm Gustloff Foundation, 27 October 1936.   **32.** Heinz Adler's biography in Stein and Wohlfeld, pp. 36–7.   **33.** Kater, p. 214.   **34.** Schley, 'Weimar und Buchenwald', p. 34.   **35.** 'Massive, natural water reserves in Thuringia' – Report of the NSDAP Gau newspaper, 23 October 1936.   **36.** Lernort Weimar. 'Ein gefährliches Geheimnis: Rosa Schmidt'.   **37.** Carl Weirich's Diary, 3 July 1936.   **38.** Quoted in Kirsten, p. 59.   **39.** Letter from Weimar Mayor Walther Felix Mueller to the Gau Organization Office of the Nazi Party, 15 November 1935.   **40.** Kirsten, p. 59.   **41.** Newspaper report, 29 April 1936.   **42.** Gau newspaper report, 23 May 1936.   **43.** Summary of costs for the 10-year anniversary of the first Reich Party Rally 1936.   **44.** Gau newspaper report, 23 June 1936.   **45.** Quoted in Kirsten, p. 60.   **46.** Adolf Hitler's speech at the State Reception at Weimar Palace at 5 p.m. on 3 July 1936.   **47.** *Jenaer Volksblatt*, 4 July 1936, p. 1.   **48.** Joseph Goebbels' Diary, 4 July 1936.   **49.** Quoted in Kirsten, p. 61.   **50.** Carl Weirich's Diary, 4 July 1936.   **51.** Quoted in Domarus, p. 628.   **52.** *Jenaer Volksblatt*, 7 July 1936, p. 9.   **53.** Ibid., 6 July 1936, p. 2.   **54.** Kirsten, p. 63.   **55.** Harry Stein, 'Eine Stadt für die SS', pp. 25–6.   **56.** Quoted in Schley, *Nachbar Buchenwald*, p. 25.   **57.** Loos, p. 89.   **58.** Ibid., p. 95.   **59.** Kirsten, pp. 64–5.   **60.** Loos, p. 64.   **61.** Das Gauforum in Weimar – Ein Erbe des Dritten Reiches.   **62.** *Jenaer Volksblatt*, 7 June 1936, p. 8.   **63.** Joseph Goebbels' Diary, 5 June 1936.   **64.** Carl Weirich's Diary, beginning of 1936.   **65.** Ibid., New Year's Eve 1936.

1937

1. *Jenaer Volksblatt*, 3 May 1937, p. 1. **2.** Ibid. **3.** Ibid., p. 5. **4.** Ibid. **5.** Kirsten, p. 66. **6.** Loos, p. 400. **7.** 'German Festive Day under glowing May sun.' In: Gau newspaper, 3 May 1937. **8.** Carl Weirich's Diary, 1 May 1937 and beginning of 1937. **9.** *Jenaer Volksblatt*, 3 May 1937, p. 6. **10.** 'Professor Hecker as a Scholar'. In: Gau newspaper, 3 May 1937. **11.** Rehbein and Bosse, p. 49. **12.** Ibid. **13.** Quoted in ibid. **14.** Ibid., p. 50. **15.** Baldur von Schirach's Goethe Speech, 14 June 1937. **16.** Award of honorary citizenship to Baldur von Schirach. **17.** Observations from pictures taken by Criminal Police Weimar on 15 July 1937, Fotoarchiv Buchenwald. **18.** Quotes and information from Harry Stein, 'Eine Stadt für die SS', pp. 12–13. **19.** Gedenkstätte Buchenwald. 'Weimar im Nationalsozialismus. Chronik'. **20.** Löffelsender, p. 17. **21.** Quoted in ibid. **22.** Harry Stein, 'Eine Stadt für die SS', p. 13. **23.** Schley, *Nachbar Buchenwald*, p. 26. **24.** Harry Stein, 'Eine Stadt für die SS', p. 13. **25.** Schley, *Nachbar Buchenwald*, pp. 26–7. **26.** Kater, p. 255. **27.** Schley, 'Weimar und Buchenwald', p. 35. **28.** Quotes and information from Merseburger, pp. 355–6. **29.** Letter from Theodor Eicke to Heinrich Himmler, 24 July 1937. **30.** Schley, *Nachbar Buchenwald*, p. 29. **31.** Quoted in Riederer, p. 80. **32.** *Jenaer Volksblatt*, 12 August 1939, p. 7. **33.** Kater, p. 254. **34.** Schley, *Nachbar Buchenwald*, pp. 29–30. **35.** Günther and Hoffmann, p. 121. **36.** Ibid. **37.** MDR Thüringen, 21 March 2024. **38.** Löffelsender, p. 84. **39.** Kater, pp. 258–9. **40.** Günther and Hoffmann, p. 203. **41.** Information and quotes from Riederer, pp. 61–2. **42.** Information and quotes from ibid., p. 62. **43.** Quoted in ibid., p. 80. **44.** Quoted in ibid., p. 75. **45.** Ibid., pp. 59–85. **46.** *Jenaer Volksblatt*, 30 September 1937, supplement. **47.** Quote and information from Dietrich and Dell, pp. 18–21. **48.** Lüttgenau, Hotel Elephant. **49.** Quoted in Loos, p. 358. **50.** Hinrich Holtz's petition to grant Emmy and Hermann Göring honorary citizenship, 27 April 1937. **51.** Draft letter of Honorary Citizenship for Emmy Göring, 29 May 1937. **52.** Göring, pp. 127–8, 131–2. **53.** Göring, p. 132. **54.** Ibid., p. 127. **55.** Telegram from Otto Koch to Hermann and Emmy Göring, 3 June 1938. **56.** Naake, *Nietzsche und Weimar*, p. 126. **57.** Loos, p. 191. **58.** Naake, *Nietzsche und Weimar*, p. 126. **59.** Ibid., p. 124. **60.** Ibid., p. 125. **61.** Loos, p. 191. **62.** Quoted in ibid., p. 192. **63.** Carl Weirich's Diary, November and December 1937.

1938

1. Günther and Hoffmann, p. 107. **2.** Sabine Stein. **3.** Quoted in Löffelsender, p. 16. **4.** Quoted in Fischer, p. 79. **5.** Quoted in Sabine Stein.

6. Fischer, pp. 80–81. **7.** Lernort Weimar. 'Marstall'. **8.** Extract from the Interrogation of Gestapo Officer Junge by the Criminal Office Weimar, 19 May 1945. **9.** Hans Eberling's report to the state leadership of the KPD Thuringia, 17 October 1945. In: Stein and Wohlfeld, pp. 38–9. **10.** Ibid. **11.** Report by the President of the Higher Regional Court in Jena to the Reich Minister for Justice about the Attitudes of the Population to Protective Custody, 2 March 1938. **12.** Kater, p. 269. **13.** Schley, *Nachbar Buchenwald*, p. 41. **14.** Ibid., p. 51. **15.** Details in this paragraph from Kater, pp. 266–7. **16.** Weber, p. 18. **17.** Quoted in Schley, *Nachbar Buchenwald*, p. 37. **18.** Ibid., p. 45. **19.** Ibid., pp. 70ff. **20.** Riederer, p. 61. **21.** Schley, *Nachbar Buchenwald*, p. 44. **22.** Riederer, p. 60. **23.** Ibid., p. 67. **24.** Quote and information from Schley, *Nachbar Buchenwald*, p. 48. **25.** Joseph Goebbels' Diary, 4 August 1938. **26.** Ibid., 30 August 1938. **27.** Merseburger, p. 354. **28.** Chorus of the 'Buchenwald Song'. **29.** Carl Weirich's Diary, March 1938. **30.** Ibid., 10 July 1938. **31.** Ibid., 24 May 1938. **32.** Loos, pp. 97–8, 509. **33.** Carl Weirich's Diary, top of 1938. **34.** Ibid., 29 May 1938. **35.** Ibid., 7 August 1938. **36.** Müller and Stein, pp. 102–3. **37.** Aryanization Questionnaire for the Buyers of the Department Store Sachs & Berlowitz. **38.** Müller and Stein, p. 101. **39.** Quoted in ibid., p. 119. **40.** Ibid. **41.** Letter from the Reichsstatthalter in Thuringia to the Mayor of Weimar about the sale of a Jewish company. **42.** Quotes and information from Müller and Stein, p. 106. **43.** Lüttgenau, Kaufhaus Sachs & Berlowitz. **44.** Kirsten, p. 69. **45.** *Jenaer Volksblatt*, 7 November 1938, Special Inlay. **46.** Ibid. **47.** Gau newspaper, 6 November 1938. Quoted in Kirsten, p. 69. **48.** *Berliner Tageblatt*, 9 November 1938. Quoted in Loos, p. 360. **49.** Quoted in Kirsten, p. 69. **50.** *Jenaer Volksblatt*, 7 November 1938, Special Inlay. **51.** Quoted in Kirsten, p. 70. **52.** Quoted in ibid. **53.** *Jenaer Volksblatt*, 7 November 1938, Special Inlay. **54.** Ibid. **55.** Longerich, p. 232. **56.** Quoted in ibid., p. 283. **57.** Carl Weirich's Diary, top of 1938. **58.** Joseph Goebbels' Diary, 10 November 1938. **59.** Quoted in Longerich, p. 288. **60.** See summary in ibid., p. 288. **61.** Carl Weirich's Diary, 9 November 1938. **62.** Telegram from the Gestapo Office to all State Police Offices, 9 November 1938. **63.** Quotes and information from Lernort Weimar. 'Das Paradies war in der Teichgasse 6'. **64.** Quoted in Müller and Stein, pp. 131–2. **65.** Quoted in ibid., p. 148. **66.** *Jenaer Volksblatt*, 11 November 1938, p. 1. **67.** Quoted in Müller and Stein, p. 125. **68.** Quoted in ibid., pp. 132–3. **69.** Quoted in ibid., p. 125. **70.** Quoted in ibid. **71.** Schley, *Nachbar Buchenwald*, pp. 113–14. **72.** Riederer, p. 62. **73.** Quotes and information from ibid., pp. 63–5. **74.** Gedenkstätte Buchenwald. Chronologie des KZ Buchenwald. Massenverhaftungen. **75.** Gedenkstätte Buchenwald. Chronologie des KZ Buchenwald. Sonderlager Novemberpogrom.

1939

1. Carl Weirich's Diary, 12 February 1939. **2.** Quoted in Schley, *Nachbar Buchenwald*, p. 66. **3.** Quoted in Nielsen and Freienstein, p. 122. **4.** Quoted in Schley, *Nachbar Buchenwald*, p. 66. **5.** Quoted in ibid. **6.** Quoted in ibid., p. 65. **7.** Nielsen and Freienstein, pp. 122–3. **8.** Riederer, pp. 80–84. **9.** Quotes and information from Schley, *Nachbar Buchenwald*, p. 118. **10.** Carl Weirich's Diary, top of 1939 and March 1939. **11.** Application from the Gestapo to the Thuringian Finance Ministry about the Installation of Further Prison Cells in the Basement of the State Police Office Weimar, 18 January 1939. **12.** Plan for the Rental of a Coach House from the Grand Ducal Estate Management for Conversion into a Temporary Prison, 25 March 1939. **13.** Report: 'Four cells of special construction'. **14.** Hans Eberling's report to the state leadership of the KPD Thuringia, 17 October 1945. In: Stein and Wohlfeld, pp. 38–9. **15.** Zuschlag, p. 60. **16.** Quoted in *Jenaer Volksblatt*, 24 March 1939, p. 10. **17.** Quoted in ibid., 30 March 1939, p. 7. **18.** Zuschlag, pp. 60–61. **19.** Ziegler, p. 16. **20.** Quoted in Pollmann. **21.** Quoted in Longerich, p. 289. **22.** Excerpts from Hitler's Speech before the first 'Greater German Reichstag', 30 January 1939. **23.** Quoted in Longerich, p. 292. **24.** Carl Weirich's Diary, 13 May 1939. **25.** Quoted in Ochaba. **26.** Kirsten, p. 67. **27.** Fritz Sauckel on 'The Old and the New Weimar', 24 August 1939. **28.** Stutz, p. 94. **29.** Göring, p. 11. **30.** Ibid., p. 12. **31.** Ibid. **32.** Carl Weirich's Diary, 3 September 1939 and end of 1939.

EPILOGUE: WAR

1. Carl Weirich's Diary, 9 February 1945. **2.** Quotes and information from Kater, p. 273. **3.** Günther and Wallraf, p. 631. **4.** Carl Weirich's Diary, 11 March 1945. **5.** Field Judgment against Kurt Nehrling, 23 September 1943. **6.** Ibid. **7.** Kurt Nehrling's farewell letter, 22 December 1943. **8.** Alexandra Greulich's report from the Thuringian State Office for Race Questions, 18 June 1942. **9.** Lernort Weimar. 'Ein gefährliches Geheimnis: Rosa Schmidt'. **10.** Letter from Arthur Schmidt to Business Police, 6 May 1943. **11.** Müller and Stein, p. 184. **12.** Ibid., pp. 184–5. **13.** Rosa Schmidt's Death Certificate, 14 December 1944. **14.** 'Ruchel' appears as Rosa Schmidt's first name in files relating to her incarceration and death at the hands of the Nazis. Her passport, tombstone and any other available documents name her as 'Rosa Schmidt'. **15.** Quoted in Müller and Stein, p. 185. **16.** Arthur Schmidt's Obituary, 2 February 1945. **17.** Letter from Clinton C. Gardner to his parents, 16 July 1945. **18.** Carl Weirich's

Diary, 28 April–1 May 1945.   **19.** Ibid., 16 April 1945.   **20.** Ibid., 12 April 1945.
21. Ibid., 28 May 1945.   **22.** Ibid., 24 June 1945.   **23.** Ibid., 9 August 1946.

CONCLUSION

1. Carl Weirich's Diary, 1971 on inserted additions to the bound diary.   **2.**
Ibid.   **3.** Carl Weirich's Diary, reflecting on 1939 on inserted additions to the
bound diary.   **4.** Carl Weirich's Diary, 24 June 1976.   **5.** Carl Weirich's Diary,
reflecting on 1939 on inserted additions to the bound diary.

Acknowledgements

When I told my dad that I was writing this book about Weimar, he smiled at me weakly and whispered: 'You'll spend much time in Thuringia, then. I like the thought of that.' He'd had a stroke and life was draining from him fast. A native Thuringian, he would never see the deep green mountains of his home state again. I thought about him often as I researched the lives of the people of Weimar, pondering the roles of individuals in history, the way humans are remembered and the traces they leave behind. I never thanked him for the traces he left in my life. Johann Wolfgang von Goethe, Germany's national poet and Weimar's most famous resident, once said that children should get two things from their parents: roots and wings. Papa gave me both, and I will always be grateful for that.

This book would never have come about without the many people who have supported me along the way. My brilliant editor, publishing director Casiana Ionita, has been as patient, constructive and empathetic as any author could wish for. I'd also like to thank senior publicity manager Corina Romonti, senior marketing executive Rosie Brown, editorial assistant Maria Green, senior editorial manager Rebecca Lee, copy-editor Tamsin Shelton, head of production Katy Banyard and the other members of the Penguin team for their cheerful efficiency. My agent Toby Mundy and his team are incredibly good at what they do and helped the project take shape, plying me with coffee, ideas and advice when I needed it.

Local support in Weimar has shaped the book. If Jens Riederer, the director of the Weimar Town Archive, hadn't shown me the diaries of Carl Weirich right when he acquired them – they had not even been catalogued yet – you would hold a very different book in your hands. A brilliant archivist with a wealth of local knowledge and a great sense of humour, he was always happy to answer my questions, accommodate my requests, point me in new directions, and discuss ideas and research.

I would also like to thank the staff at the Thuringian Main State Archives, particularly Frank Boblenz and Katja Deinhardt, who both greatly assisted me in finding my bearings in the subject matter. They were generous with their time and interest in the project. The professionals at Klassik Stiftung Weimar, the Goethe and Schiller Archive, the Nietzsche Archive and the various museums around town were all happy to help, providing friendly advice and access to documents and sources. Local historians took time out of their busy days to provide their expertise. My special thanks to Christian Faludi and Michael Löffelsender. Further afield, the Bundesarchiv and the Deutsche Kinemathek were very helpful in tracking down individual documents and people.

I'm grateful to my long-suffering family and friends for tolerating my obsession with Weimar for a few years, for allowing me to stress-test ideas and findings with them, and for joining me on 'holidays' to Weimar during which I would vanish for a few hours by just popping into the archives quickly.

Writing is by its very nature a solitary profession but it feels a little less so when authors are supported by great professionals, colleagues, friends, family, cats and of course you, dear readers.

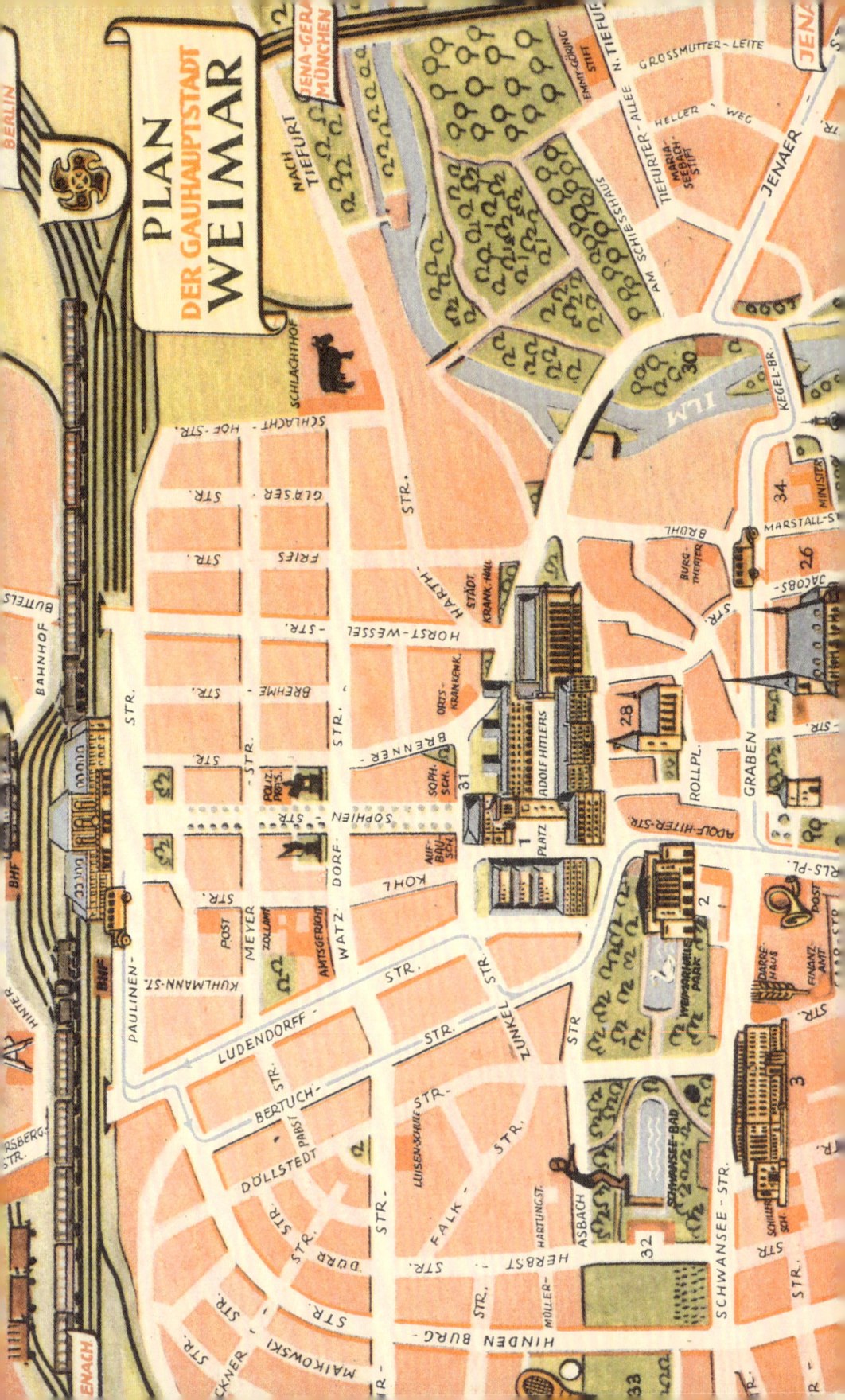